ALSO BY LAWRENCE WESCHLER

Seeing Is Forgetting the Name of the Thing One Sees:
  A Life of Contemporary Artist Robert Irwin

The Passion of Poland: From Solidarity Through the State of War

Shapinsky's Karma, Boggs's Bills, and Other True-Life Tales

A Miracle, a Universe: Settling Accounts with Torturers

Mr. Wilson's Cabinet of Wonder

Calamities of Exile: Three Nonfiction Novellas

A Wanderer in the Perfect City: Selected Passion Pieces

Boggs: A Comedy of Values

Robert Irwin Getty Garden

Vermeer in Bosnia: A Reader

Everything That Rises: A Book of Convergences

True to Life: Twenty-Five Years of Conversations with David Hockney

Uncanny Valley: Adventures in the Narrative

Strandbeest: The Dream Machines of Theo Jansen

Domestic Scenes: The Art of Ramiro Gomez

Waves Passing in the Night: Walter Murch in the Land of the Astrophysicists

Abelardo Morell's Flowers for Lisa: *A Delirium of Photographic Invention*

And How Are *You*, Dr. Sacks?

And How Are *You*, Dr. Sacks?

A BIOGRAPHICAL MEMOIR OF
OLIVER SACKS

Lawrence Weschler

FARRAR, STRAUS AND GIROUX   NEW YORK

Farrar, Straus and Giroux
120 Broadway, New York 10271

Portions of this book were previously published in "A Rare, Personal Look at Oliver Sacks's Early Career," *Vanity Fair*, June 2015.

Grateful acknowledgement is made for permission to reprint the following material:
Lines from "Epilogue," from *Collected Poems* by Robert Lowell. Copyright © 2003 by Harriet Lowell and Sheridan Lowell. Reprinted by permission of Farrar, Straus and Giroux.
"The Panther," from *The Poetry of Rilke: Bilingual Edition* by Rainer Maria Rilke, translated and edited by Edward Snow. Translation © 2009 by Edward Snow. Reprinted by permission of North Point Press.
Thom Gunn letters courtesy of the Estate of Thom Gunn.

Illustration credits can be found on page 385.

Library of Congress Cataloging-in-Publication Data
Names: Weschler, Lawrence, author.
Title: And how are you, Dr. Sacks? : a biographical memoir of Oliver Sacks / Lawrence Weschler.
Description: First edition. | New York : Farrar, Straus and Giroux, 2019.
Identifiers: LCCN 2018060824 | ISBN 9780374236410 (hardcover)
Subjects: LCSH: Sacks, Oliver, 1933–2015—Health. | Neurologists—England— Interviews. | Neurologists—United States—Biography.
Classification: LCC RC339.52.S23 W47 2019 | DDC 616.80092 [B]—dc23
LC record available at https://lccn.loc.gov/2018060824

Designed by Jonathan D. Lippincott

Our books may be purchased in bulk for promotional, educational, or business use. Please contact your local bookseller or the Macmillan Corporate and Premium Sales Department at 1-800-221-7945, extension 5442, or by e-mail at MacmillanSpecialMarkets@macmillan.com.

www.fsgbooks.com
www.twitter.com/fsgbooks • www.facebook.com/fsgbooks

10 9 8 7 6 5 4 3 2 1

In memory

During the four years in the early eighties

that I spent in his often near-continuous company,

Oliver Sacks would sometimes refer to himself

as a clinical ontologist,

by which I came to understand

he meant a doctor whose entire practice

in relation to his patients

revolved around the question,

How *are* you?

Which is to say,

How *do* you *be*?

For, as he had come to understand:

Being is Doing.

Contents

Part II: How He Was (the Passing Months)

Part III: Afterwards

Note: Where indicated in the text with ^{SB}, excerpted letters and other writings can be accessed in their entirety in an online SourceBook for this book at www.lawrenceweschler.com.

And How Are *You*, Dr. Sacks?

Prologue

Heading out to City Island that first time in late June 1981, I'll grant you, I was trawling, vaguely, for another story.

I'd only just transplanted myself to New York City from my original stomping grounds in Los Angeles, largely owing to the success of my previous tale, which a few months earlier I'd somehow managed to sell, pretty much over the transom, to *The New Yorker*.

While still back in California early that spring, only recently turned twenty-nine, I'd come home late one evening to my Santa Monica apartment to find the light blinking on my answering machine. Answering machines must have seemed pretty newfangled in those days, because the feathery voice on the tape began haltingly, "Mr. Weschler, is this Mr. Weschler? . . . Mrs. Painter, do you think he can hear me? Should I leave a . . . Mr. Weschler? This is William Shawn of *The New* . . . aaaah, Mrs. Painter, how can I tell if the thing is working? . . . William Shawn of *The New Yorker* magazine, and I am just calling to say that we all very much admired the piece you submitted to us a few months ago and we were wondering if . . . oh dear, Mr. Weschler, if you are getting this message could you please call us back at the following number"—and so forth—"Mrs. Painter, I don't think he got any of that *at all*."

However, I did, I had, and in later years I'd be very grateful for the momentary filter of that answering machine: Had I happened to have been home and picked up the ringing phone, I'm sure I'd have assumed it was one of my friends pulling my leg and blurted, "Yeah, and I'm Bernardo Bertolucci" or something and just hung up.

The piece in question, a book-length midcareer biography of the California Light and Space artist Robert Irwin, had been four years in the making, as I subsequently explained to Mr. Shawn on a visit to New York a few months later, when he invited me to lunch at his usual haunt, a corner banquette at the Algonquin, from which he could survey the entire room while pretty much disappearing, mouselike, into the background. He urged me to sample anything on the plank-long menu the waiter had just extended—nervously I chose the first thing that caught my eye, the day's special, lobster-stuffed filet of sole—at which point Mr. Shawn ordered "the usual" (cornflakes, as it turned out). He then turned the full force of his penetrating curiosity upon me (that of the Iron Mouse, as I'd subsequently hear him called).

"It appears that you currently live in California," he said, "but, I mean, where were you *born?*" (His was hardly an unusual New York prejudice in those days: My Irwin book had by that point garnered more than half a dozen rave rejections from New York publishers, all assuring me that they definitely wanted a look at my *next* manuscript, though they couldn't very well see how they could be expected to succeed in publishing anything about a *California* artist.) "Van Nuys, California," I responded, "in the San Fernando Valley suburbs of Los Angeles." Still confounded, Mr. Shawn bore down: "But, I mean, where did you go to school?" Birmingham High, in Van Nuys. "And college?" Cowell College at the University of California at Santa Cruz. Things clearly weren't adding up, but Mr. Shawn, a first-rate reporter in his own right, continued probing until he was able to establish that all of my grandparents had been Viennese Jews who'd variously arrived in flight from Hitler (indeed, my maternal grandfather had been the eminent Weimar-era émigré composer Ernst Toch)—a category, at last, that he *could* comprehend.

Following that lunch meeting, Mr. Shawn offered me a job as a staff writer at *The New Yorker*, and soon thereafter I moved to New York. The magazine would eventually publish half of my Irwin book across two issues, but as things developed, before that I'd also begun reporting for the magazine from Poland (at the height of its Solidarity passion) and soon afterwards would be submitting a whole variety of one-offs (one on the marvelous Louisiana Museum of Modern Art in Humlebaek, Denmark, for example, and another on the antic nonagenarian musical lexicographer Nicolas Slonimsky). But I was still looking for a subject upon whom I could direct the sort of slow, long-term attention I'd previously lavished on Irwin, and in the back of my mind I thought that this at the time still barely known, clearly quite idiosyncratic neurologist, out there on City Island, might just be the one.

☀

Nor was I calling entirely out of the blue: He and I had already engaged in a few rounds of correspondence during the preceding year.

I'd first heard of Oliver Sacks during my last year at Santa Cruz, in 1974, the year after his remarkable chronicle *Awakenings* was published. It's worth recalling that Oliver's second book was hardly a bestseller when it first appeared (any more so than his first book, *Migraine*, published a few years earlier and marketed, to the extent it had been at all, to a relatively limited niche market, had been). Although *Awakenings* had been fervently hailed by literary critics (W. H. Auden, Frank Kermode), it had gone largely dismissed in medical circles, and in any case did not really catch fire on either side of the Atlantic. But Maurice Natanson, the lead phenomenologist at Cowell College—a Husserl scholar who looked more like Buber—started touting it almost from the start, which would have been just like him.

Come to think of it, the entire Awakenings drama had been taking place during the very years I'd been studying in Santa Cruz—starting the spring just before my arrival at Cowell, in April 1969, when Oliver, back at the institutional home he was calling Mount Carmel in the book, had become convinced that eighty of the place's five hundred hopelessly lost causes (catatonics, assorted other demented, Parkinsonians, stroke victims, and the like) were not like the others, that even though they seemed to be "human statues" (locked in deep trancelike states from which they had apparently not emerged for years), some achingly attenuated form of life seemed to be persisting there deep inside. On that hunch, he'd resolved to bring them together, segregate them from the rest of the population, and study and care for them as a group. Even before that ward was established, though, Oliver had begun hearing reports of a remarkable new "miracle drug," L-DOPA, which was said to be having surprising results with severely impacted Parkinson's patients. So with some trepidation (for he was suspicious of such claims), he decided to try the drug on his patients. The results that summer were astonishing—a complete springlike Awakening—patients who had neither moved nor spoken in years suddenly emerging joyously active and voluble, and the ward veritably brimming over with blithe energy. The springlike summer did not last, however, and by September (just as I was entering Cowell), the ward at Mount Carmel had descended into the phase Oliver would come to call Tribulation, a bedlam of horrific and screeching side effects and side effects of side effects. Some of the patients never made it through to the other side, though over the years others did, at length achieving a measure of surcease—Accommodation, as Oliver was to call this extended final phase—nothing ever again as wondrous as their brief summer resurrection nor quite as bad as the prior decades of their deep winter freeze.

I'd taken the better part of a year off during my time at Cowell (tending to my composer grandfather's estate in the wake of the death of my grandmother), so I was still there when Oliver published *Awakenings*, which in turn is how it came to pass that during the last weeks of my senior year, Natanson, glowering, as was his wont (a glower that was at the same time a kind of benediction), thrust the book into my chest as we passed each other in the hall. "Read this," he commanded.

It would still be a few years before I got around to reading *Awakenings*. However, the impact of reading the book when I finally did proved utterly galvanizing, and I couldn't stop thinking about it. I was quite overwhelmed, albeit a bit puzzled. Because (and it took a while to narrow in on the precise nature of that sense of perplex) for all the drama and fellow feeling evoked by the text, the figure of the doctor himself was remarkably fugitive, held back, subdued. What, I wondered, must all those awakenings and their churning aftermaths have been like for *him*? The more I continued to ponder the question, to hone and focus it, the more I came to sense that the true deep drama of the story had less to do with his decision to administer the drug and all that followed from that but rather with the mystery—what could it have been about him and his professional formation and his own past?—behind the fact that before all that he and he alone had proved to have the (what?) . . . the perspicacity to notice those particular living statues as somehow distinct from all the others, and then the moral audacity to imagine that there might in fact be ongoing life persisting deep within those long-extinguished cores.

Being a good little instance of my own specific type in that specific time and place (a free-floating would-be intellectual back in my hometown of Los Angeles in the late 1970s), I responded to those questions in the way we all seemed to be doing in those days: by writing a preliminary screenplay treatment. And that was what I'd first mailed to Oliver in the fall of 1980 (around the time I'd completed my Irwin project and was beginning to shop it around), asking if anyone else had approached him about the idea of turning his book into a film, and, if not (and if upon reading the treatment he found it worthy), whether he might be willing to let me pursue the matter.

There followed several months of silence, but then, early in 1981, in fact on February 13, my twenty-ninth birthday (when he would have been forty-seven), I finally received an envelope containing a letter he'd written some months earlier but somehow misaddressed, which got returned and then mislaid, but eventually, according to the cover note, recovered and was now being sent off once again. "I am most grateful for the kind things you say," the letter began,

> and happy that AWAKENINGS apparently found some deep
> resonances in you. One always has the fear that one lives/works/
> writes in a vacuum, and letters like yours are very precious as
> evidence to the contrary. Indeed, I never regard the writing of
> anything as "completing" it—the circle of completion must be
> made by the reader, in the individual responses of his heart and
> mind—then and only then is the circle of the Graces—of
> Giving, Receiving, and Returning—complete.

The letter graciously went on to explain how there had indeed been occasional interest in a film version of his book, though nothing definitive and nothing specific at the moment, so he was not averse, but that we should at some point in the months ahead try to get together to discuss things further. Which was fine by me: I was still mainly busy trying to place that Irwin manuscript (it was a few months out yet from Mr. Shawn's phone call).

Oliver and I continued to correspond sporadically through this period, and though I somehow misplaced those letters during my ensuing move to New York, I remember one in particular in which I suggested that I understood why he'd assigned the institutional home in question the clever pseudonym of Mount Carmel (Saint John of the Cross, *Dark Night of the*

Soul, and so forth), but that it seemed to me that his text was much more kabbalistic (shades of Natanson, again), which is to say Jewish rather than Christian mystical—was I wrong? To which he replied with the first of his mammoth multipage handwritten responses. For indeed, as he went on to explain, the actual place was named Beth Abraham, in the Bronx, his family was deeply Jewish in all directions, in fact his first cousin was the legendary Israeli foreign minister and polymath Abba Eban, the Balfour Declaration had first been broached and stenographically massaged in various London family basements before he was born, and perhaps most important, the great inspiration of his medical life was the Soviet neuropsychologist A. R. Luria, who, who knows, may perhaps have been a descendant of the great sixteenth-century Palestinian Jewish mystic Isaac Luria, one of the principal students and explicators of that ur-kabbalistic text, the Zohar.

After that exchange, our contacts became more and more cordial (even though the initial pretext of a possible screenplay gradually seemed to fall away as I became more consumed with my dawning *New Yorker* responsibilities), until that day in June 1981 when I rented a car and drove out to meet Dr. Oliver Sacks in person in his own relatively new home on City Island.

Later that evening, I recorded my impressions of the visit in the first volume of what would become a veritable shelf of notebooks chronicling our deepening friendship. Here follow some extracts from that first entry:

> Sacks lives today out on City Island, an approximately thirty-minute drive out of Manhattan, through the Bronx, and out onto a small almost quaint fishing island. He has lived there for about nine months, having slowly migrated across a succession of stages, from Greenwich Village, where he lived when he first alighted in the city, on through Mt. Vernon, where he rented an apartment just before this. His house, at 119 Horton Street, is near the end of the island, the terminus of this somehow unexpected urban appendix jutting out into the Sound from the Pelham Bay district of the Bronx. It is a brief walk to the narrow beach at the end of the street, a walk he tells me he takes often. He thinks of himself as only partially terrestrial, or rather, as entirely amphibious.
>
> Indeed, he says, in the old days not too long ago, when he still

lived in the Bronx, he used to set out swimming from Orchard Beach over there (pointing north) on the mainland, sometimes circling the Island, for example. And one day not that long ago he came ashore on the pebbly beach at the end of the Horton spur. He ambled up the short street, dripping wet, slogging along. He saw a quaint red house. He thought, What a quaint red house. He saw people moving boxes out of the house. He saw that one of the people was a former student. He ambled up and was beckoned in. "No, no I'm dripping wet." "But no, please, do come in." He acceded. He liked the house, was told that it was on the market, walked back out, said goodbye, walked on up Horton, turned left on the main drag, continued walking on up the road, trailing drops from his sopping trunks, walked into a realtor's office, inquired after the house on Horton St., and somehow bought it on the spot.

The house itself, with its rickety front porch and little back garden—and its eccentric occupant—reminds me of the pictures I've seen of Joseph Cornell's out on Utopia Parkway.

Sacks is a large robust fellow, given to impish childlike outbursts, his chest proportioned like a squat child's, his motions and postures often awkward like a child's, as well.

When we first meet I tell him he does not look like I'd expected. "My physical look changes radically over time," he replies. "Sometimes I'm bearded, sometimes I'm not; sometimes I weigh 190 pounds, sometimes I weigh 300" ("That must be some beard," I hazard). He is currently somewhat closer to the former. He has severe back problems, the result of several accidents, "worldly infelicities"—and when we go to dinner, a brief walk to the nearby fish restaurant, he carries along a narrow square curved lumbar support pillow ("something of a cross between a prosthesis and a transitional object," he jokes). At dinner he suffers recurrent heat flashes, his face reddening and his brow glistening with sweat, and when we return to his home he heaves himself before the air conditioner in his study (there is one in every room) and basks in its shivery flow, relieved at last. He kneels before the thrumming machine, as if in ecstatic prayer (a contented seal).

He tells me he had to get a house for his home—this is his

first—in part to house his "secret production." He points to a long shelf parallel to his bed, atop which at least thirty notebooks are neatly arrayed. "At most times I am either talking, listening, or writing: That's from the last six months."

In other rooms, hundreds of casebooks—notebooks devoted to individual patients whose names appear on the spines—are piled one atop the next. In one room, by the study, there is a veritable tilework of audiotape cassettes in their plastic boxes, a wailing wall of contained pain. There are also dozens of videotapes.

He is thinking of writing a book to be entitled "Five Seconds"—a detailed study of the myriad, speeded up lives that a single ticcing Touretter can live through in any random five seconds—he needs to use high speed video equipment in order to even begin to capture it all. He insists every face-change or yelp is significant: and that they all relate, one to the next.

His bookshelves teem with philosophy: Nietzsche, Schopenhauer, Leibniz, Spinoza, Hume, Heidegger, Husserl . . .

He tells me that as a youth he read philosophy uncomprehendingly, but that afterwards he tended to drift away, focusing instead on his scientific studies. His patients, he says, coming to him with their "philosophical emergencies," forced him back to philosophy.

He respects facts, and he has a scientist's passion for precision. But facts, he insists, must be embedded in, entired by stories. And stories—people's stories—are what really have him hooked.

And music. In his later work, he explains, he has come to appreciate the vital qualitative role music can play in the Parkinsonian's or Touretter's life across his recovery:

Music, he insists, is in some profound way healthful.

In his living room, an elegant vintage stereo: The bequest to Sacks of his friend W. H. Auden.

On the irrational and the rational—Sacks has no romantic love of the irrational, nor does he worship the rational. The irrational, he says, can overwhelm a person—he's seen it happen and he doesn't romanticize the consequences—the irrational needs to be mastered into personality—otherwise it merely fractures and scatters. But at the same time, those who have been visited by these irrational firestorms and surmounted them can somehow become deeper human beings, more profound persons, for the experience.

He points to a postcard reproduction of *St. Francis Receiving the Stigmata*, by Van Eyck. "That," he says, "is the painting's actual size! What a miracle of compression! That is the kind of thing I would have liked to do with that book on five seconds in the life of a Touretter."

He prefers to work in institutions. ("I wouldn't work anywhere else but in the back corners of asylums: that's where all the treasures are.") Such as Beth Abraham, the old chronic-care facility in the Bronx, the Mount Carmel of *Awakenings*. Though he also works for the State & the City. His other principal employers are the Little Sisters of the Poor. His parents and a niece, all doctors, all worked for the Little Sisters in other areas. "I like them," he tells me, "because they are implicitly religious without being explicitly religious."

Thus he has very little income. And it's not as if he couldn't use the money. He points over to a wall (shelves & shelves) of EEG readouts. "There are incredible discoveries in there," he assures me, "if only I had the time, if only I could afford the time."

I ask him why he doesn't take private patients. "Well," he says. "I do. I mean, if someone calls up in need, of course I'll see them. But usually it ends up that I see them here, at the house, and often the first session can take five hours—I mean, it takes that long to begin to know someone—and after you've spent five hours with someone, it's just awkward—how can you ask them for money? It makes me too uncomfortable. And then later I always seem to forget to bill them, anyway."

I ask him if he would accept a grant if one were tendered. "Oh," he squirms, "it would arouse as much guilt as anything. I mean, there are people who *need* the money."

Oliver faced a major crisis in 1972. He was fired from Beth Abraham, lost his apartment, and had his mother die—all in the space of a few weeks. He returned to England, sat shiva for his mother for a full week, and "then a strange calm descended and I was able to complete *Awakenings*."

Six months before that crisis, bounding up some basement stairs, he'd crashed his head on the ceiling and been hospitalized. The final 11 case studies in *Awakenings* derived from the notes his secretary had taken at his sickbed as he recounted the stories of the patients.

"Prokofiev," Oliver tells me, "said he could never read *Oblomov* because he couldn't relate to Oblomov's lack of energy. Well, I seem to alternate between periods of Prokofian energy and Oblomovian sloth."

And there *is* a certain ursine melancholy to the man.

He had been institutionalized himself between ages 6 and 10 during the war, in a very bad institution. The experience cast its dark shadow. He was the youngest of four children, and was, for all intents and purposes, raised as an only child by his two doctor parents, his father a jovial GP, his mother a tremendously accomplished gynecologist and one of the first female surgeons in England.

Three older brothers, two of whom also became doctors, and the other . . . The third son, Michael, who'd been with him at the same very bad institution, several years older and indeed on the cusp of puberty, had been destroyed by the experience and is to this day, for all intents and purposes, a schizoid shell of his former self, living in London with their father.

After attending Oxford and then medical school, Sacks himself left England, seemingly in a hurry though he is conspicuously vague about why, landing in California in 1960, where he completed medical residencies in San Francisco and Los Angeles, engaging all the while (he suggests in passing) in binges of drug-taking, muscle-building, speed-motorcycling and all manner of other extreme behaviors, before finally settling in New York.

As I get set to take my leave, Oliver points to a book of Frank Kermode's on the table that he refers to as *The Genesis of Silence*— "When I first saw this book I sat down and composed a letter to Kermode but I never mailed it. I guess I considered that it might be deemed a bit impertinent sending someone a 30,000-word letter on the basis of the *title* of their book alone! I still haven't read it. I lent my copy, bought six more and somehow managed to lend *them* all. Well, I just got a new copy. Do you want it? Or maybe, on second thought, I should keep it and read it this time."

As he pulls the book away, I notice that he's gotten the title slightly wrong. It's actually *The Genesis of Secrecy*.

All of that, as I say, from the first entry in my notebooks. There would be many more—presently fifteen volumes across four years as, pretty much on the model of my three previous years with Irwin, Oliver and I would get together several times a month, if not a week. Fairly early on I resolved to feature him as a subject for a future profile (Mr. Shawn immediately approved), a profile that grew into a prospective book as the months passed. Oliver was agreeable, if a touch wary. I would travel with him to London, join him on rounds (encountering, among others, the last remaining living Awakenings patients), dive with him into natural history museums and botanical gardens on both continents, join him for meals in New York City, or head out again and again to City Island, where he'd give me free run of his files. I would start recording interviews with colleagues and friends from his youth, and others.

It was an odd period in his life. As I say, he'd already written what would in time (though not yet) come to be seen as his masterpiece. In the meantime, though, he'd fallen into an excruciating siege of writer's block on the book immediately following that, an account of a leg accident of his own and its philosophically and therapeutically fraught aftermath. That terrible blockage (which actually often took the form of graphomania, as he spewed forth millions upon millions of words, just not the right words) would eventually take up almost a decade of his life (our first four years being the final four of that siege). Sometimes, a few days after one of our dinners, I might receive a bulging envelope, featuring a dozen-paged, typed (two-finger pecked), single-spaced amplification on some of the things we'd been discussing. He was tormented by feelings of wastage and use-lessness. Indeed, he was at times floridly neurotic on all manner of themes, swinging wildly between feelings of grandiosity and of utter failure. He was pretty much a recluse out there on City Island, still as I say largely unknown, church-mouse poor, entertaining relatively few visitors (and still fewer friends), finding what surcease he could (often, in fairness, quite considerable) in his daily outings to see his patients. He and I kept up our conversations: He seemed to enjoy, by and large, dredging through his past and showing off his wards.

Four years on, his blockage would finally lift and he'd at last complete that damned Leg book of his—with a whole flood of long-dammed-up material clearly just waiting to burst forth in its wake. Indeed, a year after that, in 1985, he would release his breakthrough collection, *The Man Who Mistook His Wife for a Hat*, with almost a dozen other volumes to follow, celebrated bestsellers all over the world, and by the end of the decade *Awakenings* finally would see its translation to the screen, nothing to do with my treatment, alas, with yet more fame and celebration to follow— anyway, just before all of that, I decided to take a retreat of my own, put my notes and transcripts in order (the *index* to my notes ended up taking up more than 250 pages), and finally embark on the writing of my long-gestating profile.

At which point, Oliver asked me not to.

He wouldn't, he assured me, care what I did with all the material after he was dead, but he couldn't live with the prospect of encountering it while still alive. He was wracked with compunctions about one particular aspect of his life, which—well, that's the story, or an important part of it anyway, isn't it? As you will see.

Instead, he hoped that we could remain friends, and indeed we did. I married and he welcomed my bride into his life (and she, somewhat more forbearingly at times, him into ours). She and I had a daughter who became his goddaughter, and the girl grew to adore him (of which more anon, as well). We continued to have splendid adventures together. And then on the far far side of all that, just a few years ago, as he was dying, he not only authorized me to return to that long-suspended project. He positively ordered me to do so: "Now," he said, "*do it!* You *have* to."

※

It would necessarily be a different project. Back then I had been imagining something of a midcareer biography and was taking notes toward that. But life intervened, other things started consuming my attention, decades passed, and I stopped chronicling things Sacksian in the way I would have had to if I were going to be launching into a full-scale biography. In any case—have I mentioned?—the man was a graphomaniac. Talk about shelves groaning under the weight of notebooks! Someday someone is going to take on the project of a full-length Oliver Sacks biography, and it's going to be an extraordinary book when it happens, but that person is going to have to be a lot younger than I am now. I wish him or her well—and I envy them.

Instead, what I propose to offer here is at its core something more like a memoir, in particular of those four years in the early eighties when I was serving as a sort of Boswell to his Johnson, a beanpole Sancho to his capacious Quixote.

Even that prospect was complicated quite late in Oliver's life, however, for indeed just before he issued his command that I now return myself to the fray, he'd published his autobiography, *On the Move*, spilling many of the very tales that for so many years had seemed my own exclusive preserve. And yet perhaps not as complicated as all that, for Oliver's late-life telling of his own tale was suffused—and how can one not celebrate this?—with a certain hard-won grace and serenity, whereas the Oliver one encounters in my notebooks from that time almost forty years earlier was a decidedly other creature, far more wildly (and sometimes, dare I say, delightfully) various, and the furthest thing from serene. In addition, my notebooks teemed with the kind of immediate "table talk" so often elided from more conventional biographies and autobiographies. Here was a sublime empathizer entrammeled in his own self-obsessions, a grand soliloquizer who often soared right past his audiences, blind at times to their very faces, an unparalleled clinician who nevertheless at times couldn't help falling back into the role of a studiously detached naturalist, a chronicler who, while he would never consciously shade the truth, was nevertheless not averse to admitting, proudly, that on occasion he'd had to infer or even to imagine it into being.

Nor had these been just any random four years in his life. In retrospect one sees the first half of the eighties as the virtual hinge of his professional and creative progress, as he seethed and churned to escape the demons of self-involvement veritably blocking any further advancement: By the time they were over, in 1985, this virtual hermit would be on the precipice of worldwide fame, and somehow becalmed and integrated enough (at long last centered rather than merely self-centered) to endure it. (By uncanny coincidence, these were also the years when I myself—albeit at a much less spectacular scale—was consolidating the lineaments of my own professional career, growing from a journeyman California scribe to a regular fixture at *The New Yorker*.)

As I've reacquainted myself with my notebooks during these last few years, and considered how best to organize this book (whether, for example, to reshuffle everything into a sort of conventional biographical order), I came to feel that I ought rather to largely honor the chronology of the entries from those four years, giving the reader a lived sense of how all those often seemingly contradictory details gradually came together for me, offering the reader (and perhaps that future full-scale biographer) a chance to make evolving sense of it for themselves.*

The passage of those four years will thus form the meat, as it were, of this volume. Once they have been forded, I will offer a considerably tighter summary of the years thereafter, at least from my point of view, and some wider thematic meditations as well (not least crucially on the sometimes contested question of Oliver's credibility, among other such topics).

But in the meantime, there's this . . .

---

*There has been some light editing, especially to remove redundancies, and the occasional reordering of material for sense and flow, especially in the first part of the book. But the majority of what follows tracks with the way things happened at the time. For reasons of privacy I have occasionally altered minor details. I have also tended to use pseudonyms for most of the patients referenced in this book, aligning those pseudonyms, where pertinent, with the ones Sacks himself used in his own publications.

In addition, I have radically excerpted from some of the letters and other sorts of texts I will be citing, those of Oliver and of others. However, many of the texts are quite fascinating in their own right, and I have compiled those in their entireties into a sort of SourceBook for this book that is posted online on my personal website, at www.lawrenceweschler.com. The texts that appear at greater length in the SourceBook are indicated with ^{SB}.

PART I

Getting to Know Him

Going for a Row

My next time out to the island, I arrive a bit frustrated because I've just been caught by the local police in an unconscionable speed trap. Oliver sympathizes, takes me out to his driveway, and points to the grille on his car, out of which a little clear plastic spur protrudes.

He tells me how he was always getting tickets for speeding, too, but that one day in Canada he was pulled over and told by the cop himself, "Look, our radar had you clocked at eighty-five."

"Radar?"

"Of course. You should get yourself a Fuzzbuster."

"A Fuzzbuster?"

"Sure. Look, we use electronic surveillance; you have to use counter-surveillance. It's only a game."

Oliver pauses, dreamily, before going on. "For a while I had the rec-ord for motorcycle speeding tickets in California. I used to belong to a semiprofessional racing club in San Francisco, and one afternoon I came tearing off the northern spur of the Golden Gate Bridge rounding that gentle curve right past a highway patrol car that must have been going about half as fast. Later they said I was going 122, although I think that must have been an exaggeration: I could swear I wasn't going a mile over 115.

"It's not an antinomian tendency," he goes on to clarify. "I just *like* speeding—you know, the sense of movement."

Our conversation shifts to the current state of play with his Leg book.

"Like Gaul," he says, "my Leg book falls naturally into three parts.

One: A prologue, Encountering the Bull on the Mountain, fall, and rescue. Two: The ordeal in the hospital in a single room, largely inside my head, provoked to a climax by relentless introspection. Three, and now yet to be composed: A rural Turgenev-like pastoral recovery, making peace, expanding.

"I love Turgenev. My mother used to read me Turgenev.

"My friend the poet Thom Gunn reports that when *his* mother was pregnant, she read him the whole of Gibbon."

Which brings us around to a wider discussion of Thom Gunn and Oliver's doctor colleague Isabelle Rapin and their roles in his life.

"With Thom, as with Isabelle Rapin, I started out imagining them as the sternest people I'd ever met, and now see them as the kindest— stern, that is, but *compassionate.* In both cases, grounded in integrity.

"With both of them the integrity can be felt as sternness or sweetness, depending on which side of the integrity you were on—I mean, over time I had occasion to show them prose occasioning responses of both kinds.

"Thom is relentless on falsehood."

Oliver leaps up to show me a copy of Gunn's new book, a volume of autobiographical essays, inscribed:

> To Oliver, a book of limping prose
> to a man whose prose strides, runs . . . leaps!

At which point, as if taking a cue, Oliver suddenly asks me, "Shall we go out for a row? I mean," he continues, "there will be no problem with speeding out there. At best you can only row three miles per hour!"

We head out to the clapboard garage on the side of his little backyard— inside, a series of oars lined along the wall, one of them with its handle shattered clean off. We pick up the oars and oar grips and walk down toward the narrow beach at the nub end of his street. (I roll up my dress slacks, Huck Finn style.)

The boat, a fifteen-footer, is moored upside down in a little sand alcove, the new keylock jammed with sand. "Only a Jewish intellectual," Sacks grumbles, wrestling with the mechanism, "could get himself into such a fix." And yet we two Jewish intellectuals finally manage to free the thing.

And soon we are out on the water (with my notebook curled in my lap at the prow of the boat, I feel like a damsel with her parasol), Oliver pulling with a clean steady rhythm as the boat slices out toward the open channel. Oliver proceeds to row for well over two hours, a continuous steady rhythm, talking cheerfully all the while. A spangle of sweat soon appears on his brow, but not once does the conversation flag for breath—there is no change whatsoever in his breathing, despite the fact that such exercise would quickly exhaust anyone else I know.

Back in California, in his Muscle Beach days, Oliver recalls, he was known as Doctor Squat or Doctor Quads. He had the strongest legs in the state—he has a photo of himself winning the state weight-lifting championship, hoisting *six hundred pounds!* (In the photo he shows me when we get back, he is huge, his large face ballooning with exertion—he is sporting a trim Abraham Lincoln/Amish beard.) "Mine was called a 'dead lift,' and for good reason—it kills. And indeed, in time I damaged a disk in my back. My legs were stronger than my back! My back wasn't weak—it, too, was strong, only strong *and* vulnerable."

We continue on out. The Empire State Building glistens in the distance, on the far horizon to the south—a paperweight souvenir of itself. "My neighbor, whose boat this is," Oliver tells me, "is an old sea captain: Sometimes he rows it to Wall Street, which is about sixteen miles.

"Over there," he continues, indicating over his shoulder, "is the Throgs Neck Bridge. This is my favorite swim: from the island out to the pylons and back, about six miles altogether" (two beats) "although it can get a bit hazardous since the people in their motorboats don't normally expect swimmers in these waters" (two beats) "especially late at night."

A brief pause as he turns around, reconnoitering our drift.

"Swimming runs in the family," he goes on. "My father loves to swim. The poor man's equivalent of crossing the English Channel was a fifteen-mile course off the Isle of Wight—a race for which he has held a succession of records by decile, for swimmers in their twenties, their forties, their sixties, and, currently, for ninety-year-olds."

And your mother? I ask.

"My mother was not so much into swimming." (Two beats.) "She held several English records in the standing long jump."

I can't quite tell if he is kidding regarding this last. "Well, yes," he avers, "obviously a very un-Edwardian thing to do. But my mother was very well coordinated, you see, not like my father, who like me is clumsy.

"I love to write as I row. Back in 1979," he says, referencing a happier time, as if it were ages ago, "especially on Manitoulin Island in Canada, the rhythm of writing and rowing seemed in perfect unison—I was working on a version of the Leg book—I finally stopped short because my fingers got numb from so much typing, or maybe because I couldn't write about getting better, about returning to the world, about ceasing to be the frantic solitary investigator in the laboratory of myself.

"Rowing allows an investigation of posture and action from the inside. I love performing experiments on and with myself. I also love to write as I swim. Sometimes I have to hurry ashore to scribble what I've thought—and then head out again!

"I'm not a fast swimmer. But steady. And I can swim forever."

As we continue to slice through the water, Oliver indicates over his shoulder, to the west. "Beyond the dunghill, that's Co-op City. It's a public housing project that's radically rotten. Architecturally dishonest. It's not organic and it never quite became a community—no wonder."

At one point he notices that he has the metal oar holds on backward and his attempts to resolve the situation turn progressively more slapstick—the oar splashing about, coming unhinged.

"You see how wrongheaded I am," he giggles, "though hopefully on the right side of lethality.

"For its part," he resumes, "City Island was originally a nautical community—its indigenous industry is nautical gear—this boat, all my boats were made on the island. Also living on the island, because of its proximity to Einstein [the Albert Einstein College of Medicine in the Bronx, where he has an occasional affiliation] are a number of doctors—and then also, a number of strange folks. It's a schizophrenic's paradise.

"I've always loved islands. Do you know D. H. Lawrence's story 'The Man Who Loved Islands'? It's about a wealthy man who sequentially isolates himself on more and more barren islands—his stabs at utopias, I suppose—till he dies on a craggy reef. It's another story my mama used to love to read me. She also loved reading me ghost stories."

More on his mother: "As for medicine, I was already a colleague of hers when I was nine."

At approximately age twenty, Oliver ghostwrote with her a book on menopause that did very well.* "Far better than anything I've ever done since: over 200,000 copies in print. You might recognize the style. Odd, of course, considering that at the time I had and, notwithstanding my subsequent medical education, *still* have no idea what women have down there. It's a complete scotoma to me." (*Scotoma* being one of his favorite words: not only a pathological hole, as it were, in one's visual field, as in certain forms of migraine, but at times an uncanny gap in one's very awareness that one is experiencing such a hollow.)

From there he drifts into a general chronology of his secondary education: Scholarship to Oxford 1950, Oxford 1951 to 1955. Middlesex Hospital in London from 1955 to 1958. Medical degree in 1958, followed by three six-month house jobs (English internships).

We round one of the pylons beneath the Throgs Neck Bridge, and head back toward City Island, his rowing steady, still not the slightest hint of labored breathing.

"Then in 1959, I launched out on a visit to Canada which I am still on.

"One reason I left England was that I was due to be inducted into the army in August 1960—one of the last inductees in a draft which was set to end that September.

"I felt a tremendous sense of injustice and yet, arriving in Canada, I decided I would *love* to serve—only on my own terms. So I decided to apply for service as an MD in the Canadian air force. I was taken to Ottawa and interviewed by a senior officer who ended up saying, 'We'd love to have you, only we're not sure—and we *are* sure *you're* not sure—what your motives are.'"

He recommended that Oliver travel for a few months, which he then did. He bought a motorcycle and cruised cross-country, a time he subsequently memorialized in an unpublished long piece titled "Canada: Pause," culminating, in compensation perhaps, with a stint fighting brush fires in British Columbia. After which he surfaced in San Francisco.

"I've always wanted to, and feared to, belong—I suppose it's part of the Jewish thing. I deal with this, for example, at Einstein by belonging to the staff and never being seen. Or else, I would live in a Jewish neighborhood and work for the Little Sisters."

---

*Muriel Elsie Landau, *Women of Forty: The Menopausal Syndrome* (London: Faber, 1956).

Presently we make landfall back on the little strip of beach at the nub of Horton Street and drag the rowboat ashore. Then walk up the spur of road, stop for a moment at his house to retrieve his prosthetic/transition wedge of a back cushion, and head on up the road, turning right on the main drag toward some restaurants, and establish ourselves in one, where Oliver orders calamari. Which sets him to talking about his days back in secondary school, at St. Paul's Academy in London. He, the antiquarian bookdealer and *Times Literary Supplement* columnist Eric Korn, and the doctor/dramaturg (and Beyond the Fringe veteran) Jonathan Miller were all chums in a legendary biology class in high school. They'd each adopted a favorite grouping: Jonathan—sea worms; Eric—sea cucumbers; and Oliver—cephalopods (including his favorite of those, the cuttlefish).

One day, while summering with Jonathan's parents, Oliver recalls how he and Jonathan were walking past a fish market and heard a monger hawking "Cuttlefish!" at a cheap price. Oliver procured approximately a hundred of them, which the two boys then placed—without preservatives—in a sealed glass jar that they left in the basement of the Millers' home.

"Well, after a few untended weeks," Oliver relates, "of course, the jar exploded with a deep rumbling belch, unleashing what must be the worst smell in the world, that of putrefied cuttlefish. We tried desperately to cover the smell with copious quantities of lavender, so that the room became filled with alternating layers of smell—overripe lavender and rotten cuttlefish—smells that no amount of subsequent cleaning seemed capable of dislodging. We overnight reduced the value of the place, I'm sure, and I don't think Jonathan's parents fancied me around the house quite so much after that."

His earlier passion, he tells me, when he was about ten, had been for chemistry. Returning from a hellish few years at his terrible school outside London, he'd been dazzled at the science museum by his "vision at the periodic table.

"Looking at that table, I saw the logic of the entire world, as if at a moment's glance, and I soon had a lab at home. My parents were generous even though they were in constant danger of being blown up—I was careless, even then, and more than once some sulfur I'd left in the kitchen sink exploded, terrorizing our cook."

Later, however, at St. Paul's, his interest shifted to biology, though that interest was never as intense as had been the initial rush with chemistry.

"Perhaps," he surmises, "the relative decline in the level of such passion was connected with sexual disturbance" (he was entering puberty) "or perhaps because I was now forced to deal with others. Everything I'd done earlier, I'd done in secret and by myself. Jonathan Miller, for instance, first encountered me in a corner of the school library, curled over a book on electrostatics, utterly rapt."

When Oliver arrived at St. Paul's, avid for science, he was at first discouraged by the headmaster and steered onto a more conventional classics track. "But general education stopped when I was thirteen—after that it was pure science."

Well, where then had he gotten all the philosophy?

"Between sixteen and nineteen, as I became less sure of science, I read outside, motivated by a philosophic urgency and need. I went through an enormous amount of useless, hopeless philosophic reading and really none of it helped. Later, at Oxford, where I lived across the street from the library, I read Keynes, the Bloomsbury group, Kierkegaard, but never through the college. In that sense, it was different for me than for Jonathan at Cambridge, where he was a member of the Apostles, a group that engaged in fundamental discussion. And I envied him for that.

"Though, as I say, nothing really held. I was moved by the transparency of Hume, though he didn't give back anything positive. A decade later, in 1966, I experienced an intense Spinoza love that provoked a whole part five to the migraine book as a sort of 'radiant afterspurt,' much like Rilke after *Duino*, which I ended up leaving out, however, because it would have unbalanced the otherwise classical proportions of the book.

"My Leibniz illumination came much later still, in April 1972, a gloomy month when every day seemed filled with sunshine." (This would have been in the midst of the Awakenings drama, well before he'd completed that book. It was also soon after Auden left America: Oliver had accompanied him to the airport that April 15.) "I wandered into a little bookshop on Third and Eighty-Eighth, and in a strange somnambulistically sure way pulled down a volume of Leibniz's correspondence with Arnauld—and my universe blew up. Dewey, you know, had been likewise detonated by Leibniz. I think both of us were attracted by the organic inner activity in Leibnitz. (Thank God I hadn't read Russell on Leibniz before that—it would have killed him for me.)"

He is silent for a moment, stirring the last of the calamari about with his fork. "The thing is, I need a philosophical framework, otherwise my patients would always be blowing my mind. And as I've been composing the Leg book, uniting the clinical with the philosophical, I can't think why I didn't hazard such a framework before—nor why everybody doesn't do it all the time."

We get up and head back toward the house. How's the Leg book going? I ask. His mood turns suddenly dark and gloomy, and he is pretty much silent the rest of the way.

2

Early Childhood, a Harrowing Exile, Cruel Judaism, Homosexuality, and a Mother's Curse

During the ensuing weeks, I got clearance from *The New Yorker*, and permission from Oliver, to begin pursuing a profile, and one of our next meetings took place in the New York Botanical Garden, across (and under) the Bronx River Parkway from Beth Abraham. Oliver began by noting that he comes here three hundred days a year, evincing a love of the botanical that verges on the primordial if not the downright primeval (both in terms of what he loves—ferns, mosses, cycads: the more ancient the better—and in terms of the love itself, which he insisted went back to his earliest days in the backyard garden of his family home).

At one point, I mentioned that I was going to California the next week to deal with the upcoming release of my book on Robert Irwin by the University of California Press, and Oliver in turn suggested I might take advantage of the trip to visit with two of his closest friends from his medical-residency days in California during the early sixties (in San Francisco from September 1960 through July 1962, and then Los Angeles through October 1965): Bob Rodman and Thom Gunn.

Oliver explained how he and Rodman had first met around 1962 at UCLA as residents who shared a vivid common interest, a passion for landscape photography ("California aroused in me a photographer's lyricism"). "And Bob," he assured me, "has detailed memory for periods which I have entirely occluded—I have, or at any rate pretend to have, complete amnesia for the period from 1948 through 1966."

They subsequently shared their writing with each other. And he regards Rodman's daughter as his goddaughter. Rodman's wife died in

1974, during the very time of Oliver's leg calamity. Oliver suggested Bob turn his own anguish into art, which resulted in Bob's book ("a very fine book") *Not Dying*. "There is no doubt that by way of the intensity of shared feelings during those years, we encountered each other at a deeper, stricken level."

As for Gunn, the eminent English transplant poet who I would subsequently be meeting in San Francisco, Oliver explained: "I met Thom through his poetry: his first collection, *Fighting Terms*, and then especially the next one, *The Sense of Movement*, which appealed to me enormously. Indeed, seeking him out was one of the things I'd had in mind when I first headed down to California from Canada.

"Let's see, I arrived in September 1960 and we met some while after that. I saw much of him at the time. I did a lot of traveling on my motorbike, wrote many travel pieces—I was enchanted and verbose, and would show stuff to him. He would criticize some pieces in terms that at the time I found cruel: I approached him raw and vulnerable, as a student or acolyte, and his criticism perhaps made me retreat.

"Still, I'd see him on occasion, at intervals. We were reunited by my publication of *Awakenings*. He sent me a letter that at the time obsessed me: I kept it in my pocket or wallet for months. I wrote reply after reply, eventually well over two hundred pages, none of which I posted."

What had Gunn said?

"Basically, he wrote that when he'd first encountered me in 1961 he'd thought me the cleverest man he'd ever met and yet he'd found something lacking, and precisely the most important—a sympathy, a humanity—something whose lack made him despair of all the rest. 'I despaired of you,' he wrote, '*and now this*. What happened? What changed?'"

I asked Oliver, What had?

"Well, that would require an autobiography, wouldn't it?" Oliver hesitated, holding back, stammering, wondering, it seemed, how open he should be, should allow himself to be. I assured him that I would let him review anything I submitted prior to publication with regard to any eventual profile. He sighed deeply and went on.

"Well, and um . . . what had excited me in Thom Gunn's poetry was its homoerotic lyricism, a romantic perverseness. The perverse transmuted into art. He gave a voice to things which I'd imagined singular and solitary, and this filled me with admiration. The other side of this being that he dealt with elements with which I had never come to terms in myself. And still haven't."

Another long, considered silence.

"At the time—I mean back in the early sixties—I'd been doing a good deal of writing about sex, often satirical portraits, and Thom found some of these (especially one about a mutual friend) cruel and hateful. Perhaps he was right. Indeed, I did a lot of writing about sex between twenty-two and twenty-eight, writing which had a certain power and perverseness. But this all stopped twenty years ago."

Another pause. "The thing is, Thom depicted things with compassion which I depicted hatefully. I mean, there were some things he'd liked: a long lyrical piece on fetishism that he prized.

"Furthermore, both of us were English, but more, we were both Londoners, and still more, we are both specifically from Hampstead Heath—the same hillocks make up our mutual primal landscape. And I hold him very dear."

Ever so tentatively, I tried to ease Oliver back into a conversation about his sexuality. "Closed book," he snapped. "Has been for years. I have not been with anyone for over fifteen years now." There followed a long pause as he hemmed and hawed. "Celibate. Celi . . . bate." He loped over to a drooping sunflower, gently lifted its seedpod to his face, and began delicately palpating the pod, his hems and haws morphing into hums and awws.

"By the age of five," he continued at length, conspicuously changing the subject, or so it seemed, "I had become quite fascinated with the sunflowers in my father's backyard. I didn't know the word for it then, but what intrigued me was the way the seeds in the pod tended to organize themselves in variations of prime numbers. Which in turn got me thrumming on the character of the primes themselves. And also burrowing into the notion of pi, which I'd eventually calculate to several hundred places. In my head.

"Funny," he said. "Just the other day I was reading a book on freak calculators—a fascinating book, of course, but I'm afraid I disagree with the whole approach. The author fails to understand the crucial distinction between calculation and numerical contemplation. I was a calculator myself as a child, which is to say I could accomplish mental arithmetic of a high order—I was very good at long sequences of multiplication, at determining roots, and so forth (my father, too, could add long lines of figures at a glance)—but I was also fond of numerical contemplation: the sense of being at play, adrift in a Pythagorean landscape.

"So much of the literature deals with the exhibition of freaky aptitude, with exhibitionism. But there's very little on the numerical temperament. For instance, Zacharias Dase, the number prodigy who was otherwise a dullard, could look at a handful of peas thrown on a table, it was said, and immediately say, '117,' and it's usually imagined that he counted out the peas very quickly—that he 'counted' them 'at a glance.' But the real question Dase raises is 'What is a glance?' Because I'm convinced he saw them immediately as 117 *in* his glance."

Oliver released the sunflower stalk, which now bobbed, presently reverting to its droop.

"Or take the case of the Fin twins, whom I've met on several occasions over the years: The calendrical landscape simply lies before them and they wander through it as you would a park. For a numerically prodigious child, numbers can form a nursery country in which the figures are friends. And in my own case, such numerical contemplation proved the precursor of a similar engagement with the periodic table and then scientific wonder, generally.

"But it is exactly the notion of 'freak show' which should be disbanded. The Fin twins could tell me what day I last saw them on ten years ago. But they are numerical *artists*, not algorithmists. And theirs is an art which is all the more impressive for being of such a low order."*

Oliver went on to describe a precipitous fall from the paradise of these early years. At age six, not long after the death of a beloved Hebrew teacher, he and his older brother Michael, upon the onset of the Battle of Britain in June 1940, were hastily bundled off to "that hideous boarding school in the country," as he now characterized it. "The headmaster was an obsessive flagellist, his wife an unholy bitch, and the sixteen-year-old daughter a pathological snitch. The place was called Braefield, though Michael quickly took to calling it Dotheboys, after the Dickensian hellhole in *Nicholas Nickleby*, and does to this day; he committed vast

---

*Sacks would presently write up the case of the Fins in his "The Twins" chapter of his forthcoming *The Man Who Mistook His Wife for a Hat* (New York: Summit Books, 1985), 185–203.

passages of that book to memory and can recite them at the drop of a hat . . . We were beaten. I was beaten *every day*. When our parents finally came to visit, I rushed to my mother and clutched fiercely at her knees shrieking, 'Never again! Never again! Never leave me like this again!' But she patted me, assuring me things couldn't be as bad as all that, and soon departed. It was the last strong emotion I ever expressed to her."

What of his parents? What were they doing?

"Well, as a child, I imagined that they were utterly occupied in abandoning me. In fact, they were enormously busy, as I came to understand intellectually years later, though never completely emotionally."

They were both doctors, frantically working through the Battle of Britain.

"My mother was a surgeon, so that she was busy cycling from one scene of devastation to another, operating under appalling conditions. This before the days of antibiotics, when surgical complications were a horror.

"But this separating of the children from their parents—a decision had been made: The Youth of the Empire would be safeguarded at all costs. Anyway, I believe in retrospect this was bad psychologically. It've been better to have faced the bombs with our families."

How did his parents feel about it?

"My father doesn't speak his feelings. Mother did, but only posthumously. She kept a journal during the fall of 1940, which I discovered after her death, in which she repeatedly expressed her distress, but the journal stopped after a few months. She was just too busy.

"We were beaten," Oliver repeated, almost mantra-like, cringing at the memory. "I was beaten *every day*. We were black-and-blue but our parents didn't see it, and for some reason, we didn't complain. Everyone else complained—complained and was removed. We were the last two there. Finally, they just came and closed the place down."

During the war, his aunt Helena Landau, his mother's sister, had a forest school in Cheshire. "The Jewish Fresh Air School—the JFAS—whereas Jewishness is usually stale air." The school where he and Michael were incarcerated was approximately forty miles out of London, hers another forty. Just as the school where he was kept was an infernal experience, hers represented for him a paradisal haven. Every child, he told me, had his or her own garden. He'd go there on holidays and other leaves from his hellhole.*

He had mentioned the uncle who saved him after the war by introducing him to the periodic table. Had he been saved in some sense by this aunt as well?

"Absolutely. She was almost the only good person, the only good reality during those years. She stood for reason, humor, affirmation." He went on to talk at some length about this wonderful maiden aunt, Lennie, as she was universally known throughout the family. ("By age eighty-two, shortly before her death, she would have eighty-seven nieces and nephews and three hundred twenty grandnephews and grandnieces.") She continued to play a major role in his life, standing for one pole of humane decency as against all sorts of other extremities of dereliction. For example, he wanted someday to write a book about homes versus institutions—her school representing an originary home, Braefield a primal institution. Likewise, he said, she stood in, in his mind, for a Judaism steeped in nature.

He paused. "In dying, her last words to me were: 'Don't ignore the minor prophets—Amos, Micah—don't just stick to the big ones like Isaiah.'

"My own parents," he now shifted gears slightly, "though not fanatically Orthodox, lived in a ghetto of their own making. My father to this day is always amazed when a goy turns out to be human."

Oliver cited, for example, their bitter opposition to the marriage at age forty of his brother Marcus in Australia to a *converted* gentile! "They were repelled by a radical uncleanness." Oliver interceded angrily and the marriage occurred (and survived). Just one instance of "an incredible streak of Jewish cruelty which years earlier had fallen on Uncle Benny, my father's brother who I didn't even know existed until my adulthood. He, too, had married a gentile, been hounded out of the family, moved to Portugal. The two brothers, estranged for fifty years! Finally, the woman died and during the years before Benny's death, reconciliation of a sort finally occurred."

This cruel Jewish streak "curiously stopped completely when it came to patients, who were all treated with equal humanity." Both of

---

*I never did understand why their aunt hadn't simply rescued him and Michael herself back then, and now, alas, it's too late to ask anyone.

his parents were involved, for instance, with the chronic-care homes of the Little Sisters of the Poor, as he himself would also be many years later.

He paused for a moment, taking in a bank of ferns. "My mother was sensitive but inhibited," he said. "Lennie used to consider her a dedicated surgeon, overwhelmed into rigorous distance on account of being too sensitive. I don't know."

Their own relationship, his and his mother's, was by Oliver's account way too intense, too close. He was her youngest and a prodigy. She showered him with attention, often deeply affirming but at other times wildly inappropriate. Reading him D. H. Lawrence stories that were decidedly beyond his ken, for example. Or how one of the first buried memories to emerge during his psychoanalysis years later was how she used to bring home monstrosities from surgery—deformed embryos, fetuses in jars—this when he was ten, and then, when he was twelve, how she brought him along to perform the dissection of a child's corpse.

A sudden bracing of resolve now seemed to sweep over him, as if he were only just then remembering my original prodding questions.

"When I was twenty-one and home for a visit from Oxford," he said, "I accompanied my father one evening on his rounds. We were driving in the car and he asked me how things were going. Fine, I told him warily. Did I have any girlfriends? he inquired—now he was the one being wary. No. Why didn't I have any girlfriends? I guessed I didn't like girls . . . Silence for a few moments . . . Does that mean you like boys? Yes, Father, I replied, I am a homosexual, and please don't tell Mother, not under any circumstances, it would break her heart and she would never understand.

"Not that I'd yet had *any* actual experiences.

"At any rate, the next morning my mother came tearing down the stairs, shrieking at me, hurling Deuteronomical curses, horrible judgmental accusations. This went on for an hour. Then she fell silent. She remained completely silent for three days, after which normalcy returned. And the subject was never mentioned again during her lifetime."

He was silent for a long while, shuffling pebbles in the path about with the toes of his shoes. "At twenty-seven, in 1959, at the end of Oxford and medical school, I ran belatedly away from home, to Canada. Dishonestly so."

How come "dishonestly"?

"I left with no intention of returning and without telling them so. My frequent letters were rich in botanical and geological detail, although empty of the personal. But soon I'd be in San Francisco, and then Los Angeles."

3

Conversations with Bob Rodman
and Thom Gunn in California

At the outset of my own July 1982 trip to California, I sat down with Oliver's old UCLA friend F. Robert Rodman, who had in the meantime become a distinguished psychoanalyst and Donald Winnicott biographer, in the garden of his Pacific Palisades home; I didn't tape-record our conversation, so what follows derives entirely from my contemporaneous notes.

We met in 1962 when we were both serving out residencies at the UCLA Medical Center, me in psychiatry and him in neurology. He was a great big barrel-chested oddball who was treated as a freak by the other residents, the three other neurologists who were a bunch of obsessive-compulsive conformists. Oliver wouldn't behave, he wouldn't follow rules, he'd eat the leftover food off the patients' trays during rounds, and he drove them nuts.

One time I was there when he presented a case with exquisite precision and care—his capacity for clinical description was so impressive—but they weren't impressed.

He aroused tremendous hostility; on occasion still does.

To me the greatest thing Oliver represents is the compelling need to reunite art and science. And yet this is what galls some people: "Damn it all, he's not being a scientist, he should rid himself of the pleasures of art and language."

His entire passion is to *make whole*, to give himself as an example of wholeness as against fragmentation. But people, and especially his fellow

Bob Rodman

doctors, are addicted to their fragmentations, their specializations; they resent creativity and are rewarded for their obsessive-compulsive avoidances.

Much later, just recently, when we went to a coffee shop, at one point he was accused of stealing a soft drink. He was abashed, pitiful: He didn't know what to do. Later he asked me, "Is there something different about me?"

And, of course, there is: He's like a big, free-ranging animal. He strides around with his head up in a perpetual state of wonderment.

He can be stunned by an ice plant: "Wait a minute—it's giving off more light than it is taking in!"

He's constantly raising things to a higher power: That's his gift.

One day, I hesitate to mention this, but, ah well, he drank some blood. He kept staring at it and then, "Oh, the hell with it," he exclaimed, and drank it down, chasing it with milk. There was something about his need to cross taboos.*

Back in those days, in the early sixties, he was heavily into drugs,

---

*Talk about *trayf*! Milk and blood being the very definition of kosher-transgressing.

downing whole handfuls of them, especially speed and LSD, not so much marijuana. He was very self-destructive.

At UCLA, he spent a lot of time in the darkroom, developing pictures. He'd go to the roughest bar in town and plop his camera on the counter and start snapping photos, as if he were just looking for trouble.

He was a motorcycle enthusiast in his big lumbering leather jacket, given over to very long rides at very high speeds, would think nothing of cycling up to San Francisco and back in a single day; he once took a young patient with highly advanced MS for whom the drugs were no longer doing a thing out of the hospital, strapped to his back, on a motorcycle ride in the hills, at her request. Which caused another huge scandal.

One time some guy in a car was giving him trouble—car guys are always giving motorcyclists a hard time—and at the next light, Oliver reached in and tweaked the guy's nose!

He used to live out in Topanga Canyon in a very isolated cabin, two or three rooms, a sun porch overlooking a knoll. A piano that he subsequently gave us. He could be wonderfully hospitable up there, offering you lovely things he'd prepared himself, served with the greatest delicacy.

He's a person one has the urge to take care of, to shelter. When you are with him, and he's feeling comfortable, he can be so wonderfully expansive, but then when he goes back onto the street, he veritably seems to contract—a terrible sadness seems to overtake him as he returns to his life.

One time I visited London with him, had Friday-night dinner with his Orthodox Jewish family, the disturbed brother reciting lengthy prayers in Hebrew. A strange hypocrisy around the mother ("Don't smoke at the table, save it for later on"). At one point the father took me upstairs to see the *OED*—there was clearly a great love of words. Great culture, but extremely neurotic. The passive father, the domineering mother. She was very ambitious and driven; he, a GP, the more practical one, asked me straight out if I needed any money (I felt like a child: well cared for). On the other hand, even before medical school Oliver ghostwrote his mother's gynecological text: I think she saw him very much as a tool and an extension of herself.

When he was twelve years old (has he ever told you about this?), his mother had him dissect a body—a child's body!—something he remained ashamed of and confounded by. I mean, can you imagine such a thing? The crazy-making stamping of a mind at that age. The seduction. The privileged access to a body. The excitement of it, alongside the sense of being putty in someone else's hands, his mother's.

Though he deeply grieved after her death.

Freud wrote *The Interpretation of Dreams* shortly after his father died and Oliver wrote *Awakenings* right after his mother died, and not that long after came the incident in Norway.

※

Norway is of course supercharged for him. The first time he told me of his experience there with the bull, we were sitting right here, and we spoke of a possible "paranoid transference," his fear of his originality being snatched away from him. No more than thirty seconds into that conversation, he went all flush and we had to be off and walking.

And then, walking, he spoke of his fear of being "endunced," as he put it, how some people can "bedunce" you, somebody else can formulate you into a box—this gnawing feeling that he was nothing but a blowhard, which is what many people in fact thought him to be, such that he stayed out of reach (frantically soaring, like an eagle) so as not to be bedunced.

Of course this went side by side with a sense of special privilege, going back to that charged relationship between his mother and himself.

Which I've often thought in turn allows for an interpretation of that Norway experience as a sort of oedipal provocation, with the bull (his father) castrating him (his leg). In which context, to me it seems entirely possible that part of this whole paralysis was psychosomatic (it did all take place the summer right after his mother's death).

Which may in turn help account for why the book has become so loaded for him: the fantasy that his very conception had rendered his father—whose originality he stole—the passive man he is, the benign passive sweet figure. And Oliver lives in fear that his own originality could be taken away again.

※

The first time Oliver was in the paper, his father was far from delighted, in fact mildly annoyed: "The goys will get you!"

His father's fearfulness being most prominent: "Don't stick out, don't be potent."

And yet there Oliver had been as a child, already manifestly potent.

His conflicted partial shame in later years at displaying himself, his occasional disgust at his own dazzle.

*

Dinner with Oliver: At table he begins with great delicacy, progressively dispensing, though, with knives and forks, becoming more and more animal-like, till he's just mauling not only his own plate but yours as well.

*

His letters are masterpieces. That stutter of his—it's in the letters too, the reaching out after the correct expression, the hesitation, stopping and starting over . . .

He used to destroy his manuscripts, the work of years, in fits of self-disgust. He writes at a tremendous pace but can destroy in an instant. It's a good thing that now he's learned to deposit copies with others.

*

When I'm talking to him, I sometimes feel that he is not talking to me—he becomes so absorbed in expressing himself that his interlocutor disappears. He can be exquisitely attuned one minute, then utterly self-absorbed the next. Or maybe it's just that he's reverting to the only peers with whom he truly seems to engage in continual conversation—Kierkegaard, Leibniz, Thomas Browne . . .

On the other hand, when he is with patients, he attends to *them* perfectly. It's as if the patients rescue him from his narcissism, drawing him back into the world, delivering him every bit as much as he is delivering them.

But only with the sorts of patients he finds in institutions: He belongs to and with the Community of the Refused.

*

He is subject to migrainous attacks, during which he becomes physically overwhelmed. He is conscious of his physiology in a way that few are. That way, for example, he will suddenly bound up and simply *have* to be out walking . . .

And yet there is an overarching benignity to him: a larger-than-life person organizing himself toward a delicate gesture, a goodbye kiss on the cheek of my little daughter.

※

A strange consciousness and awareness in him of his own oddity, which I think has been in him since his childhood—being a genius like that since childhood must have rendered him very lonely—and yet, in spite of the pressures and the ridicule, he has developed autonomously (he sees himself as integrated, and he may be right, he being the integrated one and the rest of us the oddballs).

Sure, he's stunted and yet in another sense he has this incredible autonomy, *like a gigantic bonsai tree*, an awesome survivor.

※

He really came to my rescue when my wife was dying back in 1974. He was the one whose interventions meant the most—the immense breadth of his ego, its sheer capacity to wrestle with the tragedies of life, made him an ideal interlocutor. He wrote some letters that I published in my own eventual book on those months simply as a demonstration of how it is possible for one person to help another.*

※

July 3, 1982 [handwritten, Sacks to Weschler]

Dear Ren,

I am glad you had a good meeting with Bob Rodman—and I am glad you will be seeing Thom Gunn. That leaves only my friends on the East Coast—and above all in England!

I am sorry I got neurotic on the phone at the Botanical Garden the other day, but (especially being a portraitist myself)

---

*Thus, for example, definitely seek out Rodman, *Not Dying* (Random House, 1977), 84–86.

I find it a bit scary to find myself the subject of a (potential) portrait—and fear disclosures of all sorts. But equally, indeed far more strongly, I know that I can trust your discretion and dignity no less than your exceptional gifts and penetration—and I suspect too that the darker sides of myself may not be too relevant to what I sometimes am—at best. Or, at most, through a mysterious alchemy and sublimation.

✻

After meeting with Rodman, I traveled to San Francisco, where I saw Thom Gunn, the British poet whose journey west had presaged and in some senses occasioned Oliver's own.

Born in 1929 (four years before Oliver), in Kent, England, Gunn graduated from Trinity College, Oxford, in 1953 (two years before Oliver received his undergraduate degree, also from Oxford, though from a different college and they do not appear to have met there). The following year Gunn published his first book, Fighting Terms, *and shortly thereafter he left for America, initially to study with Yvor Winters at Stanford, after which he settled permanently in San Francisco, where his next book,* The Sense of Movement, *followed in 1957. One of the truly eminent poets of the English language during the latter half of the twentieth century, he wrote verse that blended his English roots (especially formally: for the first decade of his career he restricted himself to iambic pentameter, striving as he quipped at the time, to be "the John Donne of the Twentieth Century") and the light of his transplanted California home (in terms of subject matter, especially, mirroring the likes of Gary Snyder and Robert Duncan in the way he celebrated popular culture and the vagaries of daily life). In later years, he would produce one of the great acts of witness to the AIDS epidemic,* The Man with Night Sweats *(1992), but that horror still lay in the future, or rather was only just beginning to make itself enigmatically felt, when we met at a little Italian espresso place in the Castro, on July 3, 1982. What follows is a condensed and edited version of the tape of our conversation.*

How'd you first meet Oliver?
I met Oliver here in San Francisco in it must have been 1961, shortly after he'd arrived in California as a medical intern. He rode a motorcycle and called himself "Wolf," which is apparently his middle name. One time he

Thom Gunn

kiddingly said, "What would my maternal grandfather think if he knew the way I am using his name?" It sounded nicely ferocious. And he wrote a great deal. He wanted from very early on to be a writer, and he kept extensive notebooks. *Extensive.* I remember at one point there being something like a thousand typed pages of journal. One summer he decided to chronicle the trucking life, had gotten on his motorcycle, which broke down, and ended up hitching with truckers and coming back with a long account of what it was like to be a trucker.*

Another time he took his motorcycle down to Baja, Mexico, very remote, I'm not sure where he even got his gasoline, but he told me about it when he came back, how he'd slept in his sleeping bag by the side of the road. I said it must have been wonderful, and he said, yeah, except for all those vultures circling overhead. And I said, yeah, but everyone knows that vultures don't attack a living person, to which he replied, "Yes, but it kept

---

*A lengthy excerpt of that story, "Travel Happy," from 1961, is included in Oliver's autobiography, *On the Move*, 81–95.

crossing my mind that there might be the odd schizophrenic vulture that didn't know that."

I don't know what happened to that journal, at one point I had the whole thing, I wish I could show it to you right now, it may well have gotten inadvertently thrown out a while back when I moved, I know I haven't seen it since I've been living in this house, which has been ten years.

What was he like, especially on just arriving?
Well, this is something I really wanted to tell you about, because he has gone through the most extraordinary changes of anybody I've ever known. I wasn't present for the change, but I witnessed both the before and after. Going back to the journal, for example, there was one bit that became quite notorious among his acquaintances, because he wrote a scathingly satirical piece about a sadistic eye doctor, a guy who in the meantime unfortunately has gone mad, but at the time he was sane, or as sane as he was ever going to be, though slightly odd. I mean, he wasn't a sadistic doctor; he was sexually sadistic. So Oliver wrote this satirical piece on him, referring to him as Doctor Kindly, and the piece *was* quite funny. But it was very unsympathetic toward someone whom Oliver basically liked personally. And then he went and showed the piece to the guy. And the guy didn't like it at all, was actually quite hurt, as who wouldn't be, nobody would like being made fun of in such a way. And Oliver was quite taken aback by the reaction.

My criticism of him at the time, and I don't know how overt it was but it was there, was that the piece was well written, wonderfully observant, obviously good training for some kind of writing career, *but* . . . It was as if he was the only person there, everybody else was being judged so harshly, so contemptuously, and so sarcastically. He seemed to have a great inability to put himself inside the skin of others, or even to be able to imagine how they might react to him. Not that he did this so much in person, it was entirely literary. I mean, obviously it had something to do with what he felt about people, but it was not at all what he really felt about people: He was a much nicer man than he appeared, than he presented himself as being in his writing. He was much more transparently self-dramatizing in those days. I mean, there is of course still a sense of drama about him, though you don't feel it is in any sense posturing. It was never unpleasant

posturing at all, he was always nice, but in his youthful enthusiasms he
was always trying on poses.

Then he went down to Southern California, and I saw less of him. I
didn't start seeing him frequently again until after he'd moved to New
York, by which time he was an entirely different man.

This would have been before he wrote Awakenings?
Oh yes, but he was obviously the man who would be able to write *Awakenings*. The first Oliver I knew would have been the last person I would
have thought capable of writing *Awakenings*. It was precisely his problem
that he couldn't sympathize with people enough. It wasn't that he was lacking in kindness; rather he was lacking in sympathetic imagination. And
that is of course what he has now—in his conduct and his talk and his life
and his writing—more than anyone else I know.

Now, what happened in between, I don't know. I'm sure it was a great
complex of things. There was obviously a maturing. When he arrived in
California, he still had no sense of who he was or what he wanted to be—as
I suppose none of us do when we are young and everything is changing.
And he was unhappy. Maybe it's just that whatever we mean by maturing, the sort of thing most people go through in their early twenties, he
still hadn't gone through any of that.

*Perhaps it had to do with his having been something of a prodigy, the way that a
child who is already the intellectual equal of adults at, say, age five is likely nonetheless to lack the emotional maturity to go along with it, and indeed may still
have the emotional maturity of a five-year-old well into his adulthood.*
I think that could be right, and that other maturity didn't really come till
his late twenties or early thirties, though when it did, finally, it was a much
deeper and more meaningful and more thorough-going maturity than
maybe any I've ever seen.

As to how it could possibly have arisen, I know it's unfashionable and
dated to say this kind of thing, but I think Oliver might support me in
saying this: I think it may have had something to do with his taking a lot
of acid, at a time when we were all taking a lot of acid. We didn't exactly
coincide in this, he'd already left San Francisco by the time I myself
started, but he did do a lot of chemical experimentation, I mean, outra-
geously extreme, far more than anyone else I knew.

His old slogan: "Every dose an overdose."
Right! Precisely. And I think that may have had something to do with it.
I mean, there are a lot of outrageous claims made about acid. Nevertheless, I find that it helped me get insight into myself and my life and other
people that I might not have attained otherwise.

*But going back to the before version of Oliver, when his brilliance was coupled to
a certain—what shall we call it?—shallowness.*
A bit, yes, maybe, but any word I could use makes it sound more vicious
than I intend. Self-centered? Perhaps, but it wasn't so much self-centered as
there was an inability to get beyond the self. There was that cleverness at
the expense of others, an inability to recognize how he might be hurting
others, as with Doctor Kindly. The sort of thing we all go through perhaps
in our teens, being smartasses as a way of proving ourselves, defining ourselves by scoring off others, but here he was approaching thirty. He was
never very nasty, if anything I was sometimes nasty to him. He was always
generous, but there was this other . . . Actually, I often found him a bit
irritating in those days, and embarrassing because he was so enthusiastic
about me, and I just didn't feel there was much to be enthusiastic about.
He seemed to be finding things in me which I honestly didn't think were
there.

What kinds of things?
Wisdom and stuff. I don't know. The motorcycles in my poetry. I know
Jonathan Miller first got him to read me.

*One thing he has said about you is that in your poetry you were so much more at
ease with issues that were still causing him grief, the homoeroticism in particular
being what I suspect he is referring to.*
Well, he did seem to be just beginning to come to terms with that, fitful
terms perhaps. I'm sure he wouldn't mind my telling you how he seemed
to fall for a series of what struck me as rather silly little boys, who were
immensely attracted to his motorcycles. A series? Maybe it was only two
or three, but it did seem endless, and they were all very butch, and very
nice-looking, and very young, and very rough. They seemed to be off the
streets, and obviously he was a great big burly father figure to them, and a
wonderfully romantic figure.

What with the motorcycles and all, did you have the sense that he was living dangerously?
I think he is a dangerous rider, yes, or a reckless driver, let's put it that way.

And also dangerous in terms of the people he hung out with?
I don't know that they were dangerous. I mean, I don't think they had knives. As I say, they tended to be more like little street boys. But no, he hung out more in leather bars, as I did, and they're not dangerous. He was a boisterous presence, and I suspect he probably charmed half the people and annoyed the other half.

I could easily imagine him getting into trouble with those he annoyed.
Well, yes, no. I mean, he might have gotten beaten up, though remember he was very strong, still there was an obliviousness to danger with him. On the other hand, you're really no more likely to get yourself beat up in a leather bar than anywhere else, it's all just for show.

And then, of course, he got to know Mel, I guess you know about Mel . . .

Not that much.
Well, Mel was the . . . a wonderful boy. He was probably about the same age as the others, physically he looked like them, but he was—is—a person of great sensitivity and intelligence, and they did live together in Southern California. I found him rather attractive myself. I didn't get to know him that well, since they were down there, the last time Oliver visited here was with him—that was many years ago. Mel seemed to me, without over-sentimentalizing things, to be *the* great love, and a worthy love he was, too. I don't know what difficulties there were, or I suppose there must have been, since he never moved to New York with Oliver. They are still friends, I believe, and they obviously feel a great deal for each other. He struck me as very fine, on the few occasions I met him, I liked him a lot. Today he lives somewhere up north, Oregon or something. I don't know whether Oliver has had any love relationships since then. My sense is he hasn't.

Did you have a sense of his living a very split life in those days, with his medical work to one side and the rest to the other?

No, I didn't see it as split, on the contrary it seemed wonderfully integrated. All of the enthusiasms would spill over into each other. Part of the richness of his mind comes from the fact that there are all these interests, and all this knowledge of different sorts, and none of it is categorized. He's not like the professor of eighteenth-century literature who hasn't read any of seventeenth- or nineteenth-century literature since having taken his PhD. He's more like Ezra Pound or somebody like that.

Indeed, he strikes me as coming from the period before the sciences and the humanities split apart. Leibniz and Browne and people like that seem his contemporaries. Just the other day he was quoting William Harvey on the musicality of movement.*

Yes, it's as if they were all his contemporaries and he was merely adding his observations to theirs, almost as if he were expecting them to reply, and sometimes even hearing their replies.
Pretty early on, I think before the migraine book or else immediately afterwards, he said to me how he longed to write a book that would be good science and good literature. Maybe not exactly those words, but something close. And then he went and did just that.

Though of course this capacity of his is still all tied up with the most remarkable sense and pressure of compulsion. I mean, I recognize a certain compulsiveness in myself, the sense sometimes that I just have to do things, or that I can't write, or whatever—but nothing like him. My blocks are never so lengthy or so absolute. On the other hand, when I do then write, I could never write the way he does either, you know, through days and nights, nonstop, thousands of words all perfectly ordered in just a few

---

*Oliver was often citing William Harvey, the great seventeenth-century Oxford anatomist (best known perhaps for being the first to have properly worked out the circulation of blood), as in this footnote from Oliver's essay "The River of Consciousness," published in *The New York Review of Books,* Jan. 15, 2004.

[M]usic, with its rhythm and flow, can be of crucial importance in such freezings, allowing patients to resume their flow of movement, perception, and thought. Music sometimes seems to act as a sort of model or template for the sense of time and movement such patients have temporarily lost. Thus a parkinsonian patient in the midst of a standstill may be enabled to move, even to dance, when music is played. Neurologists intuitively use musical terms here and speak of parkinsonism as a "kinetic stutter" and normal movement as "kinetic melody." Harvey, writing in 1627, referred to animal motion as "the silent music of the body."

weeks. *Migraine* in nine days, that kind of thing: the ability to tap into demons like that. The epic blockages, on the other hand, seem in some way allied to his feeling of sympathy with the patients in *Awakenings*, who are more completely blocked than anyone else one can imagine. When he describes how they are running and their steps are getting so much smaller and smaller until, ultimately, they are just running internally—one sees this imaginative sympathy, perhaps also coming in some way from his brother, who I sometimes think he conceives of almost as an alternative self.

Indeed, what about his brother?
Well, as you may know, he is, I don't know the word, maybe schizophrenic or something. Oliver once apparently overheard him say, "I went mad so the rest of you could stay sane." Most extraordinary remark. I'm not sure what one makes of that, though I am sure he means a lot to Oliver, over and beyond his just being a relative.

{A long silence, and then, as if to leaven the gravity of that last remark, Gunn breaks into a wide smile.}
The funniest thing he ever told me, or I should perhaps say the strangest, though he was himself laughing when he told it to me, was how at a very early age, maybe six or seven, maybe even earlier, he conceived a sort of presexual desire for a blimp. A sensual desire. I mean, who but Oliver could desire a blimp?

But he was serious, he was not making this up, this was not a retrospective fantasy. I cannot imagine Oliver lying, when I think about it—almost less than anyone else. And if he were to exaggerate, he would *believe* the exaggeration.

As I am getting set to leave, I ask Gunn if he still has a copy of the letter he wrote Oliver after Awakenings *came out in 1973; he rifles through some files, finds it, makes a copy, and hands it to me, graciously offering permission for me to cite or reprint it. And I have included it in its entirety in the SourceBook.**

---

*The SourceBook can be found at www.lawrenceweschler.com and in future cases, material amplified in the SourceBook will be indicated by [SB].

4

A Visit to the American Museum
of Natural History in New York
and Lunch at a Japanese Restaurant

August 1982

We have developed a pattern, Oliver and I. He comes over in the evening
to my apartment. I begin by offering beer and cheese and crackers, which
he consumes with considerable gusto. Then we go out to dinner, then we
return and I offer him ice cream (he's already eaten a Granny Smith apple
on the way home).

He then seems to veer along a narcoleptic precipice, he starts yawning
compulsively nodding, gasping to wakefulness. I quickly ply him with
coffee—two, three, four cups. Eventually he's awake enough to drive home.

After our most recent dinner, I get a letter from him dated August 7.

> Lovely seeing you last evening—I do greatly enjoy our evenings
> together and wonder if the sudden, peculiar collapsed feelings
> I seem to get toward the end are not because of the "forbiddenness"
> and anxiety involved— Your probing concern to elicit my
> substance and reality and draw a good appreciation to me,
> where my fearful-deprecatory part says, "No! It's a lie—you're
> nothing—not real—lie low—shut up—be mute—stay
> hidden . . . *Die!*"

❈

A week that had started well for Oliver (he'd quickly completed a new
middle portion of his Leg book) has turned sour. (The earlier tripartite

division has been metastasizing new sections, such that the book will begin with the drama on the mountaintop, which is to say the dread confrontation with the Bull, before then proceeding to chapters on his helicoptered return to the very Middlesex hospital in London where he'd once interned, only now as a patient, the whole phenomenology of that unsettling transformation, compounded in turn by a terrifying postsurgical siege of "limbo," in which he experiences a complete bodily dysphoria, as if his own leg were somehow utterly alien and other, the ensuing vertigo in his entire sense of identity, and then by turns the stages across which his bodily integrity ever so gradually returns—a musical quickening, extended physical therapy and convalescence, and only then, finally, the complete return to blessed health.) He is badly stuck again on the last section ("healing, the return of proportion, the convalescence on the Heath at Hampstead"), and as if in empathy (or by way of re-presentation), his back has now gone badly out.

Still, as previously planned, we set out for a Friday-morning walk from my new digs on far West Ninety-Fifth, and Oliver relates how this palsy with the Leg book has him worried—and with good reason. He's been blocked on it for years (ever since soon after the incident itself, in 1974, though most recently in a concerted fashion, since 1979) and everything else (the Tourette's book, the dementia book, etc.) feels all blocked up behind it. His friend Eric Korn had thrown up his hands in exasperation when Oliver told him earlier this summer that he intended to pursue the theme one more time during this vacation. Korn would rather he gave it up already, but Oliver can't: He feels the loss would be too great, and everything seemed to be going well until he got to this last section, which he sees requires a soft lyrical touch, one which he doesn't appear to be able to muster, the Talmudic intellectualizing always seeming to surface and blot everything over— So, yes, he's very worried and disturbed, all gloom and moody.

"When the writing is flowing well, I am powerful and cheerful and can't imagine it ever being otherwise," he tells me as we amble down Riverside Drive, "and when the writing becomes blocked, I am crestfallen and palsied and there, too, I can't imagine it ever being otherwise. In either case, my visions of the future are at all times characterized by a spurious permanence."

As I see it, his current problem with the Leg book is that it needs to end on this airy, ventilated, open-ended note, convalescence and recovery; only, as he approaches the end, Oliver's inhibitory neuroses and misgivings become more and more pronounced—he becomes tight and constricted and dark and brooding, just the opposite of what he's trying to describe, so that, self-fulfillingly, he can't.

We continue on, talking about nothing much.

By Seventy-Ninth Street we decide to cut east, to the American Museum of Natural History—to which he used to go often, though not so much recently.

Once inside, Oliver's disposition brightens considerably. We head over—of course—to the hall of mollusks and stop before a case of squid, nautiluses, and octopuses. Oliver is by now positively chipper.

I ask him what he'd always so liked about them. For a moment, he stares at the case thoughtfully—the polymorphous, slightly goofy octopus, the sleek propulsive squid. "I mean," he finally erupts, jocularly, "you can *see* what I liked about them.

"With octopuses," he continues, "I suppose it was partly the face—that here, for the first time in evolution, appears a face, a *distinct* physiognomy, indeed a personality: It's true that when you spend time with them, you begin to differentiate between them, and they seem to differentiate between you and other visitors.

"So there was that, this mutual sense of affection for the alien.

"And then there was their way of moving, which is jet propulsion.

"And their eyes, which are huge.

"Their birdlike beaks, which can give you a nasty nip.

"And their sexual habits—the male, you see, donates an entire sperm-filled leg to the female . . .

"That, and their ancientness . . . and their simultaneous adventurousness, how they threw off the repressive shell and moved out, to float free.

"And then, I guess, their sliminess." He giggles like a child. "I mean, I *do* like the slimy."

Gazing some more now at another octopus, Oliver sighs. "Wasn't it Freud who wrote somewhere of 'the beauty of an existence complete in itself'?"

A few moments later, we are standing before a demonstration of the mathematics of the nautilus shell: "This was my earliest delight, back in

London: my preschool childhood ecstasy—this discovery of the regularity of forms in nature—life as a mathematical ejaculation."

A bit after that, looking at an exhibition of clay models of prehistoric protohuman heads, Oliver notes: "Their eyes are more benign than they were in my generation . . . hmm . . . charming. Charming faces, even with no cranium to speak of. At my college at Oxford, we had a collection of brains in jars: the Brains of the Great. Turgenev's was huge, almost three thousand milligrams. Poor Anatole France's not much more than eight hundred."

At one point, we pass a portal labeled EDUCATION HALL. Oliver frowns. "Oh, that's too bad. At school I loved to be on the wards, in the museums, but I hated class."

They have some truly marvelous dioramas at the museum, exquisite reproductions of desert- and forest-scapes—foliage, detritus, wildlife, bark—and we pause to admire them.

"It's like the sudden return of vision at the hospital, after Norway," Oliver recalls. "After the weeks of being confined in my narrow little room. The way everything suddenly seemed to pop out again once I got outside: I mean, one *needs* the third dimension. Before it popped back out, a sort of attenuated perspective had persisted but without the *edible chunkiness* of the world."

Oliver now smiles wistfully. "The richness of the world is unbelievable! I'm afraid I don't have a comparable feeling for the richness of social tissue, the kind of thing which must make New York City such a marvel." And indeed, that seems right to me: Oliver is forever marveling at the natural world and for that matter at the world of natural wonder within any particular individual's skin—but not at the world of possibility between individuals.

Or anyway, mere human individuals: We find ourselves pausing at a diorama of a standing grizzly bear. "Ah," Oliver sighs. "I do wish to be loved by a larger animal—all of us, siblings together." He goes on to relate how once, in Yellowstone, Eric had had to physically restrain him, to hold him back in the car, to prevent him from chasing after a passing bear.

※

As we leave the museum, foraging vaguely for a place to lunch, our conversation turns to Jewishness, nature, family . . .

"Does Jewishness cut one away from nature?" Oliver wonders. "Life is a great lyrical diorama, but *not* in the Talmud. And yet it was in the convalescent home.

"I do have a set of cousins in Canada of whom I am inordinately fond. They light the Sabbath candles in their cabin in the woods—they have it right, but I'm afraid my ghetto parents did not . . . or anyway, my father did not. My mother, maybe.

"At any rate, it was only in Manitoulin"—his sometime Canadian retreat—"seven years after her death, that I suddenly remembered my mother's face and her voice—her presence."

From there, he free-associates backward. "Nature brought me to California," Oliver says. "I love Muir and Burroughs. California made me realize what a wonderful planet this is."

For a while, back then, he thought he might have the makings of a novelist. "But my own last attempt at a novel, in California, floundered in a profusion of characters—after six hundred of them, I gave up.

"I mean, really, I never meant to become a neurologist. I meant to be a naturalist. I got deflected into medicine, into neurology. So that I had to treat neurology as if I *were* a naturalist.

"Our entire family went to synagogue on Saturday. My parents and the older siblings had moved from the East End (a poor district) to Northwest London in 1930, three years before I was born. They all knew the Bible. But in our family there was a distinctly different feeling between Friday night, which was lyrical, and Saturday, which was all Deuteronomical proscriptions.

"Both my parents grew up in Orthodox environments—both with rabbis for parents—though my mother's upbringing was especially so. My mother's father was born in Russia in 1837, came to England in 1859.

"My mother may have been the least observant of the seventeen. Observation was myth and ritual for her, which is to say, Friday nights. In fact, on her tombstone, it says 'Friday nights will never be the same,' and it's true, they haven't been. She was the keeper of the totemic. She knew the Bible but had no feeling for Midrash. She liked the Psalms and the Song of Solomon, which I connect with her own fondness for nature.

"My father was more interested in commentaries. Meals were a continuous inquisition on Hebrew grammar and medical practice. With him I connect it to a passion for roots.

"I myself am illiterate in Hebrew, the only one in my family. I know by heart a lot in a gabbled meaningless way. Perhaps this is owing to a turning away, during those terrible war years at that hideous country school, or maybe because of the loss, just before that, when I was six, of my Hebrew teacher. The feeling of *profound* abandonment."

Oliver also lost an especially dear music teacher when he was twelve, a sudden tragic death in childbirth. He claims he faked his way through his bar mitzvah the following year. Perhaps, he surmises, there was a resistance at work. "Because later, during a break from my last year at Oxford, after nine months on a kibbutz in Israel, I was completely fluent. Though coming back on the plane, I instantaneously forgot it all and have not remembered a word since.

"But that clear difference between Friday and Saturday—the loving, pastoral, mythical Jewishness of Friday: Welcoming the Bride. Saturday, by contrast, was a rabbinical day, full of slaps" (as he says this, he slaps his own hand so abruptly, a loud smack, that I jump) "and prohibition. And indeed, perhaps it was Saturday that fed my later antinomian passions. It was Superego Day.

"One Saturday, Eric and I went to the airport, took a flight to Amsterdam, just to eat bacon sandwiches!

"Later, much later, my father, who has an extraordinary library of Judaica, asked me if I wanted any of his books. I asked for a Zohar" (one of the fundamental texts of kabbalistic mysticism). "He was embarrassed, somehow thought my request deeply inappropriate, but he managed to rummage up one volume out of a set.

"The thing is, everyone in the old neighborhood was Jewish. And biology wasn't Jewish—that was one of the things I liked about it—the West Coast wasn't Jewish." (His obviously having been a different West Coast than the one I was growing up in at the very same time.)

"Rather than a doctor, I'd have been a nineteenth-century naturalist, or possibly a nineteenth-century doctor," he concludes, reverting to an earlier theme.

"Actually, as a physician, I *am* a nineteenth-century naturalist."

※

We find ourselves standing before a Japanese place, gazing at the food dioramas, "by turns horrifying," as Oliver characterizes them, "and mouthwatering."

After we've gotten seated and ordered our sushi, I pick up and ask him why he became a neurologist rather than some other kind of doctor. The question, to him, hardly makes any sense.

"I mean," he stammers, "obviously I became a neurologist rather than, say, a cardiologist, because there's nothing for an intelligent man to be interested in in cardiology. The heart, I suppose, is an interesting pump, but it's just a pump. Neurology is the only branch of medicine that could sustain a thinking man."

Okay, but why neurology rather than, say, psychiatry?

"I pretend that at the outset it was a need to immerse myself in the abstract rather than in particular living patients. But rather, I suspect my sense of origins was too strong, coming from a family of physical doctors. My mother incidentally also trained as a neurologist with the great Kinnier Wilson. He gave her, and later she gave me, his reflex hammer."

Indeed, both of his parents toyed with the idea of becoming neurologists. Did they feel bad about not having pursued the specialty?

"Well, my father had an apologizing part. He showed an ambivalence toward specialists, a definite deference, although at the same time he knew he was a far better doctor and diagnostician. This comes through in my own feelings about specialists.

"My mother achieved eminence early. She was one of the first women admitted to the Royal College of Medicine. By 1920, in her late twenties, she was already powerfully established. (This gave rise to an occasional embarrassment at ceremonial dinners—'And what does your husband do?') She was a brilliant surgeon who became a much-loved surgeon—as she grew older she developed her humanity."

Oliver is silent for a few moments, pondering that last thought, working his way through his sushi pads. "For all my failures and the suicide which will probably end it all, I do have a feeling of *developing*, though, of being different at fifty than I was at forty, at forty than at thirty. I don't know how people who don't develop bear it."

How does he feel he has developed?

"I think I'm deeper. I have a stronger sense of depths and abysses and what is surely felt and experienced though difficult to put into words."

He pauses, sighs. "But, of course, in fact I haven't gone forward. I've gone back. I present a sorrier state each decade."

At which point he absentmindedly starts working his way through *my* sushi pads.

Does he feel bad he's not a GP?

"Yes," he responds without a moment's wavering. "Back in 1979, in Manitoulin, they offered me the job—their old doctor, a fine New Zealander, was retiring and they urged me to come up. I fantasize about it: I'd have gone up and apprenticed myself to him—it might have taken about six months to master the skills. It would have been a good life. My father is a very 'fortunate man.'"*

Speaking of fortunate men, I mention that my artist friend Robert Irwin will be in town from LA later in the week and suggest that he join Irwin and me for dinner at my art-collecting aunt and uncle's at the weekend.

He hesitates. "Probably I'd sit through the whole first hour mute, in an excruciation of silence. Then suddenly I'd burst forth, so vociferous no one could get a word in edgewise. Either way—mute I'd be a great embarrassment, or megalomaniacal perhaps an even greater one."

And we have reverted to the gloom with which we began the day. Interestingly, at this point he free-associates back to his youth: "Partly I felt like a queer alien growth arising unprecedented from my background—a bewilderment, an embarrassment to my parents and teachers. But I myself have always felt vaguely freakish. The writing passion, for example, was peculiar to me in the family.

"In 1946 or so, when I was thirteen or fourteen, during my chemistry passion, I became fascinated by thallium, which features a bright green line in its spectrum, and I became obsessively charmed by it. In the car I would rhapsodize about it for minutes at a time: A quarter of an hour into my celebration, my parents would say something which indicated to me that they had no idea what I was talking about, and indeed that they mildly disapproved.

"Which would only confirm my set-apartness.

"I sometimes compare their attitude to that of Yehudi Menuhin's parents, who always struck me as so sensitive and sensible about their genius son.

"I don't know that my parents knew what to make of me," Oliver

*A reference to John Berger and Jean Mohr's classic evocation of general practice in their *A Fortunate Man: The Story of a Country Doctor* (London: Allen Lane, 1967).

finally says with a sigh, pushing away the empty sushi platter, "although that may just be grandiosity or melancholia or Japanese-lunch syndrome.

"You see," he says, "part of me wants to regale you with tales of my background and part of me feels it's totally irrelevant."

Our day winds down. He hails a cab for the ride back to the parking lot where he stashed his car, suggesting that he may head on up to Canada later for a few days, to try to shake his mood.

❋

During the day at the Natural History Museum, I'd urged Oliver to explain primes and sunflowers to me. He had demurred—he wasn't in the mood. I call him that evening to remind him, and a few days later get this handwritten missive:

August 28 1982
Dear Ren,
    [. . .] Sorry I was a dull dog today—I felt both a bit ill and a
bit depressed—*acutely* so (both organically and morally) after the
MSG . . . It is this *sort* of thing which led me to *MIGRAINE*
and in general to Neurology—
    I have no interest (tho' sufficient competence) in "ordinary"
neurology—perhaps I should call myself a "neuro*psycho*logist,"
like Luria: but this is not so either— What I am (have always
been) interested in are the effects ("resonances") of disturbed
bodily function on the mind—"What will become of thought
itself when it is subjected to the *pressure* of sickness?"
(Nietzsche). Or, more generally, the effects (reciprocally) of
Bodily States and Being [. . .]—a study of Being in the way
that a physician is peculiarly equipped and circumstanced to
do. Absurdly, I know scarcely any other contemporaries with so
general an interest—and yet it would seem so *obvious*—and
exciting.
    [. . .]
    There may be a novelist manqué at work—I do see myself
(at times) as a queer sort of "neurological novelist"—and I see a
whole *genus*: "The Neurological Novel" (and now Pinter has
given us a neurological *play*). ["A Kind of Alaska," Pinter's one-act

riff off of *Awakenings*, the script of which Oliver had recently received.]

The "novelizing" impulse is very strong indeed—but the "neurologizing" impulse is equally strong. [. . .] I suppose I am interested in "Neurological Fate"—*but only insofar as it is opposed by Freedom*. For whatever reason, the eternal fight of Fate vs. Freedom—which one sees played out on so many arenas and stages (social, political, psychological, etc.), the *drama* of Impersonal Force vs. the Individual—which is the center (say) of the Marxian or the Freudian epic—is, for me, most poignantly fought out with one's organic (neural and psychological) endowments, i.e. on a "Lurian" stage.

[. . .]

Anyhow—these thoughts come to me (incoherently, it has lasted too long for MSG, I must have flu or something) in delayed response to yr questions as to why I turned to neurology . . .

As for sunflowers, etc., I take the liberty of enclosing D'Arcy Thompson's chapter on this. In a curious way, I can only think of such things when I am *happy* (or *well*). In Manitoulin, in that good summer of '79, I was continually collecting and examining pine cones, delighting in their logarithmic spirals, Fibonacci series, etc. (or perhaps giving myself to an "inexcusable Pythagorism"). Many people,—especially the old anatomy professor I mentioned today—compared me to D'Arcy Thompson—this love of the mathematizing organic was always central in me. But, *unlike* D'Arcy T, and perhaps "inexcusably," this love has always associated itself to a sense of "mystery," and mystical idealism, which as you can see, he strongly reprehends. But for me, these *are* "the thoughts of the Old One," starting in numbers and spirals, conceiving this whole Universe in ideas (I think this sort of "mystical idealism," and Pythagorism in particular, is strongly developed in my mother's side of the family, but obviously most intensely developed in me).

Forgive this inordinate letter! Oliver*

---

*For the full version of this text and all others marked with an [SB], consult the SourceBook for this book posted at www.lawrenceweschler.com.

Over the ensuing Labor Day weekend, Oliver disappears without a trace, and without any prior indication. I call and call. Dark fantasies play across my mind: Has he actually gone and committed suicide, as he'd teasingly suggested? Would a prospective suicide leave his answering machine on? Likely not, but then perhaps has he gone swimming toward the bridge, thrown his back out but good, and drowned? Or flipped his car, barreling around some curve? It gets silly, all this worrying, and yet I can't stop, and it only gets worse.

Monday evening I get a call: It's Oliver, his voice faint and thin with self-loathing. He'd been in the Adirondacks, it had been wonderful, the only good writing days of 1982. Why, he wonders, he positively hisses at himself—why had he come home?

5

Oliver's Cousins Abba Eban
and Carmel Ross

One day our conversation turned to Oliver's first cousin Abba Eban, or "Aubrey" (his given name, as he always seems to be referred to in the family). They shared a common grandfather, Eliahu Sacks, Oliver's father, Sam, being the brother of Aubrey's mother, Alida.

Aubrey (born in 1915), the second oldest of his siblings, was almost a full generation older than Oliver (born in 1933), the youngest of *his* siblings. But Oliver likes to recount how they share more than a remarkable physical likeness. He describes how once they were having lunch with a large group of family relations. "It was uncanny," he recalls. "I would suddenly get up and head toward the buffet and simultaneously he would be doing likewise, heading for the same place. We had to laugh. He said the sight of me had startled him. Aubrey was raised pretty much by our grandfather, whom I never met—there's a photo of him in Aubrey's autobiography. But Aubrey said that when he first saw me walking in (I was in one of my bearded phases), he could have sworn it was our grandfather come back to life.[SB]

"Meanwhile," Oliver continues, "the speech therapist at Beth Abraham, who's a quite canny observer of mannerisms, one day out of nowhere came up to me and reported that she'd been 'watching TV when they showed this back view of a large, awkward, lumbering, and yet somehow decisive figure and I was sure it was you, Oliver. Only it turned out to be Abba Eban!'"

I never got a chance to interview Aubrey on the subject of his cousin, but as it happens, he had published that autobiography only a few years

earlier, in 1977, and though at that moment in their respective lives, he'd
still had no occasion to mention Oliver in the book's more than six hundred pages, their mutual grandfather did turn out to play a prominent role
in the book's first chapters.

Born in the Lithuanian shtetl of Yanushki (near Kovno), Eliahu Sacks
and his wife, Bassya, were the parents of eleven children of whom only
four (including Aubrey's mother and Oliver's father) survived past childhood. Like many Lithuanian Jews during this period, the family presently
decamped for South Africa in search of greater tolerance and wider material prospects, though as Eban reports dryly, his grandfather Eliahu "seems
to have been the only Jewish immigrant to South Africa who achieved no
affluence whatsoever," and soon thereafter he moved on to London with
much of the family, though they left their daughter Alida behind in the
company of her husband, Abraham Meier Solomon ("a solid merchant with
a meticulous passion for founding Zionist societies wherever he went"), and
their two young children, Ruth and Aubrey. Alas, only a year after Aubrey's
birth, his father was stricken with a fast-spreading cancer, and though
the young family repaired to London as quickly as possible in search of
medical help, Abraham died within months of their arrival. Alida began
working part-time as a translator at the newly established Zionist Office,
soon becoming a special assistant to Chaim Weizmann's chief colleague,
Nahum Sokolow, and in that capacity was called in one evening in early
November 1917 to urgently translate successively evolving versions of the
Balfour Declaration, which would come to memorialize the British Foreign Office's commitment to promote the establishment "of a Jewish national home in Palestine." Much of the rest of the time, Alida worked as a
lab assistant to her brother, the newly minted Dr. Samuel Sacks (a few years
later she would be by his side during his "real blooding as a clinician," as
Oliver sometimes refers to it, tending to victims of the terrible influenza
outbreak at the end of the war). A few years after that, she married one of
her brother Sam's colleagues, Dr. Isaac Eban, who adopted her first two
children and with whom she had another two.

For his own part, during those years, Aubrey seemed to divide his time
between St. Olave's, a prestigious middle school where he was securing a
superb classical education, and the ministrations of his grandfather Eliahu,
still somewhat hapless in any material sense but a singularly devoted
Talmudic scholar who, Eban reports, "had decided that his legacy of

Hebrew scholarship should pass to me, and that the transmission of it would henceforth be his life's sole purpose." His grandfather, Eban writes,

> was so learned that by sticking a pin into a standard Vilna edition of the Talmud text, he would be able to tell you what was written at the corresponding position six pages ahead. But he was at heart a son of the Enlightenment, captivated by the Hakalah movement, which had stressed Hebrew studies more as a humanistic discipline than as a school for ritual. His attitude to religious observance was correct but without fanaticism. And while he respected Zionism for the active reverence that it gave to the Hebrew language, he was not very sanguine about its political prospects.*

It's tempting to contemplate what it would have been like for young Oliver to have interacted with this formidable figure (who, based on the photo Aubrey includes of him in his book, does indeed bear an astonishing facial resemblance to his grandson), but Eliahu died, alas, when Aubrey was only fourteen, which is to say four years before Oliver was born.

❄

I subsequently did get a chance to visit with Oliver's cousin and closest relative in town, Aubrey's half-sister Carmel Ross, for tea at her third-floor apartment, around Lexington and East Sixty-Third Street. She was approximately ten years older than Oliver, a short sweet woman, something of a madcap flibbertigibbet though apparently quite competent beyond the patter, at least in her day, when she was a theatrical agent. She is surrounded by the clutter and paraphernalia of her life in the theatuh.

"The thing you have to understand," she insisted at the outset, "is that both of Oliver's parents arrived in England with *nothing*, not even money for bootlaces. So that the acceptance by the medical profession became a strong factor in their lives. The more successful, the more concerned they became that nothing should disturb that success. Which is why David, the oldest son who became doctor to all the film stars, was regarded by their father, Sam, far more highly than Ollie.

---

*Abba Eban, *Abba Eban: An Autobiography* (New York: Random House, 1977), 6.

"Theirs was an impossibly Orthodox home, but all on the surface—talk about the creation of a Jewish neurotic! My own branch of the family was different. We never had Friday-night dinners—which they never failed to have. Our Judaism was somehow internally strong if externally nonexistent.

"All this relates, I suppose, to this business of being first-generation. My grandmother was illiterate. Grandfather was a Talmudic scholar who came to England when Sam was ten or eleven. There was no heat in winter, they were totally poverty-stricken. Much of the family's idiosyncrasies relate to this background. Grandma was illiterate in a strange country trying to raise four children. And Oliver's father has tried to put it all out of his mind, pretend it never was, hence his devotion to upper-middle-class proprieties, hence their prizing of David. He was in some ways the only son, the golden-haired boy. David is six foot two, a handsome Van Johnson, with that bubbly euphoria of competence and success."

What of Oliver's mother?
Elsie was a handsome lady. Ollie's the image of her, although with Sam's gait. (My brother Aubrey and Ollie walk identically, I'm sure you've been told about that.) Her emotional life, however, was tied up with her patients. What remained was cool-not-cold-withdrawn, correct, imposing.

She was much more brilliant than Sam but very much a product of her time: You could be either a doctor or a woman. Her idea of being a good mother was to bring twelve-year-old Ollie bottled fetuses to dissect—you see, she knew he was special but this was the only way she could think to respond.

Ollie was a lovely boy, an angel with brown, brown eyes, extraordinary sensitivity and openness. He had a terribly lonely childhood—he was abandoned to an incredible solitude. He was much younger than David and Marcus.

What about Michael? And what about what happened to the two of them at that school during the war?
In Michael's case, I think what followed Braefield was even worse. English prep schools are abominable to children who are different—the one that Michael went to was especially terrible to him.

It was a good school with a house for Jewish boys where Michael was apparently frightfully abused. Michael had been a cherub of a boy, though he came back from that place no longer there. Ollie was lucky in being sent to St. Paul's instead.

Oliver's solitude, however, did give him time to read. Though by his time in Oxford, the main thing I remember seeing in him was his lonely gaze.

Years later, around 1964, Ollie arrived on our doorstep here in New York, his motorbike having been stolen during a cross-country jaunt from LA. He looked awful. At the time, he showed me some pieces that he'd written on drugs. They made my hair stand up on end. They were so graphic, so de Maupassant!

I told Sam that Ollie was a great writer. Sam whinnied and harrumphed, "Well, yes, but how's he going to hold down a job?"

My own stock in the family plummeted. My mother called to ask, "Why did you upset Uncle Sammy?"

Were you afraid for Oliver during his time in California?
One is afraid for Ollie for every minute of every day of every year . . .

It's true, though: During California he was wild, on a different wavelength. He had so cut himself off from everyday norms that he seemed to be floating in outer space. He was very unkempt, we took him to buy clothes. It was never a wildness destructive of other people, though, only of himself.

Later, around the time of *Migraine*, Ollie called to ask advice: Faber and Faber was apparently lax on PR, so I offered to do some. We got him superb coverage in all the London papers. At which point Sam called up, blanched and hysterical: "How will he ever get a job *now*? His name's all over *The Times*!"*

One last sip of tea, and a long sigh. "They *still* don't know what to *do* with Oliver."

---

*Ollie subsequently confirmed this last, how his father "came in one morning, white-faced and quivering, feeling it was an utter scandal to be mentioned in *The Times*."

6

From California to New York (1962–1967)

Another afternoon around this time, I ventured over to Oliver's place on City Island and found him sitting in the shade of his front porch, deeply engrossed in Charles Darwin's *The Formation of Vegetable Mould Through the Action of Worms*, a pile of folders by his side. He'd been aimlessly leafing through his files the previous night, he told me (rising from the Darwinian loam), and found something he wanted to show me. An unpublished manuscript from his California days, during the early sixties: a celebration of his motorcycle passion.

He handed it to me, it was dedicated to Thom Gunn, and as he watched me scanning the piece's epigraph (from T. E. Lawrence's "The Road"), he recited the lines by heart:

> A skittish motor-bike with a touch of blood in it
> is better than all the riding animals on earth,
> because of its logical extension of our faculties,
> and the hint, the provocation, to excess . . .

Whereupon (turning the page) his own typescript launched out:

The Road is straight and white. My shadow gesturing, sweeps before me. I sing aloud in the brilliant sun, but the wind steals my sound before I can hear it. I sit up, in state, upon my saddle. I lie flat and hug the bulbous tank. I swerve inanely to and fro. The bike swings easily with my hips, translating feeling into motion.

Rediscovering the piece himself the evening before had put him in a nostalgic frame of mind. "When I came down to LA, at first I missed the communal outings with my regular cycling mates over the bridge and up Mount Tam, through the fogbanks and out to Stimson Beach. In LA, I reverted to my solo adventures, quitting work Friday evening, saddling up, and heading out into the desert—Death Valley, the Mojave, not infrequently I'd even ride through the night out to the Grand Canyon. Huddling down flat against the tank I could achieve speeds in excess of a hundred miles an hour, at which point, racing after the cycloptic light beam piercing the empty road ahead, one began to experience all sorts of curious spatial reversals and illusions, though that might just have been the drugs kicking in. I'd spend Saturday hiking in the canyon and then race back on Sunday afternoon, returning in time for work Monday morning."

Ah, youth. (Another time he told me of one weekend jaunt, entirely hepped up on speed, all the way up to Crater Lake in Oregon, where he'd circled the lake and then just aimed straight back down, accomplishing the journey of close to 1,500 miles without stopping once except for gasoline.)

"I needed the landscape of travel," he said. "Strange, in those days I had always to be off, in continual external flight. Now, rather, I am so inner-directed." The bike passion was tied, too, to that other one, for landscape photography: He took thousands of photos, developing them himself in various makeshift darkrooms, often in otherwise abandoned janitorial closets at the hospital. He wished he could show me some of the resulting images, he still prized them in his mind's eye, though alas, typically, the suitcase containing his photo archive (both prints and negatives) had gotten lost or misplaced—or who knows what—somewhere along the way amid his many moves. He still harbored the vague hope it might resurface someday.

Speaking of photos, though, he reached into his pile, stammering (was he blushing?), he had come upon a thin folder of shots of himself posing at the peak of his muscle-building days. Handing the folder to me, he seemed proud and abashed in equal measure. And they *were* something! Grade-A beefcake: Charlie Atlas in a black Speedo, with bulging thighs, as prized from below. "By my LA days, as you can see, I'd become a frail calcareous creature dangerously oversheathed with muscle."

Whereupon he launched into reminiscences about his months of living in a little apartment in Venice, right alongside Muscle Beach, spending mornings at Gold's Gym and evenings among the weight lifters in the outdoor cages by the sand, training for his successful siege on the California State heavy-weight-lifting record (600 pounds from a full squat).*

He had many friends there, including several Olympic champions, he says, pretty much all of them oblivious of one another's ulterior lives, though there was one fellow in particular, clearly a remarkable mathematician, who died tragically young.

And it was in this context that he himself ever so gingerly broached the topic of his own great chaste love from this period, the young working-class sailor from out of Minnesota named Mel to whom both Gunn and Rodman had previously alluded.

They'd met, Oliver explained, in San Francisco, and initially Oliver had "fancied molding and educating the boy, who in turn I think himself fancied the prospect." Their relationship, Oliver said, was not so much sexual as "increasingly daring—riding motorcycles farther and farther, diving deeper and deeper, climbing higher and higher," and presently Mel joined him in LA, moving into Oliver's studio apartment and getting a job in a nearby carpet factory. They'd share breakfast and head off to their own days of work. Mel was confused about his sexuality, as wracked with Catholic shame as Oliver had been larded in Jewish guilt. But he loved wrestling, and Oliver loved wrestling with him. After which Mel ("I loved that his name meant 'honey' in Latin") loved having his back massaged, and Oliver would sit astride him, loving doing so, kneading his broad shoulders, approaching the edge but never going over the brink of orgasm, until one late afternoon (and this part he only imparted to me many years later) he did accidentally climax, spurting all over the young man's back. Mel stiffened, and without a word got up and took a shower, not speaking to Oliver for the rest of the evening. (Oliver recalled his anguish, falling straight back through to his mother's dark and accusatory silence—he even

---

*Back during our San Francisco conversation, Thom Gunn had recalled how "at one point during his craziest stage, maybe 1963 or so, he announced he was going to train himself to get the California State weight-lifting championship. At which point he put on a huge amount of weight. At one point, I was quite shocked, he waddled across the room, just like Jell-O, he was veritably wobbling. I said, 'God, Oliver, what would your mother say if she saw you?' To which he replied, 'She'd probably say, "So you're really taking after your father now, are you?"'"

found himself suddenly noticing how Mel's appellation spelled out the initials of his mother's maiden name: Muriel Elsie Landau.) The next morning Mel told him it was time that he moved out and got a place of his own (there may have been a woman involved). And Oliver was devastated.

Oliver soon moved out of the Venice apartment himself, decamping to a cabin atop a remote ridge along Topanga Canyon, where partly owing to the failure of that relationship, and partly as a result of "the waning effectiveness of the travel experience generally," his involvement with drugs now started to explode. "All my friends on the beach were drinking and smoking marijuana," he told me, "neither of which did anything for me. My experience with amphetamines, on the other hand, was altogether different, indeed involved a virtual conversion of the will: If I took two, I had to take four, six, eight.

"I was a weekend addict, entertaining long sustained controlled solitary hallucinations. Come Friday evening, by my peak involvement, I'd take upward of a thousand milligrams. Now, a tablet is five milligrams, so I was taking doses of hundreds of tablets crushed and laced into a milk shake. After which I'd experience a pounding orgasmic heart for thirty-six hours straight.

"Another drug I liked was called something like Hackamine; Jonathan Miller for this reason used to refer to it as Wankamine.

"But this was truly my autistic sexual liberation."

Over the years he regaled me with countless tales of his drug-fueled extravaganzas (which years later he would unfurl in considerably more detail in his book *Hallucinations*, so I won't rehearse them all here). During the last year of his time in LA, however, Augusta Bonnard, a psychiatrist (a student and collaborator of Anna Freud) who was also a friend of Oliver's parents, was dispatched to California as a sort of "emissary of the family" to check on things, and she was appalled at the spectacle of Oliver's self-destructive behavior. "She insisted that I get myself to a shrink immediately," Oliver recalled, "and I did, though this first attempt at analysis failed, in no small part owing to my utterly sarcastic and haughty attitude." He paused, giggled to himself, and as if to confirm the characterization, noted: "The man's name was Bird, which seemed to me entirely appropriate, since all he seemed to do was peck, peck, and peck."

The thing was that for all the extravagance of his druggy excursions, Oliver was an exceptionally high-functioning addict and still had much to be professionally haughty about. Working with a colleague at UCLA, he managed to pull together a remarkable exhibit for the spring 1965 meeting of the American Academy of Neurology in Cleveland, offering up extraordinary Kodachrome transparencies of the microscopic appearance of various types of vastly extended axons—a display that, with Oliver himself offering guided tours of all the marvels, became one of the hits of the convention. As a result, job offers poured in from all over the country (his UCLA residency was set to expire in June), and Oliver ended up choosing the lab of a dynamic young neuropathologist named Robert Terry at New York's relatively new Albert Einstein College of Medicine, a researcher whose work on the electronic microscopy of cells associated with Alzheimer's disease had impressed Oliver when Terry had paid a visit to UCLA the previous year.

"But an abyss of three dangerously unstructured months yawned between my leaving California and my reporting for work in New York," Oliver recalled, and he went on to recount how he ended up selling his BMW motorbike in LA and buying another one in Europe, where he spent part of his vacation on one last extravagantly meth-stoked affair with a German theater director in a Paris hotel, the drugs inflaming not only the sex but a seemingly heartfelt mutual love that appeared to soar and soar across the ensuing exchange of letters during the months after Oliver returned to America, but then, following an actual visit by the young man late in the fall, came crashing to earth, leaving "a taste of ashes" in its wake. Reeling from yet another broken heart, Oliver's drug use amped up even higher, "and one day, I found myself looking at my face in the mirror—this was December 31, 1965, so it was a sort of New Year's Eve glance—and I heard myself say, 'Ollie, old boy, you keep this up and you will not make it another year.' This wasn't some melodramatic cry—rather, a calm, passionless diagnosis, as a physician might give to a patient.

"Whereupon I resolved to put an end to my sexual life—and did—and to begin to come to terms as well with my drug habit and all the roiling deeper life issues that seemed to be compelling it. And so early in 1966, I went in search of another analyst—this time, all I was saying was 'Help!'—and by sheer luck came under the care of a truly remarkable one, Dr. Leonard Shengold, who completely independent of the transference, seemed to me, and still does, a good, compassionate, *sane* man. And he saved my life."

Notwithstanding their three meetings a week, however, the transference took a while to take—for one thing, Shengold was not much older than Oliver, which initially discomfited the latter (how could such a young man be truly wise?). Or maybe that was just an excuse, for in actuality Oliver was not truly ready to give up the drugs.

And yet in many ways Shengold's wider interests and deep well of cultural reference (Shakespeare, Kipling, Chekhov, Dickens, and so forth, all of whose works and lives he drew upon and explored in his own writings) seemed to meld perfectly with a patient like Oliver. In 1963, Shengold had published a paper on "The Parent as Sphinx," and in 1967, soon after he began treating Oliver, he published an analysis of Freud's Rat Man under the title "The Effects of Overstimulation." More than fifteen years later (when Oliver was still seeing him twice a week, as he would for the rest of his life), and not that long after Oliver began telling me about Shengold, he turned up as an admirable expert side commentator in Janet Malcolm's *New Yorker* reportages entitled "Trouble in the Archives" (December 1983), where she quotes him saying, "It is in no way to condone or minimize the often heartbreaking damage done to observe that some victims of soul murder have been strengthened by the terrible experiences they have endured. Talents and, occasionally, creative power can arise from a background of soul murder." As indeed, Oliver told me how in the ensuing years Shengold had helped him to see his own Second World War hellhole, Braefield, in much the same light.

But not yet. For one thing, the drugs still seemed to be enhancing his workweek performance. As his work focus, Oliver had decided to zero in on diseases associated with myelin, the fatty material that sheathes large nerve fibers, enabling them to conduct nerve impulses more speedily, and since earthworms, as it happens, had unusually thick myelin sheaths around their exceptionally conducive long nerves, and also because he just liked them (as had his hero, Darwin), Oliver chose earthworms as his experimental subjects, as a result of which he was regularly outside in the Einstein gardens, amassing thousands of them, which he then had to individually kill so as to extract the sheaths in question, "like Marie Curie processing tons of pitchblende to obtain the decigram of pure radium." It would end up taking him nine months to painstakingly harvest the relatively tiny amount of purified myelin soup in question.

In the midst of all this (and he still remembered the exact date:

March 15, 1966), he woke up "with an entirely altered state of mind—I felt tremendously energized. I wrote a cosmological poem. I began devouring texts on cosmology, physics, chemistry. In analysis, I'd talk hyperphysics for days at a time rather than anything about me or other people.

"I experienced a sudden upsurge in knowledge. At seminars at which I used to cower in the dark corner, I was suddenly blurting out identifications on microscopic slides, complete with bibliography—I was experiencing a great exaltation of memory. For about six weeks I, who could never draw, drew anatomical drawings effortlessly. I experienced, in addition, a great exaltation of smell.

"Furthermore, I was able to communicate this excitement. My sudden enthusiasm galvanized the entire department of neurology. No less than six major experimental projects were launched, each with me at the head. The entire thing was like a sudden, wondrous nova—for the first time in my adulthood I seemed to be tapping back into the scientific energy or the ecstasies of my adolescence—all of which, just as suddenly, from one day to the next, went dead.

"I woke up one morning about six weeks later, and there was nothing there. Which dumped me into a great depression and indeed dumped the entire lab into a great dejection.

"And to this day I don't quite know what it all meant, whether it was principally a manic reaction to the ongoing drugs, or what."

The dejection persisted, his energy utterly drained. Meanwhile, his research began going almost comically off the rails. He had been filling a large green notebook with painstaking records of his myelin extraction program, which one evening he took home to study and the next morning, having failed to secure it sufficiently to the bike rack, he managed to lose as it went flying off his motorcycle and into the rampaging traffic of the Cross Bronx Expressway. Not a total disaster, though, since he still had the precious myelin itself, though he then somehow managed to lose that as well when absentmindedly cleaning his lab bench a few weeks later. He was breaking microscopes, strewing stray bits of hamburger all over the lab and even into the sterilized interiors of the sacrosanct centrifuges. (Strange in recalling all this how he doesn't even think to blame the drugs, instead attributing it, perhaps correctly, to his innate and age-old ham-fisted clumsiness.)

At any rate, by the fall of 1966, his bosses at Einstein decided to cut everyone's losses and to transfer him instead to clinical settings—the nearby Montefiore Headache Clinic and Beth Abraham—where it was thought he might do less damage working with mere patients. "I was expelled from academic medicine for being too extravagantly clumsy to be allowed to continue," he said as he concluded this portion of our conversation, "and my banishment proved my salvation."

His drug addiction persisted a bit longer. How, I asked him, had he finally kicked it? "Well," he replied, "for one thing, the medical effects were becoming more and more dramatic, and I was clearly in manifest danger. I mean, some weekends I was giving myself a pulse rate of two hundred plus for forty-eight hours at a time. More important, Shengold told me emphatically: 'You are putting yourself out of reach. If you continue, we can't go on.' And the prospect of such an expulsion truly terrified me, because by then I had become convinced that he really was my last hope. But then there was a curious third factor. Because the fact is that through all of those drug experiences, I had been trying to get somewhere, and finally I *did*, and what had previously been a febrile incandescence, a sterile awakening, became a *fertile* awakening. And after that, I didn't need the drugs anymore."*

---

*For more on this period of Oliver's life and much else, see my conversation with his colleague and one true friend at Einstein, the pediatric neurologist Isabelle Rapin, in the SourceBook.

7

The Migraine Clinic (1966–1968)

Another day, this time as we sat on the back porch overlooking his postage-stamp backyard on City Island, the bright sunlight pouring over our shoulders, Oliver commented, "Who, looking at white light, would imagine that it has parts? And yet a spectrograph reveals them, in slices. Similarly, perception seems a seamless endeavor: The world comes to us, is delivered to us through our senses. But migraine is an unusually good decomposer of perception—it acts to decompose the world of perception at every level, stretching and distending and upending and confounding all sorts of processes which we usually take for granted, but only for a finite period—within minutes the patient is 'okay' and can describe what he has been through, thus providing a spectrograph, as it were, of the very activity of perception."

I asked Oliver to talk a bit about his days at the Headache Clinic.

"Well," he said, palming a tall glass of water, "in October '66, flung out of lab practice for everyone's sake, I arrived at both the Headache Clinic and Beth Abraham, though for the first two years most of my work was focused on the former.

"Patients were referred to the Headache Clinic from all over the Bronx, New York City generally, even Connecticut. It may have been the only one in the area, founded maybe ten years earlier by an eminent specialist named Arnold Friedman and by then well established in a small wing of its own over at Montefiore.

"It was mostly a place where doctors who were getting defeated by their patients could 'send them to those wizards'—there were six or eight of us. Most of the referrals were seen on an outpatient basis; occasionally some would be brought into hospital for diagnostics or specific therapies."

Oliver recounted how he started out doing two to three and later four clinics a week, in addition to one research session. Between them, the doctors were seeing fifty and sixty patients an afternoon.

He raised his eyebrows. "So you can see, it was quite a mill. It was partly sponsored by a company that had cornered the headache market, so there was an unseemly pushing of drugs, in many cases their own.

"It was a Headache Clinic—not a migraine unit per se—so we also had to diagnose for tumors and the like, so the tendency was to do skull X-rays, CAT scans, and so forth, besides the EEGs, and all of this before the patient was even seen. The EEG man there, for fear perhaps of being thought useless, diagnosed everyone as suffering from a midline cerebral tumor . . . and everyone was therefore EEG'ed. The charts would be presented to the patients, without comment, and naturally they'd become terrified. Indeed, that's why I had to learn how to read EEGs, so as to be able to reassure them. I tried to convince Friedman not to require an EEG of every patient, but the profit motive was overweening and I was told to mind my own business."

Oliver paused for a moment, sighed. "I was honed as a neurologist, a good one, maybe even a great one, in the most squalid circumstances: at the Headache Unit and at Beth Abraham.

"Research at the Headache Unit was extremely modest and limited to two long-range studies. That at any rate wasn't the draw.

"Friedman regarded himself as the King of Headache—the head don of the Migraine Mafia. He was a veteran neurologist with vast experience in headache and good clinical judgment when he was non-neurotic—an expert is *always* interesting. But he was often neurotic and had had several similarly ambivalent situations before me.

"The thing was, he stood in need of bright young people as companions, animators, laborers: people who would write papers on which he'd then put his own name.

"And he was impressed, puzzled, and finally resentful of someone like me coming in with the intention, perhaps, of uncovering the Grand Scheme of Migraine. Saturday morning he'd have me to his posh midtown office, like Charcot receiving a would-be disciple.

"One such Saturday morning, I began talking about migrainous bellyache, and he exploded, 'Sacks! You're in a headache unit! Migraine means headache. By definition you cannot have a non-headache migraine.' And yet later, he would take my chapter on migraine equivalents and secretly publish it *verbatim* under his own name."

Oliver paused again, took a sip of water, and continued.

"Over two or three years I saw twelve hundred patients. By the end of several visits, they always left clarified though seldom cured. Central to the therapy, as far as I was concerned, was *talking* to patients about the will, matters of courage, fortitude, humor—in essence about *dealing with one's fate*. Sometimes there was a happy ending, though usually not.

"Some patients demanded a *cure*. I'd say, 'Go see my colleague next door, he's more your sort of man.' Conversely, my colleagues would occasionally foist patients on me: 'This fucking patient wants to *understand*!'

"Quite a number of patients did not know what they had. Such that a single expository meeting, in which I was able to tell them, 'This is migraine. Nothing else,' proved entirely enough.

"Migraine aura or scotomas can be terribly frightening," he went on, "and simple understanding can be immensely comforting."

Had he himself ever suffered from those particular versions of migraine?

"Oh yes. And it can be a horror, especially doughnut vision, where the center of the visual field disappears, along with the very idea of a center. Indeed, one of my earliest memories—at age two or so—was looking up at my mother as she was holding me and she had no face! Beyond that I regularly experienced pre-migraine scotomas. I would be out in the backyard and the pear tree would no longer be there. At age three I remember having a dialogue with myself: 'Was there a pear tree there or did I make it up?' It was a great comfort the day my mother acknowledged my anxious look and told me that, yes, that kind of thing happened to her as well."

Returning to his practice at the Headache Clinic, he recalled, "No two patients were ever alike. Though I did get tired of headaches. There's a little footnote in *Migraine* in which I mention how seeing that I was bored with headaches and fascinated by auras, my patients developed more and more auras—one woman even had a zigzag dress made up especially for me, a pattern so intense that it almost gave *me* an aura!

"But as I say, the main thing was talking to the patients and listening to them. By the end, I was doing five afternoon-to-evening clinics a week.

I tended to stay longer than the others (another thing held against me, another way I caused trouble). Patients got to know: If you come toward the end of the day, he may be an hour late but by God he'll listen, he pays attention.

"It didn't actually pay, though. The clinic's rates were $30 an hour, $20 a half hour, and $15 a quarter hour. My sessions were seldom less than an hour long, and often an hour more, which drove my colleagues crazy."

And how had his migraine book come about?

"Well," he said, going back into the kitchen for a moment to top up his water glass, and then returning. "As I think I mentioned the other day, though I had sworn off sex a few years earlier, I was still engaging in drugs to a quite considerable degree when I arrived at the Headache Clinic. And one weekend, in February 1967, I was preparing for my standard weekend of stoned onanistic hedonism, but instead of the usual sexual fantasy, that weekend I had happened to have checked out of the library Liveing on migraine."

Which is to say Edward Liveing (1832–1919), another great English Victorian neurologist, and his book, *On Megrin, Sick-Headache, and Some Allied Disorders: A Contribution to the Pathology of Nerve-Storms.*

"And I was taken into a realm of enchantment: I read through the six hundred pages in one sitting as if at a single glance! The whole subject opened up before me as a great firmament, the firmament of neurology, with—crystal clear—the constellation of migraine. The landscape of migraine. The landscape of Liveing. For that matter, the landscape of Victorian science. All of it so clear!

"I put the book down and thought, 'What a wonderful, wonderful book, but it's a century old. This must all be re-seen, for the present, but by whom?' I reeled off a dozen names, sarcastically dismissing each in turn until a voice deep inside welled up, saying, *'Dummy, it's you!'*

"Ordinarily, at the end of thirty-six hours of such star-tripping, I'd descend, rocket-like, with empty hands. This time, however, the drug passion did not go away, not then and not six weeks later. I came down with a sense, as real as during the trip itself, a completely solid residue as to what I should do and *could* do, had it within myself and had the power to do.

"And the addiction ceased that weekend. Ceased with the experience of a *good* trip, a *successful* trip. I'd gotten there, I didn't need to try to get there anymore. And it's from that weekend really that I date the final end of what I often describe as my grayout."

He outlined his migraine book quickly, completing initial work back in London in July 1967, and securing a contract from Faber and Faber, whereupon he sent off an excited buoyant telegram to Friedman, and got back a furious telegram in reply: "STOP. DO NOTHING!"

"*Don't you realize that all this is mine?*' Friedman thundered when I got back. 'This is *my* clinic, these are *my* patients, all your thoughts are *my* thoughts.' He was a very powerful man at that moment, the head of the headache section of the American Neurological Association. And he was absolutely forbidding me to publish: 'If you do publish, I'll blackball you, and you'll never get another job in the field!' Whereupon he had all my charts locked away and I was forbidden and physically prevented from seeing them."

For a while Oliver lay low, simply doing his job. In June 1968, however, "I determined secretly on resuming the project, though I had to half plead, half bribe the night staff into letting me back into my files, such that working between midnight and four a.m. on successive nights, I copied out my case histories without his knowledge."

Meanwhile, unbeknownst to Oliver, Friedman had had his secretary secretly lift Oliver's 1967 manuscript and photocopy the entire thing, whereupon he'd begun publishing entire chapters under his own name.

"In July 1968, I took a month off, at which point Friedman fired me. For some weeks, I fell into a terrified darkness. But then suddenly, on the last day of August 1968, it all became clear to me: I realized that my forbidder was now powerless.

"'Ollie,' I said to myself, 'rewrite it, reconceive it, but it must be on Faber's desk in ten days from now or else we're going to have to kill ourselves.' This worked. It scared me into starting, but within minutes, hours, I'd become entranced with the writing itself, and I managed to write the whole thing, thus entranced, in nine days."

(Huh. I couldn't help but notice that the same sort of thing would subsequently happen with *Awakenings*, which he'd likewise only been able to complete after being fired.)

"The people at Faber and Faber prevailed upon me to include a final section on therapies, which as you may recall I hadn't originally felt was going to be necessary, and that delayed things a little." But the book was finally published in the fall of 1970. Which, as we shall presently see, was just around the time that a letter he'd written to *The Journal of the American Medical Association*, regarding the pervasive L-DOPA side effects among his Beth Abraham patients, was starting to kick up a terrible ruckus, ruining Oliver's enjoyment of the publication of his first book.

Friedman, for his part, fared somewhat worse. At first a few of the reviewers began writing Oliver and asking if he'd earlier published some of the chapters under the pseudonym "A. B. Friedman." Presently, though, it was Friedman himself who was being confronted with charges of rampant plagiarism. (It quickly became clear who had copied whom, if nothing else on the basis of consistency of style.)

"Shortly thereafter, Friedman left Montefiore for Tucson to found the Southwest branch of the Migraine Mafia," Oliver concluded, setting the empty water glass on the deck table. "It had been an extraordinary situation: I suspect he'd been betting on my self-destructiveness, that I would not live to publish or to notice."

8

The Awakenings Drama (1968–1975)

It was striking how often, during our conversations in those days, Oliver's accounts of his earlier life seemed to prefigure the coming drama of his Awakenings period—his first encounter with those postencephalitic "living statues" at Beth Abraham in the Bronx (individuals in their sixties and seventies, scattered among the wider population, who'd apparently been frozen like that for decades), his decision to bring them together in a separate ward and eventually to offer them the reputed wonder drug L-DOPA, their seemingly miraculous coming to life, the calamitous tribulations that followed, and the slow hard-won road to a measure of accommodation thereafter. As early, for example, as his years at that Dickensian boarding school Braefield, where one afternoon he remembered having written a paper— he would have been eight or nine years old at the time—entitled "Recalled to Life," on the character Manette in *A Tale of Two Cities*: Alexandre Manette, that is, the brilliant physician who had been buried in the Bastille on trumped-up charges, incommunicado, entirely lost to his family for more than eighteen years before his eventual release. "I must have related," Oliver surmised. "It was, I suppose, a way of trying to telegraph my own personal situation in terms of his, not that anyone was paying attention, although it has not passed my own notice since then how neither was Manette's situation entirely dissimilar from that of the patients I would be encountering at Beth Abraham thirty years later."

Recalled to life, indeed.

Or during his days in the late fifties at Oxford, across his nascent (and presently aborted) laboratory practice, how he was simultaneously

keeping track, out of a corner of his eye, as it were, of the progress of researchers in Sweden, led by Arvid Carlsson (who would share in the 2000
Nobel Prize in Physiology or Medicine for the discoveries), in isolating
dopamine in the brain and beginning to identify its crucial role as a
neurotransmitter.

Or how his first residency in an American medical center, at Mount
Zion in San Francisco, "even before I had my long-term visa, had been with
a unit that did stereotactic surgery on Parkinsonians—a common treatment in the days before L-DOPA—making tiny lesions in the thalamus,
a couple of neurosurgeons and myself, and I worked with them for nine
months."

Not to mention his own subsequent drug excursions. Once, when I
asked Oliver how much his own lavish experiments with hoary pharma-
ceuticals might have been of help in relating to the experiences of the patients he would subsequently be encountering at Beth Abraham, his
answer was both simple and immediate, interrupting me before I could
even finish the question: "Very."

He then paused a moment before continuing, "Had I not myself been
through all sorts of such experiences, had I not been a head myself, I might
never have appreciated the tenor of their lives both before and after they
were given L-DOPA. Granted, though I haven't actually experienced Parkinsonism per se, I often tell my students, 'Do you want to know what
Parkinsonism is like? Take Haldol.' And I had sampled a good deal of
Haldol. I had sampled a good deal of a whole lot of things. And as for
L-DOPA, in many ways its nearest pharmacological models are amphetamines, with which I was of course prodigiously familiar. More to the
point, though, I'd known for myself both the promise and the threat, the
attraction and the danger, of cerebral stimulants. And I also understood
the economics of stimulants: I knew that you had to pay for things. As
Havelock Ellis once said regarding such drugs, 'They don't give, *they cost.*'"

Something Oliver would have been quite aware of as he arrived at Beth
Abraham, in the fall of 1966, when he was still abusing drugs himself at
a considerable rate.

"As I've described to you," he recalled during one of my afternoon
visits to City Island, "I arrived at Beth Abraham in October 1966, during
a kind of crisis period for me, having been cast out of academic medicine,
for everyone's sake.

"Now, at medical school back in England I'd seen occasional post-encephalitics whose cases wended back to the twenties, but never this many, and never like this, never these living statues. I'd even spent those nine months with that Parkinsonian unit in San Francisco in 1960, so I was disposed to be interested. Leonard"—the pseudonym he gave in his even-tual book for the patient who would come to be played by Robert De Niro in the Hollywood film*—"was the first of these postencephalitic patients that I encountered, but it developed, at length, that there were at least eighty others of them dispersed among a population of five hun-dred—a uniquely high concentration. Indeed, Beth Abraham had been founded for them—for postencephaletics and permanent neurological war injuries—in 1920, when it was opened as a 'Home for the Incurable'" (the characterization still chiseled over the entryway) "though over the years all sorts of other individuals suffering from all sorts of other dire maladies had been added to the mix, and I don't think any particular notice was any longer being given to the postencephalitics as such—Beth Abraham was simply seen as an asylum for chronic patients, which is all they were thought to be.

"Nevertheless, they did stand out, or at least they did to *me*, even though I was still highly ignorant and had no idea what to make of such a high concentration of such almost catatonic people."

How so?

"Well, they stood out by their strange isolation, stillness punctuated by sudden explosions of movement, for instance"—Oliver jumped with a start, my pen went flying out of my hand in startled response, which made Oliver laugh, I picked it up, he continued—"occasional sudden acrobatic flights, as in the completely mind-blowing case, early on, of one fellow who hadn't moved, seemingly, for months. One day, as I was checking on a pa-tient near him, he suddenly exploded into a riotously funny imitation of a berserk neurologist—me—grabbing one of my own instruments, quite a complex tool, out of my bag and strapping it to his own forehead, performing this whole uproarious shtick, carefully returning the scope

---

*Although in our conversations Oliver regularly toggled back and forth between the actual names of his Awakenings patients and the pseudonyms he gave them in his book to protect their privacy (I eventually had to fashion a big wall chart to keep track of the doublings), for the purposes of this book I will hereafter confine myself to the pseudonyms Oliver gave them in his text.

to its case, and then reverting to his eerie stillness, as if nothing had happened.

"And within a month of first seeing them, I had developed the sense that they were quite extraordinary and endlessly fascinating, this door between the grotesquely disabled and the seemingly completely normal opening at random and then closing just as abruptly with a complete return to utter stasis, but impervious to any medical or surgical treatment. They were, in short, an amazing *spectacle*, these sentient statues, even before I developed any sense of them as individuals—they would of course be even more so later when I'd brought them all together, and especially so later still, when they were to open up so very widely—briefly . . . pregnantly.

"Beth Abraham was in fact a treasure house of remarkable patients, and I became their curator! Like Jonathan Miller, I feel that my greatest interest resides in the back wards of asylums. Hughlings Jackson, the father of modern neurology, did his best work there—you have all the time in the world, he used to say, no one is expecting anything, and the patients are hungry, yearning for any attention that is not insulting. Indeed, later on I would partly regard L-DOPA as an irritating interference in the calm, careful, timeless study of postencephalitics which I might otherwise have wished to continue. I would spend hours sitting with them, one at a time in my office, trying to infer their sense of reality. I was more into stillness in those days (only later with the Touretters did frenzy truly come into my purview, though when it did come up, it served to enrich my study enormously)."

Thus, for example, as with Leonard, how Sacks would spend hours at a time patiently sitting with him—Leonard seemingly frozen in time—as ever so slowly the stunted patient dragged his trembling fingers across a sort of Ouija board; once, having asked the palsied man what it was like in there, Oliver sat, astounded, as achingly slowly Leonard eked out the reply: R-I-L-K-E-S-P-A-N-T-H-E-R. Leonard, it turned out, had been a brilliant young librarian, just starting out, when years earlier the disease had felled him. Oliver, for his part, was familiar with the reference from Rilke's poem "The Panther":

> His gaze has from the passing of the bars
> grown so tired that it holds nothing anymore.

It seems to him there are a thousand bars
and behind a thousand bars, no world.

The supple pace of powerful soft strides,
turning in the very smallest circle,
is like a dance of strength around a center
in which a great will stands numbed.

Only sometimes the curtain of the pupils
soundlessly slides up—. Then an image enters,
glides through the limbs' taut stillness—,
dives into the heart and dies.

(translated by Edward Snow)

A week later, during a late-afternoon early-autumn walk from out of my apartment into Riverside Park, Oliver picked up the story where he had left off (post-"Panther").

"In February 1967," he recalled, "I first began to hear from *them*, my postencephalitics, or at any rate from the more conventionally Parkinsonians scattered among the rest of the hospital's population (there were approximately a hundred and twenty others of *those*), about the work of George Cotzias on L-DOPA, a synthetic precursor of dopamine, which was said to be having remarkable results with more typical Parkinsonian patients at his labs out at Brookhaven on Long Island. Leonard himself, in moments of arousal, was soon referring to Cotzias as 'the chemical messiah.'"

As it happens, this was also the month Sacks indulged in that very last epic drug-infused weekend of his, finally achieving the high he'd been seeking all along through immersion in the pages of that long-forgotten nineteenth-century text on migraines. As a result, though, for the next eighteen months "my main involvement was with the migraine clinic and the migraine book project which grew out of my work there, on which I didn't do my final reworking till September 1968. But once the migraine book had gone to press, I was ready to concentrate on the postencephalitics at Beth Abraham."

The summer of 1968 had been unusually sweltering, Oliver recalled.

"None of the wards were air-conditioned and dozens of patients had died of heat stroke while others were suffering critical swallowing difficulties. L-DOPA up to that point had still been too expensive, but now I began to feel we really had to give it a try. In order to do that, we still had to get a number and a license from the Drug Enforcement Agency and that was going to take a while, six to nine months we were told, but in anticipation we began reviewing files with their ancient case histories and bringing all the postencephalitics together in a single ward.

"This would have been approximately October or November 1968, and the hospital basically was proposing a double-blind ninety-day experiment to see if L-DOPA would work on this kind of patient."

Oliver and I paused to gaze out over the Hudson, toward the Jersey Palisades on the far side. The river was flowing seemingly in reverse, as high tide pushed the sea up toward Albany.

"Still, I was conflicted from the outset. For one thing, I didn't know whether L-DOPA would even work on patients with Parkinsonism of such severity. I didn't want to raise the hopes of patients and families unrealistically. And then, too, I was concerned about the depth of the trance the worst of them had been subject to, a sleep that was both personal and historical, over and beyond and no less than animal and physiological: If the treatment did work, what would it be like existentially for some of these individuals who had been out, as it were, for decades, to suddenly be wrenched back into the present? The sort of thing Pinter would subsequently fasten on.

"But even more so, reading between the lines of the euphoric reports coming out of Brookhaven and the other labs about this new 'miracle' treatment—well into 1969, there had been hardly any articles documenting negative instances, and the tone was overwhelmingly optimistic, but I was a bit suspicious. I felt the 'side effects' were probably more significant than mere side effects, and might be worse yet with patients whose conditions were so much more pronounced. I didn't know what sort of Pandora's box we might be opening."

Why did Oliver think he might have been less susceptible to the drug's millennial expectations?

"I'd run into this sort of thing with a lot of the migraine patients, and I was thoroughly fed up with purveyors of magic, both patients and doctors—credulous patients and unscrupulous doctors. The migraine scene is full of conscious and unconscious fraud. Both at the Headache Clinic and Beth Abraham, and ever since, I was and am interested in the natural history of complex disorders with many causes and cures—more so at any rate than in therapy alone. In fact, if you go back and look, you'll see that already in the opening paragraphs of my migraine book I had written how one cannot expect magic for migraine *or Parkinsonism.*"

Had he ever discussed any of his misgivings with Cotzias directly?

"I had only one contact with Cotzias, a few years before this. One of his patients came into my hands, a woman named Helen: She had been given DL-DOPA in 1965; the history she gave coincided with that given by all her relatives and subsequent doctors, which is that she had gone ape bonkers on DL-DOPA, had escaped from Brookhaven, had spent ten nights lost in the ditches of Long Island (luckily it was summer), had been completely psychotic for a year: a terrible, terrible reaction. I wrote Brookhaven for her records, but they said virtually nothing: 'She became a little anxious and discharged herself against our advice,' that sort of thing, is all they would admit. So I phoned Cotzias, exchanged courtesies, then mentioned, 'We have Helen here.' I asked if he perhaps had further details. 'Dr. Sacks,' he insisted, 'I am no clinician. I am a chemist.' The man was *lying.*

"I'm told that when *Awakenings* eventually came out, he leafed through it quickly, looking for references to himself, and then closed the book, never to open it again."

Oliver paused before resuming. The tide was calming, getting set to turn, the river almost still. "Anyway, so the patients were being brought together during the winter of 1969—as usual I was relying on the nurses and the therapists, especially a new speech therapist who'd arrived a few months earlier named Margie Kohl. Originally, we were going to be given a floor in a new building—instead, at the last minute we were switched to 5ZP, an older and shabbier ward. In my own mind, they were being brought together with the idea that they would or at least could be given L-DOPA. Of course, first I had to speak to patients, relatives, and therapists, and this took time.

"But then, in January 1969, a new patient, named Sophie, arrived at Beth Abraham from the Neurological Institute on One Hundred and Sixty-Eighth Street, where more of the L-DOPA work was going on. And she'd been reduced to the most terrible gibbering and motor psychosis. I was appalled at her state. The Neurological Institute, where the Basal Ganglia Club held its monthly meetings, was one of the centers of all of this euphoria. She was one of theirs, and she was a real horror story, would go on to die during the coming summer. Which of course gave me further hesitations and was of course quite frightening to the patients."

So why *did* he go ahead?

"I felt that we had to at least try because without L-DOPA they were more and more incapacitated, and as during the previous summer, with markedly rising rates of mortality. And, also, notwithstanding all of that, I thought something remarkable might happen—as I say, I'd seen remarkable instances of kinesia paradoxa already, this sudden brief bursting to life, which gave further evidence that, despite all indications, they were fully alive in there, deep inside their trances."

What of the problem of consent?

"As for telling the patients of the possible dangers in advance, I was warned off by Charlie M, our executive director, and others: 'Don't tell them too much.' He was already showing signs of incipient messianic tendencies and would quickly become power-crazed as the experiment proceeded.

"To be sure, delicate questions of competence and the morality of choice were raised. I was fairly sure about the patients' intellectual competence, but here I was offering fantastic hope to the previously hopeless. No matter how guarded my presentation, the whole thing was fraught with millennial expectations, which I partly shared even as I partly shunned them.

"In general, I said to the patients, those I could reach, 'This thing has come up which appears to have a chance of breaking the akinesia, the motionlessness. It has been described as having remarkable effects. You may have heard about it. We'd have to start very slowly and see what happens. How would you feel?'"

But how could he be sure he was reaching them?

"From my hours with them over the previous months, I had come to feel that most of them could hear what I was saying. Although infinitely preoccupied, they could sometimes focus when needed.

"And several of them were indeed eager. Leonard called L-DOPA 'ressurectimine.' Others were compliant without much feeling: perhaps simply for lack of affect (they couldn't help appearing indifferent). Others wanted to wait and see about its effects on their colleagues.

"I talked to patients, I talked to relatives. I tried not to coerce, nor was there an implicit coercion. The creation of the special ward was separate from the L-DOPA experiment, both in my mind and in reality.

"I had no funds and I was using my own money for the initial L-DOPA, the extra hours for the therapists, and the camera and film with which I was documenting the condition of the patients in the months prior to the administration of the drug."

The sun was setting over the Palisades and the river water now completely stilled, a warm evening breeze rustling through the overhanging branches of the park's trees. We took a seat on a nearby bench.

"By March 1969, we had gotten permission from the DEA and we were ready to begin. But slowly and double-blind. Three patients were given placebos and the three first patients who, as it turned out, were actually given the L-DOPA were, as I named them in the book, Leonard, Hester, and Aaron. And the results were almost immediate, within hours, at most within days. I recorded everything and put together a spectacular film—and spectacular it was—which I now showed to the Federation of Jewish Philanthropies, from which I was able to schnorr . . . I mean, raise $55,000 to keep the experiment and its documentation going.

"With Hester, I saw complications the first moment, though not so much so with the others, Leonard and Aaron, such that there was a strong movement toward optimism and rather quickly the double-blind framework got thrown out. A conventional scientist would have persisted with the double-blind, but it was immediately obvious that the L-DOPA was working, it was inconceivable we were witnessing a placebo effect, and to have continued with the double-blind trial would have been both scientifically useless and therapeutically negligent."

And how did the other patients react?

"Seymour, for example, had been hesitant, he'd held off. But he was very fond of Hester, and he said he couldn't believe his eyes at her transformation: 'If it did that for her, I'm going to try it.' Many who'd sat on the fence now took the plunge, and in some instances, I did some pushing. With Eda, I suppose I committed a bit of a crime: I had it administered to her by stealth in her applesauce. She had been negative, but she's the one who later said, 'That dopamine is a mitzvah. Thank God you gave it to me.' By mid-spring, pretty much every Parkinsonian at the hospital wanted L-DOPA, and in good conscience one couldn't very well deny them.

"And thus the work progressed toward infinity. By the end of April, it was clear we were dealing with something spectacular, and by the early summer, most of the postencephalitics had been started. So it wasn't so much a rising curve as an explosion. I was spending twenty, twenty-two hours a day on the wards."

How did he manage to keep up?

"Not on speed, for a change; just on adrenaline. Seriously, I'd given up drugs and I'd given up sex and I was into *medicine*—but what medicine! I'd hit the jackpot!"

Thank God, he was now living close to the hospital. Back in March he'd still been living in Manhattan, on Seventy-First (the farthest north of a succession of apartments that had begun in the Village), but that month he'd suffered a burglary, and the hospital had offered him an apartment a hundred yards from the ward (as a result of which, he'd also had to take on, on top of everything else, the duty of signing death certificates for the entire place and being on call pretty much every night).

May, June, and July would prove "the most turned-on period for the patients, and for everyone," as Oliver described those high good days of the initial Awakening: the uncanny lifting of blockage and the return of ease, of grace, of joy and delight and resolve. Leonard, for instance, took to a typewriter and began banging out a heartrending autobiography that eventually stretched to fifty thousand words (Oliver subsequently showed it to me).

Over the years of our work together, Oliver regaled me with countless such specific stories—of the awakenings themselves, and the subsequent harrowing months of Tribulation, and the eventual hard-fought and hard-won attainment of a sort of Accommodation. But there's no point in re-hashing all of that here; in this case, the reader is advised to consult Oliver's narratives (both in the original *Awakenings* book and in his late-life memoir), where he details the particulars with matchless depth and verve. I do remember one tale that I think he neglected to commit to writing himself, that of "a woman who spent her entire rejuvenescence sitting outside on the Beth Abraham front porch, guarding my motorcycle. 'No no,' she'd say, when anyone approached. 'Leave that alone. That's *Doctor's* motorcycle.' She'd sit there, day after day," Oliver recalled, smiling, momentarily lost in remembrance, "safeguarding my steed."

But things began to turn, inexorably. "Already in April we were beginning to see unsolicited variations. With Hester, as I say, we saw side effects as soon as we saw effects. Thus there was an intensified conflict early on, for we saw both therapeutic effects beyond our wildest expectations and incipient catastrophic effects beyond our direst fears."

The temperature dropped quickly now that the sun had set (the river waters had begun to turn, the tide was going back out) and I was cold (even if Oliver of course wasn't), so we decided to head back.

At first, Oliver continued to relate, at first it seemed possible that the progressively rampaging side effects—oculogyric crises (which are inexorable deviations of gaze, often skyward), stampeding festinations (forced, irresistible accelerations of walking, talking, or thought), sudden abrupt stoppages, panics and spasms of all sorts—might just be a question of titration. Already the postencephalytics had been receiving dosages far lower than those administered to ordinary Parkinsonians, but now Oliver and his nurses and the pharmacologists tried to modulate the dosages yet further. "The fine arts of titration were something I was well familiar with, both from my experiments on some woebegone hens back in my research days at Oxford and from my subsequent experiments on myself." He told me of his mounting horror with one patient in particular, how at one dosage she would seize up into oculogyric crises, which went away at a lower dosage, only to be replaced by blithering festinations, which went away at a slightly higher dosage, only to be replaced by resuming oculogyric episodes—how the caregiving team kept trying to achieve a perfect knife-edge balance, which they finally did, though, alas, the patient now began experiencing *both* oculogyric and festinating crises simultaneously.

Was there a point where he thought, My God, what have I done?

"Yes, it came to me many times that this was tampering, meddling with human lives on a large scale. But I dealt with that by saying, first and last, without this there would be no life whatsoever, and turbulent life is better than none. With Hester: She would have been dead. It had been getting so that she couldn't swallow. In a medical sense, we were dealing with a frail and dying population. I had a feeling of unprecedented responsibility—and yet, I told myself I am not responsible for someone's physiology.

"I must have been repressing, I suppose.

"Our director, Charlie M, somehow managed to close his eyes to the negative altogether—he was becoming avid for publicity in the roiling mania." Later that summer, he landed a visit from a reporter with *The New York Times.*

Was Oliver himself immune to such messianic delusions?

"I was embarrassed by the power of the tool that had been placed in my hands, and embarrassed by the power of the emotions and the transferences my tool was eliciting. Partly I dealt with my confusion and guilt with my therapist.

"Beyond that, though, one of the main things that made it possible to live with what might otherwise be unbearable therapeutic pressures is that ultimately, as I say, I'm a naturalist before I'm a doctor. I didn't enter medicine for . . . Freud talks about 'the lie of salvation'—and this business of feeling myself a naturalist in the landscape of postencephalitics enabled me to work amid atrocious affliction and insoluble therapeutic dilemmas.*

"Granted, there was always a conjunction, sometimes a collusion and sometimes a collision, between the naturalist and the therapist. I often thought of Jane Goodall watching that sad neurotic monkey with his mother—clearly, she'd perceived that this could come to no good end, and yet she did not intervene. But one of my functions as I saw it was to bring the patient into the position of being a naturalist with regard to her own illness, which implied a neutrality of interest and description wed to the love of phenomena for their own sake. And my colleagues said they had never heard patients speaking with such precision and dispassion about their own illnesses."

We exited the park and headed across Ninety-Fifth toward my apartment and his parked car. "At any rate, there had been building up, partly unconsciously, a feeling of moral complexity, of existential complications, of intellectual excitement, during the five months from March into July: consuming, ravishing, frightening, full of promise and full of threat. I was averaging three hours a night of sleep. I was being overwhelmed and succumbing to a sort of moral indigestion.

"By the end of July, I had seen an inconceivable amount, my mind had been blown in all directions, and I was close to a nervous breakdown and

---

*The great art critic Leo Steinberg speaks somewhere of "that moment when the artist stops asking 'What can I do?' and starts asking 'What can art do?'" And surely there must be something similar in the practices of science and medicine.

collapse myself. During August, therefore, I left for London, where I wrote up the first nine case studies (writing itself being a way of thinking things through), while Margie, our speech therapist, held the fort.

"And I'll tell you the rest next time."

※

Around this time, I had occasion to reach out by telephone to Oliver's collaborator Margie Kohl. Though she had in the meantime moved with her husband and family to Memphis, she recalled her years at Beth Abraham vividly. She related how she had graduated from Boston College as a speech therapist and then gone on to secure a "more scientifically and psychologically based" master's at Columbia in 1968, at which point she'd applied for a job at Beth Abraham to found "a speech-therapy department of one," arriving there, as she described herself at the outset, "fairly conventionally rigid."

When she'd first arrived, she told me, "it still said 'The Beth Abraham Home for the Incurable' over the entryway, though the place had a newer official name. Still, one doctor told me, 'Our youngest is eighteen and no one ever leaves here, they all just eventually die.'

"Charlie M was the medical director; Jack S, the chief of medicine. It was generally said of doctors there that if you'd ended up at Beth Abraham, career-wise you were likely as badly off as your patients.

"Oliver being the exception, of course.

"He was odd, odder than today: huge, a full beard, black leather jacket covering T-shirts riddled with holes, huge shoes, his trousers looking like they were going to slide off his body. He was deeply eccentric. A number of times he was fired and rehired the same day—in part the result of the place being administered by a director who was going progressively senile.

"Oliver was still doing drugs in his early days at Beth Abraham, though they were trailing off. He clearly had an addictive personality: 'If one is good, three are better.' Though with his patients he was scrupulous and very, very careful—the opposite of how he was with himself.

"When I first met him, he was still living in this rat hole in the East Seventies and would come motorcycling up, even in the worst ice storms. Beth Abraham eventually gave him a nearby apartment, in 1969. As I say, his clothes were a mess, and as the Awakenings drama began to take hold and he was having to make public and media presentations, I really

Margie Kohl with Oliver

didn't want people laughing at him and writing him off, so I took him
out, buying him suits and ties. Tried to get him off the motorcycle, at least
in winter, even got him to buy a Rover roadster at one point, though that
proved a fiasco."

What had been the deal with the director? I probed.

"Well, Charlie was sixty-two or sixty-three, seemed a sweet old man,
and indeed could be quite warm and caring, but then would flip out at
the most arbitrary moments, would become a real control freak (which may
have had to do with the fact, only recognizable in retrospect, as I say, that
he was progressively losing his mind): 'Ollie, you do this and report back
to me that you have done it!' He'd be furious when Oliver came in late,
oblivious to the fact that he'd been there till one a.m. the night before. He
sensed Oliver's brilliance, but this only aggravated things as he grew immensely jealous.

"But it was similar, with the administration as a whole, especially as
we began asking for special funds and supplies in the midst of the whole
Awakenings drama: They felt threatened, and then began to connive at finding ways of getting press coverage and taking credit. 'Let's get the *Times*—
hell, let's get Geraldo Rivera!'"

Ms. Kohl sighed, seemed to smile audibly, shifting gears.

"Our Monday staff lunch meetings were a marvel. Oliver wanted everyone in there: the therapists, the aides, the nurses, the orderlies, the janitors. 'If we want to get a sense, for instance, of Hester,' he'd say, 'we need to pool everyone's input.' And the change in the help, the nurses, and so forth was immediately apparent: how they all became so proud.

"Ollie would draw people out: 'How does Seymour's wandering around like that affect you? What can we do to help with that?' We started sharing responsibilities. The notes became so rich. We were like one big flourishing organism up there, with Ollie as the father and me as the mother, with me keeping all the notes (because Ollie would misplace them).

"And then Charlie would flip out, shrill with suspicion, and come storming through, disrupting everything."

I asked her about the awakening itself: the flourishing and presently the mounting crisis.

"Well, I'll tell you one thing," she responded, "the experience forever changed my own outlook on illness. Here were these people: I mean, by any conventional understanding, they were disgusting. I am thinking for instance of the Rose of before: drooling, crumpled over in a perpetual slouch, bearded, with patchy skin. Who could possibly care about her, or most any of them, really?

"And then to have someone emerge from all of that, to suddenly find this person who'd been stuck there inside, voracious for news, warm, very human and tender and sweet and concerned, brimming over with reminiscences which could presently give themselves over, for example, to incredibly lewd songs.

"Or Leonard, our sweet involuted Leonard, who became veritably ravenous, lunging at anyone with breasts! 'Our Parkinsonian Portnoy,' we called him."

That's right, I suddenly realized, since of course 1969 had also been the summer of *Portnoy's Complaint*!

"And Seymour, our Talmudic scholar, who was so sensitive, a part of him entirely otherworldly and completely untouched by his imprisonment: He had been having vast Talmudic arguments in his head for years; his had definitely not been an idle seclusion. But now he imagined or maybe he did have a woman friend on the outside and he'd repeatedly try to escape. He'd be frozen stiff when suddenly, like a bat out of hell, he'd be off and running, he'd look like he was going to crash but he'd use walls to stop and redirect himself—watching, one's heart would be in one's mouth, and one had to wonder if an institution had the right to prevent a mentally competent patient from leaving . . . He was also unduly fond of his hallucinations, one in particular of his father's voice advising him to kill himself. Most everyone else saw him as schizoid and dangerous, but I knew that when he got like that, I could talk to him, he'd calm himself and listen and he'd talk back . . .

"And Maria, whose fate became a veritable nightmare. At one point, I had to physically restrain her from killing someone else, she was violent and strong and growling and snarling, and then just as suddenly she collapsed into sobs, and I had to hold her as she cried for two and a half hours, rocking her, rocking her . . .

"Or Ida, as we called her. She was very hostile toward everyone, except for Oliver: She liked his size, and I think there was a parallel side of him that liked hers.

"With Hester, once, she was in such a frenzy of upper-body ticcing that I grabbed her and held her in my arms in a fierce bear hug, and I could feel her starting to relax when suddenly, to my own horror and hers, her legs started flailing.

"The sheer drive of energy demanding release somewhere, anywhere—legs, arms, hands, neck, voice. Later on, gradually, things would begin to standardize, and you and they could discern patterns, but at first it was just sheer chaos."

Another long silence, the telephone wires humming.

"Our relationship to the patients," she resumed, "was sometimes oddly parent-childlike. 'I know you want to run outside and be free, but you can't run in traffic like that and you have to stop trying to or we'll have to strap you in.'

"Which was an especially ironic situation for Ollie, because he was himself so childlike; it must have been comforting for him in a sense for once to be an inverse of the usual. Neither of us was or will ever be more loved than we were when we were on that floor. They were at once our grandparents, concerned about our welfare, the way grandparents can be, and our children, and we simultaneously their parents and their kids.

"Some days they'd go completely silent. Others they'd start talking, and if they were talking that day, he'd stay for as long as they were. Hence those one a.m. departures.

"Early on, after the administration of L-DOPA, during those great good days, everything was so charming, it was like a beehive up there, family visits, outings, they'd tell you what they'd made that day, they were all reading and gossiping.

"And then you'd walk in on a bad day, and it was bedlam, a termite hell, all these insects clamoring all over each other, incredibly noisy with barks and groans and curses and moans—and even those who weren't yet afflicted stunned in terror: *When is all of that going to happen to me?*"

We went on talking like that for hours—it was clear that in part of her life, Ms. Kohl was still entrammeled back then, as increasingly I felt myself to be becoming. At length, past midnight, we signed off. SB

⁂

"Of course, I'd had misgivings about leaving for London that August," Oliver resumed the following week, when we met for dinner at a Chinese place, "and returning at the end of the month, many of my worst ones were borne out.

"At the time I'd left, a quasi-delusional messianism had been threatening Charlie M, but by the time I came back, complete disaster had set in. M's tyranny would brook no moderation. He wanted patients with swimming eyes looking up at him and saying, 'Thank you, God bless you, Dr. M, our savior!'

"He fired the head of medicine for standing in his way.

"And then there came the terrible case where he broke a patient's leg. Her name was Anna Perlman, and she was deeply submerged in a fixed lucid despair which had already lasted thirty years. She'd turned from the world in many ways. Poor rigid thin Anna, bright and brooding: She was the most death-loving person I ever met. She started to unfreeze a little, but really she'd never been reacting so well. And finally one day, Charlie took to screaming at her, '*Bend your leg, bend your leg, goddammit!*'—and then proceeded to do so himself, breaking it! After which she reverted completely, slumping into a depression from which she never emerged, not once, across her remaining ten years."

As for the other patients, the last quarter of 1969 and on through 1970 was characterized by a sort of subsidence, a grudging coming to terms:

never again as bright and brilliant as the great albeit tragically truncated hope-filled days of Awakening, but not as desperately dire as the harrowing horrors of Tribulation; a spent becalming, more lucid and engaged in general than the decades of trance that had preceded it, but not by terribly much. An Accommodation, as Sacks came to think of it.

Thus, for example, the case of Rose R, the woman who'd suddenly become entranced at age twenty-one in 1926, only to awaken briefly in July 1969, a sudden and full-fledged flapper, vivid and vivacious, completely given over to the lingo and the dance steps and the lewd songs of the time, only to spiral clean out of control in the days that followed, mortified by the prospect that she might in fact not be the young woman she knew herself to be, subject to ever more violent oculogyric crises, until she curled back to bed, barely responsive when called out but seldom more than that. As Oliver reported some years later at the end of his account of her story in the book (and I quote at length here, in part to further tempt readers to return to the source):

> She indicates that in her "nostalgic" state she *knew* perfectly well that it was 1969 and that she was sixty-four years old, but that she *felt* that it was 1926 and she was twenty-one; she adds that she can't really imagine what it's like being older than twenty-one, because she has never really experienced it. For most of the time, however, there is "nothing, absolutely nothing, no thoughts at all" in her head, as if she is forced to block off an intolerable and insoluble anachronism—the almost half-century gap between her age as felt and experienced (her *ontological* age) and her actual or *official* age. [. . .] She continues to look much younger than her years; indeed, in a fundamental sense, she *is* much younger than her age. But she is a Sleeping Beauty whose "awakening" was unbearable to her, and who will never be awoken again.

The book, however, was still several years off. Meanwhile, during the first half of 1970, Oliver composed a narrative account of the entire drama for *Brain: A Journal of Neurology*, "a glorious, nonjudgmental noncondemnatory piece on our postencephs, containing a wealth of description, including many things which hadn't been seen in *years*," a piece that was rejected in a letter of three lines: "Paper unsuitable, so unsuitable that no revision is recommended."

Regarding which, Oliver added: "Across the early sixties, *Brain* had held out as the last bastion of description, the outlet, for example, of Wilder Penfield's marvelous papers, but by 1970, it had clearly fallen completely under the sway of scientism, with its charts, its double-blinds, and its relentlessly specious narrowings of focus."

After that, in the early spring of 1970, Oliver dispatched five letters to the editor of *The Lancet*, in England. "They'd all been composed in a single evening, were descriptive and noncontroversial, and began appearing one at a time in the months thereafter" (May 9, June 6, June 27, July 25, and September 13) "to relatively mild effect, although the third letter, 'Incontinent nostalgia induced by L-dopa,' got released by the *Lancet* people to Reuters and eventually found its way to the *National Enquirer*, which bannered the headline DOCTOR BRINGS DEAD TO LIFE, to my horror and my patients' pain.

"There then came an absurd blowup with Dr. M—he was damned if I was going to be publishing in England like that—and he pushed me into submitting a less satisfactory and far more peremptory piece to *The Journal of the American Medical Association*, which in turn ran it in their September 28, 1970, issue, and led to my break with the profession.

"The thing is, no one had been put on the spot by the *Lancet* letters, whereas everyone was put on the spot by the *JAMA* article. Out of sixty patients, I reported, every single one given L-DOPA had shown therapeutic results and every single one had shown 'side effects' so pronounced that one wondered whether they should be called 'side effects' at all or perhaps something deeper. *Nobody* wanted to hear this."

Oliver stabbed at his scallops in garlic sauce with his chopsticks, and then over at mine. "A few months later, an issue of *JAMA* came out devoted to outraged letters about me. I answered each letter personally but chose not to answer in *JAMA*. Quite how I dealt with my own conflicts I don't know—but I'd certainly aroused the reaction of others with that *JAMA* article.

"One Southern California doctor, for example, wrote to the effect that 'This should not have been published. It disturbs the atmosphere of therapeutic optimism.'

"I sent him a letter: 'Although poor, I'd gladly send you a ticket and you could fly here to Beth Abraham and see for yourself.'

"To which there came no reply."

Oliver paused before continuing. "In the most recent edition of *Awakenings*, I've included a phrase to the effect that things denied in 1970 have increasingly been seen to be the case. But back then the *JAMA* thing came to a head at precisely the moment that *Migraine* was published, and I felt paralyzed, paranoid within my profession, the entire atmosphere poisoned, my writing stoppered. As things would remain until September 1972, when Mary-Kay Wilmers reached out and invited me to write a piece for *The Listener*."

⁂

Another evening, Oliver recalled how "I once challenged Cotzias's young colleague Dr. [Paul] Papavasiliou at a symposium on L-DOPA. Someone had asked Dr. Papavasiliou about so-called yo-yo reactions, and he claimed they were 'very rare and easily dealt with,' to which I countered, 'I've seen them in two hundred of two hundred patients and found them very difficult to deal with.'

"It was a fairly gladiatorial exchange.

"At a subsequent dinner, he commented to me: 'If we'd had as many doubts as you, we'd have been paralyzed and could not have done any work and the world would have come to a stop.'

"To which I replied, 'If I'd had as few doubts as you, I'd have blown from one project to another frenetically and the world would have blown off its axis.'"

Oliver paused for a moment, considering. "Both types are needed, I suppose, the gung-ho researcher and the doubting contemplator." Two beats. "Let it not be thought, however, that I am the more pessimistic. I am about *medication*, but there is a whole universe of other therapeutic possibilities."

⁂

Late in the summer of 1972, Oliver took a three-month leave from Beth Abraham, which he spent in London, in part to celebrate his parents' golden wedding anniversary.

During this period, Colin Haycraft, the chairman of Gerald Duckworth and Company, who'd been hearing about Oliver's Awakenings travails from Jonathan Miller, increased his gentle pressure on Oliver to turn them into a book. It is probably either he or Jonathan who would have told Mary-Kay Wilmers about the prospect—all of them lived within meters of each other on Gloucester Crescent—hence her feeler that September, to which Oliver quickly seemed to respond. Likewise, he now poured himself into fashioning the eventual book's final eleven case studies, actually dictating them to a stenographer as he lay bedridden, suffering from the whiplash he'd given himself bashing his head against a low beam rushing up the cellar stairs, the transcripts from which he would edit, read to his mother, and then pass on to Colin.

Back in the United States, scarcely did Oliver have time to savor the small triumph of his *Listener* piece, published October 26 ("This doctor's report is written in a prose of such beauty that you might well look in vain for its equal among living practitioners of belles lettres," raved Frank Kermode, a few days later in *The Daily Telegraph*), than he faced three major crises, one hard on the next. On November 8, Dr. M evicted him from his apartment (which, the director explained, he suddenly needed for his own ailing mother), and when Oliver objected that the apartment was intended for doctors working at the hospital, on November 10, M fired him for insubordination, for good measure. (Although, having decamped to a small rented house in Mount Vernon, Oliver would continue to tend to his patients at Beth Abraham for free until his reinstatement, on the far side of Dr. M's retirement, in 1975.) Then, on November 13, he received word that his mother had died of a heart attack while on a visit to Israel, hiking in the Negev Desert.

He often told me, in those days, how this was the greatest blow of his life, the loss of his "deepest and perhaps most real relation" (albeit, just below the surface, a highly charged one; the two of them had never again broached the subject of his homosexuality after that one horrible outburst, almost fifteen years earlier). After the funeral, at which the four brothers carried the casket, they all sat shiva with their father for a full week, Oliver, almost inconsolable, poring over the Bible and John Donne's *Devotions*, after which, he recalls, "a strange calm descended and I was able to complete the allegorical overview sections of the book—Perspective, Awakening, Tribulation, Accommodation—which were to follow and synthesize all the themes raised in each of the earlier case studies, and then the epilogue, which in turn brought things up to date, in a matter of weeks," delivering the finished manuscript to Colin Haycraft by the end of the year. "Whereupon I dispatched four hundred additional footnotes in rapid succession across the weeks immediately thereafter." Colin, noting how their cumulative mass well outnumbered the pages of the entire text, completely overwhelming the narrative, allowed Oliver twelve and told him that *he* would have to be the one to choose.

The book now hurtled toward publication. Oliver had gotten it into his head that the book had to appear before his fortieth birthday, that coming July 9, and Colin obliged him with a June 28 publication date, with a celebratory review of the book by Richard Gregory appearing in that week's *Listener*, which also included an essay by Oliver celebrating "The Mind of A. R. Luria."

Awakenings was well reviewed in the cultural pages though largely dismissed when not simply ignored by the medical profession. A decade later, Oliver was still remembering "a neurologist named Marsden who appeared on the *Kaleidoscope* program over BBC Radio shortly after the book's release and more or less said: 1) It's amazing, this Sacks fellow must have spent hours and hours attending those patients; 2) Obviously we working neurologists can't lavish that sort of time on our patients; and 3) Who needs it, anyway?"

On the other hand, on July 19, making up for all of it, an immaculately handwritten letter arrived from Moscow, signed Dr. A. R. Luria— the first of what would become many such missives, and a veritable occasion for rapture on Oliver's part. Auden would die a few months later (on September 29, in Austria), and one senses in Oliver's recollections of this period a powerfully tidal transition from one validating father figure to the next.

The other immediate result of the book's UK release was a phone call to Oliver from Duncan Dallas, a television producer based in Yorkshire. Oliver invited him over for a visit and the two quickly agreed to attempt a documentary, Oliver's recent firing notwithstanding (a firing which, as I say, Oliver was pretty much ignoring in any case, right up to the moment of his eventual reinstatement).

I tracked Dallas down at his Yorkshire offices, by phone, and he recalled how "at first, I was shocked by the seeming squalidness of Beth Abraham, and indeed as I was taken around, I was introduced to people who at first glance seemed not quite derelict but certainly incomprehensible and plainly uninteresting. Now, granted, again, that this was several years after their full flowering, but the thing that most amazed me from the start was that Oliver should ever have discovered interest in such people in the first place.

"Seriously, when you first saw the patients who'd survived the time of Tribulation, you didn't really believe all the things Oliver was ascribing to them, but the more time you spent with them, the more you began to realize how their inner lives were in fact still quite *dense* with experience, and then, when coupled with the films Oliver himself had been taking earlier on, both before and after L-DOPA, you could see that it was all true.

"Meanwhile, I too was concerned, because the television lens can be quite ruthless, and when I was first getting to know them, I was sometimes painfully embarrassed—for them, for myself—and they would grow embarrassed for me. But Oliver had this uncanny capacity to put all of us at ease, and we got through that."

Dallas paused and took a deep breath before concluding: "Caring doesn't begin to encapsulate it. He's *interested*, and vitally so: He's continuously imagining what could be going on, but—and this is the thing—testing his imagination against the real."[SB]

The film proved a terrific success when it aired that fall in England, but Oliver's triumph notwithstanding, the end of 1973 and continuing into 1974 saw a period of growing crisis and disintegration at Beth Abraham. "The mad director eventually resigned," Oliver recalled for me one day as we sat in his City Island living room, "but he was replaced by a somewhat abstracted fellow who went around with his yarmulke, muttering phrases which were either Hebrew prayers or biochemical equations, one could never be sure.

"Meanwhile, Beth Abraham began facing disastrous cutbacks. When Medicare had first come into being in the late sixties, it had connoted a strong infusion of money for the hospital. While at first we had been oblivious to the attached strings, those strings now began being pulled hard. Severe cutbacks led to many layoffs, including that of Margie Kohl. One of the patients in *Awakenings* died immediately as a direct result of the firing of his therapist, and more generally, we were seeing rampant disruptions in what had been a delicate physio-psycho-social ecosystem.

"Partly because of these cutbacks, a sudden edict mandated the release of any patients who were ambulatory. Some of these patients had been at Beth Abraham for over thirty years, but the language of Medicare's bureaucratic enforcement required the arbitrary separation of ambulants and non-ambulants.

"The first effect of this was a sudden universal simulation of paralysis." Oliver let out a gentle laugh at the memory. "But even in the short term, that failed to work, and the terrible result was that most of the community's livelier participants were transferred, leaving only the truly miserable, and thereby devastating morale.

"In the process, valuable symbiotic relationships were trammeled. Thus, for instance, one Parkinsonian, a severe catatonic who could sit frozen for hours on end until called upon, whereupon she would suddenly come to and respond in normal, fluid fashion—for example, she was often called upon to perform some errands at neighboring stores, which she would cheerfully do, after which she would return to her chair and her catatonia—anyway, she had developed a close friendship with an utterly paralyzed MS patient.

"The MS patient would call out to the Parkinsonian, pull her out of her trance, ask for and receive assistance. *Helping her helped her*, can't you see.

"So suddenly these two were separated. The Parkinsonian was remanded to lodging in Co-op City, where she had no one who needed her, no one who would call out to her—so that she sat for days on end without moving until one afternoon she fell, broke her brittle hip, and within a few weeks was dead.

"The woman with MS, meanwhile, back at Beth Abraham though without the benefit of her friend's ministrations and now relegated to the inadequate care of a sorely overworked staff, likewise went into a precipitous decline and was likewise dead within months."

Oliver stared out the window, grimly. "Two deaths—and I assure you these were not the only ones—caused simply by somebody's idea of bureaucratic efficiency."

There was a long pause, the grandfather clock ticking loudly in the corner, before he resumed. "Because of the hideous way they were being treated, the staff at Beth Abraham launched out upon a strike in 1974, and I was quite torn. On the one hand, I shared their horror at the turn things were taking, and I completely agreed with their grievances. But at the same time, I couldn't participate in the strike" (notwithstanding the fact that he was still at that moment technically fired and only volunteering at the home) "for the sake of the patients. Their community was so delicate, their care so precarious as it was—and many of them could not be expected to understand what was happening.

"At any rate, not only could I not honor their picket lines, I threw myself into an emergency effort to recruit students at Albert Einstein to come assist in the care of the patients across the duration of the strike. We worked round the clock for eighteen days.

"The strike was finally settled, and on the last afternoon I returned to my car, only to find all its windows smashed, with a banner wrapped around the steering wheel—'WE LOVE YOU DR. SACKS BUT YOU'VE BEEN A STRIKEBREAKER'—which they had every right to do. I didn't begrudge them that for a moment. None of us could have done otherwise."

In the wake of his dismissal from Beth Abraham, Oliver had had to cobble together an alternative existence, and he did so in what would become two fateful ways. For one thing, he joined another neurologist, a certain Dr. F, in setting up a part-time (and presently quite spectacularly ill-fated) private practice (of which more anon). Beyond that, he ramped up his ongoing work with the Little Sisters and the nearby Bronx State Hospital as well. The latter was focused particularly on the no less ill-fated Ward 23 (again, of which more anon), in desperate flight from which Oliver (still grieving as well over the death of his mother less than two years earlier) would presently flee for a brief and, alas, equally portentous trip to Norway, where on August 24, 1974, he would shatter his leg during that fateful encounter with a mountain bull, in turn launching a series of events that would still be obsessing him many years later, as I was first beginning to know him.

Notwithstanding the publication of his masterpiece *Awakenings* and the success of the Yorkshire Television documentary based on it, Oliver was still decidedly outside the medical mainstream during those years in the early eighties when I was spending so much time with him. At one point I'd asked Dallas Duncan what other doctors made of him in England, to which he'd replied, "Most don't reject his work so much as they simply don't want to know anything about it. And in that sense, I'd say ninety-five percent of doctors don't know anything of him; the other five percent maybe concede, 'How interesting.'"

As Jonathan Cole—a young British doctor, himself somewhat idiosyncratic (as he'd be the first to admit), who after happening upon the book had come over to study with Oliver a few years earlier—confirmed when I subsequently asked him the same question: "It wasn't that he was embattled, so much as he was just ignored . . . and still is: He just doesn't fit the mold. Most neurologists, then and now here in England, see their ten or twelve patients a day, never really get to know them as people; most neurology is much more mechanistic, merely physical diagnosis, perhaps pharmacology, some therapy. But one patient after the next, like that, day in and day out."[SB]

And Isabelle Rapin, the pediatric neurologist who was perhaps Oliver's closest friend and colleague at Einstein and Mount Sinai in New York, came to much the same conclusion, though in somewhat more nuanced terms, when I asked her what her fellow doctors in America made of Oliver.

"I think those who know of him—which again, is not that many, most really don't—can see how creative he is and realize what a contribution he is making, even though they are nonplussed because what he is doing is so different from what everybody else is doing. There's no doubt that many people don't see his work as serious science. But, for example, remember how he described that very rapid change in some of his patients, how they would go from being totally Parkinsonian to completely not, just like that, in an instant? When he described that in *Awakenings*, people thought he was making it up, but today this phenomenon is called the 'on-off effect' and is well known and well recognized. So you see, I think he's an excellent observer.

"Now, many people would call him a naturalist, and they would say he *just* observes. Such people feel that in medicine, in order to progress you have to have a theory, and then you must try to find facts that either support or destroy your theory. And of course Oliver doesn't have a theory a priori: He observes what he sees and then tries to figure out what's going on. And he is much less shy about great flights of the imagination and great hypotheses that are supported by nothing than most other people are. And that's why people think he is a romantic."

And that was a common view of him among medical people she knew?

"Yeah. And because he takes these great intellectual leaps, this makes people in science very uneasy, because they say, 'Well, you have no data to support what you're saying.' People in science tend to be *and have to be* very, very cautious. [. . .] And they can be very suspicious. 'Sure,' they'll say, 'that's all quite lovely, but what if it turns out to be wrong?' And in fact it may well turn out to be wrong. I don't think you can believe everything Oliver sees as a fact. I think a lot of it is inference. And I don't think he's always clear in his own mind where observation ends and inference starts. He makes a lot of inferences and a lot of leaps. But they're so exciting! And you need people who can do this. You need the Darwins: Talk about somebody who made tremendous leaps; of course, he accumulated a lot of bricks too. Oliver for that matter has accumulated his own share of bricks, because he is also a very astute clinical observer and records things meticulously. Indeed, I think a lot of people don't realize how many bricks he has brought in, they don't give him credit."[SB]

Summarizing his own thoughts about the whole arc of the Awakenings experience, particularly as they pertained to his reputation among his colleagues in the medical profession, one day Oliver commented, "At one level I am fascinated by the perverse, the antinomian, the apostatic, the sabbatian, the upending of all order. And yet I am profoundly rooted in the *tradition* of antinomianism, and indeed in tradition itself. This is why being well received at the Royal Society in London this past February [1982] was so important. It was as if my fifteen years of work with the fringe zombies had not been in vain—it was almost a consecration."

I'd asked Cole if he had attended that session.

"Indeed," he'd replied, "I did."

And what had it been like?

"Well," Cole continued, "it was at an advanced medicine conference at the Royal Society, to which Oliver was slated to address the topic 'After Awakenings.' Purdon Martin, the foremost authority on postencephalitics in Britain, now a very old man, and Oliver's father were both there, so it had something of the air of a homecoming for Oliver, I feel sure. A very good neurologist introduced him, and Oliver was initially somewhat stilted, quite nervous, there were these long pauses as he reached for words, but then he showed some films of the Awakenings patients, before and after, and that seemed to center him, and at the end, his last paragraphs were on the subject of Pinter's play, delivered quite playfully.

This to an audience of doctors who spend most of the rest of their week reading graphs and charts and most likely weren't capable of quite appreciating what they were witnessing. But he was very proud that his father had been there.

"Truly an amazing bloke," Cole concluded, "truly amazing bloke."

9

On Rounds with Oliver at Beth Abraham

Oliver comes over one day in quite a good mood. I give him a silly novelty toy that has started to show up all over on Fifth Avenue: Wacky Wally, a gooey polymorphous octopus that, when thrown against a wall or window, squirms and shudders its way down, an astonishingly lifelike mollusk. Oliver is completely beside himself, rapt, childlike, throwing it at mirrors and squealing at its downward progress. He can't wait to try it out on his charges.

As agreed, a few days later, I meet up with Oliver on an unusually brisk autumn morning at his little office in Beth Abraham (the windows thrust wide open, the office somehow even cooler than outside, a pile of blankets stacked neatly off to the side for the use of patients and nurses), just as he is finishing his morning office hours. He is wearing an uncharacteristic white medical coat. "I'm playing doctor," he explains. "I never used to wear these, but it helps the demented ones figure out who's who and what I'm doing here.

"On an average day here, everything comes my way and I have all the time in the world."

He reviews the file of one patient he's just seen, "a nice lady with a time bomb in her head, a tumor that will soon claim her. I've seen many people like her, whose days are measured and who have started to live gracefully: Whatever neuroses she may have had have fallen away and she's living fully."

While he writes up his notes on this patient—or should I say, tears off, as he is a fierce two-finger typist—I look around his office: plain white linoleum floor; beige walls; very spare; "DR. SACKS" Marks-A-Lotted on a card taped to the door; a green-blue striped awning (like on a cheap little Italian café) as the window shade. A breeze.

A nurse comes in to ask him about the effect of a particular new drug. "Oh well, it killed six patients and made one markedly better," he laughs. He rifles through the day's pile of files, making sure all is in order. "I could have written a book on each patient," he muses, almost to himself, "and they'd each have been worthy of it."

For example, he recalls one recent patient with a consuming arithmetical compulsion. "We got her hooked up to the EEG and I asked her to make a relatively complicated computation in her head, and as she scrunched up her face, I could hear the EEG needles chattering behind me. It took more than twenty seconds but then she announced 'Done!'

"'What do you mean?' I asked.

"'I got there.'

"'Got where?'

"'It was like a flashing billboard, one hundred separate computations on a blackboard before my eyes.'

"I went over and looked at the EEG record and, sure enough, there were precisely one hundred spikes in the reading on the visual area."

The "gooey octopus" I gave him the other day, he tells me, "has caused acute panic and perplexity but also much pleasure."

Oliver packs up his briefcase: a reflex hammer (his mother's, which is to say Kinnier Wilson's), periodicals in several languages (Yiddish, Spanish), and a foam ball (which he actually stuffs into his coat pocket)—that's it.

"My main neurological tool is the ball," he explains. "You can learn much from how the patients play—and many patients who will do nothing else will open up to a gently tossed ball. I never cease to marvel at the wondrous way in which shattered people are integrated in action and in play—also in dancing and singing."

As we close up the office and head into the hall, we pass the head nurse, Miss Costello, a holdover from 1968. They give each other a fond greeting.

In the hall, we pass one patient whom Oliver tells me writes poetry and another, Yetta, completely stiff and contorted in cerebral palsy, whom Oliver tells me edits the Beth Abraham patients' newspaper—with her teeth!

"When the California filmmakers were here," Oliver recounts (another set of filmmakers has begun to probe the possibility of turning *Awakenings* into a feature), "they asked, quite stupefied, 'Is *everyone* here writing books?'"

Looking back at Yetta as we continue to amble, Oliver sighs. "The cerebral palsy patients fight a battle whose central challenge is the refusal to be passive. They're making films, writing books, editing papers. They're lucky in a way: Cerebral palsy has power and funds—a whole foundation to itself. The other patients get $16.00 a month, an amount that wouldn't even satisfy a child."

Beth Abraham's wide halls resemble a slow-motion version of bumper cars: the shiny floors, the fluorescent haze, the metal wheelchairs jostling in submarine ultimity, the patients like shell-shucked creatures, scuttling or frozen still, tired vacant gazes, a strange and eerie scene through which Oliver glides with consummate grace, the sorry halls blossoming with greetings as he passes. It is so clear that he is loved here. "Hello, doctor," these sad crumpled patients somehow manage to grunt, and he hellos them right back as if they *were* people, not as if they were *like* people. Or rather, neither of those: He interacts with them simply as the people they are.

We pass one who, Oliver informs me, is listed as "patient number 20" in his file and who has been here since the hospital opened in 1919. "What's your name again?" she asks. "Dr. Sacks," he answers with a smile. "Oh yeah, I like *you*," she says. "I like you too," he replies, and we move on.

One patient walks up to us, a bright intense woman with very clear eyes, who suddenly launches into a gibberish tirade, presently slams her palm to her forehead, mutters "Shit shit shit," and walks off. "She is suffering from jargon aphasia in the wake of a stroke," Oliver explains. "She thinks she is making sense, but she can see from your eyes that you don't understand her and this frightens and frustrates her, hence the cursing at the end."

"A few years back," he recalls, "I was giving a tour of the ward to some interns when I spotted another such patient up ahead, similarly a stroke victim with all sorts of complications who was gradually recovering. 'This man,' I explained as we approached him, 'is still suffering from jargon aphasia so that everything he says sounds like a cross between Finnish and Sanskrit.' The fellow started talking his gibberish and suddenly one of my students interrupted, 'But Dr. Sacks, he *is* speaking Finnish,' and proceeded to merrily converse with him!" Oliver is visibly delighted by this joke upon himself.

"Most of the Awakenings patients are now gone," he says, his mood sobering. "In the last two years, thirty of them have died, and in fact only eight of them are left. And they are not that old: several still under seventy. But they are frail, and alas, the standard of care has been declining."

He clearly has more to say on that subject, but he interrupts himself as, rounding a corner, we begin to approach one of the postencephalitics: Miriam in the book. In advance of meeting her, Oliver relates how he's recently modified the new edition of *Awakenings* on account of her angry comment to a colleague of his. She'd said that she felt the portrait of her was "cruel and a pack of lies."

"I had called her misshapen—that being the word that had so wounded her—and I have since toned down that physical description."

In the event, Miriam *is* bearded and hunched. But she has a book by her side (a paperback on World War II), and it develops that she is quite active in the hospital library and reads everything. She also tells us about outings to the racetrack, where she recently won $40 on a $2 bet; she also went to *Evita*. Her voice is clear. She festinates in counting—onetwothreefourfivesix—and slurs a bit, but is terrifically fast. As we prepare to take our leave, she taps Oliver and thanks him for correcting the new edition, bound galleys of which he'd left with her the previous week ("It's much better").

Several yards ahead is Hester, a doughy, scrunched mono-mass, her tongue dangling, swollen, and cakey dry. No movement, no expression. She seems to acknowledge Oliver as he is passing by, however, and he pats her shoulder compassionately. Presently he reaches into his coat pocket, retrieves the foam ball, and throws it to her; instantly she unfreezes, lunges for it, catches it, and tosses it right back, in one clean motion, whereupon she refreezes. Oliver hands her a clipboard, asks her to sign her name— she freezes, he urges her again, and she signs it with powerful, confident authority, whereupon she reverts. "I'll see you again next week," Oliver declares, to which she manages a fond, wan smile.

As we proceed down the corridor, Oliver relates how last week, when a doctor from England had been visiting, it had proved most gratifying, all the postencephalitics behaved splendidly, and one of them in particular (he wasn't around today), even though he has now completely lost the ability to speak, when asked how he felt, wrote, "I feel . . . I feel . . . I feel . . . ," jamming nine times before finally coming unstuck, with a flourish, "I feel *fine!*"

Around another corner we come upon one more of the Awakenings patients, an older woman this time, likewise crumpled into her wheelchair in a deep slouch, and Oliver introduces her to me as . . . well, in this context we'll call her Gertie, her name in the book. Oliver excuses himself, he has to attend to a piece of Medicare bureaucracy, but I kneel down to converse with Gertie. Her voice is a breathy whisper, her delivery slightly slowed, but she is completely present and engaged and happy to talk. Once again it is clear how deeply fond she, too, is of the doctor. Presently I ask her if she remembers what it was like the day that she suddenly came to, following the administration of L-DOPA.

"Oh yes," she says.

What was it like?

"Well, suddenly I was talking."

Does she remember her first words, after all those years of frozenness?

"Oh yes."

What were they?

"'*Ooooh!*' I suddenly heard myself saying, '*I'm talking!*'"

And gazing up at me from her slouch, she smiles broadly at the memory, a merry twinkle in her eye.

Oliver returns, we bid Gertie a good day, and we walk out of the building and over a bridge across the Bronx River Parkway into the enchantingly unexpected, pristinely Thoreauesque botanical garden. "As I think I've told you, I come here three hundred days a year," Oliver alleges. "It is a bit like Hampstead Heath," he continues as we establish ourselves at a picnic table by a rushing creek, "a retreat into nature." And it *is* astonishing how the city is bustling just over there, over that ridge, maybe a quarter mile away. Unlike at Central Park, here you have no sense of it.

I reach into my satchel so as to be able to pull on another sweater. Oliver takes off his white coat and his jacket. We go to the walk-up counter of the Snuff Mill Restaurant to order. Or at least to try to. The counter boy does not emerge from the back room to take our order. Suddenly Oliver unleashes a convulsive, incredibly loud—and utterly fake—sneeze. "I'm too shy to say 'Hello' or 'Ahem,'" he explains, but his sneeze blows everybody away and the counter boy comes running up in a virtual panic.

Over lunch (Nova Scotia salmon for him and Westphalian ham for me), Oliver seems to pick up now on the dropped thread from earlier, during rounds, as he notes, "When I first arrived, the average age of the patients was in their forties. Yes, they were incurable, but they'd come there to build a life. Subsequently the population grew old, the ambulatory patients were evicted, and now the average age feels like it's swelled into the eighties or nineties. Recently I discovered that three-quarters of our patients live less than three months beyond their admission. They come to die . . . of broken hearts."

※

The skies have suddenly darkened with the approach of a fast-scudding storm, and Oliver grows almost frantic with the need to escape the dark brood (uncanny the way he feels the weather, the falling barometric pressure, deep inside himself; it's as if there is no membrane and any sudden outer turbulence quickly becomes his own). We race back across the Parkway to the parking lot in the nick of time and dive into his car just before the heavens open.

10

Auden and Luria

The Awakenings years, as one might think of them, running from roughly 1969 through 1975, around the hinge of Oliver's fortieth birthday in 1973, were enormously consequential for Oliver psychologically, comprising not only the death of his mother but both the entrance into and then passage out from his life of two major father figures: W. H. Auden and A. R. Luria.

※

One afternoon, walking in the Village, Oliver and I get to talking about Auden—"Wystan" as Oliver would eventually call him, though for the longest time he remained, deferentially, "Mr. Auden"—in whose home on St. Marks Place Oliver was a frequent visitor in the late sixties, throughout the Awakenings drama, and in the years immediately thereafter. They'd been introduced by Orlan Fox, a close friend of Auden's and a drug and motorcycle buddy of Oliver's from his earliest days in New York.[SB]

Oliver referred me to an essay he'd contributed to Stephen Spender's volume of posthumous tributes to Auden, and a few days later sent me a more detailed letter, summarizing other aspects of his relationship with the great poet:

> I met Wystan, first, at Orlan's apartment—I don't think you ever
> met Orlan Fox. (He was Wystan's closest friend, I would think,
> for the latter, the last 15, years of Wystan's life—and a *fairly*
> close friend of mine from the time we first met, in November '65.)

W. H. Auden and A. R. Luria

I am afraid I cannot quite date the meeting—(something to date it may occur to me)—it was either in '67 or '68.

I had seen Auden before—in June '56, when he gave his first lecture, his Inaugural, as Professor of Poetry [at Oxford]. It was in this term that I had my first—and before the later sixties—my only sight of Auden.

I had certainly never seen him at close quarters before. I was petrified, mute, with fear and awe, that first time—I was fascinated by his furrowed, Jurassic face, I had never seen a face which so resembled a geological landscape—at the same time trying not to stare. I was fascinated by his memory and wit—which reminded me, strongly, of Eric's* (indeed I never ceased to feel, here, an almost physiological resemblance between them). But, and here he differed sharply from Eric (and perhaps I felt there was something more akin to myself), the flow of wit, the gossip (he loved gossip!), might suddenly cease, if something *deep* chanced to be brought up. The memory, the wit, were prodigious, phenomenal; but what really moved me,

---

*Eric Korn.

what excited awe, was to see Wystan *brooding*, to see him
suddenly silent, *arrested* by thought (I often saw this later, I
loved to see him ponder; I saw it first, but forget the precise
occasion, that evening at Orlan's in '67 or '68). Eric doesn't
ponder—he's quick as a flash. He's as clever as Wystan—but he
lacks (or disallows, or is disallowed) that strange depth. And
Wystan himself had to struggle to find it—he often railed at
"cleverness," especially his own, how this would tempt one to
clever instantaneous solutions, how it stood in the way of
genuine thought; and how he himself, in his early work (so he
thought) was often "clever," but at the expense of genuine poetic
depth. I do not remember—Orlan might—that I exchanged a
single word with him that evening, other than saying "Pleased
to meet you" and "Goodbye." But Wystan noticed me—despite
silence and shyness; he was himself often painfully shy, and
knew very well how to be patient, to wait, for the shy . . .

It may have been a year or more before I ever met him
alone—I'm inclined to put this sometime in '69. He got me to
speak of my *Migraine*, then in press, and was fascinated that I
had given Groddeck so central a place.* He then brought out
something he had translated, but never published—a work
of Groddeck's on massage (Groddeck's father ran a sort of
gymnasium-sanatorium), with unexpected insights on the
somatopsychic effects of this, and the somatopsychic and
psychosomatic in general . . .

It was in relation to this Body/Mind theme that I lost
my own silence and shyness, and found myself talking, for the
first time, quite freely, with him. In particular—[since] he
was endlessly, though tactfully curious—[I remember] being
"pumped" on clinical and personal experiences. I spoke freely
of the clinical, reluctantly of the personal: Wystan himself
seemed to equate them—and I saw then what perhaps I had
only sensed in certain poems, how profoundly, even essentially,
"clinical" he himself was . . . But not in a glib sense (though

---

*Georg Groddeck (1866–1934) was a German Swiss physician and early pioneer in psycho-
somatic medicine.

he was sometimes glib); in a *deep* sense, which combined mind and heart.

So, I met him as a friend of Orlan's; and then, so to speak, as myself. Curiously—this is often the case with me—there seemed to be (until close to the end) more *letters* between us than actual meetings . . . and a sort of decorum was there for—for years. He was always "Mr. Auden," I was always "Dr. Sacks"—I am not sure that we used first names until '71.

(I'm glad you liked the "Dear Mr. A" piece [in the Spender book]—your letter made me glance at it, for almost the first time in ten years.)

[. . .] I'm getting numb fingers, I think I must stop.

Love, Oliver

A few days later, this time at his City Island home, we continued our conversation about the poet. Oliver complained about a documentary that was recently made on Auden and in which the only section they used of their interview with him was of some comments on Auden's obsessive chronological punctiliousness (how tea was *always* at four o'clock, and so forth).

"It's true," he said, "that my favorite was to visit him at teatime, which was always from four to five, on the dot. He was tremendously stereotypical in that sense, yes, but what happened *between* four and five was wild, was utterly spontaneous. I saw Auden bubbly, I saw him deep with anguish, I saw him *motionless with wonder.* Okay, I may not be good at anecdotes, but that which they used of me in that documentary I resent: likewise the first Auden biography, which was a string of anecdotes when in fact his life was *one long thought,*" continuing sotto voce, almost as an afterthought, "like mine."

Oliver looked over at me (he needn't worry, I looked back, the comment had registered), paused, and sighed deeply. "He and Gunn have stood for me for a fundamental virtue in the face of my own, of my mother's primal accusations."

He then went on to describe how Auden regularly described himself as a drunk but not an alcoholic ("When I asked him the difference," Oliver recalled, "he insisted that an alcoholic undergoes a change in personality when he drinks, whereas a drunk can imbibe as much as he fancies and never changes, and he, he concluded, with immense satisfaction, was *a drunk*"); how early on they'd had spirited discussions about migraine, or "the megrims" as they both enjoyed referring to them—Oliver was just finishing his book at the time and sending it to press—and how when Auden subsequently reviewed the book (for *The New York Review of Books*, under the title "The Megrims"), it was really the first time Oliver felt "that someone of grand powers had taken public notice of me," and how thrilling that was; how important Auden proved during the Awakenings days themselves as a sounding board, and "an avid one at that" (Auden's eminent doctor father, George, had in fact been a medical officer in Birmingham in the late teens and early twenties and was one of the first to have described the rampaging spread of the encephalitis lethargica and in particular its effects on children); how Auden had urged Oliver to write up the stories of his patients but told him, "In so doing, however, you will have to go beyond the clinical: be metaphorical, be mythical, be whatever you need!"*

By 1972, however, Auden had resolved to decamp from his American home and return to Europe, though to Austria rather than England, and toward the end, Oliver and Orlan had converged on the St. Marks Place apartment to help him pack. "At one point," Oliver recounted, "Wystan came over to me and suddenly commanded, 'Take some books, no really, any you like.' I was stunned by the gesture, and clearly stymied, so he just reached for two, his libretto for *The Magic Flute* and a much tattered, heavily annotated volume of Goethe's letters—'These are two of my favorites,' he declared—thrusting them into my arms."

A few days later, Orlan and Oliver accompanied Auden to the airport, several hours early ("Have I mentioned, he did have a thing about time"), where they indulged in a meandering conversation around themes of leave-taking ("After all, he had been here in America over thirty years, half his life"), and at one point "a complete stranger walked up to him, just like that, and declared, 'You must be Mr. Auden . . . We have been honored to have had you in our country, sir. You'll always be welcome back here as an honored guest, and a friend.' They shook hands, Wystan

---

*"Oliver's friendship with Auden had a tremendous impact on him," Margie Kohl had told me. "He distinctly changed as it grew. In the absence of validation by his colleagues, he felt tremendously privileged, admitted, *recognized*."

was clearly touched, and the fellow concluded, 'Goodbye, Mr. Auden, and God bless you for everything.'"

Auden's penultimate collection, *Epistle to a Godson* (1972), included one poem recounting a visit to an "Old People's Home" ("All are limitory, but each has her own / nuance of damage . . .") and concluded with a major poem, "Talking to Myself," the first from his transplanted home ("Spring this year in Austria started off benign, / the heavens lucid, the air stable . . ."), which he dedicated to Oliver.

The following year, in February, Oliver, back in England for the final edits on *Awakenings*, met up with Auden again when the latter happened to be visiting Oxford, and Oliver was able to give him a copy of the book's galleys. "And a few days later, I got a letter from him"—Oliver bounded up and rifled through some folders (he clearly kept his correspondence with Auden close at hand) and retrieved the hand-scrawled letter ("Oh look, he sent it on February 21, which would have been his birthday") and handed it to me.

Dear Oliver.
    Thanks so much for your charming letter. Have read
Awakenings and think it a masterpiece. I do congratulate . . .

While I was reading that note, Oliver continued rifling through the folder and laughed, pulling out his own response, or one of them anyway, dated March 31, in which he began by stammering at length and to great comic effect over his inability to remember for sure whether he'd already answered Auden's original note (the two usually corresponded by hand, at Auden's insistence, but that was why Oliver could no longer remember whether he had, he was horrified that he might not have, and now he was going to type his response, so that at least he'd have a copy, in case he forgot again), going on to thank "Wystan" profusely for its contents, he (Auden) being the first and only other person besides his publisher to whom he'd shown it, and there being "*nobody* whose favourable response could make me happier than your own." He then went on to note his growing despair at the prospect of finding any real sympathy within medical circles "(especially the barren neurological ones to which I belong)," but expressing hope, nonetheless, that there may yet be "a mass of real, *alive* people outside of Medicine who *will* listen to me, and with whom I can enjoy the delight (the *necessity*) of real converse, what (if I remember correctly) Dr. Johnson called 'a streaming of mind.'"

After I'd finished reading that letter and given it back to Oliver, he noted that "Later that spring Auden, back in Austria, had written to say that his heart 'was acting up' but that he hoped I'd come visit him in the house he was sharing with Chester Kallman, and I so had hoped to that summer, but one thing and another, I failed to make it, and he died on September 29. I've always regretted not having made it." He sighed. "Oy, and aye."

⁂

Meanwhile, time and again during our conversations about the Awakenings period, another name would also recur, that of Oliver's great idol and master, the Soviet neuropsychologist Alexander R. Luria (born in 1902).

"I had revered him—'admired' is too mild a word—for years," Oliver recounted one evening over dinner. "I'd first encountered him, or rather his work, at Oxford, by way of his first major book, *The Nature of Human Conflicts*" (Luria's doctoral thesis, published in the States in 1932, though in the Soviet Union only in 2002, and subtitled *Or Emotion, Conflict, and Will: An Objective Study of Disorganization and Control of Human Behavior*). "His was a liberated physiology—conflict, you have to understand, is a distinctly nonclassical notion, and he would, for example, describe Parkinsonism in terms of 'intense conflict.'

"Most moving, perhaps, was a piece I read just out of medical school, an affectionate tale of identical twins with speech and intelligence disorders. I was moved by his preface, its fusion of science and poetry. The piece was called 'The Regulatory Role of Speech'—a typically dry title, you wouldn't think it contained such an enchanting tale.

"And amidst my desolate cynical despair after three numbing years of medical school, here was this obviously *good* man—one of the thirty-six Just Men, it seemed to me.

"Not that he had any particular reputation," Oliver muttered, adding, under his breath, "then *or* now.

"Then I forgot him somehow"—this being another of Oliver's so-called "lost continents," lost, that is, in the penumbra of his gray decades—"set him aside. And it wasn't until 1968 that I checked out all of the Lurias

from the Einstein library—his dry texts and his so-called 'romantics'—
and devoured them all, once again encountering the greatness, the consistency, the beauty of his life's work.

"So I revered him all over again, and then, panic-stricken one night, I
gasped, '*And what place will there be left for me?*' Which led to a peculiar
rage where I actually destroyed three of his books.

"Around this time, I was going through something of an identity crisis. It was the beginning of the Awakenings project. Before that I'd been
fucking around—the migraine book, face it, was just fucking around. But
it now became possible to admire and employ Luria, to demonstrate him
to my students as a new way of neurophysiology and neuropsychology.

"The thing is, he would grasp the character or nature of various things
as a *whole*. A sentence of his that truly resonated for me was 'The body is
a unity of action'—since for others it's just 'a mass of tissues'—'and that
which is cut off from the unity of action is *unbodied*.' You can see why I
might subsequently have been especially drawn to *that* sentence. Another
favorite word of his was 'syndrome'—a natural running together—not like
a world, rather like a *cosmos*. He was the first to understand syndromes in
this fuller sense, in so doing becoming a geographer, an astronomer of the
mind. Similarly, he was drawn to the qualitative, not the quantitative, as
a result of which, with him, this enormously rich landscape emerges. In
The Mind of a Mnemonist,* for instance, a quantitative project became a
qualitative landscape. Luria's work is comparable to Piaget's: It involves
tests, but not tests that disintegrate, rather tests that aggregate, that
somehow show the *essential integration of character*. One sees the person,
whole, almost as a work of art. He had a method, I suppose, and yet there
are descriptions of him where he sounds on his rounds like a magician.

"There was a great aesthetic feeling for truth in him as well, and for
reality. He *melts*, at times, at the beauty of things. He had a feeling for the
sublime—beyond the beautiful. Medicine, in general, pitches its work well
below the sublime, but it needn't have to. And Luria showed the way,
though he would never have used a word like 'sublime'—it would have
embarrassed him.

"He was highly regarded in the Soviet Union, although there were periods when he was in disgrace: He was effectively excommunicated after

*Published in 1968, subtitled *A Little Book About a Vast Memory*.

his first book, not allowed to practice psychology for fifteen years; instead, he went to medical school and became a physician. During the war, his great clinical work brought him into contact with the constellation of the five great Soviet neurologists—this was truly a time of genius in Soviet medicine, in part, alas, on account of the great number of head injuries they were being forced to minister to, not unlike the way the Civil War here in America had brought out the likes of a Weir Mitchell. That whole group of Russian medical geniuses, though, also reminds me of the great Russian novelists—they were novelists who'd been shoved into science, but the novelist still shines through.

"Right after the war, Luria brought out four books in rapid succession, then another gap. After 1958 he was able to bring out the first of these volumes of 'romantic science'—deeply felt yet passionately precise case histories. And through the rest of his life, his work was divided between these monumental overviews and the case histories."

We wrapped up our meal (sometimes Oliver would get like that: lecture mode, as I would come to think of it, with me privileged to be a class of one) and ventured out for a walk, with Oliver resuming.

"In 1972, *The Man with a Shattered World** appeared, just around the time my own *Awakenings* was about to, and Mary-Kay, my *Listener* editor, said, 'You've been yammering on and on about this guy for so long—okay, so review his book.' Which I did, my review of Luria appearing in the same issue as Richard Gregory's review of me.

"Practically by return mail I received two letters from Luria, one hot on the next, the envelopes festooned with stamps with images of paintings from the great Russian state collections—each letter rendered in his beautiful Victorian handwriting—one on the review, and the other on *Awakenings*. And it was a complete shock—*like getting a communication from Freud* (Luria was the only other person in this century who I'd mention along with Freud in the same breath). I ran around showing the letters to everyone—never had I encountered such a combined feeling of dearness and greatness, of clearness, strength, and *kindness*, such a *cordial* mind.

"I mean, his contemporary Nikolai Bernstein's mind might have been more powerful, any sentence of his being laser-like, like Wittgenstein. Luria on the other hand is less of a light and more of a *voice*. And the voice

---

*Subtitled *The History of a Brain Wound.*

can't aberrate as much as the eye: *Things either ring true, or they don't.* The musical part of one is not easily deceived, and while a prestidigitation of metaphor can dazzle and fool, there is a *tone of voice* that is a guarantee."

With this last sentence, Oliver was suddenly brought up short. Crossing a street, we paused in mid-island, cars whizzing by on both sides. He stammered for a few moments, presently explaining, "Actually, that's not quite right."

What?

"My description of his first two letters. Back in 1973."

We resumed walking. "The thing is, I don't like to let things go to press without reviewing them. But that happened with my *Listener* piece about Luria where I had in one passage, in context, called him 'cruel.' When I saw it in type I fell ill and proceeded to feel ill for five years, until his death, which I was convinced it had caused."

The mood of the evening had suddenly curdled as a result of this confession, and Oliver soon found his car and left for home.

A few days later, I received a packet with this note:

> Here, before prevarication sets in, a copy of *The Listener* with
> my article on Luria, and Gregory's on me (the circle would have
> been completed by Luria on Gregory!). Its publication date,
> June 28, was that of *Awakenings*. I came (even before it was
> published) deeply to regret the article, which I felt unfair,
> unappreciative, when not downright distorting. I spent the
> entire summer in an agony of guilt about it—it entirely
> engulfed the natural joy I might have had from [the release
> of] *Awakenings*—and not the least of Luria's human qualities
> was delicately to help me out of this self-accusing hell.

Not only did the packet include the issue of *The Listener* in question but the photocopies of Luria's first two handwritten letters as well.

Curiously, I couldn't find the word "cruel" anywhere in Oliver's article, which began by putting Luria in the context of two earlier giants of Russian psychology, Sechenov and Pavlov, the latter of whom he implied was Luria's teacher. While celebrating Luria as "the most significant and fertile neuropsychologist alive," one who "has raised neuropsychology to a subtlety and simplicity which could not have been imagined thirty years

ago," he went on to describe him, nonetheless, as a "divided man," one part
(the part responsible for such "monumental and systematic works" as *Higher
Cortical Functions in Man*) "in absolute allegiance to Pavlov and Sechenov,
to Descartes and Locke, to the notions that the human mind starts as a
blank, a tabula rasa, which is then imprinted by experience with 'images'
and 'facts,' and that thinking consists of nothing but analysis and synthesis, connecting, disconnecting, reconnecting, performing operations," and
so forth. This is the part of Luria, "marked by a certain impersonality and
coldness of style," that is most admired by professional neuropsychologists
today, Oliver suggested. "The other part of him," Oliver went on, however, which "strives to escape the domination of the atomic, the analytic,
the abstract, the mechanical," and is marked by "a lively sense of personal
style and expresses itself naturally in the form of stories or biographies,"
has grown more and more pronounced in Luria over the years, despite being seen as "unscientific and slightly embarrassing" by many of his more
conventional colleagues. (Oliver dated the beginning of this second, "romantic" side in Luria to 1956, with the account of the twins he himself
had so admired, then only just recently out of Oxford.) After which he went
on to explicate both the *Mnemonist* and the *Shattered World* books as ster-
ling instances of this second type.

Luria began his first note to Oliver (July 19, the longer of the two,
consisting of two large pages of densely packed, exquisitely inked hand-
writing laid out in unfailingly parallel lines) by expressing his "deep thanks
both for your attention to my work and your review, but first of all—for
the fact that you studied a whole series of my publications. Please be sure
how high I appreciate it!" However, he went on to say that "I really cannot
agree with an over-evaluation of both my publications and my personality. I am one of Soviet scholars in psychology and by no means an outstanding one . . . my abilities are just medium, and the only what I have
done was to study the brain basis for human conduct for a long time,
ca. fifty years, that is true, and there is nothing of false modesty in this
statement." He then went on to insist that he had never been a student of
Pavlov's, only met him twice (under almost comically dismal circumstances), though he was a proud disciple of Lev Vygotsky ("the real genius of Soviet science, a scientist who died very early in 1934, being only
37 years old" whose seminal work "had *nothing* to do with Pavlovian
psychology!"). Mainly though, he wanted to insist that there was not such

a difference in substance, beyond that of style, between his own two sorts
of writing, and that the science, and the allegiance to science, ran equiva-
lently throughout. All expressed in the most collegial, albeit firm, of terms
(and, needless to say, nothing to have gotten so bent out of shape about).
Indeed, he concluded the first letter by saying that though his copy of
Awakenings had not yet arrived, after having read Oliver's piece describing "The Great Awakening" in an earlier *Listener* and Gregory's review of
the entire book in the more recent issue, he already felt confident in as-
serting that "I feel the Awakening is a great event."[SB]

An estimation he confirmed less than a week later (July 25), having
since received and read the book "with great delight," a phrase he returned to three times in the paragraphs that followed, while celebrating
the evident revival of the great nineteenth-century tradition of clinical
case studies, a tradition he had feared was going moribund—but no
more!

(Incidentally, for my own part, I can think of no finer reflection of
Luria's temper and character than the fact that he—and he alone, as I can
think of no one else who would have used the term, then or since—chose
to characterize Oliver's Awakenings saga as "delightful." And he is *right*,
for no matter how harrowing and unsettling and terrifying the particulars of the tale, it is also, in Oliver's telling, precisely that.)

"I never met him," Oliver told me on another occasion. "I was always
wanting to and never quite making it. Although I regarded myself as
the one and favorite son, I was in fact one of twenty or thirty, in half a
dozen languages, with whom he kept up a voluminous correspondence.
He always handwrote his letters—I imagined him using a quill. He
would take in what everyone was doing and reflect it back in the kindest light."

Oliver figures he eventually received upward of twenty to twenty-five
such letters.[SB] There was an exchange of four or five pairs of letters about
the Leg book alone.

"Once," Oliver recalled, "in the middle of an eighty-eight-page letter,
I mentioned to him that I was thinking of writing a text 'From Luria to
Luria'" (in other words from Isaac Luria, the great sixteenth-century kab-
balist from Safed in the Galilee to A. R. Luria, of twentieth-century Mos-

cow). "He didn't respond. The next time, I apologized for the length of the previous one but then went on to compose a further thirty-three pages of single-spaced type."

Following a pause, Oliver continued, "In 1976, he had a massive heart attack—he suffered from angina—so that thereafter he regarded his days as numbered, a situation he viewed with great sadness. But in his last years he brought out five books, an autobiography, thirty scientific papers, all this while his correspondence kept expanding.

"His was a model of How to Die.

"At news of his death, in August 1977, I wept for three days." (Oliver had received word of the death from a cousin who'd suffered a stroke, was aphasic, and was only able to tell him haltingly, over the phone.)

Oliver subsequently showed me a copy of the letter he'd thereupon sent Luria's wife ("I have known other men of genius, but never one with such a beautiful and affectionate openness of heart, simplicity and modesty of spirit, and such humor and courage in the face of grave illness and other troubles. He was a most lovable and loved human being, as well as being a very great one"), telling me, "There had been an obituary in *The New York Times*, although none in *The Times* in London. So I instantly wrote one which they presently published. That one was dry-eyed, but then I spilled out a twenty-five-thousand-word memoir which I've since misplaced.

"I couldn't believe it, in some ways still can't. I often dream of him, endow him with a voice (though I knew what he looked like, I'd never actually heard him). I converse with him during my rounds. He suggests comparisons, makes associations, he has an eye for the singular. I've incorporated him. He's never rough with me.

"He's like an *ego*, not a *superego*."

A few years later, in a letter to me of January 21, 1984, in answer to my question of which teachers he'd felt had been the most influential in his development, he returned, at length, once more to the subject of Luria:

Obviously human beings differ profoundly here, in all sorts of ways, at all sorts of levels. There are those who are profoundly *influenced and influenceable*, for better or worse; and those who while perfectly accessible and friendly pursue an essentially

solitary track through their whole lives. *You*, say, are full of
grateful memories of teachers . . . who were influences, inspirers,
"awakeners" to you. So, for that matter, is Isabelle. I am (half)
afraid, (half) ashamed, to say I am *not* . . . that I feel, at the
deepest level, uninfluenced by anybody. Certainly, in my school
and college days, what would usually be accounted one's most
"formative" or "impressionable" period, I cannot think of *anyone*
that "meant" much to me—those whom I most liked, and am
most grateful for, were those who *allowed* me to go my own way,
and provided a sort of wisdom and support, an encouragement,
an affirmation . . . though not an "inspiration." There was *nobody*
in my first forty years who was too important—even in this
"permitting," encouraging, affirming way . . . nobody, at least,
whom I knew personally: only Luria, "out there."

And then in 1973, around (or even on) my fortieth
birthday, there came that first letter from Luria to me. The
correspondence with Luria was different from anything I had
ever known—it was the *sole* experience of a personal/scientific
"intercourse" in my life. It was an enormous privilege; it was
deeply "good" for me. I felt quite heartbroken, "orphaned," when
Luria died. *And yet*, affirming and encouraging as it was, in the
highest degree, I do not know that it/he "influenced" me in any
way. I think I would have "developed," gone on in my own way,
even if I had had no contact with him . . . But it *fortified* me, it
gave me a certain strength and assurance—and, with this,
lessened my insecurities, my paranoia . . . If I were to give a
"follow-up" on the personal "story" I told in the *British Medical
Journal*, which ended with *Awakenings*, [regarding my] *unresolved*
relation to "Neurology," as this was exemplified in the majority
of my colleagues—"the profession"—this follow-up would
accord Luria a central position.

Why should I care what the little idiots in "the neurological
establishment" said or did, if a man like Luria was "on my side,"
was "with" me? Grandiosity was not stimulated, but *tempered*,
by this.

※

The first Duckworth edition of *Awakenings*, in England (1973), was dedicated "To the patients whose lives are here depicted," a dedication that was reconceived for the 1976 Vintage edition in the United States:

> To the memory of
> Wystan Hugh Auden
>
> 'Healing,'
> Papa would tell me,
> 'is not a science,
> but the intuitive art
> of wooing Nature.'
>
> W.H.A. (from *The Art of Healing*)

But after 1977, every subsequent edition was dedicated, quite simply:

> To the memory of W. H. Auden
> and A. R. Luria

11

A Visit with Oliver to London, including Conversations with Eric Korn, Jonathan Miller, and Colin Haycraft

My profile of the Louisiana Museum of Modern Art in Denmark ran in The New York *in late August 1982, and in October Mr. Shawn and I agreed that I should head back to Poland to report on the country in the wake of martial law, with its attempted suppression of Solidarity. On the way there, I was to join up with Oliver, who was already in London (working on his Leg book with Colin Haycraft at Duckworth and getting set to attend the premiere of Harold Pinter's one-act version of* Awakenings, "A Kind of Alaska"), *so as to accompany him on visits through his old stomping grounds, and to meet some of his family and friends, gathering further insights into aspects of his life that we had been discussing.*

❋

I call Oliver a few times from my hotel, but he's not yet answered. I haven't heard from him, a fact I gauge darkly to signify that things have not been going well with the Leg book, a surmise he confirms when he finally does reach me on Sunday morning.

However, things seem to be easing up now, being home, renewing contact with friends. His father is at synagogue this morning, this being the day of Rejoicing the Law. Last night, when Oliver had gone along, he'd been called on to read from the Torah, which he did "clumsily, with some howlers and with frequent sudden loss of auditory volume."

He suggests that we go to a concert with his father this evening. His father "likes to go to a concert every evening," enjoying "an indiscriminate love of music." And that in the meantime I should come over to the house to spend the afternoon with him.

＊

The house at 37 Mapesbury Road, the home of Oliver's infancy and still the residence of his father and brother Michael, and the place Oliver stays when he is in London, is just off Shoot Up Hill (!), between Jewish Cricklewood and Kilburn—a two-story red-brick Edwardian house in a neighborhood of Edwardian tract homes built in 1905, "which is to say," Oliver explains as he meets me and we launch out on a quick walk around the block, "twenty years too late for the intimate corners of Victorian manors, a home which achieves vastness without spaciousness, a home which never, ever achieved comfort."

Oliver is limping. His back has been giving him a lot of trouble and the doctor he finally consulted before coming to London warned him of an impending calamity if he didn't start taking care. He is furious at his lot: "I want to kick my Achilles tendon to teach it a lesson." (Granted: a funny thing for a man blocked on a Leg book to say.)

We pause on our walk, Oliver unconsciously sliding his hand along the bark of one of the plane trees lining the road. But he is clearly tense, something is bothering him beyond the back, and he keeps hinting at a guilty conscience vis-à-vis one aspect of our earlier conversations in the context of what he suddenly characterizes as "a rampant tendency to confabulate." ("Sometimes I no longer even know the difference, the lie becomes habit.") But for a time he does not get any more specific, instead scurrying on to other subjects.

He cites the chapter "Writing, the Turning Point" in Luria's *The Man with a Shattered World*, then seems to change the subject—he speaks of "a sense of homelessness, most pronounced when at home," before returning to Luria: "Once, when I was obsessing on the Leg book, I sent Luria a five-hundred-word telegram ($200!)—Was this all right? What of such-and-such an approach? What if I did it this other way? Was that acceptable?—and received a blessed two-word reply: 'Do it. A. R. LURIA.'"

As we return to the house and enter through its imposing front door, Oliver returns to the theme of his recent fascination, by way of Hannah Arendt, with Duns Scotus (1266–1308), the great high-medieval philosopher theologian, and specifically with his notions about "the delight of doing." He notes how "Luria's was a pure Scotian thing to say," and later crows, "I'm doing long-neglected thirteenth-century work!"

Oliver and Pop

In his father's study, a photo of a burly Oliver, all in leather on his motorcycle, is prominently displayed alongside those of others of his brothers (in photos of himself as a youth—at home, at college—Oliver is usually seen beaming a muscular smile) and one of his mother, "still not gray, though that's the only way I remember her." She was thirty-eight at Oliver's birth.

His father arrives, fresh from a house call on one of his patients to which, as ever, he drove himself. He's a short, roly-poly man with a little squib of a mustache, his round head bald on top with thin hair graying to the sides (a physique like Wimpy's in *Popeye*, and come to think of it, an identical waddle and manner). He is joyfully oblivious (when I attend a performance of *Hamlet* a few days later, I recognize a family resemblance to Polonius as well). He started his practice in 1917!

Michael the mad brother flits about the edges of life, emerging every now and then from his room upstairs: a heartrendingly raw being, his posture erect, dressed in a full dark suit at all times, a daft semi-crew haircut, a nervous, clipped, but proper speaking manner. Oliver tells me how on this visit when he asked him how he was doing, Michael had replied,

"All compulsion and contradiction." Another time, he declared, apropos nothing in particular, "I live in Little Ease" (the cramped torture cell in the Tower of London whose inmates could neither stand nor stretch out lying down, that is, never posture themselves at ease). And still another time, when I visit him in his room alone, he confides, "I am the favorite of a sadist god."

※

In the backyard, Oliver is at home at last among the ferns and the ivy. "It's wonderful how this yard has reverted to the Mesozoic, before the age of flowering plants—to ferns and mosses. One expects a diminutive little dinosaur to come poking out." A pause. "I disapprove of decoration and hence of mannerist flowers. They're post-Jurassic and I disapprove. If I was making a planet, I wouldn't let it get past the Mesozoic."

It emerges that Colin Haycraft at Duckworth has achieved something of a muddle over rights with Harold Pinter and Methuen, his publishers, over the book version of "A Kind of Alaska," to be included with two other one-acts as *Other Voices*. As a result, Oliver is completely flummoxed over how, if, and when to approach Pinter. I suggest he simply call and greet him.

"Ah yes," Oliver says. "Greet. To greet. Not to apologize, nor to accuse. To greet. What a wonderful word. I must remember it. 'Hello, Mr. Pinter. This is Dr. Sacks, I am calling to *greet* you.' Yes."

※

Evening comes and Oliver and his father (whom Oliver always calls "Pop") and I set out for the concert. His father insists on driving, so it's something of an adventure. London taxi drivers train for months on a bicycle until, after arduous research and practice, they are said to have acquired knowledge of the city, or "the Knowledge." "Pop," says Oliver, as his father careers around corners and up side-alleys, "has the Knowledge."

At the concert, during intermission, Pop stages eruptions of garrulousness. He walks up to pregnant women he's never met, pats them on their bellies, letting his palm rest on the bulge, and then announces, before even introducing himself, their predicted due date, unfailingly accurate within a day or two. The women, unfailingly, are amazed and charmed. Pop is delighted; Oliver, embarrassed.

❋

Later that evening, back in the kitchen after we have put Pop to bed, I finally confront Oliver: "So what specifically is this confabulation that's been eating at you?"

Oliver hems and haws and, at length, nervously confesses. "Several weeks back, I remember telling you that both my grandfathers were rabbis. This is not strictly true. Indeed, it's not at all true. My mother's father was a shohet, a ritual slaughterer. And my father's father was a Talmudic scholar, but no rabbi. I mean, they were as-if rabbis. There *were* great-grandfathers who were rabbis. But this is a long-standing confabulation, one so steeped that I have long since come to believe it and only rarely do I see it for the fantastification it is."

Much relief at the confession, and the balancing of books.

And so to bed.

❋

The next morning, as on all occasions, Oliver's father addresses me cheerfully as "Mr. Weschler." He is preparing a lecture on Chagall's Jerusalem windows. A slide projector and screen bisect his bedroom.

Later, conversation with Oliver reverts to his childhood and school years. I ask him what sorts of books had captivated him as a youth.

"*Moby-Dick*," he replies, without a moment's hesitation. "What can you say about *Moby-Dick*? There's Shakespeare and there's *Moby-Dick* and that's that.

"We liked *Cannery Row* and *Sea of Cortez*, for the marine biology." (Funny that, as bookends go: *Moby-Dick* and *Cannery Row*.)

"Early on an editor told me I was too florid, to be more spare, to be like Hemingway, which among other things prevented me from liking Hemingway.

"Dickens wasn't Dickens: He was life.

"My parents met at the Ibsen Society.

"My mother read more than my father. I liked it when my mother read to me. As I think I told you, she read me a lot of D. H. Lawrence, including a lot of stuff utterly unsuitable for my young age.

"I learned Shakespeare by heart in huge chunks along with multiplication tables. But I can't recollect ever being 'taught' English.

"My school reports were strangely varied in their judgment, but in one thing they all concurred: That I could not draw. That the marks I made bore no relationship to reality, real or imagined, that in this regard I was utterly unteachable."

He recalls fondly how Eric and he would regularly go to Hanover Terrace, off Regent's Park, and spy on the home of H. G. Wells. "Once we caught a glimpse of him—of *an* old man, at any rate, if not *the* old man. Eric did once call on Julian Huxley, I think I'm sure, or maybe that's confabulation."

He gets up abruptly. "That reminds me, I was going to show you something, found it in my bedroom last night." He goes to fetch it, returns with a program.

Colet Club Revue
1951—St. Paul's
[. .]
15. Round the World with Radio
J. R. Miller and M. E. Korn
16. At the Piano
O. W. Sacks

At St. Paul's, he goes on to recall, he, Jonathan, and Eric founded a tremendously successful literary society, which quickly eclipsed the staid Milton Society "which had been founded at St. Paul's, years earlier, by Milton himself."

"We were a ravenous Jewish overgrowth," he goes on, "and one day the headmaster called me in and said, 'Sacks, you're dissolved, you don't exist,' as simple as that, a phrase that has persisted within me, hauntingly, through the years."

※

Talking about St. Paul's, which "used to be in Hammersmith, in a magnificent Gothic monstrosity," to which Oliver would bike or bus ("the 28, the bus of my childhood, whose fare has in the meantime jumped from one penny to forty P."), puts him in mind of the Natural History Museum in nearby South Kensington, which he would often skirt on the way to and from school—and he proposes we head over for a visit.

On the drive, he explains how, though his romance with motorcycles began in adolescence, he really only got his first one on his twenty-first birthday. During his last six months in England, stationed for a residency in Birmingham, he would gun his black Norton down the Birmingham–London highway. Eventually, as virtually his last act in England—he starts to laugh at the memory—he "stepped off" his bike, at eighty miles an hour, slid a hundred yards on the slippery road, and survived, protected by his leather swaddling. (The bike was destroyed.)

Then, the minute he got to America, he got another, "an off-road scrambler."

Arriving at the Natural History Museum, a huge imposing stone secular cathedral built in high confident Victorian Gothic, Oliver relates, as we approach the ramp, how "beneath the visible museum, there was a vast underground one, crammed with anatomical samples: The New Spirit Building it was called, and Eric and I were frequent visitors. The place used to be so unpopular, it was a delight," Oliver says. "There were *no concessions* to popular presentation," he continues, punning.

"I hate this brightly lit stuff," he grumbles as we pass winking blinking displays of ecology and Nature and Man just past the entrance. "It was so dull and minute before.

"Quick, let's find the invertebrates!" he interjects, hurrying along, pushing past the tarrying throngs. "Let's find some place that's *not concession*. In those days, we just had a passion for cataloging. The fact that there was Courtship and Mating and Feeding"—Oliver mimics the titles of the new displays, mincingly—"was not the least interesting to us.

"The passion was systematic: It was for *evolution*, for cataloging—we couldn't care less about habitats." He veritably spits out the word, but then pauses on the threshold of the largely empty invertebrates hall. "Funny though, now that I think about it, because conventional neurology nowadays is like a parody of systematic thinking, whereas today, I am much more interested in issues which might be described as the cerebral habitat."

We cross the threshold.

"I was once almost killed by a *Cyanea*," Oliver announces, dreamily.

A what?

"A *Cyanea*. A jellyfish. Eric's phylum was the echinoderms: starfish, sea urchins, the sea cucumbers. How we loved their names. I remember one— yes, that one over there—called penny-agony [*Peniagone*].

"There's much too much space in these cases now," Oliver complains.

"They used to be filled with hundreds of examples illustrating the slightest variations. Now everything has gone into deep storage. It's too bad: This allows for a *superficial* enchantment. We used to come to a *profound* enchantment at what was simply a *zoological* museum."

We continue to roam the cases, as Oliver becomes more thoughtful. "Reluctantly Jonathan and I left zoology and went on to medicine, but even late I considered abandoning medicine and Jewishness to become a gentile zoologist in California."

In what did he think this love for classification had consisted?

"Forcing or finding order in an imagined chaos. Basically, it was a love of *names*, there was a lot of *name magic*, an Adamic passion.

"We also had a passion for dissection. Jonathan was an extraordinary dissector, achieving dissections of great aesthetic beauty and delicacy. He could have been a wonderful surgeon. As dissectors, Eric and I were fast, mad, and messy, eager for essentials.

"Ah here, one of our favorites: a prized rarity. Only two known cases." (I didn't catch the name.) "We preferred ugly creatures. We tended to despise shells because they were too pretty.

"The staff were Victorian—ancient, taciturn, attuned to earnest visitors, *pre-ecological*."

As we continue to explore a room full of fossil cases, Oliver delights in the presence of an old woman, stooped before successive cases on the far side of the room. "The only act of concentration I've so far encountered in this museum today," he huffs. "The way it used to be: We were *pilgrims*."

Was the activity devotional?

"Yes, if devotion and play are not seen as opposites."

We drift out of the invertebrates, through the Hall of Amphibians ("I loved *Eryops*: clumsy amphibians out of water who took on grace and ease once back in it") and presently into a room featuring a display of stuffed hippos. "Ah, my friends!" exclaims Oliver, rapt. "I used to have erotic fantasies of all sorts here, and by no means all human (*hippos in the mud!*); indeed, not all organic (*the mud!*)." He sighs dreamily, only barely self-parodic: "A hippo would make a wonderful bed partner," he pronounces definitively.*

---

*There may have been something in the water, or the mud, as it were. For in his book *Grand Hotel Abyss: The Lives of the Frankfurt School* (London: Verso, 2016), the cultural historian

We continue on next door to the Geological Museum. "The geology museum had a wonderful dullness." We make our way over to a case full of geodes, before which Oliver pauses transfixed. "I love the idea of something dull on the outside, and spectacular and crystalline on the inside."

Later: "Gorgeous stibnite! I used to worship a huge phallic one upstairs!"

After which we venture next door to the Science Museum, in the vast interior vault of which we are immediately confronted by huge engines. "Wittgenstein loved it here, as did Auden. Wittgenstein could think of no afternoon more pleasant than one spent fixing a friend's toilet."

Before biology, Oliver had loved chemistry and optics. "I love the brass and gold and old nineteenth-century apparatus. I hate plastic and twentieth-century apparatus.

"And here," he says, "is the wall where they used to have their periodic table, the table before which I had my salvational vision. Each element was listed, and alongside, in a succession of elegant Victorian bottles, samples of each element. I would come here and gaze, entired by a feeling of natural (as opposed to arbitrary) order—of *holy order*. I was nine then. I would think out the properties of the messy ones. I had many of these elements in my lab at home, including a bar of lithium, which is highly unstable."

Meaning?

"One had to keep it immersed in oil or it would spontaneously ignite."

Oh.

"I would spend all my pocket money on chemicals. Tungsten, I loved: I had an uncle who ran a lamp factory who would slip me an occasional sample. It has the same specific gravity as gold, a fact I found extremely pleasing.

"I loved combines: For example, I would make a teaspoon out of a combine of tin, lead, and bismuth, which would melt if one put it in a cup of

---

Stuart Jeffries records how at least two other prominent Jewish intellectuals of the period seemed to have a similar fixation. To wit, according to Herbert Marcuse's stepson Osha Neumann, "[Marcuse] 'would sit with this one stuffed hippo on his lap, and project this image of a non-genital, non-aggressive sexuality.' Marcuse shared that fondness with Adorno, who . . . in letters to his mother would address her as 'My dear, faithful Wondrous Hippo-Cow' and sign himself off as 'Hippo King.'"

tea—to my great delight. The same thing happens, of course, with spoons made of gallium.

"I indulged in extravagant anthropomorphisms, just as I had earlier when it came to numbers, and I used to fancy, for instance, how three 37s yearned, just *yearned*, to merge to form 111. When it came to the elements, I felt sorry for the inert gases—they fascinated me perhaps more than any other elements, but I felt sorry for them—for example, for xenon, which it was thought at the time could not merge with anything, although I suspected it could with fluorine. I used to muse: The passion of fluorine should be able to overcome even the aloof coldness of xenon—and years later this was proved so. In 1960, xenon hexafluoride was derived, just as I'd predicted in 1944. 'Hooray, it exists,' I remember thinking, I knew it would. I merely couldn't command the pressures and the temperatures.

"The fact is, I simply doted on the elements, just as I later read Mendeleev had. There is a love of truth, which is chemistry, but there can also be cranky truth, which is alchemy. Both of them, strangely, were strong in Newton.

"I was fascinated around the same time by stereoscopy and became quite inventive, contrived a variety of mirrorscopes which upended vision."

He pauses for a few moments. "And here I confabulate *not*: My grandfather Marcus Landau did invent a miner's lamp which used to, at any rate, be on display right here at the museum." Whereupon there ensues a mad, fruitless search for the very lamp in question.

Presently we give up, but just as we are walking out of the museum, he spots a special exhibition off to the side of protective clothing, and utterly possessed, he makes a beeline for it, all agog, racing right past the cashier (to whom I, the eternal Sancho, rush to apologize and settle accounts for the two of us).

Inside the darkened space, he is hushed, rapt, and giddy.

"Leather is very modish today as a fetish," he tells me, at length, "but I disapprove. Somehow it must be tied to use: to danger and speed and motorcycles. Otherwise it's completely inappropriate."

We move among parachute gear and spacesuits, scrub equipment and firefighters' garb. Oliver is delighted, beads of perspiration on his brow. "Had I not become a doctor, I'd have loved to design protective wear for extravagant environments."

❊

Later that night, Oliver insists we go to a Chinese place so we can have squid and bêche-de-mer (sea cucumbers), the latter of which are distinctly squishy-odd: all slippery and sinewy. "Very primitive," Oliver rhapsodizes as he tries to frame a bite between his chopsticks. "Very rarely does one get to eat something this primitive." (Having seen them at the museum, he had to *eat* one at a restaurant.)

Conversation caroms about, to begin with his father, who calls to check in, "a combination of anxious attention (for example, calling us here at the restaurant to tell us he's got home safely)," Oliver observes, "alongside a propensity for being completely oblivious to the obvious danger (for example, when Michael and I were being beaten at school)." Oliver spears another slurp of bêche-de-mer. "Like a hypochondriac in denial about the real illness: a nasty business."

From there we free-associate (how? I wonder, maybe just from one nasty business to another) to the subject of a rogue cousin. None other than Al Capp, the late cartoonist behind *Li'l Abner* and a notorious, almost operatically pro-Nixon anti-hippie archconservative. Who is not only a cousin of Oliver's but a cousin of Abba Eban's as well. They are all cousins!*

Oliver goes on to speak of the strange sad story of his second cousins the Capps, how they'd all been fervent leftists during the thirties but with the coming of McCarthyism, Al had maneuvered things such that his brothers would take the rap while he emerged clean, a reactionary convert who to the end of his days professed a particularly cynical, and especially *transparently* cynical and self-loathing, form of conservatism. (Myself, I told Oliver, I'd always wondered if it wasn't some sort of grimly sustained act: *You want to see a conservative, I'll show you a conservative!* Oliver isn't so sure.)

A moment's pause, another slurp of bêche-de-mer. Another curious free-association: "Once I was with a patient who was intently watching his hand slowly monstrify into a ticcing machine. Laughing, I told him he

---

*Technically, Ollie's grandfather Eliahu Sacks had a son, who was Ollie's father, and a daughter, who was Eban's mother. But Eliahu also had a sister who was Al Capp's grandmother. Thus Ollie, Abba, and Al share a set of great-grandparents.

looked like the Werewolf of London watching his nails becoming talons with horror and amazement. I then threw him a ball, which he caught—springing him out of his Parkinsonism. For a moment, *he forgot to behave like a Parkinsonian.*" (I mention Sartre's notion of the waiter who is continually engaged in acting like a—what?—*a waiter!*)

Later, palming the tea and slowly making his way one by one through all the orange slices that have arrived with the check, Oliver concludes the evening by discussing an article, or maybe even a book he's been pondering—if only he could get past the Leg book. "I would like to do for the demented what Piaget did for children, which is to say to survey the slow deconstruction, as opposed to construction, of personhood. Or phrased differently, to bring out how the demented are no less human for being demented—which is to say, *how to love a demented person.* How even when tasks are no longer possible, play still is. How the very last thing to go in dementia is the signature, the home of personhood."

Themes, he concludes, of dignity and indignity.*

✻

Conversation with Eric Korn

The next day I pay a call on Eric Korn, the renowned polymath, antiquarian book dealer, and regular keeper of the Times Literary Supplement's *much-beloved Remainders column. He proves a short fireplug of a fellow, fierce, voluble, droll, genially self-mocking. In suggesting I talk with him, Oliver had early on written me that "Eric and I have known each other from infancy, and he has a quite perfect and undistorting memory, unlike my own. We have a 'hereditary' relation, because our fathers were close friends as far back as 1912, having been medical students together." We meet amid the teeming clutter of his quarters on Lady Margaret Road*

---

*Oliver had clearly been thinking along these lines for some time. All the way back to his
Listener piece about Luria's *The Man with a Shattered World* (1972), he'd speculated:

If we wish to find a comparison for Zasetsky's condition, we should seek it, not in the state of innocent but expanding childhood, but in the blight of senile dementias. [. . .] One meets old gentlemen completely unable to read, write, or add two and two, who retain the courtesy, the bearing, the social and histrionic sense, which constitute their characteristic "presence." Thus one sees in old age the reverse of childhood: one sees that the structure and sense of personal identity subsist long after all "secondary" aptitudes are lost, as its original development, in earliest infancy, far precedes all learning and training.

Oliver and Eric in California

in London. In this adaptation of the transcript of a taped conversation, he excuses himself to rustle up some cheese and crackers from the equally teeming and cluttered kitchen, emerging as well with a pot of tea and in high mid-peroration.

He can get so exasperating at dinner, you know how he is. "Oh come on, Oliver, take the whole thing, instead of cutting it into progressively smaller pieces all of which you know you're going to end up eating!" The other day at Claire [Tomalin]'s house, Oliver was charming everyone, reaching for food at all the tables, and presently he'd landed on a cookie jar, filled with crayons, and Claire was at a complete loss as to how or indeed whether to tell him. One hoped he would figure it out for himself, though one can never be quite sure.

Of course you knew him all the way back. What was his childhood home like?
Ah yes, the incredible morbidity of 37 Mapesbury Road. It was like something out of a Hitchcock movie, like a morgue even when full of people, always incredibly cold, incredibly vacuous. The furniture, although it had been there fifty years, looked like it had been rented the day before. This kind of emblematized the family's relationships. The piano was covered in

the drawing room with these awful—it was the Jewish equivalent of a
North England parlor, a room which was only used on Friday nights. And
it was a particularly cold, pompous, and inhuman room.

Was this especially unusual for English Jewish families?
No, they just took it to extremes is all. Oliver, of course, confabulates enormously, and it's difficult not to follow him in this. I mean, in fact there is
no doubt that they were jolly . . . they would entertain enormously. The
house was full of jolly people much of the time. As adolescents, we really
rather loathed being in his house, even though or maybe because we spent
a good deal of time there. The dining room was full of tens of . . . what, I
mustn't exaggerate, scores, grosses of photographs of Sackses in academic
robes and the like, celebrating whatever achievements they had, which were
numerous. And yet somehow it was more like a trophy room, the Jewish
equivalent of moose heads.

It was a musical house, I will give it that, considering again that
awful inhabited vault and the acoustics of that drawing room, which actually prevented breathing.

But one didn't get the impression that there was any real pride or
affection in anything anyone had actually done. Oliver's mother was awful,
a veritable spider of a woman, in spite of being a very good doctor and a
very kind woman outside her family, as far as I could understand. But a
bearer of doom to her entire—

How do you interpret that in her? What was that about?
I don't know at all. Obviously, you'd have to go into the relationship between her and Sammy. And the strains of being a woman doctor, God
knows that can't have been that easy when she started. Have you met the
siblings?

I have met Michael.
One gets the impression that Michael is the elected member, that it might
have been any of the others. Marcus is more or less fine because he got out
of there, went to Australia. And David is—I don't know, I don't know
David all that well. Oliver presents him as a monster, which he may well
be. Sammy, the father, is cheerful, tender, blundering, perhaps more
blundering than I think is forgivable, even in somebody whose function

in life is being the roly-poly jolly blunderer. He was constantly taking the
rest of us aside at parties when we were fourteen or fifteen and asking,
"What do you think about Ollie?"

Meaning what?
"Is he happy, is he intelligent, is he bent? What should we *do* about
him?"

Was he bent as a child?
No. He was very deeply eccentric. I remember his being a kind of oddity
at school, though the school was tolerant of oddities and there were a lot
of them. He wasn't particularly persecuted at the schools at which I knew
him, though his earlier school seems to have been quite phenomenally
frightful. Again, one doesn't know what the actual truth is, but as far as
he is concerned, terrible things were done to him when he was six, seven,
and eight. And I have no reason to doubt him.

And he feels that that's what did Michael in.
I think so, too. I mean, Oliver obviously is immensely good at creating
and living by his own mythology, but I think he was right in that instance, in particular about his parents' obliviousness about what was
going on. It's rather curious because after that, we were both enrolled into
the Hall prep school, which is where we first really got to know one another, and he must have been coming straight from that other place. And
you might have thought that our parents might have been sensitive to
the fact that the headmaster there at Hall had recently been put on pro-
bation for interfering with *his* pupils. But there was a general feeling
that he was an old man and he was kind and it was wartime and not all that
serious: This was a sort of gesture by the community to trust in him, to
give him a second chance. And in fact, his behavior, as far as I could make
out, was more or less impeccable, at least by the standard of English prep
school masters, which were pretty weird anyway. Certainly didn't do me
any harm, or Oliver as far as I know. But it may have some bearing on the
kind of solicitude which his parents showed or failed to at the time: that
they chose to send Oliver to this place shortly after the man's appearing
in court might seem puzzling, especially after their immediately prior
failure.

And that's where the two of you met?
Well, in fact our families knew one another. I have actual memories of a fistfight with him in 1938.

Who won?
I think he did. I'm not sure, he might remember it differently. But then we met again at the Hall, and then more seriously at St. Paul's, where we became moderately close friends. He was a year ahead of me, I suppose, and so went to St. Paul's a year before me, but there the forms tapered toward the top, where we coincided and became closest friends in our adolescence, from fourteen on or so.

You were talking about Oliver being somewhat eccentric.
Well, at St. Paul's he was a little tedious, just being kind of odd and ingrown and following his own interests, which were themselves slightly odd, so he was teased a little, but we were all odd.

St. Paul's was one of the two or three public schools on the English scene—our public being the equivalent of your private—where there were hardly any boarders, since it was a London school. It had a very high academic reputation and was liberal-minded in that it wasn't a branch of the navy or the army or otherwise given over to the lash. And there was a lot of freethinking of various kinds. It had a fair number of Jews and didn't seem to mind about that, and it was not horrifyingly reactionary, as most English public schools are. So it was a very good place to grow up in: You could be eccentric and bad at games and not suffer too much, particularly if you were good at something else. I mean, jocks existed, but the school was as much or perhaps even more concerned with its scholarship record and its record for getting students into Oxford and Cambridge. You developed a group of friends. There were about half a dozen in ours.

This was the biology group?
They weren't all biologists, though most of them were: Dick Lindenbaum, Jonathan Miller, Oliver, me, we had the odd historian, though he drifted off with time.

It's striking how all of you pretty much stayed close through the rest of your lives.
Oh, absolutely: It's Mary McCarthy's *The Group*.

Was that common in English schools?

I suspect not that uncommon. I mean, at the time we thought, as all groups do, that we were quite unique. And our first activity was to start diarizing: From the age of fourteen we saw ourselves as living a vast communal novel. Of course, actually we knew almost nothing about one another or indeed about ourselves. So as our group got going, it gelled fairly rapidly and shed outsiders, although it took on various others and certain hangers-on and women on a semipermanent basis. It renewed itself—you've been an adolescent—from party to party, the great thing being the parties. And in such an apparently close environment, there was also a lot of room for hiding. So that Oliver was both protected and he could happily secrete himself in such a group, pretending to go along with the mob while actually not really participating much necessarily.

And was Oliver's role to be the oddest of the odd in the group?

Probably, yes. He was physically odd. He was famous for being very large and immensely strong and immensely clumsy. There are a lot of silly stories—natural history outings upon which he would break train doors, that kind of thing—and he played up to them. He got access to a car rather early, at seventeen or so, which rendered him immensely useful and in demand. There were a lot of parties at his house too, where he appeared to be pursuing women with the same enthusiasm as other people, at least for several years, though as I say, there was room for a good deal of camouflage in those situations as well. And I think he found them nonthreatening.

And academically?

Well, he took classics, as I did, till transferring into the biology form, as did I, where we were actually exposed to physics and chemistry for the first time. And Oliver had this spectacular laboratory at home in which he would do all sorts of morbid things like spilling enormous quantities of sodium all over the lawn. It was all largely lethal, rather than constructive, that and his fascination with bizarre metals.

And then, as for biology, I'm sure you've heard about Pask's group,* and how we each had our own phyla—mine being sea cucumbers, Oliver's

---

*Sid Pask, their biology teacher at St. Paul's.

being cephalopods, of course—we would memorize the hundreds upon hundreds of genera and subgenera and still know them all to this day. This whole Jewish Adamic passion for naming and calibrating and listing and distinguishing between things into ever finer distinctions. Though if anything Oliver has now gone to the complete other extreme, there perhaps being an element of reaction in that refusal of his nowadays to make measurements of *anything*: his constant emphasis on the immeasurable, the imponderable, the intangible.

And from St. Paul's you both went to Oxford?
Actually, he went right away while I went into the air force for three years, during which time I would only see him on holidays, such that I only arrived at Oxford, same college, three years into his time there. So we really only overlapped there for the year when he was doing his blighted research on hens: some study involving organo-phosphorous poisons, which evince some sort of nerve effect, though I'm not sure I have that quite right.

Anyway, he started with a very large number of hens as his experimental material. Only, they kept dying. So he kept redesigning the experiment to yield results with fewer and fewer hens until eventually he had some scheme so elaborate that it involved injecting, as it were, a single hen with the poison, the antidote to the poison, the antidote to the antidote, a further poison, a further antidote, and so forth. And provided the creature survived, the entire chain of hypotheses would be proved. But it died. Possibly of mishandling, possibly of needle shock from all those injections, or maybe that's just what hens do.

Was Oliver already experimenting with drugs at that time?
Well, in fact it was just around then, maybe a bit later, when Oliver was back in London already, and I was still at Oxford, doing research on neurotransmitters (immediately after you graduate they say, Fine, you've got yourself a splendid degree there, here's a laboratory, now go discover something), that somehow I got my hands on a tube of ten grams of LSD, which was a preposterously large amount, which came straight from Sandoz labs, it was actually the authentic stuff. Virtually nobody had yet heard of it, with the exception of Huxley and a few of his friends. Anyway, with immense timidity, we made up a tiny dose and sat around observing reactions, which were virtually none. I remember vividly that

we'd made up two hundred milligrams and each taken fifty milligrams for starters, and at some point I must have gotten up to look out at the stars or something, because when I came back Oliver had gulped down the remaining hundred milligrams. He was famous for being quite greedy back then. Of course, his entire attitude to drugs was like that, one of uncontrollable orality. But I guess we'd miscalculated, because even that wasn't enough to provoke much reaction. And Oliver didn't get into really serious experimentation till several years later, in the States.

Curiously, I carried the remainder of those ten grams around with me for six years thereafter, never finding suitable circumstances to do anything but inject the stuff into snails.

What happens when you inject it into snails?
Not a whole hell of a lot. I mean, you can't really tell if a snail is hallucinating. I was just tiddling around. And it wasn't till I got to Liverpool that the whole remaining batch was finally stolen by somebody's student. Somebody must have looked into the fridge and noticed that it contained well over £1,000 worth of LSD, though it had probably gone off by then and become quite ineffectual.

Returning to Oxford for a moment, can you characterize Oliver's time there in any further way, since he claims to have forgotten all of it.
His eccentricities became a bit milder, seems to me, though he became quite unsociable, only had a small group of his old friends, one or two new Oxford ones. There was one sort of monstrous extrovert and bon vivant with whom Oliver had an unlikely camaraderie—he often surrounded himself with friends who were a lot bigger than him, must have been some sort of identity crisis going on there in very submerged ways—a man called Tosh whose only claim to fame is that he made Oliver look positively elfin. But I don't think Oliver had a very good time at Oxford.

Whereas Jonathan, for example, had the most wonderful time in university at Cambridge, very stimulating, effervescing in every conceivable way, I don't think Oliver's time at Oxford was anything like that. He did badly with teachers generally, though he was always affectionate with his supervisor, who was a man generally known as Uncle Cyril, which suggests affection rather than respect. He didn't speak much of his other teachers. He did go into a research project at one point with a charlatan name of Sinclair or some such, who headed a department called the Laboratory of Human Nutrition and managed to so annoy people at Oxford that they actually took his department away from him, as it were, between Saturday and Monday. Just closed it down. Which left Oliver in something of a lurch. I hadn't thought about it till now, but that may have been the first of that series of awful fraudulent bosses that Oliver so obviously seems to seek.

What do you think that's about?
Well, I mean family, I suppose. It does make things easier if you can blame your father. Though doubtless there's more than that. But the sheer skill with which he selects them! Though who knows, I've not met any of these trolls, and they may be the most benign and harmless figures. Or he himself may just induce crazy behavior in them. No, I think he picks monsters: that recent ex-partner of his who got them both into all that trouble with the IRS. And there's no way that you can ever say, "Oliver, get away from that one, he's bad news." Because on the basis of five minutes of conversation, he can build up the most astonishingly convincing, detailed, sympathetic, and rounded vision of a person's character, its etiology and origin, the prognosis, the whole thing—which sometimes bears no relationship to the individual whatsoever.

Often?
Well, one doesn't often have a chance of testing it. Certainly, it's worrying that his judgment is often wrong and sometimes spectacularly wrong. It's because of the haste, and the immense richness of his confabulatory life, his imaginative life. Means that he seldom actually tests reality.

What kind of relevance, if any, is that when judging a book like Awakenings?
Have you seen Duncan Dallas's movie? Because it's all there. No, it's a very shrewd question, because one does say, "Maybe he invented the whole thing, no one else seems to have seen it." Except that in that instance I think the eye and the observable object have met and married perfectly and that indeed he has seen what others failed to see. I think his migraine book is a very sound piece of work as well. I think his Leg book is nonsense.

Nonsense because it's taking him so long to finish, or because—
I don't think there's a rich objective datum upon which the whole thing is based. Look, his musings are always fascinating and rewarding and rich. But I think they always need to have some objective, clinical groundwork to come back to. And I don't think that is present, at least not in the part of the Leg book I've been shown.

Today as it happens is the anniversary of his first walk after his recuperation, so he is out walking the Heath at this very moment. This extraordinary calendrical fixation of his. Myself, I am at the other extreme, I never know what makes me feel some way, or when I first felt that way. But if you say to Oliver, "Does fish ever give you a stomachache?" he will say, "Well, on August 5, 1980, and again previous to that in 1978, which may itself have been a reminiscence of that awful disaster"—because of course you are supposed to be familiar with all of this—"of August the 9th, 1964."

Coming back to Awakenings, *it is striking that the prize it received, the Hawthornden, was for "imaginative literature." Which was a fascinating insight on the part of the committee that awarded it.*
The reception of the book among medical authorities, on the other hand, was very odd. One strand of it, I think, was a kind of Stone Age ignorant, philistine refusal to accept that anything well written could be reliable. This was exacerbated, I think, by Oliver's own refusal to tabulate, diagramatize, to offer statistics or do anything else that might have made them happy. Which he certainly would have been capable of doing; he may not feel quite as at ease, but he certainly has the intellectual capacity for such things. In addition, he'd grown out of sorts with the hierarchy in various ways, was badly treated because the book hadn't come up, as it were, through *The Lancet* or other such journals in the appropriate fashion. And, too, there were people who were just jealous of its success. But another strand was the feeling that while yes, this is beautifully described, is there any objective datum there?—and his refusal to reconcile himself to this concern of theirs.

He seems to have a similar problem with Medicaid: He doesn't present his data in a form that they demand. I think he does it to be a martyr, not because he can't do it.

One doctor I was speaking with a while back, when I told him I was preparing a profile of Oliver Sacks, sniffed, "Well, he's not a doctor, he's a romantic."

He *is* a romantic, certainly. What worries doctors is whether he is also romancing, or rather romanticizing. I don't think he is. It's entirely a matter of sympathies with him, and I think when his sympathies are engaged, his observation is superb. When they're not, when he's bored or indifferent or senses hostility, then I think he can bizarrely misinterpret what's going on.

I often find his descriptions of friends or people he respects, especially older people, remarkably astute. On the other hand, his descriptions of foes, imagined or otherwise, often seem off the wall. The other day I was with him and his father, and his father was talking to some fellow who said one word that got Oliver going. And by the end this man had transmogrified into a veritable Hitler, to hear Oliver tell it.

Absolutely, that is it. It's the sense of being persecuted. We had a trip to the north of Ontario once where Oliver really did seem to be much more persecuted by mosquitoes than I was. And he took to identifying the mosquitoes with various doctors who were giving him a hard time at the moment. They were at the same time anti-Semitic in their attacks on him and Jewish in their persistence. And he was very angry that I wasn't complaining sufficiently loudly. Indeed, he reckoned that I was somehow casting doubt on the reality of his experience, when not suggesting that I was in fact in league with them.

Ah well, I mean he is highly sensitive, and the fact is, even paranoids do actually get bitten by mosquitoes. In what way he attracted them, I don't know.

Of course, too, there's his enchanting ability to parody himself when he realizes he is going over the top. Sometimes he will do it for comic effect, and to break the tension. Other times, however, it becomes a kind of serious self-parody, and this can be dangerous. I think that is what gets him into some of those situations.

Speaking of off-the-wall, why do you think he is so stuck on the Leg book? Is that the correct category, the tendency toward going overboard?

Yes, well, I don't know, God knows I wish he would get off it and back onto something more substantial. Of course, the quality of the effort he's put into it is really admirable. But at this point, it's how many words? He passionately disbelieves in editing, as you know. And there's a willful element there. The number of times I've gone through a text with him and said something like, This is good, but see if you can't make it tighter, cut out, say, a thousand words. One time I really got angry with him, this was on the migraine book, we went through the manuscript together and marked up about three thousand words' worth of passages that were to be taken out and all he had to do over the weekend was to add a couple of linking phrases to make continuous prose of the remainder, but come Monday morning, with a kind of self-conscious naughtiness, he declared, "Well I haven't gotten around to any of the linking passages, but I've written another ten thousand words that need to go in."

Mary-Kay Wilmers, now at the *London Review of Books*, is very good with him in this regard. Immensely tolerant. I don't think he realizes how much tolerance is called for. But she can also be tough, and Lord knows he needs that, too.

But it's the same thing here with Leg. Because once again, the more he writes the greater the block becomes, as though he were in fact piling up a barrier in front of himself. He needs to turn off the creativity and get to work with a scraping trowel. And to me, the original leg experience simply can't bear the burden of the huge weight of interpretation that is being put upon it, coming on ten years of considering and reconsidering, thinking and rethinking about what he once thought . . .

There's also the problem of it being about himself as opposed to other patients. And indeed, there are all kinds of psychoanalytic sorts of issues that rise up when you begin to put the chronology together, this having been a trip he took shortly after his mother died and then he gets attacked by a bull and loses his leg. No wonder it's all so loaded for him.

It's funny you should put it like that, since it has frequently occurred to me to wonder if it actually was a bull. In view of the fact that he always calls my dog—I mean, the reason she hates him so much is that he always calls her "him." Another willful refusal to recognize . . .

Was the writing of Awakenings *accompanied by similar sorts of blockages?*
Much less.

What was it like when he was telling you those stories before they'd become the book? Are there stories about that?

Fabulous, very striking, but not really, no, because those stories very quickly achieved their final shape.

Was he feeling guilt at the craziness these people had been woken into, or doubts as to whether he should have administered the L-DOPA?
Not a lot, no. I think mainly there was a sense of stupefaction, excitement, amazement, and a sense of privilege. A certain self-doubt that he was in fact observing this correctly. But he was gaining confidence that others, too, could see what he was seeing, that it was happening and that he was describing it accurately. Anger and distress, to be sure, at the medical abuses and messianic fervor among doctors surrounding the introduction of that new drug, how other doctors were refusing to see the complexity of the reactions in their patients, simply because they had no way of registering them on their charts.

Still, some of the hells his own patients were opening onto after those two weeks of euphoria, it must have been—
But there he was at his most professional of any time in his life. A doctor must feel compassion but not passion, and at that time I think he did. He wasn't swayed improperly. He felt privileged to have served at something so miraculous and astonishing. He felt that he was doing right, I think. He never expressed guilt.

Changing subjects, I wanted to ask you about your trips into nature with Oliver.
Yes, for how many years now Oliver and I have spent several days every January or February, at the tail end of whatever antiquarian book fair in California, driving into the desert or into Mexico, picking up the debate at whatever point we'd left off the year before, probably covering the same ground from year to year, on the nature of individual style, say, or the limits of determinism.

Are those trips about your friendship or are they about the desert and nature, or are they a commingling of both?
Oh, very much the latter. Though it sometimes seems to me that we are both pretty insulated from the environment, me perhaps less so since I am not on the sort of quest that he is and I need much more external stimulus. So I am constantly both listening to him and watching the outside

world and occasionally trying to get him to shut up, which is a totally impossible thing to do, totally ineffective, since he is hell-bent on some line of reasoning that he is following, which will not let him rest and will come between him and whatever is outside the windscreen. In fact, it is tremendously good for him when one does finally get him out of the car and can force him to come face-to-face, as it were, with a cactus.

But it's good for him, to get him out to actually feel or smell something new. And in fact, he can be childishly and simply grateful and enjoy simple things in the nicest possible way when they actually get through to him. In that sense, he's actually a rather good traveling companion.

The other day we were walking through the nature dioramas at the natural history museum in New York, and he took to rhapsodizing about them, how they'd done a really good job with them, and talking about the desert- and the lake-scapes, culminating with the comment, as we were walking away, that he loved the natural tissue whereas he lacked a sense of appreciation for the social tissue, the sort of thing he said that must make New York so fascinating.
Though what he really loves are dioramas. He builds his own dioramas out in the wild. By which I mean he doesn't need more than a touch of nature to be able to reconstruct, to model internally, the whole of the natural world, albeit quite accurately.

Again this interest in the intimate vista as opposed to the vast landscape.
He loves anomalies of order and disorder. There was a whole trip several years ago where what took us away were these fields upon fields of cactuses that appeared to be growing in ordered rows. We couldn't decide whether we'd stumbled upon some sort of cactus plantation. Since then I've been given to understand that it's simply because the soil is so poor that they cannot grow close to each other, you can't get temperate forest densities, and instead everything is just naturally repelling everything else, and you end up with these patterned distributions. But Oliver is completely delighted by such signs of natural orderliness. No doubt he'd go mad at coral reefs as well, though not so much at their profusion and density as at their patterns and arrangement.

What about Manitoulin, this island he keeps raving about?
Have you been there?

No.

It's no great shakes.

Oliver describes it as paradise on earth. Where is it?
I mean, it's pleasant enough. It's an island in the Georgian Bay, which is part of Lake Huron. It happens to be the largest freshwater island in the world; it's part of Canada and to my mind is very like rural Ontario. There are a couple of Canadian small towns and a strong Indian presence, a lot of pleasant nineteenth-century wooden farm architecture and fences. The towns he gets so excited about because the people were friendly and he felt accepted were just like any small towns. But they were *his* small towns. He was even fantasizing about moving there as a GP. Until that business with the woman.

Yeah, what was that about?
Again, who knows what actually happened. But he was extraordinarily funny about that, even though he only seems capable of giving a curiously egotistical account in which the poor woman's feelings count for nothing compared to the disturbance she caused him by cutting off the whole of northern Lake Huron for a long period. One could grow impatient with him. But I must say, when we actually ventured back a few years later and he started doing his number—"We're getting close now, within ten miles, you can probably already notice the way the landscape is turning bleak and ugly. Look, there's a blighted tree, and all the cows have plague. The heavy toxic fog descending over the entire area," at which point he dove under the seat to hide, or tried to, he was a bit large to be trying . . . I mean, this is the rich kind of self-parody, and it was quite enchanting, a lovely performance.

When he goes into his deep depressions, on the other hand, it can get so total that he can't laugh or be laughed out of it.

Do you ever worry that he is going to go into one of those deep black depressions and not come out?
Oh, I think one must. On the other hand, he has a tremendously power-ful sense of self-preservation, even though it's curiously buried. It works very deeply at some instinctual level: The wisdom of the body keeps him out of the severest of trouble. Bob Rodman once said to me, "Of

course we are very lucky to have him alive at all." Which was tender and touching. But it hasn't just been luck. He's never really been ill. And he takes immense care of himself, when he isn't abusing himself in the most appalling fashion. And he's curiously transparent, even though of infinite depth.

※

The night after that, Oliver and I are joined by another old St. Paul's and Oxford pal of his, Dick Lindenbaum. Oliver and Dick had entered St. Paul's the same day, having the exact same birthday, and Dick was another of Sid Pask's biology pack; he and Oliver reported together to Oxford, where Dick branched off into a distinguished career in human genetics. The three of us begin by attending the last preview before its premiere of Harold Pinter's trilogy of one-acts, *Other Voices*, featuring Judi Dench in the lead of the *Awakenings* segment, "A Kind of Alaska," based on the Rose story in the book. Before the play begins, Oliver notes how Margie Kohl, his speech-therapist colleague from Beth Abraham, had already commented of the script, "He's caught the essence of Rose—it's not like reading Pinter, it's like reading the *truth*."

Oliver, for his part, is touched by the transformations from the actual person, his patient X, through words (Oliver's evocation of her as "Rose") on through other words (Pinter's rendering of Rose as "Deborah") and back into another actual person (Judi Dench).

Although he is subtly disappointed that first night, apparently the second night—the premiere—will go much better. A few weeks later, he will be beaming as he tells me about it, and about the gracefulness of his reception by Pinter when he did go to the playwright's home to "greet" him and his wife.

That night at dinner, Oliver is especially glad to have Dick along as someone who can testify to what he was like during the years of which he claims to have no memory. Both of them order "the internal organs of beast and fowl," as Oliver relates (and Dick confirms) how his mother loved dissecting hearts as she served them—"hearts and brains being not only tasty but also pedagogically interesting if eaten with proper anatomical attention."

In Oxford, Dick reminds him, Sacks lived on Divinity Road.*

---

*Orlan Fox subsequently told me of a trip he took with Oliver back to Oxford, and how Oliver had shown him "an apartment he'd occupied on the Iffley Road overlooking the field

Oliver's Middlesex days—for Dick accompanied him to medical school there in London as well, after Oxford—were, according to Dick, "far from colorless, verging if anything on the Tom Jones picaresque. I remember countless evenings following Oliver through the streets of Soho at six or seven miles per hour, four hundred words per minute, Oliver positively wingey on speed. Finally, around midnight, I'd peel off, exhausted, but I'm sure Oliver, now alone, continued at the same walking and speaking pace well on to dawn."

"Not only do I confabulate," Oliver interjects, a trifle defensively. "Others confabulate about me. For instance, it is not true, as was often being said around Middlesex, that I once threw a motorcycle over a bridge. I only threw the motor*cyclist*."

"But it is true," interjects Dick, "that not infrequently those of us taking breaks in the cafeteria during night shifts, say at two or three in the morning, would experience phenomenal shudderings of the entire building, emanating from above, where it turned out you were traipsing about on your rounds, with twenty-pound weights strapped around each of your calves—some sort of weight-training regimen, you assured us."

Oliver giggles at the memory, cocking his head and raising his eyebrows in acknowledgment. The dinner winds down and Dick excuses himself, he has an early conference in the morning. But Oliver and I continue on for a long walk, indeed right past Middlesex Hospital, where Oliver interned and fifteen years later found himself installed as a patient, recovering from his leg injury.

We pass a bookstore, where in the window there's a book by Richard Asher, MD, "one of my teachers, one of the few whom I respected—who later committed suicide—for having a brain in chemistry."

Another book in the window, this one about thoracic surgical technique, sparks another memory. "My happiest house residency posting in England was a surgical one in Birmingham under an inventive surgeon who'd get a new idea for a partial mastectomy at dinner which he'd proceed to demonstrate on a potato. My mother did that sort of thing, too.

"I have no feeling against surgeons. I admire them as I admire all fine craftsmen."

---

where Roger Bannister, a doctor, broke the four-minute mile in 1954, a deed which meant a lot to Ollie."

Most of his time as a resident, Oliver says, some memories coming back now, he spent with the patients or at museums—which is to say, very little at lectures, conspicuous absences that were somewhat frowned upon.

Of his years as a resident, he now recalled three particularly formative experiences involving patients.

The first was with Gerald P, a tea planter from Ceylon, who endured a monthlong descent into terminal uremic delirium, "a muttering old man, the sweet breath of uremia on his lips—and I would visit him daily. He was thought to be a rather uninteresting patient. But I was fascinated by his delirium and listened to it for hours on end, and it was an amazing privilege, like being privy to a dream. As I listened to him—for even delirium always connects with experience and motives and personality—gradually his inner landscape became clear to me. Then I started to make comments, to enter his dream, as it were. I think there had been a sort of terrifying alienation and loneliness in his delirium, and there was a lovely sort of warmth as well as illumination that became possible when one could enter it. I was able to join him, not judging, sharing, sharing his fear and his humor, and, I'd like to think, easing his way by way of the company I provided. Of course, this was regarded as eccentric behavior by pretty much everyone else: 'There goes Sacks again, listening to a delirious patient this time.' But it was a beautiful and invaluable experience."

The second involved "a youth, a fellow weight lifter, for indeed I'd started weight lifting already then, who contracted a sudden leukemia and who was vaulting toward the window to leap." Oliver wrestled him back, wouldn't let him commit suicide. Subsequently the leukemia attacked the boy's spinal column, an exceedingly rare occurrence, and he suffered an excruciating six-week death, too weak now to kill himself, and cursing Oliver every single day.

The third, Oliver recalled, was a middle-aged man with an acute heart condition who insisted on leaving the hospital, which Oliver wouldn't allow because just the walk would surely kill him. The man protested to Oliver's superiors, who reprimanded Oliver: "He has a right to do as he will." The next day he announced he was leaving, and Oliver warned he wouldn't make it to the door; the man, unheeding, leapt out of bed and suffered an acute fatal heart attack within two steps—a death for which Oliver feels guilt to this day. "The value of remission," Oliver concluded,

"the reason you want to keep a patient alive for the hope of even brief remission, is that it allows people time to make their peace."

We continue walking, the night growing quite silent around us. Oliver's timepiece is incredibly loud. "Yes," Oliver agrees when I point this
out to him. "It has caused incidents—elevators have had to be cleared, and
buses, entire airport lounges!"

He claims not to hear it, except at night when it stops, at which point
he wakes up with a start.

The dinner with Dick Lindenbaum, though, has gotten Oliver thinking some more about his time at Oxford, and his thoughts seem to return
there again as we start trudging back to his father's house.

"During my first year at Oxford, something bizarre must have been
going on in terms of reading and searching: I was *insatiable*. I read West-
ern philosophy with a sort of desperation. It didn't work. I didn't get anything, I didn't retain anything, the only value in retrospect having been
that twenty years later, I knew where to look.

"Now that I look back on it, I must have been suffering an intellectual and emotional breakdown. Or rather, I identified the two and somehow imagined that a right philosophy, if I could but find it, would be
healing. I felt that I had been blown clean away from the early adolescent
paradise of age fourteen or fifteen.

"And so I became like Eric, learning-voracious, swallowing up enormous obsessive amounts. I was like the moronic Fin twins who lived in
almanacs: I carried about the 4,000-page *Handbook of Physics*, every page
crammed with indices of which I had memorized every one. I knew
every table by heart but it didn't work. If one could dig out the record
of the library from that year, one would see what kind of strange, futile
frenzy it was."

We paused for a moment to look into the vitrine of a medical supply
store.

"It stopped after my first year," he went on, "leaving a dullness, or
simply despair."

A few moments later his mood seemed to have lightened. "My closest friend was Kalman Cohen, a mathematical logician who subsequently
went to the University of Pittsburgh. One night he stayed over at the
Mapesbury Roadhouse. My mother freaked out the next morning to find
the bedsheets covered over with equations.

"Another friend was a chap named Sinzheimer, an interesting mix of a gifted man and a pathological liar. But the thing was, he usually later made good. He claimed he spoke Russian and indeed became the chair of Oxford's Russian Society, though he did not speak a word. But then later he did, and he taught Slavic languages! Still later he committed suicide, oh, fifteen years ago, which brought clear to me what a tormented life it must have been.

"Another friend, Vivien Jones, is now a London judge.

"But I was much closer to a suicide than a prodigy," he said, reverting to his earlier theme. "Things had been sour for years. The neurotic and sexual distresses which had somehow hovered, suspended, bracketed, between ten and fourteen, now sunk their fangs into me. I think of John Stuart Mill's crisis—having been pushed and pushed for years up to the point where only Wordsworth made sense to him. My third year, only the poet Richard Selig, a student of Theodore Roethke's, made sense to me.

"By my fourth year I was in a similar crisis. My experimental research was going badly, and meanwhile, Richard Selig was dying of a lymphosarcoma which I'd had the misfortune of diagnosing. He was only twenty-eight at the time. I'm told he wrote some of his best stuff under this sentence of death.

"Such that by my fourth year I was alone and dealing unsuccessfully and frantically with what I am now dealing with successfully: the inadequacy of quantitative science. I was frenzied. I'd take off on huge runs followed by all-night spates of writing, my nightcaps."

We were now ambling along a nearly empty All Souls Avenue in the direction of Cricklewood.

"My tutor told my parents I was at the bursting point. He suggested I go to a kibbutz in Israel to calm down. I went and I did, and there were no further frenzies till the mid-sixties. The kibbutz was near Haifa and it *was* soothing for about three months. I liked the structure, the community, the sense of a concrete task. In fact, it was fine as long as I couldn't speak Hebrew, intolerable once I could. I then went down to Eilat for some snorkeling, where I again fell in love with marine biology.

"By the way," he interrupted himself, "did you read that Talk piece in *The New Yorker* the other day about that institute for the study of nonviolence? Well, Gene Sharp, the head of the institute, was a friend of mine from my days at medical school in London. We liked each other. I once spent time with him on a little island off Norway—a pleasant time, neither of us central to the other. He has a Gandhian spirituality and a clear political head. It was my first experience of sharing a house without friction. I read a lot of Bakunin.

"For a withdrawn person," Oliver suddenly acknowledged, "I do seem to have run into a lot of people."

From All Souls we'd verged onto Willesden and were now turning onto Mapesbury.

"From Israel I then had my first experience of sex," he said, as if in a hurry to finish the story before we made it back to his father's house. "I came back, age twenty-two, wonderfully slim, mahogany brown, and went to Amsterdam where I was picked up, dead drunk, sprawled in an alley, by a nice man—he was thirty-seven—who told me about the life, about bars, etc. I was incredibly naïve and innocent, ingenuous, though filled with the most wicked fantasies.

"Various friends had tried to set me up with women. Kalman once set a date up for me. I had some pallid intellectual meetings with a formidable though probably in actuality quite frail lady. And then there was the Bernice episode: a plump Jewish maiden with a seven-figure dowry. A few bizarre things in which I felt I was being made to go to school with Martians. But the thing is, I was living in a world, you see, in which Kalman Cohen, one of my best friends, knew me so little after two years that he tried to set me up with a girl.

"Later on, I was very embarrassed in medical school when on the anatomy final, I was completely unable to describe the female genitalia—this even though I'd been present at countless dissections—with the result that I was down-graded to eighty-ninth out of ninety. As I say, I have no idea what women have down there—a scotoma, a discreet circle of non-differentiation—a mystery greater than which there is none.

"Notwithstanding which, a few years earlier I'd been able to ghost that gynecology book for my mother."

His family home now rose into view. "I had a poignant anniversary dream about her a few months ago, last time I was here. She was back. I said, 'Where have you been?' She said, 'On a long holiday . . .' I woke up and it was her birthday—a fact I'd forgotten till that moment."

We climbed the steps into the house, and so (three a.m.) to bed.

❈

*The next morning I head to Poland for my reporting on martial law, coming back
ten days later by way of London for a last few days of interviewing.*

Conversation with Jonathan Miller

*I pay a call on Jonathan Miller, the eminent physician, erstwhile comic (of
Beyond the Fringe fame, during his Cambridge days and immediately thereafter, alongside Alan Bennett, Peter Cook, and Dudley Moore), frequent
BBC documentarian, and inspired classics adapter (do try to catch his tele-
vised* Alice in Wonderland *or* Plato's Symposium *if ever you have a
chance), at the rehearsal space for the National Opera, where he takes a break
from rehearsing his latest opera adaptation, a reprise of his celebrated Mafia*
Rigoletto *with the English National Opera. This conversation is adapted from
a tape transcript.*

When did you first meet Oliver?
We first met in, what, 1950? 1948? I must have been about fifteen though
we didn't really become friendly till the following year. And I remember
him as a sort of strange, corpulent, clever, Ustinovian figure in a rather
capacious tweed overcoat, standing, or rather kneeling, on the edge of a
rugby field.

Was he more athletic and self-possessed in those days?
No, he was always quite awkward. As he got older he came to remind
me of Pierre in *War and Peace*: shortsighted, clumsy, given to sudden eruptions of shrill giggles. At the time I met him, he was still a classicist . . .
but soon after he passed his qualifying exams to continue on in classics,
he shifted over instead to biology, which is where I was and where I
really came to know him. We were part of a group of very competitive
young Jewish scientists who worked together in this rather hothouse
atmosphere.

Your family was Jewish as well?
Yes, though not nearly as much so as Oliver's; to this day when asked
whether or not I am a Jew, I tend to reply, Well, I am Jew-*ish*.

Jonathan and
Rachel Miller

Anyway, we had this wonderful biology teacher, a man named Sid Pask.

Oliver and Eric both talk about him as well. What was he like?
A strange sort of blond, blue-eyed, rolling-gated gentleman farmer. Rather conservative. A sort of old-fashioned Herbert Spencer–like mixture of conservative and atheist, I suspect an old-fashioned social Darwinist of some sort. But with this curious capacity to engage the affectionate enthusiasms of his students and anyone who was prepared to rise to the occasion.

There was this wonderful annual event of his, this going out to Millport, a marine biology research station on the Clyde estuary on the southwest Scottish coast, that was a very important part of all of our lives. We all did peculiar and wonderful experiments and collected things. Each of us had his own phylum. Oliver's was cephalopods, and mine were polychaete worms. Eric's were holothurians and echinoderms. I think a lot of what was exciting for all of us was this Jewish thing of cataloging and naming, the sheer relish of those Linnaean bionomical labels rolling off our tongues.

And that, too, is why museums were so exciting to us: the very fact that they cataloged every single specimen known to man, dryly labeled—we just delighted in that, it was a sort of zoological kabbalah; I mean, there was almost a rabbinical element to it.

Was Pask—
No, he was not Jewish. And he was so innocent he was probably quite un-aware that his brightest lot were almost all Jews. Not that he would have minded—I expect he'd have been quite indifferent to it.

Oliver told me to ask you what your parents came to think of him and his cephalopods.
Well, oh yes, that's right. There was that very weird little episode. Once when we were on holidays—my parents, my sister, and myself—we'd hired a house on the south coast for a summer holiday, and Oliver came down with Eric. I can remember this strange silhouetted couple, Oliver with a bowler hat and Eric wearing strange trousers, all raised up the calves, pop-ping along the seawall, coming to visit us, looking absolutely like some-thing out of *Godot*, like Pozzo and Lucky or something. And I remember how later we'd trawled for cuttlefish in the sea and gotten ourselves a lot of cuttlefish, which then remained, stinking, in this jar on the window-sill, which in turn somehow got overturned, filling the house with this terrible stench which we couldn't get rid of. Everybody else was out at the time. So Oliver, in a fit of insane inspiration, went out to a local grocer's and bought some essence of coconut which he then sprinkled, like incense, all about the house in the hopes that it would mask the stench, but instead of which just resulted in equally intolerable passages of intense coconut essence at one moment and equally intense passages of rotting cephalopod at the other.

Oliver surmises that your parents may have lost their enthusiasm for his visits after that.
I think they always regarded him as an eccentric, clumsy person. The crock-ery had to be hidden; he overturned things and he spilled things. And he also had what in fact became this established, well, eccentricity, which was an absolutely unremitting and unvaryingly voracious and omnivorous ap-petite. Such that simply to have him in the house was to set up a sort of

current of food that simply converged upon Oliver. It wasn't so much that he devoured with any sort of ferocious rapidity but that gradually you noticed that all the food was gravitating to his end of the table, where it quietly and systematically got eaten—almost like a kind of fidget, a tic. If the food wasn't there, he evinced no hunger. But if it was, it just simply and quietly got eroded. It was a force of nature really.

Where do you think that came from?
I don't know really. It's just something very special to him. His father was always very—he was a great rotund man of enormous hospitality, and visiting their place, one was expected to eat at the same gargantuan scale that the Sackses ate.

Oliver's mother, also?
No, the mother was a very impressive, big woman, but not fat. His father was very roly-poly, still is, at nearly ninety now. His mother was a rather severe gynecologist, who in fact taught my wife at the [Elizabeth] Garrett Anderson Hospital. She had this strange inability to separate or distinguish her gynecological work from her domestic work, so that you'd be sitting watching at the operating table, attending an operation, and you'd hear her talking to a sister in that strange North London voice, and she'd be saying, "Right, Sister, pass me the Spencer Wells hemostatic forceps, would you please, here we are, we're going down and getting at the pelvis now, a lot of pus in there—oh, Sister, remind me I have to pick up some crystallized ginger on my way home." So that would all get blurred in at the operating table. And then equally, or conversely, when I was over for Friday-night suppers, she'd say, "Oh, Jonathan, you'd be interested in this, I had a fascinating case this afternoon. Elderly woman, sixty, complaining of lower abdomen pain gradually moving toward the left side. And well, to cut a long story short, I decided to open her up, made a left paramedian incision and the pelvis was just overflowing with pus. Sam, pass the mayonnaise, would you?"

This was when you were still in—
Oh, I mean, I was likely in university by then, but Oliver had similar stories from when he was ten, eleven, twelve years old.
    Yes, she was steadily and quietly and undramatically interested in her

work. And equally passionately but undramatically concerned with domesticity. And the two ran into each other without any sort of margin or frame.

I mean, she was enormously domestic. She used to have a vast pantry filled with domestic stores. My wife once was delighted at being allowed to visit these stores, as Oliver's mother proudly threw open the cupboard doors to reveal twenty or thirty Brillo pads, forty scouring powders, hundreds of packets of washing detergents. The whole thing stocked against some hypothetical disaster in which the shops were all going to run out.

How was she regarded as a doctor?
She was obviously a very capable gynecologist—a stately and well-respected figure in her profession and in the hospital where she worked. She was a grimly wry lady: She didn't suffer fools gladly. But my wife, who was her dresser for a short while, had great respect for her skill and also for her kindness and her gossiping intimacy with her patients.

Do you think that's where Oliver gets some of his intimacy with his patients?
Yes, it could well be. I suspect he has a particularly striking way with a quite particular sort of patient—people, locked in some kind of incommunicado, with whom Oliver especially succeeds in communicating. They may in some way stand in as reflections of, or maybe rather serve as metaphors for, Oliver's own image of himself as being solitary and socially incompetent.

And what of Oliver's father?
I just remember him as a sort of chatterbox paterfamilias. I don't think he was in any sense an intellectual (neither was she, she was just a good practicing gynecologist, they balanced each other in that way). He was a very skillful diagnostician who took great pleasure in his patients, was well loved among the Jewish patients in North London. He always used to drive about with the boot of his car filled with dried fish, which he'd reach into and impulsively give out to people. So I mean, food was given or devoured by the Sackses with equal and opposite energy. It was just always assumed that people would desire it with the same urgency that they themselves did.

Was Oliver seen as prodigious in the family?

I don't think they . . . I mean, they admired him and thought him clever and all. They were all, except the one who was a schizophrenic, successful doctors, but they weren't intellectuals, and Oliver was. Marcus, who went to Australia, was just a good rheumatologist, and David was just a show-biz practitioner, large, handsome, blond hair, a Golem of a figure whom I never liked very much. Oliver was clearly the rabbinic intellectual.

Did he feel himself out of place?

I think so, yes. He was out of place and yet an obviously well-loved and well-admired member of the family. But he was a solitary eccentric given to exorbitant and sudden peculiar energies and enthusiasms. Suddenly, for six months or a year, he'd be the greatest living expert on stereoscopic photography. Or he would develop an absolute passion for the periodic table, then becoming intensely interested in one particular narrow band of the table, say the rare earths, sending away for specimens.

There was a sort of element of this South Kensington, Wellsian wonder of science—H. G. Wells, the first men on the moon, nineteenth-century science fiction—which to a degree we all shared. And Oliver had a laboratory just off the back of the conservatory in this rather gloomy red-brick house in Kilburn. Within this rather ordinary and conventional bourgeois Jewish house, he was a peculiar and eccentric anomaly himself, just as anomalous as the anomalous fluids and substances that he insisted on collecting. The exceptional, the peculiar, the bizarre—I mean, these always interested him.

Was he ridiculed by the kids at school?

No, not that I can recall. I mean, he was ridiculed very, very humorously by all his friends all the time.

{There's a break in the tape as we leave the rehearsal space and head out to his car, resuming a few moments later.}

. . . They were gelatinous and tentacular and pliable and boneless and I guess, now that I think about it, all these sort of wrapping and embracing creatures were perhaps for him sort of half-realized sexual partners.

Oh, hardly half realized. Nowadays Oliver will be the first to celebrate that aspect of things. What of the years after St. Paul's?
Well, he went off to Oxford with Eric, to Queens College. I didn't go to Oxford, I went to Cambridge, so I lost a little track of him during those years. But it was obviously a very important part of his life. I can remember him talking about it a lot. He was well liked and tremendously admired by some of his teachers. He wrote prize essays, got prizes, wrote voluminously, was thought to be very intelligent. But it was all upset—his scientific reputation, that is, destroyed—by a clumsiness which was his and everyone else's despair. He would destroy whole experiments by sheer Bezukhovian clumsiness. Shortsighted, inept, what we referred to as flat-footed Jewish clumsiness. Still he was an academic success, went on to Middlesex Hospital, where he became a houseman, an intern there.

Did you have a sense of Oliver's desperate excess, as you call it, at St. Paul's already or during the times when you'd see him across his college years?
No, I don't think I really saw it until later in his medical career. I think it started to happen when he went off to California, though he'd already become sort of extravagantly eccentric and experimental with himself still in London—fixing himself blood milk shakes with half-finished transfusions, frying placentas, I mean he stopped at nothing. He just experimented with himself, and as I say, this was all part and parcel of this business of finding the heaviest fluid known to man, or the only thing known to have a refractory index identical to glass, all part of this hankering after the most-bizarre possibilities and monstrosities.

And then of course later on there were the motorbikes and speed and picking up anonymous masked people, and just experiencing the excitement of coming at a hundred miles per hour. His sexual universe was entirely Newtonian: It had entirely to do with acceleration, rather than with people. In California, too, he went into extraordinarily dangerous spirals of drug taking, drugs which have probably irreversibly harmed his body in some way.

How do you account for his still being alive at all?
Well, for one thing he's superhumanly strong. One has to mention the weight lifting as well, which had already begun here in England, before

California. He was fantastically strong. And the swimming, which too was very strange. He was like some enormous urodele reptile, or rather a urodele amphibian. Plantigrade, flat-footed, incompetent, clumsy on land, who then developed this extraordinarily potent grace in the water. Because the water supported his weight and his feet became irrelevant and his hands didn't have to manipulate things delicately, he became as graceful and fluent as a porpoise. All very odd. And weight lifting too—that just involved very rapid seizures of enormously laden bars.

I can remember him weight lifting and suntanning. He used to delay his ward rounds as an intern until the night because he was on the roof taking a sunburn. And on at least one occasion he did a ward round wearing these twenty-pound weights wrapped around his ankles, with no shirt, white coat, and brown hairy chest, coming clanking like some giant Golem about the ward, doing all this at three in the morning, since that was the only possible time he could spare from his weight lifting and suntanning.

Do you think it bothers Oliver, for all his hermit-like solitariness these days, that he is not that well known, that to date Awakenings, *for example, has not proved that much of a success?*
The thing about Oliver is that he has enough of a sense of reality to actually passionately desire social acceptance and fame. If this were just a case of someone who feared that his Hasidic solitude could be upended by publicity, that would be understandable. But I think, and I hope this isn't doing him down in any way, but he wants it very badly indeed, to be famous and a social success. So that these things war in him.

That strikes me as not unlike the yawning chasm you see with him in social settings, how he can evince that crazy contrast between stammering tongue-tied shyness and even at times a peremptory prickliness on the one hand and then at other moments how he can be gracious and gregarious and endlessly expansive, sometimes seemingly shifting from one to the other and then back again from one moment to the next.
I know, half the time he can be extraordinarily graceful and entertaining and amusing, and very funny about these very things, and other times he can go very, very black, and still others he can become veritably eruptive and not be able to stop. He's a very weird man, and yet he's made a life for

himself: He's even managed to mythologize that awkwardness, so that it's become an almost heroic stance, flecked with a kind of grace. I don't know how it will work out for him in the future. He's obviously disliked by the profession; on the other hand, the profession is so repulsive that if anything that's a tribute to him.

There's one parallel I've seen in interviews I've read of you, and in conversations I've had with Oliver, this sense of obvious not just competence but really mastery in your chosen fields, simultaneously at war with tremendous feelings of not having accomplished anything.
And you'll get that from Eric as well.

Where does that come from?
I suppose from that little group at St. Paul's who had reason to believe that it was very clever and there was no limit to what they, what we could accomplish by way of scientific achievement. The thing is, we set our standards for that sort of achievement very high, by way of the nineteenth-century figures who became our models of achievement and success. I mean, ask Oliver about the people he admired in his molluscan phase or his cephalopodilic phase, these were people we all of us admired, the great encyclopedic Victorian comparative anatomists—Ray Lancester! Go mention Ray Lancester to Oliver and see what happens. Gegenbauer. The great comparative embryologists. Balfour and Goodrich. The comparative vertebrate zoologists! These were the names we thought of—grave, serious, and achieved. And I think we came to feel ourselves falling short of those examples: Set your goals high enough like that, at an early enough age, and it condemns you to a life of frustration and despair. I think all of us have that. I mean, me, what am I? A show-business flibbertigibbet. And I suspect Oliver feels the same in his area.*

---

*Jonathan Miller's son William just recently amplified on this tendency of his father's in his new memoir *Gloucester Crescent: Me, My Dad and Other Grown-Ups* (London: Profile Books, 2018). Channeling his eleven-year-old self, as of 1975, he writes, "Dad basically thinks his life has been a total waste of time. According to him, everything he has done amounted to nothing, which I've never understood because I don't know anyone else's dad who's done as much as mine. And it doesn't matter how many times everyone tells him this, he still falls into these depressions and then finds it hard to get out of them" (p. 164).
Miller also recounts regular visits of Oliver and Eric to the Miller family kitchen table

Do you suppose it has anything to do with your common Jewish upbringing?
No, not really, because our Jewish upbringings were very, very different.
As I've said, Oliver's parents were in no sense intellectuals. I mean, his
father I suppose was a sort of Hebrew scholar, but they were fairly bourgeois figures. Whereas both my parents were very, very high-powered
intellectuals, my mother an accomplished writer and novelist and Victorian biographer and my father a philosopher and psychiatrist, a good
painter and a good sculptor, and a Bloomsbury intellectual. There were
probably different sorts of expectations. But my family wasn't Jewish
the way Oliver's was. Oliver reads Hebrew and I don't know any Hebrew
at all.

And no interest?
None. None. Anti-Zionist and actually a lot of the time anti-Semitic.
Oliver himself can be very anti-Semitic with me, about Jewishness, but
nevertheless has a much longer and stronger attachment. For example,
when his mother died, when his father will die, he sat and will sit shiva. I
just don't have anything to do with any of that. I mean, I suppose I'm
glad to be Jewish because it's nice to be rootless, to the extent that one is.
But I also take a great pleasure in being English. The sound of the shofar is
anathema to me, whereas the thing that brings lumps to my throat is
English hymns.

*Whereas the last time Oliver had interest in anything specifically English was prob-
ably from the time of the Druids.*
That's right. While I just have a great passion for the peculiarities of English life. They please me a great deal, even though I know I am not truly
part of it and yet it is the thing I feel closest to of anything really. But
Oliver never particularly liked any of it.

The other difference between Oliver's upbringing and mine, and it's
partly due to the fact that they were more committed to Judaism, is

---

on Gloucester Crescent, and how (this again from his eleven-year-old vantage) "Dad and
[Oliver] are quite competitive about the things they know about science and the brain. If
Oliver is trying to make a point and gets stuck on a word [owing to his previously discussed
stammer], Dad goes straight in there and talks over him with his own theory. I once saw
Oliver get so frustrated with this sort of situation that he twisted one of Mum's silver spoons
under the table as he stuttered until it looked like a corkscrew" (p. 65).

that his house had the ugliest interior that I think I've ever seen. It had that thing that was quite characteristic of all Jewish middle-class households, where in fact there is no general culture, the objects are hideous, the furniture depressing and heavy and ugly. And there isn't one beautiful thing in the house at all.

Lots of books, though?
No, not very many.

No Jewish books?
Well, yes, lots and lots of Hebrew books, but nothing else at all. Except in Oliver's room, where he kept lots of books, of course. But his father never had any books other than the Hebrew ones. In my house, there was lots of art and a vast library, part of which I've inherited, I have lots of my father's pictures. But in Oliver's house, and Eric's was the same way, the visual was nonexistent. Maybe one reason Oliver has no feeling for England is that a lot of what is characteristic about England is what everything *looks* like. And I don't think Oliver could give a visual description of what *anything* looks like.

Although he can give extraordinary descriptions of what things feel *like.*
That's right! He lives in a sort of strange, tactile world. One can always remember moving through botanical gardens with him and his producing squeals of delight as he reached out to touch delicate ferns—*Oeyim! Oooooh!* But the thought that a fern might *look* beautiful—never. Or rather to the extent that it did look beautiful to him, this was because of the fact that its look conveyed a very strong memento of what it might feel like to touch it.

For much the same reason, he and Eric would often go on these strange gastronomic holidays together. They'd head off to Amsterdam when they were younger, to eat. They were great ones for tasting foods of strange and peculiar textures. Even now when they get together they take great pleasure in venturing into exotic Oriental restaurants. Whereas I don't think either of them ever really go to a picture gallery.

He has a great sense of music, though.
Yes, that he does.

Which is another way of being submerged, surrounded, I suppose. Eyes closed.
And he was at one time quite an accomplished pianist. His father has almost total recall for almost all the operas he ever heard, going back over sixty years. Very, very strange. They do have that together: quite a musical family.

※

He went through a completely dark, totally disintegrated phase there at the end of California and when he first moved to New York. He was depressed, violently peculiar, resentful, lived in great squalor, and I think was a danger to himself. Gradually he succeeded in reconstructing himself.
But he's also had those very peculiar and destructively paranoid relationships with a succession of bosses and associates, people who become tyrants who endanger him, perhaps castrate him in some way. And I think they probably are monsters. It's very hard to separate his fantasy view of them from what they're actually like. But I suspect they actually are vicious, tight-assed, puritanical, competitive little Jewish tyrants, who can't understand Oliver, his being the sort of person who threatens their very view of the cosmos. He finally seems to have found a modus vivendi in that regard, which is to say no longer being bossed by anyone. Except for his Little Sisters.

※

{We arrive at Miller's home on Gloucester Crescent, take seats at the kitchen table, where we are occasionally joined by Miller's wife, Rachel, who flits in and out, as our conversation turns to Oliver's sexuality.}
I mean, early on it wasn't really as if he were in a closet, since there was nothing outside that could really be called "gay" per se. But then there were these wonderful pathetic attempts on the part of his father to persuade him back into the orthodox fold of heterosexuality. Such as taking him into his consulting room and ripping open a drawer and saying, "Take these contraceptives, take any of them, as many as you like, *they're yours!*"

Oliver talks about how his mother, upon hearing of his homosexuality from his father, came storming down the stairs, launching into hours-long Deuteronomical curses—

That's right, she talked about "the filth of the bowel," a particularly piquant expression I remember his relating.

Which would be followed by several days of silence, after which the subject was never raised again.
But this is what I was talking about, probably, is that his parents were in no sense intellectual, otherwise they could have accommodated it. They lived by a very simple Yeshiva-like set of standards, and their learning was entirely confined to Talmudic sorts of learning, with no other sorts of culture being admitted. It was just halakah and that was all: It was law, law, law. And of course homosexuality is against the law, so it's bad. Whereas Oliver was drawn rather to kabbalah, because he's interested in decipherings and strange luminous secret significances.

Do you think the awkwardness you've described was rooted in the homosexuality and then spread to everything else?
But even to call it "homosexuality," especially in the early days but even to this day, implies a fairly constituted and formal degree of sexuality which with most homosexuals is actually quite sociable and therefore has elegance and grace and form. Whereas I think Oliver's homosexuality and gracelessness are both part of a curious primeval incoherence in his personality.

{Rachel, passing, overhearing our conversation, interjects, "Did you tell him about . . . ?"}
Well, yes, there was actually this wonderful moment, it was around the time he was beginning to come out to some of his friends, although I'd actually known for some time. But now he was trying to get himself back into heterosexuality, and he insisted he was going to need some help, some companionship, someone who could help him see things clearly. He said, "I've managed to pick up a couple of"—and he described them as—"high-hipped Caribbean beauties. And I'm bringing them around to your house so maybe we can all go out for a walk on the Heath. And your presence on this date will somehow assist me."

Rachel: Completely ignoring my presence in the room!
Jonathan: Whereupon he produced some strange, black, toothless hags, in
    no sense high-hipped, giggling, ski-pantsed—well, trollops they

were. And he obviously couldn't see that they were simply repulsive. He had a sexual agnosia. The thing that is so interesting is that a lot of straightforward gays can perfectly recognize what it is that heterosexual men find attractive in women, even if they happen not to. But Oliver can't.

Rachel: But he's always had that kind of thing of behaving as if he really doesn't understand anything of social reality, exposing his haplessness in this regard to you and then laughing at his own failures, in that instance to achieve romance.

Jonathan: Yes, there's a sort of Martian quality about him, as if he's visiting the earth and making sort of instrumental inferences about what it is "you people" like and then making terrible, terrible mistakes.* Rubber pants instead of leather, black latex—

Rachel: But it was all tied up too with his losing and gaining weight. He would lose a couple stone at a time . . .

Jonathan: . . . and then gain it right back again. His body image was entirely arbitrary. But you see, there he is like a Martian again, the Martians from one of his favorite Wells books, *The War of the Worlds*, who, come to think of it, were themselves like cephalopods, boneless things, with no ability to support themselves in terrestrial gravity and therefore having to inhabit enormous mechanical walking devices.

As far as the sexual side goes, though, nowadays it all gets talked about in the past tense.

Jonathan: Yes, well, he talks about himself nowadays as a burnt-out case.

Rachel: "But that was twenty years ago." The drugs, the sex . . . all of that is over.

Jonathan: He really regards himself as having been lunified, I mean like the surface of the moon, a landscape of once active volcanoes that are now totally inert craters. Which I think had a lot to do with his interest, his identification, with the patients in *Awakenings*: these other people who are now inert but still contain memories of the dramas

---

*These comments were made more than a dozen years before Oliver titled a subsequent collection of his own pieces *An Anthropologist on Mars* (following the self-characterization of one of his subjects, the high-performing autistic animal scientist Temple Grandin, in a formulation that, granted, could apply to both of them).

they once lived. As I say, many of his patients are memories of himself.

Rachel: But it's like we were saying in the car the other day, about the Borges-like quality of many of his reports. And this is where he leaves certain neurologists behind. Many I have spoken with say, "It doesn't add up. That's not what those patients actually seem to be exhibiting, and it can't be trusted." He gets dismissed as a romantic neurologist.

Jonathan: Well, he *is* a romantic neurologist. But he in turn gets at things, he sees things, that other, more conventional and reductionist neurologists don't see. He sees larger—

Rachel: But he misses things according to his projected fantasies. His description of us, his idealized romantic view of our marriage, which hardly describes us or what any marriage is really like.

Jonathan: Well, it's the same as with "the high-hipped Caribbean beauty." I mean, obviously it's not the case that she was one. And one wonders if the same thing doesn't occasionally apply to his patients. Still these fictions do become, as in the case of Kafka, strange luminous truths in their own right, and it's almost irrelevant if they are what he says they are.

Rachel: He wants people to be more interesting than they are.

Jonathan: Yes, I think he wanted the whole world to be a sort of tic, this thing ticcing away. He wanted some sort of infinity of representations to be contained in any given case that he could identify.

Rachel: That book he was intending to do on five seconds in the life of a Touretter.

Jonathan: Well, of course, he believed that in five seconds was crammed the entire history of the universe. But that takes us back to the kabbalah, how within one sentence of the book of Genesis might be contained the entire universe.

He has a postcard reproduction of a van Eyck painting at actual size on his bulletin board, and sighing, pointing to it, he says, "The compression!"

Jonathan: Well, that's right. But again, that also reflects his interest in Leibniz and his monadology: the idea that each of the monads contained representations of the whole rest of the world within.

Actually, at the time Leibniz had himself been consorting with kabbalists as he was developing his monadology. But as for Oliver, do you think that he is unreliable as a neurologist?

Jonathan: Well, he is unreliable only in the sense that it would be very difficult to accommodate some of his work within the body of neurology as it stands today. On the other hand, he also appeals to and represents some aspects of classical neurology which the modern reductionist neurology hasn't accommodated *itself* to. This curious sort of infinity that *does* exist within each individual self, which simply doesn't get treated in ordinary neurology.

Rachel: I don't think he'd be particularly good treating a child.

Jonathan: Well, his own childhood was so unrepresentative. I think on the other hand he is superb at somehow giving consolation and meaning to the life of those patients who have been so totally destroyed and desolated by many of the particular conditions he has chosen to address. As in fact it is only through communion with those sorts of patients that they can be treated at all.

He talks about the way that in the sorts of institutions in which he works, you don't choose the patients, the patients choose you.

Jonathan: Yes, and in many cases I think his patients are more like disciples than patients. So the notion of reliability is in a way irrelevant, because what's the test and criterion of reliability? What are you relying on someone *for*? In the wider sense of conventional neurology, of course I don't think he's reliable. Because in fact ultimately descriptions of most human life are coming from a sort of middle way, from the ordinary chronic sort of life that most of us are forced to live and from which most diseases are quite recognizable departures. But some of these unrepresentative disorders are so peculiar, featuring experiences which are so anomalous, that only some totally different universe of discourse is suitable from which to address them.

I once asked him why he became a neurologist and he replied that what else could a thinking doctor do, meaning, he went on, that the heart is an interesting pump, for instance, but it's just a pump.

Jonathan: Well yes, because the brain in his terms is a monad, a device whose very purpose is to re-present the entire world, compared to which the heart is just a sort of life-support system.

What about the phenomenon of his extraordinary blockages, those tremendous bursts of activity followed by—well, the way in which he really hasn't completed anything substantive since Awakenings?

Jonathan: I know, it's very strange, these paralyzing lassitudes he falls into, and the self-hatreds. Often accompanied by voluminous writings, all of which get torn up.

Was he like that already at St. Paul's?

Jonathan: No, no, he was always fluent and capable of writing.

Rachel: He went straight through to his degree, without any real interruptions.

Jonathan: That's right. I mean, he did have trouble with the research itself, he broke the glassware and failed to remember to feed the rats. But that's because he belongs to a world of pure phenomenology. Experiments, which is to say fragmentations of reality, breaking reality up into observable and quantifiable sequences—those simply weren't his interest. But the writing blockages themselves only developed later.

Have you ever tried to talk him out of one?

Jonathan: No, not really. Eric might have. Eric's much closer to him than I am, because after all he's known him since he was six.

Rachel: And Eric has a touch of the same disease. He loves wandering, cut loose.

Jonathan: Same problem. Eric himself is an exorbitant accumulator of facts, he's a bookseller, he's not a kabbalist the way Oliver is, but he's a Borgesian accumulator of indexes, a bibliographer. [. . .] And then, too, there's that characteristic thing, that both Rachel and I have noted for thirty years, his excited listening.

Rachel: Oh yes.

Jonathan: I don't know if you've ever experienced it, but the way he will go, "Um . . . um . . . yeah . . . yes . . . shhh . . . shhhh," such that your contribution is being systematically extinguished for fear of it's actually interfering with his own stream of thought.

Though he never seems to be that way with his patients.

Jonathan: No, he doesn't, I think you're right there. There, there is an entirely different sort of listening. A profound attentiveness. Most extraordinary. Most extraordinarily odd fellow.

⁜

Conversation with Colin Haycraft

The day after visiting with Jonathan Miller, I pay a call on Colin Haycraft, Oliver's British publisher, at Duckworth's offices in the Old Piano Factory at the nub of Gloucester Crescent in Camden Town, just down the street from Jonathan's home, and Haycraft's as well for that matter (as well as those of the likes of the playwright Alan Bennett; the novelist Michael Frayn and his wife, the biographer Claire Tomalin; and The Listener *and then* London Review of Books *editor Mary-Kay Wilmers, whose sister was married to Karl Miller, the editor in chief of both those publications, and whose nanny, Nina Stibbe, would write up the whole scene many years later in her epistolary memoir,* Love, Nina*).

This transcript is adapted from notes I took at the time.

Up and down we go through various staircases and warrens, arriving in Haycraft's private office, an odd misshapen room, with old beat-up stuffed lounging chairs, papers piled on desks and end tables, and shelves brimming over with books. Haycraft himself in a gray-brown tweed jacket and a bow tie, well-worn shoes, dark-framed glasses, black hair graying at the fringes, is comfortably rumpled and ruffled, given to merry digressions ("I stumbled upon a false quantity in Marvell's Latin the other day!") and other outbreaks of silly giggles and wry whimsy.

"Well," he begins, "so Duckworth was founded back in 1898 by Gerald Duckworth, the half brother of Virginia Woolf, one of the two boys who put their hands up her skirt, perhaps on that very sofa right over there, you can read all about it in her diary" (where Gerald, to a lesser degree

---

*Stibbe's book served as the basis for a comedy-drama series over the BBC in 2016. But also see the recently issued *Gloucester Crescent: Me, My Dad and Other Grown-Ups*, Jonathan Miller's son William's account of much the same terrain; as well as pretty much any of Alan Bennett's diaries. It was quite a block.

Colin Haycraft

than his brother, George, can be seen to have behaved quite grotesquely
with their new sibling, to considerably traumatizing and possibly lifelong
effect). "After having been widowed himself, Virginia's father, Leslie, married the widow Mrs. Herbert Duckworth, who brought two prior sons,
George and Gerald, into the household. That's her, incidentally, over
there"—a quite haunting photograph by Julia Margaret Cameron—"and
there's Gerald." Haycraft is given to bounding about: He can't quite settle
back into his seat before he's darting up once again, pointing to this or
spearing that. "The old offices of the publishing house served as a set for
Hitchcock's film *Frenzy*, but we abandoned those in 1971, in part so I could
be closer to my home. Now I just walk back and forth, editing and entertaining as much in the one place as the other. After moving in, we found
out that this used to be a piano factory, so we renamed the whole building the Old Piano Factory, much to the annoyance of the manufacturer of
new lampshades upstairs, who resents the *old* denomination, but who cares.
As for Duckworth nowadays, we tend to publish the Three F's, as I tell
people, which is to say Fiction, Fucking, and Filosophy. For example, this
volume here"—up he goes again to snatch a copy of *The Latin Sexual*

Vocabulary by James Noel Adams—"utterly learned, fascinating, not a single joke in the whole thing unless you include"—a barely suppressed giggle—"the little squib of mine there on the cover, 'This is a fundamental book in every sense.' It's having the duck on the spine that sells them, I suppose; it was designed by the artist David Gentleman, who also lives just down the street."

I steer the conversation toward Oliver. "Well, yes, so one evening, this would have been toward the end of 1971, Jonathan brought him over to see me. When Oliver arrives, you find yourself after about eight hours or so wondering what the hell to do with him, so Jonathan just brought him over to me. Turns out we'd gone to the same college in Oxford, Queens, he three years after me though there was a slight overlap, him reading medicine while I was getting a proper education. There's a wonderful old college photo of dozens of students from the college, all the rest of them quite stiff and formal, with only the two of us, Oliver and me, noticeably somewhat askew."

Haycraft explains how actually Jonathan had an ulterior motive in bringing Oliver over, because Oliver had been showing Jonathan nine case studies of the Awakenings patients, which Oliver had completed in 1969 before abandoning the project, torn over misgivings about patient privacy and medical reception, or rather the old-fashioned and decidedly unfashionable way he was proposing to go about relating their histories. Haycraft found the tales remarkably moving and urged Oliver to continue, but nothing more came for the next six months. In July 1972, Haycraft decided to jump-start matters by simply setting those first nine stories in type, as galley proofs, and mailing them to Oliver. "He did this without warning," Oliver would recall several years later, in a memorial essay following Haycraft's death in 1994, "in the impulsive-intuitive way he often did things. It was a most generous act—what guarantee had he that I would ever continue my writing?—and also a crucial act of faith. It convinced me, more than any words could, that he was in earnest, that he was not just talking, that he *really* thought *Awakenings* should be published."*

Haycraft went on to recount how "Oliver didn't want *Awakenings* to

---

*Oliver Sacks, "Midwife and Unmuddler," in Stoddard Martin, ed., *Colin Haycraft, 1929–1994: Maverick Publisher* (London: Gerald Duckworth, 1995), 57.

be a medical book, like *Migraine*, which he had published with Faber and
Faber, which by the way—did you ever stop to think about it?—is Latin
for Smith and Smith. Things hadn't really gone well there for him, and
they were trying to convince him to do for Parkinson's what he had done
for migraine, but, as I say, he didn't want to just bring out another medical book but rather a *proper* book, as he put it."

I thereupon pulled from out of my satchel a photocopy of a letter
from the time, which Oliver had shown me some months earlier, and
handed it to Haycraft. Dated August 30, 1972, and still somewhat formally
addressed to "Mr. Haycraft," Oliver had written how he was enclosing
another five case histories and expecting still to add several more, some
sixty thousand words in total so far. He was trying, he said, to move from
"lists," as he put it, to "stories," though with as yet questionable success.
"You're so right," he continued, "about the shape of Art and the shape-
lessness of Life—perhaps I should have had a cleaner line or theme to
them all, but they were so complex, like tapestries. To some extent these
are crude ore, which others (including myself) can dig in and refine
later."

Haycraft smiled at the "sixty thousand words" reference. "Over the
course of the next year," he said, "that figure ballooned into something
more like half a million, which I was continually boiling down, returning
the results to him, only to have him return them yet further expanded.
Luckily, I suppose, the final editing took place in a mad rush, him bashing out the ultimate version on my dining-room table down the street in
nine days. He's not all that eccentric by English standards, I suppose, but
he was quite literally *The Man Who Came to Dinner*: I mean, he will eat
everything in your house, like some sort of hippopotamus. But the point
is, he had gotten it into his head that the book had to come out before his
fortieth birthday, which was going to be in early July of 1973, as I recall.
He kept adding footnotes, which I kept shaving off, and the pressure of
the deadline meant that my decisions stood more than they might otherwise have. But that's why there are so many typos in that first edition, and
why, too, the cover is so stark and spare. We had hoped to wrap the book
in a jacket with a beautiful image of a window with sky, but again, Oliver
was frantic to get the book out before that birthday, quite superstitiously
possessed about the whole prospect, so in the end we just had the black
cover with the Frank Kermode quote in bright white letters, which

embarrassed Oliver, or so he claimed, though modesty is its own form of vanity, isn't it? What? Don't you think?"*

How, I asked, had the book been received?

"A complete flop. I never published a book with better quotes and better reviews, but it didn't sell. It's still on its first printing! It won the Hawthornden Prize, which comes with no monetary supplement, so it's naturally the most prestigious one there is, but it's like that Samuel Johnson quip on an early novel of Congreve's, 'It has been much praised though I would rather praise than read it.' In this case, it seems, they'd rather praise than *buy* it. We can't have sold more than two or three thousand copies in coming on ten years. After which, over the years, Penguin, Doubleday, Vintage all tried their luck, but nobody who has published that book has sold it! Which is something of a relief: The one case where one doesn't have to feel guilty or incompetent. But still."

He pauses, breaking into a smile. "But I control world rights for the book, which I bought originally for one hundred pounds, which accounts for the lovely row I'm now involved in with Harold Pinter. I mean, a lot of people had wanted to do the book as a play, but Pinter just went ahead and did so and contacted Oliver afterwards, whereupon Oliver sold him volume rights which were actually not his to sell, which has led to an ungodly mess. (Ah the Pinters! Pinter married Frasier, each of them mistaken in their evaluation of the other, he thinking she was an aristocrat, and she thinking he was an intellectual.) Anyway, as you can see, it's led to quite a correspondence." He rummages through the papers on one of the desks and retrieves a bulging file, which he shows me, with evident satisfaction. "It will all work out eventually, of course, but one's got to get one's kicks out of publishing somehow, hasn't one? Lord knows it won't be in sales."

I ask about the Leg book, still in progress. "It's becoming a crushing bore, alas," he says. "I mean, Oliver's a deeply neurotic man, you have to understand. The whole family are. If Freud had not existed, he'd have had to be invented to account for them. His father is clearly jealous of the son; the brother, meanwhile, at the party for the *Awakenings* book, stood stock-

---

*Kermode's cover blurb, as indicated earlier, read: "This doctor's report is written in a prose of such beauty that you might well look in vain for its equal among living practitioners of belles lettres."

still in the very middle of the room, rather than in the corner, as his way of hiding in plain sight.

"The difficulty of being Oliver's editor," Haycraft goes on, "is that when he's good, he's completely wonderful, but when he's bad, he's god-awful. I'd wanted him to do a ticcer book: Oliver in that Tourette's television documentary actually looked madder than the ticcer. But that was not to be, and now instead we have his Leg, which does seem to go on endlessly.

"Once you get into Oliver's neurotic searchlight, though, you can get into a lot of trouble. I got into trouble a while back over Luria. I was actually quite keen to publish Luria, but Luria himself wanted to see a book of his own father's published first, which I didn't really want to, but finally I announced it in our catalog, R. A. Luria introduced by A. R., *The Inner Image of Disease*, and in the event things didn't work out, at which point Oliver really went for me, I had let him down, he was beside himself. Interesting, I could tell during the entire affair that Luria himself saw it all, Oliver's madness on the subject, my own reluctances.

"Being a publisher is in some ways like being a psychiatrist: For one thing, your patients are going to be jealous of each other, so you mustn't let them meet in the waiting room; on the other hand, you do want to let them know that others exist, otherwise they'll think you're incompetent. But in the same way that you shouldn't sleep with your analyst, you really shouldn't analyze with your publisher.

"I will publish the Leg book, of course, if he ever brings it to a conclusion. But it is getting tiresome. *Awakenings* was probably easier, since I didn't know him so well; criticism could be taken less personally. It was possible to persuade him to focus, to give the material form—the three stages (Awakening, Tribulation, and Accommodation)—and then to get him to stick to that form. And toward the end we could dangle the threat of the imminent onset of his fortieth birthday, that afforded closure.

"The job of the publisher is to persuade the writer to write the right book—and I think we succeeded with *Awakenings*, at least with that first edition, all the typos notwithstanding. Afterwards, in each succeeding edition, the text ballooned once again, the footnotes began piling up ever higher, or lower. We'll see how things go with Leg."

※

The next day, it's back to New York for both Oliver and me. Sitting in the seat next to me on the Air India flight, Oliver shows me the contents of the small briefcase he is carrying (he has checked no other luggage). Inside, his supplies for a four-week stay in London: some underwear, five spectacle cases (one filled with pens), a pair of swimming trunks, goggles, and Hannah Arendt's *The Life of the Mind*.

"There," he chuckles, "there you have it. *The essential Sacks!*"

12

On Rounds with Oliver at
the Little Sisters and Bronx State

One rainy late-fall afternoon Oliver and I are sluicing, the car's wipers slapping time, toward the Little Sisters home in Brooklyn.

"I am both completely redundant and completely irreplaceable," he declares. "I have to create the need which I then satisfy, the place which I then occupy. Like a scotoma, when I leave, the space and the need may disappear too. Because, seriously, who needs a neurological philosopher? I mean, I can do the other, but I'm mainly into religious medicine, neurological play—clinical ontology."

And indeed, it suddenly strikes me, his is a practice whose principal diagnostic question is: "How are you?" How *do* you *be*?

"I am a Kierkegaardian whose practice is the category of the individual. I'm a doctor for the individual, not for the nervous system. Or rather, for both. I play ball, though, with the individual, not the nervous system."

The storm lashes clear past, and now, as we race along the Brooklyn-Queens Expressway, the sky a swirling blue, Oliver lowers the windows. He has stripped down to a cotton short-sleeved dress shirt and furry extra-warm gloves. "In summer," he acknowledges, "lying naked on my bed with galoshes and gloves and nothing else—I realize that a physiologically more absurd sight is not to be seen."

At which point, oddly free-associating: "The Little Sisters were founded during the 1840s by a French nun, Jeanne Jugan, who was beatified earlier this year. I had half a mind to go to Rome: I mean, how often do you get to witness the beatification of a woman whose picture you have gracing your bedroom wall?

"Although she founded the order, Jugan was eventually eased out of the leadership and spent her last years as a lowly scullery maid in one of the homes. And this precedent established a kind of pattern: The order is characterized by an absolute hierarchy, coupled to an absolute approachability. Everyone knows her place in the order and the order is always liable to change. Power is not sought out of ambition. Rather it involves responsibility accepted for a time.

"Indeed, once I visited one of their homes in London (ironically, both my mother and father worked for the Little Sisters in London) and I spoke with a lowly maid-nun there who seemed to know all the nuns I knew. It turns out she had once been the mother provincial for the eastern United States before this transfer, which she accepted with complete equanimity."

We arrive at the Little Sisters' Holy Family Home in Brooklyn, a surprisingly modern cube of a building (they recently moved here from more dilapidated, expansive Victorian quarters). Oliver has been going to the Little Sisters in the Bronx since 1971 (around the time he began to see the writing on the wall at Beth Abraham), to the one in Queens (the mother center for the eastern United States) since 1975, and to this Brooklyn one since 1976. He is the sole neurologist regularly visiting any of these old people's homes.

We proceed in, and Oliver sets himself up in a little office off to the side of the nursing station on the second floor. The staff are manifestly delighted to see him. He is debriefed quickly by Sister Lorraine, a merry, open, wise soul ("in no way" as Oliver says once she's left, "a castrated or stunted woman, but rather one who seems quite whole and vital").

The patients are brought forth one by one. Oliver positions himself like a great big teddy bear, a secular Santa Claus on a low rolling stool, and expansively waves as the door opens and each new patient is brought in from the hall.

The first is Terry, a former shipbuilder—both his hearing and vision are going and he is generally lost in a depressed reclusion, as the nurse who's brought him tells us—but now, when roused, he proves capable of a cheerful and generous presence.

At one point, Oliver says, "Squeeze my hand," but Terry is unresponsive. Then turning to me, Oliver says, "Now for a Lurian version of the same instruction: Make a fist." And, effortlessly, Terry does.

To me and the nurse: "You see, as soon as he thinks about it, he can't do it—he has to be tricked into doing it."

Oliver throws Terry the foam ball and soon the four of us are throwing it all around and Terry starts recalling his powers in baseball and basketball, though not football. Everyone is laughing.

Later, once Terry has left, Oliver notes: "He's becoming frozen and bewildered; he needs to play to come unfrozen. One can ascribe his condition to a lot of diagnoses—frontal lobe inhibitions, etc.—but what it comes down to is that we've got to get him moving. He needs to be active. How can we get this fine old man with a cardiac condition active?"

He looks over Terry's recent EEG: "This is too good an EEG for someone like him—deafness, blindness, and sadness. It may be easier for an old woman in this condition than for an old man, especially if he can't gossip."

Next up, a demented old lady, utterly gone, who can still juggle oranges perfectly!

And then Ola, a severe Parkinsonian. Oliver asks her to stand and she has a terrible time, struggling up from the wheelchair—but then Oliver has her sit, and he holds out both hands, an extended finger on each, and she clutches the fingers and gets up *effortlessly.*

"You see, you share your action with them."

She has little latitude in her balance, and the antipsychotic agents have been making her more Parkinsonian.

Last year, Oliver recalls, she went around "in a fever of inverted solicitude," waking everyone up to ask if she looked okay.

Now she's been feeling depressed. "Last time this happened," she says, "they gave me shock treatment. Do you think I should have it again?"

"You're the doctor," replies Oliver.

After she's left, Oliver says, "Part of me is repelled by shock treatment, shocked by it, but one does see over and over and over again how obsessive depression and melancholia can be short-circuited—it's as if the circuitry of despair gets tripped up—and the patient sometimes has more courage and sense than we."

And now, Maria the Italian shouter. A blind repeater who breaks into loud, gruff arias—she bellows except when she sings. "These head movements of the blind," he notes. "Like radar."

After she's left: "Unlike Terry, she seems locked in state."

Oliver folds up the files and excuses himself; he needs to go visit a few of the patients in their rooms.

Which gives me time for a conversation with Sister Lorraine, who always calls Oliver "Doctor," as in: "Doctor is tremendous. The *depth* of his perception (time is irrelevant)—that depth, I watch and say to myself, can I have that? Could I acquire it?

"He doesn't care about appearance: He is himself and you can be yourself." (A funny comment from a woman in a clean, starched nun's habit.)

"I love it in his notes on patients how he will write, 'The It became an I and now it's a person.' And *it did*, it was real. How many would have imagined there was an 'I' there inside that vegetable? The person he's dealing with senses that, too.

"I remember one patient, for instance, an anxious woman who from the moment she was seen by him, her world changed. Doctor comes usually on Wednesday, and so on Wednesday Ola brightens up, and if he can't make it, she goes sad.

"There is not a single person here who feels out of sorts with him—he is *so* brilliant, and yet one feels at ease. He can become totally frustrated in his own life, what with his writing blocks, and he then has to get away. But we all understand.

"My mother died and he wrote me a nice note, 'Do you have someone else to talk to? And I don't mean just among the sisters.' He was relieved when he found out my mother had a twin sister.

"He writes notes to the staff, 'Thank you very much for everything you've done.' He thanks *us* for letting him come here. *He's* such an asset and he thanks us!

"Everyone who reads his notes sees the patients differently, newly. He always types out his notes on green paper, perhaps in that a sense of hope. And the depth of his perception! Most consultants' notes are cut-and-dried, aimed at the *problem* with no sense of the *person*. Even with the psychiatric consultants, you seldom sense the total person. With him, the whole person becomes visible. Another doctor, reviewing his notes, said, 'He's a terrible speller, a terrible typist, but there's no question, the man's brilliant.'"

She pauses before confiding, "I look at Our Lord as the Divine Physician and in a way—I hope this is not sacrilege—I look at Doctor the same way: He heals, but not just the superficial problems, he heals underneath.

"One day he was looking at a woman who'd lost the feeling in her fingertips and hence could no longer finger the rosary. He just sensed what that would mean, even though he's not Catholic. He asked me, is there any way maybe we could create a bar with ten beads or bumps, would that still be valid?

"Or our Sister Geraldine, an extraordinary, dynamic social worker, Doctor's compassion for her as she was dying."

She shakes her head before concluding, "I can't imagine being that profound without profound experience: It's not just brilliance."

Our conversation shifts briefly to how precisely the Little Sisters network works: The sister provincial, Sister Lorraine explains, is in charge of thirteen homes and can transfer any of the nuns anywhere at a moment's notice. Sister Lorraine has been at Brooklyn for two years: "And I'm shining my shoes now."

The place runs on begging. Sisters go out collecting every day: "We never have enough and yet we never want—we're always in deficit, never in detriment.

"This particular building was a Bergman nursing home, part of that scandal, the money man who was busted a few years ago. The state caught up with him and forbade him to even open this one. So we rent it through begging. The food is donated—often from the Hunts Point food distribution center.

"Oh, there you are, Doctor!" Sister Lorraine's face opens as Oliver comes loping down the stairway behind me, his rounds completed. We bid everyone goodbye and head out into the early-winter darkness and toward home.

On the drive back, Oliver is subdued, apparently still thinking through one of the encounters he'd had upstairs. "To see an intelligent man lose all his faculties is something you would not wish on your worst enemy. I know: I saw it happen to my worst enemy, and all I could think was, 'Poor bugger.'" (He doesn't specify who he is talking about, but several weeks later he shakes his head one day, noting how "the Hitler of Beth Abraham"—presumably his old persecutor the director—"has recently been admitted for dementia and is being savaged by the staff.")

I ask him about Sister Geraldine, his great old friend at the Little Sisters, and he notes how when he'd first examined her seven years before her death, he had noted idiosyncrasies in her thalamus and indeed, "Seven years later, there it was, a tumor, and a horrible one. At first she fought against it, all life rebelling, but during the remission she had come to her terms." (Coming upon these lines in my notes, almost forty years later, I myself momentarily pause at the uncanny foreshadowing.)

"Hmm and hmm," he thrums. "It is so heartening to see the value of performance and play among them, the nuns and the residents alike, and in that context the value of the Mass. I have seen residents so demented they could not string a sentence together who are completely reintegrated and revitalized by the Mass. It's like spiritual dopa."

He is quiet for a few moments, as he negotiates the ramp onto the BQE. "What I love about them is that it *works*. The sisters run dozens of homes, servicing the elderly, all of them supported by begging for produce, for money. Service. Humility. Most of the homes have between eighty and a hundred residents. The ones in the New York City area are unusually large, with around a hundred seventy residents, served by perhaps thirty nuns.

"The United States is divided into three 'provinces.' The mother provincial for the eastern United States happens to live in the Queens home. And I care not only for the patients but also for the nuns who are brought in from all over the province."

At Beth Abraham, for example, he goes on to explain, he dealt only with the very ill, but at the Little Sisters homes, he deals with ill and well both—with the old.

"I love the very old. I love the tales of centenarians. One who complained that a particularly bad blizzard a few years back was nothing compared to the blizzard of '88. And another who told me tales of the flu of 1919."

His favorite home is the one north of Albany, where every resident gets his or her own garden, "which of course reminds me of my aunt's during the war."

A few minutes of silence as, at length, we approach the Whitestone Bridge, and then: "I can't imagine a strike among the Little Sisters."

※

A few weeks later, I meet Oliver at nine fifteen outside his shrink's at Ninety-Third and Park. Just as he emerges from the building, I am coming up the street, and Mark Homonoff, his friend and a fellow neurologist who's just completed an appointment with *his* shrink, is coming across it— we oughta be spies.

On the drive to Bronx State Hospital, Oliver is telling us about Bernie, the patient we are heading out to see, another sudden awakener.

"He was born in 1927, which turns out to have been a clue—that is to say, from the fact that he is fifty-five, I immediately deduced he'd been born in the last year of the influenza-encephalitis outbreak.

"He's a schizophrenic patient who's never had much of a life—a psychotic episode in 1945 at age eighteen—at that time his charts describe 'a tremor in the arms,' which might have been postencephalitic. Except for a brief period when I saw him in 1973, he'd spent almost thirty-five years as a shipping clerk, living at home, barely functioning—that is, until his blowup in 1982, when he was admitted to the hospital.

"He was admitted in an extreme Parkinsonian state, not at first clear why: Haldol-induced or aggravated Parkinsonism? He looked as if he had Parkinson's *disease* rather than a postencephalitic syndrome."

How long had he been on Haldol, wonders Homonoff, but Oliver is not sure. "I'd been asked to see him for his very severe Parkinsonian state—some odd side issues showed up on the EEG, but it was mainly that. Completely frozen, utterly removed. We weren't getting anywhere with L-DOPA or Sinemet. And I must say, I thought he wasn't going to make it—we put him into Ward 22, which is the last stop. As a last resort, we tried bromocriptine."

Oliver interrupts himself to announce that he is now dissatisfied with the letter he dispatched to the *British Medical Journal* on a recent patient's awakening. "A tissue of mendacious simplifications and overdramatizations—as is my whole work, as is the world." I glance at Homonoff in the backseat, who is shaking his head, suppressing a laugh. We both know our Oliver.

"So, at any rate, we were skeptical: He was very, very repressed and regressed."

At this point we were veering off the parkway onto a ramp and then toward a truly desolate urbanscape: Bronx State. "If you doubt the nature of the place," Oliver declares, "note the barbed wire." Across the street, the end-of-the-line yards for the subway trains are indeed surrounded by concertina wire (designed to intimidate graffiti artists, in all fairness). Still, the complex consists of a drab 1950s-ish skyscraper block, an obtruding smokestack, looking like an electric utility plant, or a prison.

Bronx State, the New York Psychiatric Institute, houses 750 to 850 patients. Oliver has been coming here since the same time as he started at Beth Abraham and is currently salaried at eighteen hours per week.

"Building 101 is over there." Oliver points, as we wend around the train yard. "Like Room 101 in *1984*: One cannot say exactly what happens there, one can only say it's the worst thing in the world."

He parks the car, opens the trunk, and pulls out a white coat. "I sometimes wear white here, too," he confesses, "especially when I'm looking even more dilapidated than usual. I've gained forty pounds in three weeks, my trousers are missing buttons . . . Around here I also like to wear a white coat to show that I'm not a psychiatrist, who here function as political messianic figures. I make as though I'm a dermatologist. Curiously, a dermatologist is the most profound doctor at Beth Abraham: He thinks more profoundly about the surface than do others about the depths!"

As we approach the entry, he says, "This Bastille-like key is the key to the wards. We have a number of patients who have developed janitorial psychoses.

"I feel a little embarrassed at your seeing me in this shabby setting."

But he now bursts into his first-floor clinic in an adjoining bungalow. The walls are institutional green, the linoleum gray, fluorescent lights. "They like to keep the temperature here at 114 degrees!" Oliver exclaims as we enter the room. Homonoff veers off on some errands of his own. The nurses all reach for their sweaters, even before Oliver walks across the room to the windows that, one after the other, he bashes open. ("Last week," one nurse laughs, "he pushed one of the windows right off its tracks!") It is about 38 degrees outside. He will see a variety of patients in this morning's clinic (before we go to see Bernie) and each of them in turn will hug their torsos, shiver, and ask whether the doctor isn't just a wee bit cold.

The first patient is a young mildly retarded black child, sloped slouchy shoulders, clear complexion, pell-mell pigtails (she was once abused, I am subsequently informed).

"Incidentally," Oliver comments to me, "they're not called patients anymore, they're called clients. It was felt 'patients' was insulting. I find 'clients' insulting."

She is, it turns out, a thirty-two-year-old child. She wants candy.

Oliver has her draw a face, write her name, identify pictures in the

Arizona Highways he brings along as a diagnostic tool, read—he notes that she needs glasses.

"I good girl?" she asks. Yes.

Now close your eyes and hold your hands out. She does so, as if at a gospel meeting.

He checks her reflexes, rolls his stick along her instep. "Oh! It tickles! Doctor is tickling!"

In answer to a question in the file, Oliver affirms that there are no contraindications to lithium. "In fact, I think there's a great deal of potential here," he tells the aide.

Next comes Mr. O'Connor, a skinny, tense, balding man who's "very desirous of being released." And indeed, nobody can figure out why he's still here. He was seen by both Oliver and Homonoff last week. "Fifty percent of the time my notes go unread," Oliver mutters in exasperation.

The patient answers all questions put to him with echt precision. "I would most assuredly . . ." "I can't say with any exactitude . . ."

It sometimes seems in these clinic exams that Oliver is just floating around, uncertain, confused—in fact, it usually develops that he's playing off the charts, trying to triangulate to the patient's sense of their own condition.

"Will somebody *please* release this fellow," he addresses an aide, after the man is gone.

With the next patient, Oliver's trying to get a sense of her awareness of current events. "I'm stuck here," he whispers to me, "because *I* don't read the papers."

"There was a war," she says, "in Beirut."

"Who's president?"

"Reagan."

"Who was before him?"

"Carter."

"And before him?"

No answer.

"Gerald Ford would be very upset," Oliver comments, "if he knew how often he is forgotten."

She is twenty years old. For months, she took PCP every single day.

"PCP is the one thing I never tried," relates Oliver, addressing me.

"Back in '66, the first time I came in contact with it, I noticed that several of the people who were taking it were convulsive, delirious, wracked with seizures—and even for me that was a bit much."

He now turns to her. "It's pushing it somewhat to take PCP every day," he hazards, tentatively. "Listen, seriously," he continues, "take pot every day but try to limit the PCP to maybe once a month."

To me, once she's gone: "I'm nothing if not a compromiser."

※

The clinic over, Oliver telephones Homonoff to tell him we will now be walking over to Ward 22 to visit with Bernie.

"We'll have to figure out what to do with him," he tells me. "It's unheard of for people to get well from Ward 22. There's usually only one way out of there—it's supposed to be the end of the line."

As we walk down the corridors of other wards, Oliver unlocks doors with his Bastille key, we walk through, he relocks them. "I find this place harder to take than Beth Abraham. The disease model here is not enough: Atrocity has been committed."

※

And now, as Homonoff joins us, we forge into Ward 22: slow-motion bedlam. Pale-skinned derelicts, their hair ratty, pants baggy or legs naked, knees knobby, bruise-blotched (not by maltreatment, I don't think, just derelict limbs), TV beaming its incongruous enthusiasm into the palsied ward, the zombies staring it down.

And over in the corner, between the sofa chairs, one skinny man is arranging pillows on the floor, then stretching out, his feet to the wall, and suddenly launching into push-ups: Bernie.

Red checkered robe, white patterned shirt, gray-green pants.

Now he gets up to greet the doctor and his "colleagues."

And it's true. He is an almanac, a bevy of sports motions. One moment he is shadowboxing ("I throw a thousand punches a day!"), the next he's miming being at bat and explaining how when he was a semipro player it was just at this particular point in his swing that the pitchers could usually get him, but he was good in right field—he mimes scooping up a grounder, then lunges for a high fly over his shoulder. Now he dissolves into football, he's the quarterback receiving the snap from center, faking a handoff, evading a phantom tackler, rearing back for a pass; now he's the receiver downfield, careening into a wall and suddenly dissolving into soccer motions, bouncing a paper wad upon the inside of his heel right down the aisle.

"This was a man," whispers Oliver, "who ten days ago could not lift a finger to feed himself."

The one-man Olympics continues. "I ran a hundred-yard dash in 10.4," he boasts, lining up at the starting line; now he's a long jumper, now a swimmer, now he's steady, dealing cards, now he's moving an imaginative chess piece across a phantom board.

This guy is like Wittgenstein on games!

Oliver and I leave him for a bit (he's now making eyes at a severely catatonic, drooling female patient, curled in a chair in the hall, deep in an Alzheimerian delirium) and go over to talk to the ward chief, a mousy, tense, but kindly, fairly unimaginative bureaucrat.

Oliver asks about the passes Bernie's been making at the women patients.

"The staff find it a bit disconcerting," the ward chief replies. "He finds it paradise.

"But I don't know, doctor," he continues, in utter seriousness, "the thing that bothers me most is that he claims to find the food here delicious. I wonder about his reality testing."

Oliver and the ward chief go on to talk about how Bernie would react were he to be released.

"Here he's king of the hill, or at least cock of the dung heap. What will it be like for him out there?" A question that is left hanging (there will be time to answer it) as we leave.

Ward 22, Oliver explains, as we negotiate the corridors back toward the parking lot, "is a gentler ward—for the disoriented, the victimized."

How do you keep from getting depressed, I ask him.

"I don't know that I do."

But by the patients, I mean, their fates?

"On the contrary," he replies emphatically. "The caretaker in me always brings me round. You remember Bridget, for example, the other day at Little Sisters? She has been subject recently to terrible, spiteful sieges where she hates everyone and everything, the hospital, her nurses, especially herself. 'You mustn't feel awful about feeling awful,' I tried to reassure her. 'These are neurological storms and of no moral import whatever.'"

He pauses, his mind wandering back to my original question. "No," he affirms at length. "Clinical reality, including the direst, never gets me down. Cruelty, though: Ward 23 I vividly couldn't bear, I had to bolt away."

13

Ward 23

Early the following week, Oliver is back in foul temper, work on the Leg book blocked once again. He'd gone up to the Adirondacks and come back, too early.

"Glades." He sighs, rallying one evening over wonton soup at a Chinese place near his house. "Glades and glens are for me an occasion for writing. Auden used to say he needed closed space to write. I do not like wide vistas, being instead drawn to intimate, close-in dioramas—mosses, lichen, plants. The reawakenings of writing for me have usually come by way of new immersions in plant life."

For some reason, our conversation wheels back toward the drama of Ward 23 in 1974, and the "scandal" of "his impermissible success." He'd often alluded to this incident, which took place in the months after his being dismissed from Beth Abraham, and though he'd yet to fill in the details, tonight he seems willing.

Ward 23 at Bronx State Hospital in 1974 was a ward of extremely disturbed youngsters—autistic, catatonic, variously self-destructive or self-absorbed—and "it was a Skinnerian hellhole, run on the strictest behaviorist principles of 'therapeutic punishment' (at any rate I never saw any cases of 'therapeutic reward').

"I, on the other hand, tended to operate on the basis of play, and with two patients in particular, I was able to make contact through play (in one case, the piano, in the other, the garden) where others had failed."

He paused, before resuming with a strange fervor. "You don't choose the patients, in such cases" (I would subsequently understand the stakes), "they choose you."

Which in turn reminded me of something he'd said another time: "My ability to actively sympathize with such patients is related to my ability not to passively identify."

Anyway, two patients there chose Oliver.

"In the case of one of them, Steve, an eighteen-year-old so heavily autistic he'd never uttered a word, I resolved to take him to the Botanical Garden. The staff insisted Steve be *handcuffed* for the outing and I insisted not—eventually the director sided with me, 'Give Sacks a free hand.' Well, Steve did not escape, nor did he erupt into the predicted inevitable violence. Instead, he uttered his first word ever: *dandelion*. The ward staff, when we returned, was black-faced that nothing had gone wrong."

Oliver suddenly turned silent, shaking his head, blocking out the rest of the story; when he resumed, he changed subjects.

"Although I have had a few epiphanies with large animals (most notably a magnificent stag in 1980), I don't much care for squirrels and suchlike. I prefer the undergrowth to the scampering in the undergrowth. I never go to the zoo, even though it's just up the way from the Botanical Garden. I enjoy plant sexuality whereas I somehow disapprove of animal sexuality."

Manitoulin in 1979, he says, had been "a riot of sexuality—the stamens, the ovules, the pistils, the . . ."

Another pause, as he pushes his chopsticks about the recently delivered moo shu pork. "One of my earliest traumatic experiences occurred at age two—I was teasing a dog, cruelly, and he bit back."

At which point his conversation turns to a patient he'd seen that morning.

"This boy is a psychotic who back in 1972, in a frenzy, savagely murdered his girlfriend and then retained no memory of the deed. In 1976 he suffered a terrible head injury, after which, coming to, he was overwhelmed by memories of the murder—which of course is fascinating: We're looking at a case in which, somehow, when the organic basis of repression was damaged or removed, the repression itself ceased and toxic memory returned!"

Does it bother him, treating a murderer?

"Although I am extremely censorious of myself, I am not at all so of others, and he talked with me . . . I wasn't interested in his murder, after all; I was interested in his seizures."

Returning to 1974: "There was an appalling sequel which caused me to leave Ward 23, after which Steve *did* escape and had to be brought down from the Throgs Neck Bridge, a would-be spectacular suicide . . . but it's too horrible to talk about."

Two beats. "I was in a horrible mood again this morning . . . Watering my garden, I imagined myself a prisoner watering his prison garden."

A rising trill: "What's the name of that *Gödel, Escher, Bach* fellow again? Hofstadter. I've become furious with that kind of materialist folly: It gives me the feeling of—what's the word?—well, 'the abomination of desolation.' He's a great fool.

"My first pilgrimage to the United States, out of Canada in 1960, was to Marvin Minsky at MIT. At the time, I stood in awe of the whole AI [artificial intelligence] enterprise. I'd like to visit him again today and attack him. Really. I can't figure out how someone as gifted musically as Minsky can square that with the aspirations of AI.

"Everything to do with AI is Golem-making. (Have you read Scholem on the two Golems?*) It's worse than perverted: It's sinister. Its highest possibility would be toward Pavlov's puppet theater.

"At Ward 23," Oliver returns to his first theme, like one's tongue to an aching tooth, "the best you could aspire to was being a good puppet. And I offered Steve and José, I suppose, the alternative, that of being a *person*.

"There was a head shrink there who established the party line. He was the Vindicator of Vindictiveness.

"But I didn't challenge them—they challenged me, accusing me of introducing license, subverting authority, breaking down respect.

"The whole thing ended horribly, in a manner *not to be talked about*."

Whereupon, he continues to talk about it.

"I had not wanted to come to that Wednesday afternoon's weekly staff conference. The entire ritual reminded me of *Darkness at Noon* at the best of times—horrible, ideological . . . But the whole thing now flared to explosion at the impermissible success of my excursion with Steve, which in just a few moments had disproved fifteen years of diagnoses, treatment, and management.

---

*Gershom Scholem, "The Golem of Prague and the Golem of Rehovoth," *Commentary* 41, no. 1, January 1966. Also in Scholem, *The Messianic Idea in Judaism and Other Essays on Jewish Spirituality* (New York: Schocken Books, 1971).

"And I guess I just lost my cool. After several jibes, instead of walking out, I began shouting, 'There is a love of punishment here which I find highly improper. The head shrink is the vindicator of the staff's vindictiveness . . .' Occasionally a dangerous eloquence can descend over me, and as far as that head shrink was concerned, I'm afraid I wiped the floor with him."

What happened?

"He resigned. On the spot.*

"And that evening, I began writing the first of what came to be twenty-seven essays, the best work I believe I've ever done, all about themes related to Ward 23 . . ."

A pause, more chopsticks stabbing at noodles. "The next week, instead of a patient being brought in for group presentation, I was placed on the chair normally reserved for the patients and subjected to a barrage of barbed innuendo.

" 'Dr. Sacks, we notice that of your six patients, all are white. How come? *Are you some kind of racist, Dr. Sacks?*'

" 'Dr. Sacks, we notice that all of your patients in addition are male. *Do you have difficulty dealing with female patients?*'

"I defended myself, cited obvious counterexamples, alluded to *Awakenings*, where most of the patients are women, insisted that I do not choose them, they choose me—indeed that just recently a new patient had chosen me, a black *girl*, as it happened.

"The following Friday, as I was approaching the ward on my next rounds, the head of the hospital stopped me in the hall. 'I wouldn't go in there if I were you,' he advised me. He was a friend, and he had supported and safeguarded my approach all along.

" 'Why?' I asked.

" 'The place is pullulating with rumors. That you abuse your patients, molest the boys . . .' "

In the midst of this story, the bill and the fortune cookies arrive. Oliver does not so much as notice his cookie. A few minutes later, when we leave, his remains unbroken on the plate—I've never seen a fortune cookie left unbroken on the plate.

---

*Oliver's longtime assistant, Kate Edgar, who'd often heard this tale, subsequently told me that she'd never heard this part about the head psychiatrist resigning on the spot.

"'Look,' the director insisted, 'these people have it in for you.'

"'But this is outrageous,' I stammered. I pointed out to him that just this sort of thing had happened to Ernest Jones. He, too, had had to face preposterous charges that he was abusing his patients, and no one stood up for him.

"My director supported me, but he said, 'Look, that place is a hell-hole, don't go back in there.'

"'*I'd rather cut off my penis than misuse it,*' I insisted.

"In my rage and my desolation that night, I went home and threw the essays, one by one, on the fire."

Out on the street, Oliver takes to recalling some of them. "The first was called 'Key.' It was about something I'd discovered in Ward 23. You see, we had some genuine microcephalics in there, kids with fifty grams for a brain, but there wasn't a single person there who didn't know the significance of a key. Even the autistic kids wagged their hands in a tic by their waist, as if playing with keys! It was an essay, drawing on Gershom Scholem, about the persistence of symbolic comprehension even when conceptual thinking has failed to take root.

"Another was called 'Desire and Delight.' All the essays were about freedom, in a way."

Smiling ruefully, he now summons Hannah Arendt channeling Duns Scotus: "*The delight that will takes in itself when it's not desiring but instead becoming love.*"

He continues: "One by one, I threw them on the fire, and as I did so, I thought of how Pope threw the first part of his *Dunciad* onto the fire, and how Jonathan Swift had been there to pull it out . . . only I didn't have a friend to pull mine out. One by one, I tossed them in and watched them burn. And they were the best things I ever wrote."

Two beats. I ask Oliver if he ever saw *One Flew Over the Cuckoo's Nest.*

"Several times."

We walked on quietly, back toward his house.

"There was a strange sequel to that whole story. One of the higher staff people there at Ward 23, one who had not taken part in the inquisition, was a very dapper, clean-cut behaviorist ideologue (he was especially clean-cut when you, as he regularly did, compared his precise demeanor to my own dilapidation).

"Well, years later, I was walking along a path and I heard a familiar voice, 'Oliver.' I turned to face an utterly dilapidated park denizen, who I only presently realized was him. He told me that he had been horrified by the inquisition to which they'd subjected me and that soon thereafter he himself had quit.

"It turned out all that orderliness had been a defense against his own inherent dishevelment.

"That day, he said to me, 'You're the survivor.' And in some ways, I suppose I am, but precariously, and at a price. I'm inhibited, isolated, haunted, unknown. However, I haven't compromised myself. And although I lie a good deal, it's mostly whimsical. I'm not living a lie, like the vindicator.

"It has been, though, a great and long strain since 1974—not to be moving, not to be writing" (he notes how it was precisely in order to escape the misery of Ward 23 that a few weeks later he had set off for Norway— "I like tundra, the austerity of tundra"—and his fateful encounter with that bull) "although internally perhaps I still am. Moving. Writing."

We pass an ATM and Oliver remembers he needs some cash, though he has to struggle to remember his access code. "Me," he grumbles, "who used to know pi to the thousandth decimal—it took me three months once, to work it out—I can no longer remember a simple four-digit access code."

Later, back at home, he starts rubbing his fingers anxiously. He has recently been worrying about the circulation in his hands. He fears he has Raynaud's disease, "a progressive corpsification of the fingers," as he puts it. After a long swim, his digits will be blanched and he will have no sensation.

Rubbing his hands, he muses about the anguish of hypochondria: "I need to be assured either that something is seriously the matter or that nothing is seriously the matter—either would be better than the endless worrying that something *might* be the matter."

And then, almost literally leaping to a conclusion, he goes on: "I have this grandiose recurrent dream in which I open *The Times* to my own obituary."

14

John the Touretter

There was a time not that many years ago (I'm writing in 2019) when the spectacle of a seemingly ordinary person in the middle of his or her day suddenly yelping or cursing or expostulating in some public place in an extravagant and seemingly uncontrollable manner was thought quite unprecedented, uncanny, unsettling, and frankly scandalous. It's hard to exaggerate how unfamiliar, even unknown, the condition characterized as Tourette's syndrome was in those days, and how misunderstood even when recognized. If that particular social scotoma has in the meantime lifted, as it were—if individuals behaving in such a manner nowadays are understood to be displaying neither willful obscenity nor some demonic curse but rather the effects of a specific neurological condition and accounted for as such—this is in no small measure due to Oliver Sacks's crusading writings and other interventions around the topic. Strange, in that context, how his pioneering work with such individuals presently got all tangled up in one of the most disastrous interactions of his career. But there you go, and there he went.

※

Over those years, in conversations with Oliver, an impinging presence almost as fraught as that of his blighted sexuality was the shadow cast by the still-smarting wreckage of a round of therapy with one patient in particular, the super-Touretter who I will call John. Splintered shards of the story would come up now and then (usually accompanied by a darkening glower and a veritable physical shudder), allusions proliferated, but I'd never gotten the full story. One day, as we sat on his back deck in City Island, I asked Oliver about it point-blank.

He was silent for a few moments, tapping his pen against the top of the red wooden picnic table. "Ah yes, the disastrous paranoic affair between John the Touretter and myself." Tap, tap, tap, after which he stuffed the pen in his shirt pocket and sighed. "I never had another relationship quite like it," he said at length. "It occupied my every Saturday for eighteen months."

Had it been his first intensive interaction with a Touretter?

"Actually not. So-called Ray, by which I mean the man I'd subsequently write about as 'Witty Ticcy Ray,' was my first Touretter back in 1971, though my piece about him only ran in the *London Review* ten years after that, in 1981. As you'll recall, 1971 was still in the middle of the busiest period of Awakenings for me. I suppose some of the wild reactions we were seeing among the postencephalitics there at Beth Abraham during the Tribulation period may have sensitized me into beginning to notice correlative sorts of behavior in the everyday wider world and wondering about those, such that by April 1974, I'd begun attending meetings of the Tourette Syndrome Association (the TSA), which were all wonderfully strange, what with their roomfuls of Touretters." A blue jay went swooshing through Oliver's backyard. "A blue jay would fly by *there* and his chirp would instantly get repeated, involuntarily, by thirty people all over the room.

"I met John at one such TSA meeting in October 1975." (This would have been a year after the Ward 23 blowup and the ensuing trip to Norway with its leg accident.) "He just came up to me, presented himself temptingly, grandiosely, masochistically, seductively, declaring 'I am the greatest Touretter in the world'—and indeed he was ticcing and contorting and gesticulating and stuttering all the while in the most outlandish ways—'I can teach you more about Tourette's than any book. You will never meet another Touretter like me. *I am the last thing in Tourette's!*' Perhaps he'd read *Awakenings* or been impressed by my contributions at the meetings. Perhaps he'd picked me out as imaginative, unorthodox, hospitable to the very strange.

"At any rate, he wooed me, though I was prepared to be wooed. I in turn brought an intellectual range and an empathic connection which delighted him, gratified him, and perhaps finally terrified him." Now Oliver was tapping absentmindedly with his fingers, gazing out into the distance. "These strange infatuations—or squabbles—these folies à deux where two people become the world for each other. What can one say?"

What did John do for a living?

"He worked in an office job at one of the South Jersey school boards. He used to teach, loved teaching, but was transferred: It was said the children were frightened of his behavior; more likely the parents were."

And his family background?

"John had been struck by how many of his co-Touretters had had overpowering fathers, and John's father was indeed a piece of work. The entire family was Tourettic: A brother had multiple tics with convulsiveness, while the father had the opposite. John's sister was the white sheep of the family and was almost discriminated against for her *lack* of afflictions. His whole life must have been a flight between the grotesque impression of Tourette's and the 'real person' under the Tourette's. But it was indeed just as he said: He *did* display extraordinary virtuosity. Indeed, he had been *compelled* into virtuosity.

"Later, when we began doing videotapes, looking at them afterwards, the 'real' John would remind me of a Rembrandt portrait, all his other iterations of an Al Capp cartoon cavalcade. He would come to the rented place where I was living in Mount Vernon at the time, where I'd mounted a bizarre labyrinth of cameras, mics, and monitors—"

Was he coming as a patient, or what?

"Well, he paid fifty dollars per session, of which his insurance covered eighty percent. Every Saturday, he was subject to, and a virtuoso at, *inspired drivel*. It fascinated me through many weeks, and for hundreds of hours, to hear, see, witness, and record his witty ticcy raving. And I felt intensely privileged."

Had they been aiming at some sort of cure?

"Well, relatively early on we exhausted the possibilities of drugs. John had had negative experiences with Haldol, but at a certain point, we decided to try Haldol again . . . And I think I almost killed him . . .

"My sixth sense had told me he might be incredibly sensitive, so I gave him an incredibly small dose, at which point he went into a coma! I got him to come back to. But it was really scary. He was then tic-free for five hours, but dulled, and then suddenly the tics just came back. It *had* been intriguing to see him tic-free. So this was a real mixture of things: With Haldol, for instance, it proved impossible to find an intermediate dose between no effect and nearly killing him. And the same sort of thing played out with other possible drugs, and eventually it was clear to both of us that due to the severity of his condition, chemotherapy of any sort was out. So medicine had failed.

"After that, we'd start each session with current problems and ascend toward general themes. Our working hypothesis was that the tics formed a kind of hieroglyphics, a pantomimic language with kinship to dreams whose meaning was clear to no one, least of all to the ticer. My bedside reading at the time were Freud's *The Interpretation of Dreams* and *Jokes and Their Relation to the Unconscious*, and indeed I sometimes wondered whether Freud had felt just like this as the secrets of dreaming were beginning to be vouchsafed to him. I still think Tourettic tics occupy a space between jokes and dreams. That they are reactions to both internal and external stimuli.

"Other aspects of things didn't feel Freudian so much as Lurian. So I sent an audiotape to Luria as a Christmas present in 1975. I still wonder what the cryptanalysts at the KGB must have made of the tape as it crossed their desks—but somehow it got through. And Luria said he'd never encountered such unselectivity of action, that it reminded him of Brownian motion: an extraordinarily funny, grotesque performance that at the same time transpired at the *roots* of both psychodynamics and neurodynamics.

"Later on, after everything had collapsed, I will say this: In all his raging and ranting, to the very end John would grant that I had spoken about him with Luria, and that somehow still really mattered."

The blue jay came arcing back into the yard, and Oliver smiled at its passage and erupted into a manic cacophony of chirps and tweets of his own, by way of greeting.

"For a long time," he continued, "I thought John had in himself the sensibilities of a naturalist and a novelist, but I may have been projecting. He'd come upon a phrase in a Balzac novel—'I can carry a whole society in my head'—and he insisted, 'So can I! In pantomime. Does that mean,' he'd go on to ask, 'that I could be an artist?' I told him the perception would first have to be disembedded from the mime.

"He had all sorts of fantasies as to what he wanted to be—lover, artist, warrior, explorer. As I say, initially he hadn't presented himself as a patient but rather as a specimen, a teacher.

"As often happens with exotic diseases, perhaps there was a sort of ambivalence in both him and me. 'You wouldn't take any interest in me if I didn't tic,' he'd say. 'I'd just be an average bright guy, whereas I'm the great-est teacher in the world!' (My brother Michael, too, sometimes speaks of 'rotten normality.') And there may have been something to that, because from the very start ours was a flawed relationship, like a bad affair: We had different perceptions of what we were about, as in natural history ver-sus an ambivalently desired cure. (I wonder how much this sort of thing arose with Freud in the early investigative days of psychoanalysts.) At first I imagined we would indulge and even encourage the pathology and phys-iology of Tourette's until we had plumbed it—but then we would some-how move on."

A long pause, the fingers tapping. "Early in 1976, a woman reporter from *The Philadelphia Inquirer* somehow got wind of John's situation and decided to do a feature on him, and she taped four hours with me. Gradu-ally, however, I began to recognize a second gleam in her eye: There was the gleam of pure interest, yes, but also the gleam of the scoop. When I saw that, a bit late, I said, 'Look, all of this is tentative, many of these thoughts are just ideas I'm playing with, some would be disquieting to publish—in particular one, two, three, and four . . .' She assured me she'd only be using a couple of lines and that she'd show me a draft. She never did. Her two lines became two pages, with one, two, three, and four as the major points, and my words recrafted in such a way that I became an obscene voyeuristic doctor grafted onto and exploiting a patient who was trapped in an endless dirty joke. She lied, sensationalized, did great damage."

Did John see the piece?

"John saw it, *everybody* saw it. You could not walk the streets of New York City in late February 1976 without tripping over it! At that point, though, John and I were still okay, things hadn't yet soured, we agreed *The Philadelphia Inquirer* incident had been unfortunate, but we let it go.

"In response to my anxiety about its forthcoming publication, how-ever, and then its actual publication, I wrote the first draft of a piece called 'Humean and Human Being' in which I referred to John as 'Motley,' hence 'M,' and keyed off of Hume's notion that we are nothing but a bundle of sensations succeeding one another with inconceivable rapidity, that any co-herent sense of personhood is hence a sort of overarching fiction, a state of affairs that may or may not be the case on average but was almost literally the case with someone like M who in that sense existed at a sort of philosophical extremity.*

"I concluded the piece with quotes from Luria's *Mind of a Mnemonist* ('Waiting, always waiting for something') and Scholem's *Major Trends in Jewish Mysticism* ('The Messianic leads to a life lived in deferment'). And indeed, I ended up wondering whether John would ever take the plunge."

It was in here, as well, Oliver noted, that he began to conceive of his own "five seconds" book—a project he might still like to pursue, if necessarily now with someone else—the high-speed recording of a Touretter ticcing and expostulating in such a way that the tape could be slowed down to reveal a veritable universe of gestures, the one related to the next, and what was provoking each, all as revealed in five seconds of tape.

As with that van Eyck postcard, the sheer compression of experience, I hazarded. "Precisely," Oliver concurred.

Oliver's thoughts about the intelligibility and interpretability of tics, though, had in the almost a decade since become more nuanced than that, as was revealed to me a few days later when I received a long, typewritten letter he'd composed a few hours after I'd left. To wit (selected passages):

> [As for your question] about the "meaning" of tics, John's in particular, about which I have expressed myself contradictorily. I again thought about this—in conversation with Mark [Homonoff] (we took off to Lake Jeff.† For a day)—but have forgotten what I thought. A tic is *convulsive*—this term is repeatedly used by Gilles de la Tourette—but it may be a convulsion (so to speak) of the Will or Passions or Imagination. This confers feeling and meaning *of a sort*, although it may be a sort which is essentially absurd.
>
> Thus, although one might suppose that every tic, or most tics, had "meaning," this was communicated cryptically if it

---

*Over the ensuing years, true to its Humean metaphor, Oliver's piece went through a whole series of alternative titles—"The Man with a Thousand Faces," "The Man with the Iridescent Mind," "The Man Who Was Simultaneously Everything and Nothing," and "The Man with the Faceted World" (the "Faceted" in that last of course being a pun on Luria's "Shattered")—none of which, as things turned out, would ever see the light of publication.

†Lake Jefferson, in Sullivan County, New York, near the Pennsylvania border, was one of Oliver's favorite swimming holes.

was communicated at all (in this way like dreams—but less coherent: delirium, perhaps . . . or like the wayward, arbitrary associations of the Luria's *Mnemonist*). [. . .]

[With John,] there was a peculiar vocal tic, an ejaculation, a crushed sound, which with "tape-stretching" and repeated playing, finally revealed itself as an admonition (in the German his father used to use) . . . *Verboten!* Followed by a lightning quick slap of the hand. I included this, I think, in the tape-segment I sent Luria.

On the one hand tics are jerks, convulsive movements; but in a ticcer like John, they can become a sort of (hieroglyphic) "language" as well . . . though a language which defeats the purpose of language by failing to communicate. [. . .]

Thus there *is*, and is not "meaning" in tics . . .

I am tired, I can't think, I am blathering . . . I fear I have confused you, or myself, more than ever. I had best stop.[SB]

"As you could see from that letter," Oliver admitted a few days later when I returned to City Island and we resumed our conversation about what happened with John, "nowadays I'm somewhat more mixed in my own mind between thinking of tics as superficial and as unfathomably deep.

"Back then, though, I was filming everything, *using up all my savings*" (just as earlier he had with the postencephalitics, it occurred to me). "And at a certain point, after so many Saturdays in the office, I began to feel that maybe I'm indulging this man and myself too much. Furthermore, I began to get bored with his repertoire of tics, just as one gets bored with any repertoire. In a way it was like, 'Okay, we've had fun, but enough now, let's try to shape up.' But every word I said along these lines he turned into tics.

"In part as a way of transcending this impasse, we decided to leave the confines of the office. He would get so ticcy describing interactions in the world, and particularly how he was received in the world, that it occurred to me it might be better just to go out with him to observe and record things in person. Perhaps we made a mistake when we abandoned the doctor's office for the outside world, for this anthropological field-work, as it were. But had we not, I might not have come to appreciate, for example, his deep love of animals: He was a ticcy Saint Francis who found all animals his brothers and sisters.

"Indeed, much more so than actual people." Oliver sighed, pausing. "One of the sinister things was that so personable a man had neither friends nor girlfriends," Oliver continued, before correcting himself. "Actually, that's not entirely true: He did have one girlfriend for a while with whom he had a terrifically complex relationship."

At any rate, the videotaping project was becoming too expensive. "Of the $10,000 I'd started with, I only had $2,000 left," Oliver related. "I'd actually spoken with a few anthropological filmmakers to see if they might like to come on board, but they all wanted too much money. So I wrote to my old friend Duncan Dallas at Yorkshire Television, describing the situation in detail, initially asking about the possibility of a grant. Whereupon, Duncan came over to see for himself, agreed that it was incredible, and though I can't remember whether the impulse came from John, Duncan, or me, at a certain point we all agreed: 'Let's do it, let's make a film together!'

"I should clarify, because from the start, Duncan, like me, also had his ambivalences. But it was almost as if we were fated from the beginning to bring John into the public realm—and in so doing to destroy everything. For now—filming took place in February 1977—things really began to intrude into John's life. The film crew were very much in his face, continuously, deploying telephoto lenses and the like—this was now indeed becoming the very stuff of paranoia.

"And no sooner had filming been completed with the crew heading back to England, than the very next day, John came into my office and showed me his 2,002nd face: acutely paranoid, in a blind fury—accusing me of having betrayed him, and so forth.

"We suspended our meetings for a while, indeed through the summer, though Duncan and John stayed in touch. At various points Duncan and I thought about shelving the entire project, but somehow it continued to stumble along. At one point Duncan wondered whether the act of being involved in the editing might not in itself have been an affirming, integrating experience for John, and he urged him to come over to England to take part, but John refused. In the end, it took over ten months for Duncan and his team to edit the program, but it was finally shown on English TV in February of 1978."

Unlike the *Awakenings* documentary of a few seasons earlier, which had aired to near-universal praise, this one received mixed reviews, and even some quite unfavorable ones which spoke of a doctor exploiting his patient—reviews which, by a terrible error in judgment, were all sent to John. ("He also received a barrage of mail, including proposals of friendship and even marriage.") But the net effect of this sudden upsurge in attention, Oliver explained, "is that John began leaving messages on my machine (by this point, there'd already been a year's break in our in-person meetings) reminding me ominously of Gilles de la Tourette's own fate—as you may know, Tourette, the first to have described the condition, back in the late nineteenth century, ended up murdered by one of his own patients.

"Presently we were brought together on neutral ground, as it were, in a psychiatrist colleague's office, alongside Sheldon Novick, the medical director of the TSA, and though we all agreed the film should and would never be shown over American television, John seemed to show himself agreeable to the film's exhibition before limited audiences. And I thought this signaled a kind of peace.

"Not long afterwards, though, he retracted the agreement, complaining that it had been achieved, as he put it, 'under medical duress.' No, he insisted, he was not happy. 'If you ever do try to show it,' he insisted, 'I want to be there to monitor what you say!' As a result of which, I have been more secretive than he'd have ever wished: I've shown it to at most half a dozen friends. He meanwhile became more and more obsessed with his own videotape copy, compulsively showing it to himself over and over again.

"The thing is, he *was* extremely ambivalent. I think he'd have liked it if I'd shown the film before the entire AMA, after which he could have emerged from backstage, proclaiming, 'The film is as nothing compared with the real thing!'

"Meanwhile, between the filming and the British TV showing of our film, another film was being gotten up by another director who'd wanted to include John and me, along with others. 'No,' John had huffed. 'What need have I of you? I am the star of my own film!' In the event, that film, *The Sudden Intruder*, featuring a fellow named Orrin, was eventually adopted as the official TSA film. At which point John really got angry, insisting that 'our film' was much better and more human than the other. That one was competent, but ours was remarkable!

"At our very last meeting, as we were still trying to sort this whole thing out, John shouted that all along I'd only been obsessed with his private life. 'I'm a naturalist,' I'd shouted back, 'not a voyeur. I don't give a damn about your private life!'

"But the next day Shengold observed, with his typically cutting intelligence, 'Don't you see? You *were* his private life.'"

✳

Going home that evening, I decided to dig back into my notes from my conversation with Duncan Dallas in London—as it happens that conversation had not been taped, but I reproduce these observations from my notes at the time. After we'd spoken at some length about Dallas's *Awakenings* collaboration with Oliver, in closing I'd asked him about the Tourette's film.

"Around 1975, Oliver told me, 'I have a new and very interesting patient I'm not going to tell you any more about.' Six months later, though, he told me of this new patient, John, who was in his own words 'a super-Touretter.' And Oliver intimated that he might indeed make for an interesting film.

"So I went back over to the States to meet John, and once again, it was the same thing. Here was this chap who, if you and I met him, we'd probably just say that the guy has a lot of problems, maybe averting our gaze and doubtless moving on as quickly as possible with the rest of our day. But Oliver had imagined himself into this fellow's situation—perhaps even a bit too much for John's comfort, as things developed. A question does arise as to the degree to which one owns one's own disease.

"Beyond that, you know how if you happen upon an epileptic in the midst of his fit, you grow frightened for *yourself*. Well, John had been having to deal with that sort of reaction to his condition all of his life, and it must have been very distressing, such that the prospect of being filmed was perhaps too much to expect John to come to terms with.

"But he insisted that he'd be happy and indeed more than happy to be filmed, so we decided to proceed with the project. Still, for various extraneous reasons, we had to put off the actual shoot for another six months, and by the time we came back, things had grown distinctly more difficult: John had in a way fallen in love with Oliver, or was it vice versa? And yet at the same time John had come to understand that Oliver was never going to be able to 'cure' him and that he was going to have to face the same old challenges for the rest of his life. In his disappointment, he began to see Oliver as just another doctor experimenting on him. And a strange dynamic seemed to have developed within him of rampant suspiciousness laced with equally rampant exhibitionism.

"Filming was difficult, and two or three times we thought of giving the whole project up. For one thing, John was entirely different depending on whether the camera was on or off, overacting as it were in either direction: At lunch he'd be completely wild and wonderful and very very funny, but the minute we turned the camera back on he became reserved, restrained, and seemed able to enforce a kind of momentary calm upon himself. Meanwhile, the good stuff we were getting was of Oliver, though even there, it seemed much more difficult than it had been with the *Awakenings* film, since he hadn't yet really sorted things out in his own mind and here we were right on top of him as he was endeavoring to do so. It was all so raw, which was enthralling for us, if difficult for him.

"Still, the final film was very interesting. We showed it over the television here in England, but if the *Awakenings* film had been very well received, this one was not so much: Critics attacked its snooping quality. And yet it did have an impact, and people do remember it.

"Then we went over to show it to Oliver and John, and initially things went okay. John seemed happy with it. But with the passing days, John grew increasingly angry and presently very, very nasty—to Oliver more so than to us. He accused him of using earlier videotapes that they had made together that were supposed to have remained private, even though he'd known of our intention to use them all along, but he now insisted he'd never agreed to that and as a result he was going to report Oliver to the relevant psychological associations and so forth. The kind of overreaction that if you are in television, you learn to shrug off and move on, but Oliver couldn't.

"I think John couldn't handle the fact that the camera in the end didn't pull the wool over anyone's eyes, and that it made evident the way treatment as such wasn't going to lead to a cure. And he lashed out. Oliver, in turn, turned completely neurotic, obsessing over the way Tourette himself had ended up being shot by one of his own patients. Oliver insisted that we not now and not ever allow the film to be shown in America 'or I'll be killed,' he said—which was fine with us. We agreed, of course, not to distribute it to the States, though eventually, apparently, relatively recently, it did show up once late at night on some cable outlet as part of some package deal, and though John didn't bother us, he did apparently vent at Oliver, and the whole thing boiled up all over again. We took pains to make sure it wouldn't happen again, but still . . .

"Which of course is all quite dismaying. Not only on its face but also because for Oliver to write, conditions have to be just right, he has to be at peace."

Pausing for a moment, Dallas concluded: "Often as you spend the post-production hours editing a big project, you become disillusioned with its subject, you come to see through them, but that never, ever happens with Oliver. He stops your life—just as he's quite prepared at any moment to stop his own."

✳

The next time I went to City Island, I asked Oliver if I could watch the video of the documentary, and he set me up in a little alcove in his basement storage area while he returned to his own work upstairs.

Frankly, I was shocked. Far from being in any way insensitive or exploitative or even discomfiting, the documentary (a part of the wider *A Change in Mind* series entitled "What Makes You Tic?") was heartfelt, charming, and intensely sympathetic to both John and Oliver. It was hard to see how anyone could have been offended or disconcerted, least of all its principals, the mutual respect and high regard and indeed pleasure they and the filmmakers were so clearly taking in each other being evident in every frame.

At one point, for example, they were all watching an earlier video from Oliver's private stash on a TV monitor, in which John can't stop tapping and poking and prodding the table mic, even though he knows he's not supposed to and has repeatedly been asked not to. He just can't help himself, he declares impishly, with Oliver guffawing in the background, behind the camera. How much of that behavior, one hears Oliver ask John, does he think is just meaningless *it*, and how much of it is *you*, such that it may stand for something? To which the John on the monitor answers, "I was going to ask *you* that!" At which point the John outside the monitor, watching the previously videotaped exchange, averred how it had been *as* incredible for him to watch as it would have been for anyone without Tourette's.

"There's a who and there's a what," Oliver speculates, "and in some ways they are separate and yet they are inseparable, they've grown up together."

"May I interrupt here," John interrupts, at which point he goes on to note how when he sleeps, he never dreams of himself as ticcing. Everything he does—playing tennis, skiing, being with a girl—he does well. And when he then wakes up, for a few moments that dream reality persists; he is calm, becalmed, content, still. "And sometimes I actually laugh to myself, thinking of myself and how I will be just a few minutes later on, making noises, making screeches, having tics and mannerisms, being looked at by people. And I laugh to myself in a genuine fashion of laughing, out loud, because I think . . . *That's not me.*"

Later on, as the camera follows the doctor and his patient on various drives and walks around town (John driving, biting the steering wheel and steering with his teeth, interacting extravagantly with passing pedestrians, whooping and pumping, putting on quite a show; the two of them traipsing through Times Square or Central Park), Oliver in a voice-over describes how, on the one hand, "John has the most incredible empathy and resonance and power to feel, indeed *to be* what other people are, and also what other nonhuman wild creatures are." (We see John playing with a passing squirrel.) "But by being everybody and everything," Oliver continues, "at the same time, he may be nothing, he may be taken out of himself and out of the possibility of being an individual because he is everybody else."

On camera, John keeps darting about, at a bagel stand in the park ("Mistuh," a kid comes up to him, "you got the fastest reflexes I ever seen—how come you got such fast reflexes?"), later at Katz's Delicatessen, where he teases the countermen and attracts the drop-jawed attention of fellow diners with his nonstop carnivalesqueries (Oliver off camera, guffawing all the while with fondness and delight and almost palpable pride). In another voice-over, Oliver notes how just plain funny and witty John is, how "he can be outrageous without outraging, his use of exhibition being like ours of inhibition. His associations are instant, sudden, surprising, immediate, without the usual deliberation, and as such they can be very remarkable."

There is a good deal of conversation about whether the triggers for such associations are external or internal. At one point, Oliver relates how on an earlier videotape, there'd come a moment when John tumbled through "a hiss, a hoot, and a twitter one after the other in quick succession" and how it was only subsequently, playing back the tape in slow motion, that Oliver was able to determine that "the hiss had been preceded by a blast of escaping radiator steam, the hoot by a car horn passing, and the twitter by a passing bird outside." On the other hand, John himself relates a story about how back in college, cramming for a test, the image of black church-goers raising their hands up to heaven and shouting "Help me, Lawd, Lawd, help me now!" came into his head and almost instantaneously transmogri-fied into repeated arm-flailing tics of his own, punctuated by compressed "Help me, Lawd" shouts, which went on for a good part of the rest of the evening.

At another point, as John grows ever more intent upon a fierce game of Ping-Pong, his tics just seem to melt away. "One sees that he is happi-est and most free and most himself, most at ease and most at home in various forms of play," Oliver observes. "This might be playing with a squirrel, playing ball, playing guitar, he is full of fun, and indeed, the various forms of play are what bring him together."

At times Oliver's observations seemed to turn wistfully self-referential—doctor and patient seeming to blur into each other. "One can only find one's repose and one's resolution in embracing arms," he com-mented at one point, "whether it's the arms of one's woman or one's muse, of Mother Earth or nature, or of the Source of Everything . . . Now in a sense this problem can become particularly intense [for individuals with especially pronounced cases of Tourette's], and the way John has it is something that in a way excommunicates and exiles and alienates and estranges him, but at the same time gives him such a sense of the rich-ness of life, as I think few people can have. Such that in one sense, para-doxically, he has so much life, and in another way he has so little."

A bit further on, Oliver confesses: "And yet as his physician, I can't give him a life. There are and will be no magic pills, and this has meant John has had to renounce certain messianic expectations. But by the same token, alongside the disappointment and the anger, together we are be-ginning to investigate all sorts of other ways of making life better and more interesting. And he is becoming more active in all of this, less passive, less of a patient and more of an agent."

As the film coursed to its conclusion, Oliver offscreen against the back-drop of a medley of sequences of John alone, making his way in the world, pulled many of these themes together one last time. "This is a man who is faced with too many possibilities. He is not simply at a crossroads; there are thousands of roads. And there's a question as to whether there's any point at which these thousands of radii all meet. I think they do meet, at least temporarily, as we have seen, in play, but as for the greater question as to what role he should play in the world, what is the role which *is* him, he doesn't know, such a thing cannot be prescribed, it can only be found . . . he has to find his own home—and I can only hope that he will."

After which the filmmakers return to the car for the final sequence, with John driving. If we asked you for the last word on Tourette's, they inquire, what would it be?

"You want it?" John shoots back.

Yeah, they say, we do, go ahead.

"That was it," John says, breaking into a smile. "Do you want Tourette's? Take mine! You want it, *you can have it.*"

※

After finishing the video, I tramped upstairs to tell Oliver that far from seeming charged or guilt-ridden, the film was lovely and loving and grace-flecked, filled with fellow feeling and fine regard. What on earth had happened?

"The absence of distance both made the illumination possible and made the subsequent intimacy terrifying," Oliver suggested, the blowup—half a decade past at that point—seemingly as vivid as if everything had just occurred yesterday. "You have to understand, the man is close to insane with ambivalence."

Speaking of which, though, Oliver too seemed almost as hamstrung over the prospect of any future book on Tourette's as he had been, for much of the past eight years, over the Leg book that he was only now verging on concluding. The John impasse still had him paralyzed: so much research material with no way to deploy it.

"For a while I thought I could just shift details—his name, the location of our conversations, his age, his gender. He positively loathed the word 'freak' and out of perversity I'd sometimes entertained the fantasy of calling the book *Freak*. More recently, I've been considering chopping him up into twelve distinct pieces, as if profiling twelve different individuals in the context of a cavalcade of several other such Tourettic portraits.

"Hmmm," he grunted, and "hmmm.

"Look at this." He suddenly reached for an old volume he'd recently been perusing: *Tics and Their Treatment*, the translation by Kinnier Wilson (his mother's teacher) of a French text from 1905, *Les tics et leur traitement* by Henry Meige and E. Feindel, a volume which included "Confessions of a Ticcer," a memoir by a patient identified as O.

Flipping through the pages, alighting on one passage and another, I couldn't help but notice the richness of O's and the authors' Victorian/Edwardian language, so obviously an influence on Oliver's own: "The absurdity of this vicious circle does not escape my observation, and I know I am its author, yet that cannot prevent my becoming its victim"; "I cannot withstand the allurement or banish the sentiment of unrest"; "abandoning himself in his moment of solitude to a veritable debauch of absurd gesticulations, a wild muscular carnival, from which he returns comforted, to resume sedately the thread of the interrupted dialog"; "he is capable of sympathies keenly felt though rarely sustained." The vocabulary! The cadences!

And then this, an extended passage that, it occurs to me, could as well apply to Oliver at times as to John:

> Alike in speaking and in writing O. betrays an advanced degree of mental instability. His conversation is a tissue of disconnected thoughts and uncompleted sentences; he interrupts himself to diverge at a tangent on a new train of ideas—a method of procedure not without its charms, as it frequently results in picturesque and amusing associations. No sooner has he expressed one idea in words than another rises in his mind, a third, a fourth, each of which must be suitably clothed; but as time fails for this purpose, the consequence is a series of obscure ellipses which are often captivating by their very unexpectedness.*

I now suggested how this might constitute a solution to Oliver's own Tourette's book problem—that is, revise this text with a foreword of his own on Victorian medicine and an afterword on Tourette's, incorporating his John the Touretter material, the entire thing to be published exclusively in France!

---

*Henry Meige and E. Feindel, *Les tics et leur traitement*, trans. S.A.K. Wilson (New York: William Wood and Company, 1907), 4, 5, 10, 21, 17.

Oliver laughed. "Aye," he said, sighing, "the problem of the ongoing existence in the world of one's subjects." At which point I laughed. And he laughed at me, all the harder.*

We both subsided. I now wondered aloud as to what Oliver would think of my trying to contact John. He hesitated, asked me to give him a few days to think about it.

And a few days later, he telephoned to say he'd talked the matter over with his shrink, Shengold, and the two had agreed that if I wished to approach John as a neutral party reporting on how I was moved by the film, that would be okay; or if I wished to approach him in the form of a neutral inquiry in the context of a profile of Sacks, that, too, would be okay; but if I imagined myself to be arranging any sort of reconciliation, that would be out of the question.

"I don't know how much you know about paranoids, how naïve you are," Oliver continued, pausing, considering. "I suspect what you might get would be an odd mixture of wistfulness, outrage, sadness, and spite . . . or he might blame it all on the film."†

There were a few more moments of silence on the line, then a long sigh. "Oomph," he concluded. "It's a pity such a wonderful disease was visited upon such a terrible person."

---

*Oliver would finally manage to slide a reference to John into a radically condensed version of his "Humean and Human Being" essay, recast under the title "The Possessed," that he would include in *The Man Who Mistook His Wife for a Hat* a few years later, recasting him as "a grey-haired woman in her sixties" he claims to have happened upon one day, "frantically" resonating her way down a city block, "convulsively" imitating everyone and everything in sight.

†In the event, for reasons that will become clear, I never did call on John. But I did subsequently produce a Talk of the Town piece for *The New Yorker*, entitled "MOMA When It's Jerking," April 10, 1995, 34.SB

PART II

How He Was
(the Passing Months)

15

The Blockage Begins to Break (1982–1983)

Early November 1982

One afternoon, Oliver calls me, wistful.

"A few weeks ago, I thought I had leukemia and it was quite wonderful. As you may have noticed, I've been dieting; I'd lost sixty pounds since my last checkup and the doctor said he wanted to take another blood test, mentioning that a few months earlier my red blood cell count had been low, that it was surely just a question of my not having eaten but . . .

"Anyway, between the two halves of that sentence, for a few fractions of a second, I was absolutely certain not only of having leukemia but that I had only three months to live. 'At last,' I found myself thinking, 'I'll be rid of my inhibiting neuroses and I'll be able to write all the books I have backed up in me.'

"Like Luria, who had a massive heart attack and yet lived on one further year during which he wrote four books, forty articles—more than he had the previous fifty years—and all of it calm, lucid, sparkling clean, nothing rushed . . . for a split second, I saw them all tumbling clear: The Tourette's book, the five-second book, the homes and institutions book, the Leg book, the dementia book . . . all in the wake of the wonderful death threat."

A pause. Two beats.

"And then the doctor finished his sentence."

﹡

A few days later our conversation turns to the shoddiness of modern living—Oliver is obsessed by the shoddiness of his leased car and of his treatment at the hands of the huge computerized alienated leasing firm.

"At root," he insists, "the problem is that of the hegemony of the computer model for thinking and organizing. People don't think like . . . or rather they start thinking like computers, and computers *can't* think. [Douglas] Hofstadter's wrong: The essential point is that a computer cannot *judge*; any attempt at judgment by a computer involves a loop of infinite regress—a program to judge the program judging the program, etc. Whereas, precisely what humans have is a *mind*, a *soul*, which puts a stop to regress and takes a *stand*. Someone needs to finish Arendt's work, the essential piece—thinking, willing . . . *judging!*"

Indeed.

He should.

November 10

Following another week in the Adirondacks, Oliver has finally broken through (once again): He has returned with a completed manuscript on the convalescence, the conclusion of the Leg book.

He is chipper: Already he is percolating. He is eager to start work on his dementia book, one which he would like to call, in homage to Arendt, *The Death of the Mind.*

November 15

He continues chipper. At a book fair in Boston, shadowing his antiquarian pal Eric, he finds a copy of Sir Henry Head's book on neurology (eight hundred pages). Head is, as Oliver puts it, "one of the grandfathers"—he was a teacher of his parents and was in fact Jonathan Miller's father's teacher as well. At any rate, Head in the early years of the last century intentionally severed a nerve in his arm to observe the process of recuperation, and Oliver naturally identifies his leg with Head's arm. He has started a postscript to the Leg book on this theme, which I joshingly suggest he title "From Head to Toe."

November 21

At dinner this evening, Oliver, starting out again from Head, reverts to describing his frantic return to London at the peak of the Awakenings drama, in August 1969, to catch his breath and try to put his thoughts in order, and how he'd indeed proceeded to tap out the first nine case studies of what would eventually become, several years later, the book *Awakenings*. (Evenings he would read the developing chapters to his mother.)

"But it was strange," he recounted, "because at the very same moment that I was drafting the most affirmative and generous of case histories, I was also contriving the most constricting, strangulating theory of experience: the culmination of my flirtation with mechanistic theory.

"Over the previous year, right alongside everything else that had been going on, I'd allowed myself to become beguiled by the work of Jerzy Konorski, a Polish physiologist whose book *Integrative Activity of the Brain*, published in 1967, was said to exist at the meeting place of Sherrington, Pavlov, and Freud. All through '68 and into '69, I was fascinated by this theory of drives and anti-drives, by the power of a scheme of simplification. And I amplified this fascination with an obsessive elaboration of my own, filled with schemas and arrows and diagrams.

"I'd forgotten all about this, but Mark* came upon some of my diagrams from those days while looking for something else downstairs amidst my files the other day, and declared them 'far along on the road to insanity.'

"Finally, though—there in London, 200,000 words into this grotesque Pavlovian folly, the torso of a massive overarching theory of human behavior—the project fell apart of its own weight.

"It was something like what happened to Wittgenstein when he was confronted by his friend's question, 'Oh yeah, well, what is the logical structure of *this* gesture?,' whereupon the entire propositional calculus fell apart and he fell from his early philosophy right through to his later work.

"My own drive scheme could accommodate everything except peacefulness, enoughness, satiety, repletion—these were totally off its (and my) path. And so the whole thing imploded.

"Thankfully. Mercifully."

Chuckling now, marveling, almost disbelieving, Oliver notes, "Some years later I wrote of Luria that he'd been a Pavlovicidal Pavlovian. To which he replied, 'That isn't true of me, but it may have been true of you.'"

For some reason this gets me talking to Oliver about Sartre.

---

*His colleague Mark Homonoff.

December 2 (phone conversation)

"I have been reading a library copy of *Being and Nothingness*, as you urged me to, and find it by turns maddeningly good and maddeningly repellent. I must get a copy of my own so I can go through and underline the good sentences—or rather, cross out the bad."

(Which he indeed presently proceeds to do, buying a copy and striking out vast passages with a thick felt-tip pen, as if he were redacting some FBI document forcibly released under a Freedom of Information request.)

December 10

We attend a Sartre documentary with Jonathan and Ibs Schell and my friend Carl Ginsburg. Carl describes Oliver as a Saint Bernard with his huge square purse dangling atop his furry barrel chest. He strikes me this evening as a child, a bearded rotund child—and I'm suffused with fondness for him.

It's two a.m., sixteen degrees, and he's just left for home—when he gets there, he says he's going to go out for an hour-long bike ride. After that he will begin preparing for a trip to Costa Rica and its rain forests, heavily laden with his beloved ferns, and coral reefs, ideal for snorkeling, where he hopes to be able to write an alternate epilogue to the Leg book, one more suffused, he suggests, with "the natural."

December 23, 1982 (handwritten letter)

In Flight (to Costa Rica)

Dear Ren

I will write you a letter—perhaps; I may post it.

I have with me the Camus essays you gave me. I read 2 or 3 of them, and threw the volume into my backpack to read here and there. The *clarity* of the writing (thinking, feeling) pleased me very much and, in the few essays I leafed through, the sense of nature's *calm*.

It is especially a sense of calm—and "Nature"—that I am seeking in Costa Rica. And it is precisely this that I miss in the

thought/writing of Sartre. I repent, however, of whatever
"denouncing" I might have done. It is, basically, that at this
time, *in this mood*, I do not want Sartre—his chargedness,
his *un*calmness, and his genius for artifice. I will see how
Camus feels . . .

Actually, I don't particularly *want* "Camus" at this time
either. What I want (just now) is the thought/feeling of a
naturalist [. . .] In particular I wanted to bring HUMBOLDT*
(who is one of my favorite people) but, infuriatingly, I could
not find my copy of his *Narrative* in the hurry of packing, and
felt I shouldn't load myself (or my poor back, which must carry
everything in a backpack) with the five maroon volumes of his
Cosmos. But it is precisely (his) "Cosmos"—combining minutest
observation with scriptural simplicity and grandeur (just like a
conjunction of the Bible and Darwin)—it is precisely *this*, and
nothing else, I now want . . . What I may be saying is that
this is what I want to write—not (of course!) the 2,000-page
summation (and crown) of a long lifetime's work . . . that is
for later (if there is any "later"), but something which *is* both
simplicity and synthesis—and can convey the arrived-at mood
of Persons and Science, as this had been reached eight years
after "The Leg"—the mood of 1982—and as its "occasion"
(have you read Thom Gunn's *The Occasions of Poetry?*), I need
natural beauty and grandeur, perhaps specifically a *mountain*,
to end where it all started . . . Whether I *will* do my "Epilogue"
in Costa Rica—a meditation, perhaps, from the summit of Mt.
Irazu, the 12,000 ft. peak which commands a view of both
oceans, I don't know. I want, also, to recapture the "Columbian"
sense of "America" . . . as the land I have reached (against all
odds and expectations) after an immense, confused, yet
(somnambulistically) sure journey to the Depths . . . the place
of Arrival, of Homecoming, after (Kierkegaard's) "70,000
fathoms"; "the Land of Reason" (Kant)—which Hume could

---

*Alexander von Humboldt (1769–1859), the epic polymath Prussian explorer and naturalist, and the author of the multivolume *Cosmos*, in which he sought to bring together all branches of science and culture.

not reach; or that "unknown continent" of which Husserl
speaks, Moses-like, in the Preface of his book—This is the
mood, the hope, the desire—perhaps it is a Dream, perhaps a
Delusion [. . .]

   The plane is starting to judder and shudder—we may be
going to crash. These are my last words. Unfortunately you may
never receive them—

   Love, Oliver

P.S. 12/30 Didn't get a chance to post this. *Now* I can, and
re-reading it (for I had forgotten what I had written), I find it
almost clairvoyant, or prophetic. I *did* write my Epilogue, and
it did come to me on a mountain, though Poas, not Irazu. I
am very thankful, very exhausted, Costa Rica was quite
wonderful.[SB]

December 31

He is back from Costa Rica, where he finally finished an epilogue to the
Leg book—"montayne to montayne"—climbing down from a Central
American volcano and witnessing a group of children huddled around a
Nativity scene: Nativity to natality. "*Quickenings*," he said, "will be the
title, either of the epilogue or of an earlier section, maybe the whole
book!"

   Meanwhile, witnessing a pack of howler monkeys communing with
one another among the trees of the rain forest, he became possessed
with the prospect of his next book (another one), which will be about
Touretters generally, pithed of John's inclusion. The title came to him
immediately, he tells me, the word jumping off a book in his guide's
satchel: *Wildlife*.

   "Their howl," he relates, "was both inhuman and primordially human,
it resonated as out of one's own chest. I said, 'Hello grandfather!'"

   In addition, he reports how out swimming one morning, he'd gotten
caught in a riptide and dragged out to sea, desperately having to stroke back
in—a quite frightening experience. Though in the telling what stands out
for me in the end is his overwhelming life instinct.

His housekeeper regularly writes him lists of things he should buy. "The other day," he tells me, "prominent on the list was the word 'FAIL.' I figured this must be some prodigiously self-deprecatory detergent and set about looking for it. But no stores had it—and I decided its name must have been self-fulfilling.

"Or so I reported to my housekeeper when I came home, to which she countered, 'No no, you idiot—not "fail"—*FOIL!*'"

January 1983

"My epilogue is going to make Kant a bestseller," crows Oliver, by way of a New Year's greeting.

My own New Year's Day, as it happens, was to prove retrospectively portentous. I go to an afternoon party in town largely attended by my friends and reporting contacts at the relatively recently formed Helsinki Watch, and their far-flung friends, where I am introduced to a young Polish journalist named Joanna Stasinska, who had been a top reporter in the Solidarity Press Agency, though I'd never met her there during any of my reporting tours. After working pretty much seven days a week for the agency, from August 1980 through November 1981, she'd taken a three-week burnout leave to Madrid, her heart's true home (she'd been a Spanish and Latin American literature major), which is where she'd found herself stranded on December 13, 1981, when General Jaruzelski declared martial law and sealed the country (where all her colleagues were suddenly under arrest or in hiding). With a hundred dollars and three weeks' worth of clothes, she'd had to reinvent her life, find work, and, on the side, represent the Solidarity underground at the Madrid Helsinki Review Conference, which is where she'd met the Helsinki Watch folk. Now, a year later, she was stopping over in New York on her way to Louisiana State University, of all places, where she'd been awarded a doctoral fellowship.

At any rate, we spoke for a bit, largely about my Polish reporting trip that past October, my eyewitness impressions of martial law there, about which I was in the process of writing, and her own doubtless much deeper and better-informed sense of things, albeit at such a sad distance. Then she took her leave and was off to Baton Rouge. Of which, more anon.

Joanna Stasinska of the
Solidarity Press Agency

Mid-January

Oliver has now taken to regular weekend trips into the Catskills.

"I never feel at home at home," he explains, "but that's all right, since strangely I do feel at home on the road, especially at inns—has anyone done a phenomenology of inns?"

January 26

Visiting Oliver on City Island, where he brings out two photos, one from when he was forty (the back jacket for the first edition of *Awakenings*) and now another ten years later, as he is approaching fifty (the proposed jacket for the forthcoming Leg book). In the first he is surprisingly youthful, youthlike; in the second he looks older, more severe, wiser than he is. "Most people, they say, get the face they deserve by age forty," he tells me. "With me it took till age fifty. At forty I was still undefined. At forty I was still Luria's pupil. Now I am no longer Luria's pupil but a master in my own right."

Speaking of photography, and of the mastery involved in portrait photography, he mentions how he has initiated a practice of including a photographic portrait in each EEG file at the Little Sisters. Some are fine but just adequate, others, those taken by Sister Joseph in particular, are special: "They are invariably pictures of how the people will grow to look."

Some years after his leg accident, Oliver relates, changing the subject, he'd read a classic Soviet treatise on neuropsychology by a colleague of Luria's, a man named Aleksei Leont'ev, entitled *Rehabilitation of Hand Function*—the compilation of a study of two hundred injuries from World War II. He found the book captivating and immediately composed a 20,000-word preface.

"When Luria was no longer there, this book was there."

Oliver relates how he subsequently undertook his own Leont'ev series of two hundred case studies of shattered limbs. He wishes he could see the Leg book buttressed by the Leont'ev book on the one side (with his preface) and the Sacks series on the other.

After all, he says, the Leg book was partly autobiographical but also partly *experimentum suitatis* (Arendt's medieval term for experiments with and on the self).

As for the Leont'ev-Luria method of therapy, it consisted not (as was otherwise usual) of repetitive exercise but rather of the recognition that function is embedded in action and that action has sense, in an exploration of spontaneity, inclination, intention. In other words, not so much in getting people to flex their muscles as in getting them to do things.

"At Beth Abraham," he goes on, by way of illustration, "I once had as a patient a blind woman who'd been afflicted with cerebral palsy since infancy—she was extremely literate and literary but only by way of talking books, she said she didn't have braille. She claimed she couldn't, what with her hands. 'They're not much as hands go,' she said, and indeed, they were curled up in a spastic clench. I tested her, did various local tests for sensation, and found that throughout the hands there was feeling but no gnosia—that is, there was tactile sensation but no perception, no exploratory ambition.

"Why? Well, she'd never been permitted to handle anything, had been thought incapable of handling anything, and therefore, effectively, *had* no hands. I took her to the occupational therapy clinic with a copy of Leont'ev's book and said, 'See if you can give her hands!' And indeed, there was a marvelous one-year transformation. She now reads braille—she learned in her sixtieth year what she should have learned in her sixth month."

From there we go on to discuss phantom limbs, and in particular a patient he's been seeing recently who had a phantom finger for more than forty years until he developed a diabetic neuropathy, a progressive paralysis of his other fingers and his hands, at which point he lost the phantom as well. "The best cure for a phantom I always say is a stroke which wipes out the representing part of the brain."

Laughing, he continues, "At Beth Abraham we have one patient with a phantom wristwatch! And another with phantom coins!"

One of the sisters at the Little Sisters, the woman who is treasurer, suffers from Parkinsonism and month by month her signature has been getting smaller and smaller, while remaining quite distinctly her signature. This of course is presenting problems with the checks she is required to sign.

March 6

Dinner at a Middle Eastern restaurant, with Oliver getting set to go to London to promote the new Picador edition of *Awakenings* (maybe this time it will find an audience).

"Back in February 1979," he reports, "I saw a man (I'm thinking of writing his case up for Mary-Kay at the *London Review of Books*). Let's call him Dr. P: he was an extremely cultured, intelligent man, a voice teacher at Juilliard, who'd been referred to me, although for the longest time I couldn't imagine why. Indeed, I couldn't imagine why until he got up to leave and mistook his wife's head for a hat: I mean, *literally*! He tried to pull her head off her shoulders, completely unaware that it *was* her head.

"Subsequently I placed a glove in his lap and asked him what it was: He studied it very carefully, clearly perplexed. Finally he concluded that it was 'some kind of container.' He described it, its 'five out-pouchings.' He speculated that it might be a coin purse with separate slots for pennies, nickels, dimes, quarters, and half-dollars.

"At length he managed to work the glove onto his hand, at which point he exclaimed, 'Oh! It's a glove!'

"He was, in addition to a music coach, a Sunday painter. His wife showed me a sequence of his paintings dating back several years, paintings which started out representational and became progressively more fragmented. His wife dismissed my finding this odd. She claimed his art had merely become nonrepresentational, but it wasn't that. The point is, he had lost representation itself.

"*Nothing had a face for him.* The glove lacked a face, his wife—even his students. He could not recognize their faces (he would wonder who he was with), he could not recognize them if they sat still, although he would recognize the *music of their movement* when they moved."

He was apparently, Oliver surmised, suffering a serious right-brain lesion. He had no body image, although he still had a sense of body music.

"My prescription for him was that he should try to lead a life consisting solely of music.

"It's strange, no one with a frontal lobe syndrome can tell you what it's like (re-presentation is precisely what they can't do). Although Parkinsonians, by contrast, retain an impudent, ironically observing ego."

From there our conversation turns to another patient he met a few years back, a young woman named Christina, referred to him by Isabelle Rapin, who had quite simply and utterly lost her sixth sense.

"She had the worst proprioceptive deficiency I've ever encountered— an extreme Guillain-Barré syndrome—her body would go completely limp, a total slump, no bone or muscle tone. The thing of it is, though, unlike Dr. P, she *knew.* And it was indeed a shocking, terrible spectacle to see consciousness in *that.*"

Oliver, in a very good mood, has taken to hoovering up the remains of both our dishes. "No," he says, "I am a veritable mine of funny and terrible neurological jokes. I am stocked and stacked with wonderful cases."

April 1

Over the phone, Oliver, back from England, tells me of his trip's success, which climaxed in a forty-eight-hour editing blitz with Colin Haycraft at Duckworth, during which the Leg book was finally beaten into shape. At the peak of the process, Oliver tells me he was able to shave fifty thousand words while adding only ten thousand—which indeed qualifies as a breakthrough past the kind of blockage he has been afflicted by up till now.

Still, once Oliver left England, Haycraft kept the manuscript, just to be on the safe side: "He wanted to make sure I wouldn't mischief it."

Later: "At least the Leg book will appear before I die. By which I mean both that I won't keep writing it *until* I die and that *it* won't kill me."

We go on to speak of the Dr. P profile over at the *London Review of Books*. I suggest that he disguise the case history by placing it in another city he is only visiting, hence the briefness and thinness of his direct observation. He meanwhile tells me of a counter-case: an engineer who had a sudden aneurism on the other side of his brain and is now a computer—brilliant but with no *soul*.

April 8 (phone conversation)

"Do I distort?" Oliver abruptly asks at the outset, clearly distraught over a recent visit with Dr. P's wife. It subsequently appears that certain details of his account of Dr. P aren't quite jibing, although the whole seems sound. Still, Oliver is in a small paranoid fit.

"I mean," he says, "perhaps it's a case that I seized on certain themes, imaginatively intensified, deepened, and generalized them. But still."

As it happens, he did see another case like Dr. P's just the other day, a man who, after two strokes, could not see and did not seem disturbed about this.

"'See?' he'd muttered uncomprehending. 'See? See?' He cannot see, he cannot imagine seeing, he cannot remember seeing—a complete visual amnesia, and he has lost everything he has ever seen.

"I called Isabelle and asked, 'Am I making this up?' 'No,' she said, 'you're describing Anton's syndrome with considerably more intensity than Anton.'"

A few days later

He is still very upset about the Dr. P piece: "Fretted, obsessed, delusionally guilty and flagrantly procrastinatory."

Mary-Kay had called him to ask, "Would you like *me* to write the postscript?" She has also suggested a swell title, with splendid Edwardian/Chestertonian cadences: "The Man Who Mistook His Wife for a Hat."

Oliver, unrelieved: "As soon as I feel better, I contrive to feel worse."

April 20

Oliver and I venture to a production of *Porgy and Bess*, Oliver still worrying the toothache of his Dr. P and Mrs. P anxieties.

In that context, he speaks of Arendt on Hobbes, how she suggests that in his conception of totalitarian man, he'd anticipated the truth by several centuries. Similarly, Oliver contends, "I don't tell lies, though I may invent the truth."

April 30

Oliver and I board the train for Washington. I've invited him along for a pilgrimage of my own to see the Vermeers at the National Gallery.

He is wearing an incongruous pink cowboy shirt with pearl buttons. "I get at random whatever is sold at Joe Tuckman's store next door to Beth Abraham," he explains. "If they're selling pink cowboy shirts, I wear pink cowboy shirts. If they sold black Nazi uniforms, I'd probably wear those."

Though, as he goes on to note, his shirts and jackets almost always feature "these large marsupial pouches, for pens and notebooks and the like."

We have a generally free-associative ride down:

The first day of his analysis, his shrink asked him, "Well, whom *do* you trust?"

"I trust Hume," Oliver had replied, "but he doesn't get me very far."

"I need to be a guest in inns and manors. My own house, I *bekafka*: I turn it into a castle."

"I had an uncle who wanted to write a book to be titled 'My First Hundred Years.' He did so, finished it, and the next morning was found dead in his bed, his completed manuscript by his side, a smile on his face."

Oliver has for the first time in his life been paying attention to politics. This is mostly because of Hannah Arendt, from whose thinking he's now moved into totalitarianism and revolution, but also, perhaps, a bit because of me and my recent writings on Poland.

At any rate, to my surprise, he suddenly asks me what I thought of Reagan's speech on El Salvador before a joint session of Congress the other day. Before I can reply, he says, "An aphasic would not have been fooled. An aphasic, you see, can pick up tone but not content. He is incapable of comprehending or reproducing propositions, lyrical sequences, the flow of argument. But he has an uncanny, an almost preternatural sensitivity to *tone,* to authenticity and sincerity of presentation. He would have seen through the demagogic vulgarity, seen through to the bad smell which would have made a dog bark. I've often felt you can't lie to an aphasic."

(This comment in turn provokes in me a flip fantasy of an alternative to the standard Brokaw-Mudd-Rather television commentaries after presidential addresses. Imagine, instead, if the camera switched over to a panel of cringing aphasics, their arms and hands brought up to shield their faces, all aghast.)

A few hours later, Oliver is taken by Vermeer during our walk through the National Gallery: "Imagine what it would be like to be a neurological Vermeer: to achieve this intimacy of portraiture while retaining tactful reserve, while refraining from the violation of privacy."

Which in turn reminds me of the final lines from Robert Lowell's marvelous late poem "Epilogue":

> All's misalliance.
> Yet why not say what happened?
> Pray for the grace of accuracy
> Vermeer gave to the sun's illumination
> stealing like the tide across a map
> to his girl solid with yearning.
> We are poor passing facts,
> warned by that to give
> each figure in the photograph
> his living name.

During an evening walk along the Mall, Oliver speaks of the Arendt biography he has been reading: "Heidegger was thirty-five and Arendt eighteen. There was a romantic if not an erotic attraction, which displeased

Mrs. Heidegger, who disliked her husband's students, especially the bright
female ones, especially the ones he liked especially."

On the train ride back the next day, Oliver speaks fondly of an eccentric muscleman colleague from his Venice Beach days, a mathematician named Jim: "I was the king of quads and he was the king of 'ceps, he
the proner to my squatter, but he was also a genius, a drug addict alcoholic conflicted ex-Mormon who later bought a ranch in Paraguay, bed a
wife, and died on the eve of paternity—a sad loss, a colleague." Oliver was
a sort of in-law in that for a time he been fond of Jim's wife's kid brother.
And he is, as he puts it, upon some extended circumspection, "the delin-
quent godfather to Jim's daughter."

Anyway, Jim was into computer chess, and Oliver recalls him
marveling at the Fischer-Spassky match: "Not just strategy: Art!"

May 10

Over the phone, Oliver relates how, in anticipation of the coming summer,
he was recently having a huge air conditioner installed. The man said they'd
be back to shore up the gap in the window the next day, but he didn't hear
from them. After they'd gone he'd become increasingly frantic. "I started
imagining, for instance, that because I'd offered them beer and sandwiches
they now hated me and had left the hole on purpose. And the hole itself
began to take on for me gigantic proportions. I called their boss. He had a
tape machine which said you could leave a message as long as you liked,
and as the day passed I left several, each longer than the previous one: 'If as
a surgeon I fail to close up my patient, leaving him with a gaping wound,
I can hardly be deemed to have performed my task!' And so forth."

What happened?

"The next day, of course, they came back and finished fixing the hole."

May 20

Oliver says, "I don't mind minor work—most work is minor, modest—as
long as it is genuine. Darwin throughout his life kept up an intercourse
with cattle breeders and pigeon-keepers—people whose lives were given
over to careful, quiet observation . . ."

June 1

Over the phone, Oliver mentions he's just come from dinner with a group of five doctors. One of them, a famous neurosurgeon, had been invited to speak at Albert Einstein College of Medicine and had said he would so long as his good friend Oliver Sacks was there. "And they'd all said, 'Who?'" So far as I could tell, I was the only one there not a neurosurgeon and not earning twelve figures.

"I saw a biblical referent this weekend while near Lake Jeff. I mean, sheep actually *do* leap. It was twilight, I was bicycling along a field and along came this Kantian moment. I just wish Kant had been there to witness it, he who was so bemused about spontaneity. I mean, here in the sunset was this flock of sheep grazing, when one made a sudden vertical movement which, as far as I could tell, was an expression of *pure festivity.*"

※

But now, just a few days later, Oliver is in a "murderous funk." Haycraft has still not edited and returned the Leg book and Oliver is, he tells me over the phone, in a "parasuicidal rage. Indeed," he goes on, "in the absence of alcohol, I have just consumed an entire bottle of Worcestershire sauce and it is making me hiccup violently."

※

A few weeks later, though, on the way to dinner with my friends Alec Wilkinson and Celia Owen, Oliver is glowing.

"I saw a patient today," he recounts, "whose case history was so remarkable and whose relation of it so clear that by the end I just wanted to lean over and hug her!"

It appears that this patient, like one other woman Oliver had witnessed a few years ago, was suffering from a form of musical epilepsy—"two old women assaulted by melody," as he describes them.

The first—an elderly Irishwoman—had become convinced that a radio station was beaming directly into her brain by way of her particular constellation of silver and gold tooth fillings. "Only, after a while she began to wonder, what kind of radio station was this which had no commercials and featured *only* Irish folk songs from her childhood?"

Oliver eventually hooked her up to an EEG and asked her to ever so slightly gesture with her finger when one of her musical sieges started— just an indication but nothing that would, in itself, register on the graph. Sure enough, "Each time she moved her finger, the needle registering the electro activity in a particular part of her brain that processes music was shooting right off the page!"

This new woman, the one Oliver saw today, was a patient with the Little Sisters. Apparently she'd been suffering for some time, and indeed suffering especially acutely because she didn't want to tell anyone for fear that they'd think she was going mad, something she secretly suspected herself. Finally she confided her tormenting predicament to a particularly kindly sister who said, "Oh gee, this sounds like just the sort of thing our Dr. Sacks would love to hear about." She assured the old lady that this doctor was very kind, very sympathetic, and would not make her feel the least bit crazy—on the contrary!

(Of course I encouraged Oliver to write this up, but we'll just have to wait and see.)

※

July 1

Oliver calls me, tremendously excited, crowing, "I'm in a pre-Cambrian bliss!" During the next few minutes, it develops that he was out swimming and was returning to shore when, putting his foot on a rock, it moved! The rock, and its neighbor, and their neighbor—the whole field of rocks—turned out to be a horde of horseshoe crabs, beached for mating.

"My people," Oliver proclaimed, "my people have come!"

※

Oliver's birthday is July 9, a Saturday. He will be fifty and he's throwing himself a party, his first since he was twenty-one. And he's gone hog wild. After days of shy withdrawal, he stoked himself up with a pint of rum and has been calling everyone in sight. "And to my astonishment, far from dismissing the invitation out of hand, everyone is being tremendously kind and responsive." He's hired a caterer and rented a tent.

On the Fourth of July, standing on the beach watching the fireworks, he confesses: "I don't know what got into me: I invited the entire block!"

I suggest he invite our friend Jonathan Schell. "Ah"—he pauses—"I'm a little ambivalent. I mean, most of these people have IQs around sixty."

Oh yeah, I ask, like who?

"Oh, neurosurgeons, cardiologists, and the like."

But he finally decides that yes, of course, he should invite Jonathan and his wife, Ibs. I mention their two kids.

"Children? Oh dear, children. How old?"

"Four and one."

"One? Oh! I better rent a wet nurse!" Oliver laughs. "I mean, I have a very sweet, kindly housekeeper, but I'm afraid she's no longer lactating."

He hires a caterer for the party. "How many will we be serving?" he is asked. "Oh gee," he replies, "I don't know. Somewhere between twelve and two hundred!"

※

July 9

The day arrives: his fiftieth birthday.

On the way to the party, Mark Homonoff, to whom I am giving a lift, recounts being on City Island during the invasion of the horseshoe crabs. "A neighbor was standing on his lawn, skewering caterpillars. 'These creepers!' he complained, 'They're bigger than ever this year. It's the weather. First these creepers, and now the crabs. Things are really weird with nature this year.'" It was, says Homonoff, like the classic beginning of some fifties sci-fi flick. In the car we all fantasize the other reels—the dissolute mad scientist on the other side of the island who was carelessly emptying plutonium into the strait—and how now everything was converging on Oliver's party: us, the neighbors, the whole *Towering Inferno* supporting cast, the huge mutated horseshoe crabs lumbering toward shore.

A few minutes later, as I describe it all to Oliver by the beach, he says, "Yes! Yes. And I'd be here fending off the hysterical neighbors, trying to calm their fears, to disarm them of their picks and shovels and rifles, trying to explain how these are *good* creatures, our *fellows*. And then I'd be turning toward them, the giant crabs, and saying, 'Yes, welcome, eat us, eat us all, the world is yours, Lord knows we've made a complete botch of things!'"

Later: "I've been feeling bad for months," Oliver says. "Remember that evening on the way to *Porgy and Bess* when I said I don't tell lies but sometimes I invent the truth? Well, this was not strictly accurate. *Imagine.* Not invent. I should have said, 'I imagine the truth.' In the sense that Tolstoy said there was only one story he ever wrote which he considered a failure, his story *Family Happiness.* When asked why, he said it was because it felt *made up.* And of course he's exactly right. I mean, *Anna Karenina* reads like a *profile.*"

Oliver describing his swimming to some of the guests: "It's slow but I *never* tire. My stroke is long, powerful, and almost entirely underwater. I come up for air, descend, and reemerge twenty yards later. One of my neighbors once mistook me for a migrating whale. Perhaps it's my destiny to die *harpooned.*"

At one point he is circulating with a large flat chunk of clear rock crystal, which he slides delightedly over a book. The book's title becomes doubly refracted.

"Iceland spar!" Oliver declares proudly. "Once Eric and I were up in northern Ontario in the far backcountry and we came upon a little gem-and-mineral store—a magic emporium. The man showed me a small chunk of this stuff and I said, 'Oh my, this would have made Newton furious.' The man looked up at me, beaming, and said, '*You're* the one!,' whereupon he descended into his basement, emerging with this lovely book-size chunk of the stuff: Iceland spar. You see, this sort of refraction could not be accounted for by Newtonian physics. When Newton was told of it, he dismissed it out of hand. He and Huygens had a huge falling out over it. (Only Huygens's undulant wave theory could account for it.) Eventually they patched it up. I asked the old man whether he'd consider parting with it, and he said, after great thought, 'For $100?' I said, 'Gladly,' reaching into my pocket and handing over the money, 'and I will treasure it my whole life!'"

The party is proceeding outside, a wonderful mingling of social classes: literary types, radical types, medical colleagues, neighbors—a love fest. At one point, women are racing up and down the narrow street, "The doctor needs chairs! The doctor needs more chairs!" Meanwhile, at another point I come upon Oliver in his air-conditioned, chilly living room, spread out on a couch, another fan propped on a chair aimed at his face.

"I could love a fan!" he announces, giggling. "What would that be? *Flabellaphilia*, I believe!"

Eric, as usual, sends Oliver a volume of nineteenth-century science, Victorian science—Oliver has a whole shelf of the stuff, arrayed as bedtime reading.

I have a brief conversation with Chris Carolan, Oliver's EEG technician. "She is a *true* person," Oliver has said. "She is incapable of falsehood." She is also bouncy, jovial, a Rabelaisian, a Falstaffian presence. She exudes joy and competence. She quizzes me as to my credentials and my interest in Oliver (she is clearly very protective). At one point she sees me berate him about something, "Oh Ollie, go ahead and *do* it," at which point she opens up, expansively, "So you *do* know him." She smiles.

"We're good together," she says. "We're a real team. I handle the difficult men and he's a dream with the little old ladies. Unlike many doctors who just come in and reel off a dozen chart readings at a go without ever meeting the person, Dr. Sacks evaluates the whole person, the EEG in the context of the person he meets. If there's something wrong, he asks, Why is it wrong? And he's very *patient*. He'll spend five minutes or three hours with a patient. It doesn't matter to him—*he doesn't know the difference*—so long as the patient's interesting.

"He's very intelligent, but often he seems to lack common sense. He is tremendously loyal to his friends, to people he sees as friendly. But if a relationship starts out wrong, he can go way overboard in his anxieties.

"He respects me. He defends me. Once, after my husband died and I was left with two kids, he tried to get me a raise. I was earning less than $100 a week at Bronx State. He wrote a letter pointing out that 'she is paid less than a garbage collector and she is concerned with life and death.'" Did it help? "No. I didn't get any raise, but it's the effort that counts."

At one point a huge watermelon is brought out. "I once had a bizarre acid trip," Oliver reminisces. "I thought the entire earth was edible!"

He is radiant, watching his party guests outside. Perhaps the most wonderful gift from the party is the softening of his attitude toward his house, his neighbors. "Didn't Arendt start out writing about Augustine's concept of neighborliness?" He has been enchanted by the outpouring of benign, affirming joy and acceptance occasioned by his invitations.

"I will have to reconsider," he tells me. "I had settled as onto a comfortable chair of spikes into my paranoid vision of the world. My analyst keeps trying to tell me that I am generally loved and that it's just the small core of self-loathing that gets projected out into the world, into these apprehensions of hostility and malignancy, so that my house appears to me a prison, a hellhole. Perhaps this will prove to have been a housewarming, as well."

※

Perhaps, but a week later Oliver's benign mood has completely evaporated and he has reverted to murderous, querulous anxiety regarding Haycraft and Jim Silberman, his current American editor at Summit Books, and the damn Leg book.

"Did they have editors in the nineteenth century," he asks me over the phone, "or are they another of these peculiarly twentieth-century pests?

"I don't ever order a fillet at a fish restaurant," he goes on. "I don't like something whose skeleton has been removed.

"Colin is filleting me and Silberman is filleting me, and I fear *you're* going to fillet me."

He pauses, ruminating. "Michael Meyer's biography of Ibsen is fine. It's not great writing but it was written in the right relation. This other biography of Strindberg is filled with excited, vulgar anecdotes apparently written in adulation."

I take this as the warning it is clearly meant to be.

"Your biography of Robert Irwin seemed all right to me. And the time I admired you most was when we were at the National Gallery and you were talking about Vermeer—you seemed to me then a whole sensibility.

"But it's different writing about a scientist than an artist. An artist is just an ordinary human being somewhat exalted, but a scientist . . ." His voice trails off. "And there's a strong scientist in me. Something rather strange about the scientific mind and sensibility which needs to be dealt with." Not to deal with Oliver-as-scientist, he seems to be saying, would be to fillet him. "It is precisely this which allows me to phone Richard Gregory" (the great English perceptual psychologist based at the University of Bristol) "in the middle of the night—his and mine!—to talk about the strobe effect on bicycle wheels, to phone and know I will find a responsive resonance."

✳

The next day he calls again, Ibsen still on his mind, how he feels that Ibsen's late play *When We Dead Awaken* may be one of the most seminal works in his experience. It concerns a sculptor and his model, and, notably, her eventual reproach of him for not seeing her as a human . . .

Oliver read *When We Dead Awaken* early, although at the time it left no trace. The title *Awakenings* may in fact come from the play, he surmises, now that he thinks about it.

Soon after *Awakenings*, Oliver was offered a big advance by Faber and Faber to write a book on pain, which he turned down. "Pain is not interesting to me. Certainly not as metaphysically interesting as nausea. I want to write about neuralgias *of the spirit*."

July 28

About a month earlier, Joanna Stasinska had resurfaced in New York, in head-long flight from Baton Rouge. As she would often say in later years, she never sought refuge from Poland, but she did do so from Louisiana. Her stay had not been particularly edifying, let's just put it that way. It turns out, however, that in the middle of her dismal semester, she had happened upon an issue of The New Yorker *at a campus bookstore, the first she had ever seen, and recalling that funny guy she had met at the New Year's party and pretty sure that that had been the name of the magazine he'd said he was writing for, she picked it up, scanned the table of contents, and sure enough, there was part one of my series of martial law reportages.*

Resurfacing a few months later in New York, she'd called a mutual friend at Helsinki Watch and in passing mentioned the coincidence. The friend called me to relate the story (and pass along her phone number), and I called her to see if she might like to go out for dinner . . . and one thing led to another. Joanna got an apartment of her own way uptown but in practice started spending most nights with me on West Ninety-Fifth. She soon got a job with Helsinki Watch, or rather (what with her Spanish) its newly founded twin, Americas Watch, and to smooth various bureaucratic details, we even indulged in a fast green-card wedding—not

*necessarily serious or permanent, we told ourselves, or at least not yet, just for im-
migration formality's sake.*

*But the point is, gradually, as Oliver kept coming over, he increasingly would
find her there with me, and more to the point she had to come to terms with that
regularly obtruding aspect of my life, and to the frequent oddnesses to which I'd
long grown inured, but in the meantime I got to experience them all over again
through her eyes. And in the end, we all got along swimmingly. As it were.*

Over dinner at our apartment, Oliver tells us of one of his patients who
suffers from an extreme form of Korsakoff syndrome—the man has no ability to form new memories (he is very intelligent, superb for instance at
tic-tac-toe but hopeless at chess), and he is also stuck at the age of nineteen, on a submarine (he had indeed been on a sub at that age). He was
and is a Morse operator in 1945. One day, several years back, as he babbled
on about these experiences in the present tense, Oliver thrust a mirror in
his face, asking, "What is that, Jimmie?"

The man was struck speechless with horror. Oliver felt terrible about
it, but within thirty seconds the man had completely forgotten the
incident.

And more recently, just the other day, which is what had brought the
story to mind, Oliver relates how he told his Russian neurologist friend
(and onetime actual student of Luria's) Nick Goldberg the story, and about
his own terrible feelings regarding the incident, to which Nick replied,
"Don't worry. That's exactly what Luria would have done."

Another day, Oliver recalls, he showed the man a *National Geographic*
that featured a photo of the earth taken by an astronaut on the moon. The
man stared at it for some time in profound confusion.

"But . . . but . . . but that's impossible. To take such a picture, a camera would have to be . . . on the moon!"

Anyway, Oliver is thinking of writing the case up, and I offer him a
possible title: "The Rime of the Lost Submariner."

July 30

I gave Oliver Lewis Hyde's book *The Gift* the other night and this afternoon,
on the eve of his taking off for a monthlong residency at the Blue Mountain

Center writer's colony in the Adirondacks, to which I have steered him
(it's in the process of being consolidated by friends on the forfeited estate
of one of them), he calls to tell me how much he's enjoying the book.

"It goes very much to the center of my own concerns—how I can't
accept a fee because it destroys the relationship of free-giving.

"This is what killed the Faber deal: They offered me a $25,000
advance and I simply froze up."

August 31

Back from LA, where I'd been working on a project with David Hockney,
I call Oliver, who is back from Blue Mountain: It sounds like he's done a
fine job up there on the Lost Submariner, which of course has ballooned
into a five-thousand-word manuscript.

I reiterate how much I like the notion of "The Lost Submariner"
because this uncanny amnesiac has precisely lost his submarine, which is
to say his sub-marine, his oceanic memory. To which Oliver replies, "Yes,
it's not that he's lost in the depths, he's lost his depth and everything for
him is a brittle immediacy, a continuous surface. Such that this piece continues my implicit critique of computers—for what he lacks is precisely
what a computer lacks."

As an epigraph he will be using a line of Buñuel's about memory, how
as he begins to lose it he realizes all the more that life *is* memory.

"A point," says Oliver, "which I then go on both to prove and to
refute . . ."

September 18

It turns out that Oliver gained twenty-eight pounds in twenty-one days
at Blue Mountain! He accomplished this thanks in part to the superb
breakfasts and dinners but especially thanks to the buffet lunches. He
started by coming down for a sandwich at twelve thirty. Later he came at
noon and stayed till one. Later still he came at eleven thirty and stayed till
two. Eventually he was coming down at eleven and staying till four. Each
new group would proclaim, "Oh, Ollie, good! You're with *our* shift," not
realizing that he was with *all* their shifts.

"I learn the latest advances from my patients," he goes on to tell me. "They read it in the paper or see it on TV and then tell me. Last year I received a cryptic note from one of my patients, a quadriplegic who'd written it with her mouth. All it said was: 'What about a monkey?'

"It turns out *60 Minutes* had had some piece about a monkey who'd been trained to help quads. Today I spent the day with the trainer and her monkeys. It was fascinating."

September 20 (dinner at a Thai restaurant)

Oliver speaks of a sci-fi novel he's been reading, part of which he likes, but then notes, "To me, empathy is the most interesting subject, and telepathy, the least interesting."

A possible subtitle for a future book: *Toward a Neurology of Identity.*

Because for him, he goes on to elaborate, psychology never had sufficient access to or interest in the organic, while neurology to date has failed in the obverse, to show regard to the *experience* of identity.

"I've long felt the need both to get out of the mainstream and to be respected by the mainstream. But a few years ago, picking up a volume of classical neurology (Head) to read on a train trip back to NYC from Boston, I felt suddenly realigned with the mainstream. Or rather: The mainstream, I realized, *is me.* It's everyone else who's strayed."

September 28

"To my great surprise," Oliver reports, "yesterday, a very dull colleague—or at least he has been an utter bore for over eighteen years—told me a fascinating story. He recounted the case of a patient he'd seen a few days earlier, who was suffering from TGA—transient global amnesia. This man suddenly couldn't remember anything for more than twenty seconds—he lost a few decades for a few hours and then, like that, became completely himself again. This produced great horror in his wife and children, although as it was transpiring he was unaware that anything was wrong. Subsequently he, too, was overwhelmed by the horror, that he could lose half his life like that, *in a moment!*"

October 3

Oliver sends me a handwritten note, complaining that he feels like he missed "the point" in a recent submission to the *British Medical Journal* on "The Origins of *Awakenings*":

> Those splendid Eliot essays you lent me,* not just that
> particular essay but almost all of them, assist me to focus, to
> remember "the point." Again and again he speaks of emotion as
> central—but not personal emotion, something impersonal,
> "artistic," and yet drawing on, drawing in the whole personality.
>
>   The center of my piece, the center of *Awakenings*, the center
> of my work (?work?), of my life—as—a—whatever (physician
> (scientist (artist??))) is exactly in this peculiar sort of (and
> elevation of) emotion (though "clinical" isn't adequate).
>
>   It is something that every real doctor feels (I hope) in the
> encounter with his patient, his encounter with their phenomena,
> the phenomenal. When I am dull, or tired, or vexed, etc., I lose
> this feeling, and the work is mechanical. At my best (which is
> perhaps over), I have known this emotion with extraordinary
> intensity—and conveyed it and shared it with the patients
> themselves, & any students or others who were around.
>
>   It is exactly this impersonal, lofty (but often very funny)
> emotion which is missing from almost all the medical
> "literature" nowadays—Luria's a most noble exception. It was
> for some reason much commoner in the past . . . if not in an
> exalted measure, yet in a genuine one.
>
>   (In its "exalted," or sublime, degree, I feel it, say, pre-
> eminently in Leibniz—perhaps I see him as the ultimate
> physician.)
>   [. . .]
>   Love, Oliver[SB]

---

*T. S. Eliot's *Selected Essays: 1917–1932* (New York: Harcourt, Brace, 1932), which includes the essay he is alluding to: "Tradition and the Individual Talent."

October 27 (dinner)

"Reading Hannah Arendt, I was utterly engrossed but it was like reading the natural history of some alien species—beautifully described, cogent, coherent, wondrous, and terrible—and it was almost an epiphany when I realized that this was *me* she was describing, my people, us!"

Conversation turns to the general lack of political interest in his life, from early on. "Eric was very interested and was in a political group in prep school—but I was oblivious, my mind wandering instead to galvanization, electrostatic currents, and so forth."

Two beats, a sigh. "No, despite all my agitation, I have been wrapped up in my own thoughts my entire life."

A few days later (phone conversation)

"It's as Goethe says in *Faust*. Theory is gray while the tree of life is green and gold. What I need to do is to infuse these writings with the green and gold of phenomenality.

"Meanwhile, though, I am in a phase of alternating rages and exhaustions. I am lying here on a hot pad with a fan six inches from my face.

"With the book finally on the verge of coming together, and the first inklings of all the coming publicity, I feel a bit like a soft-shell crab being probed, x-rayed, dissected—and I don't know if I will be able to stand having another journalist coming and making a gift of his own person, a sort of moral octopus, on my porch."

Noted.

November 14 (phone conversation)

Oliver spent the weekend in Boston at the book fair, next to Eric's booth, writing, completing the umpteenth version of his Leg epilogue.

"I was an odd figure, scribbling there beside Eric's booth, with thousands milling all about me, completely oblivious, utterly absorbed, as if I were sitting in a woodland glade.

"I do love the idea of being private in public view, whereas I fall apart when I'm all alone."

✳

November 24

He is back in his obsessive funk.

"I am living Zeno's paradox, I am in an Eleatic frenzy: I write fifty pages, add eighty-five more, take out ten, add twenty, take out five, add another twenty. I write endlessly, eat obsessively, and am sick all the while.

"I've had a strong feeling of tyrannical impulse these last few weeks, and though I may externalize it—say it was Jim* making me do it—it was an internal enslavement. He let loose the enormous machinery—part obsessive, part creative—which rises up and blots out the world, even the world of dreams."

Sounds fun. I ask Oliver how things are going with Bob Silvers over at *The New York Review of Books*. He'd earlier decided to try his submariner out on them, by way of an expansion of his previous, more circumscribed association with *NYR*'s sister affiliate in London.

"Oh, he liked it, though perhaps I made his life more difficult by sending him seventeen more revised versions."

December 3 (phone conversation)

Oliver tells me about a new seventy-page section of the endless epilogue entitled "The Tunnel" (Haycraft has completely jettisoned the Costa Rica version, "all that damn vegetation," as he characterized it, dismissingly); this new version includes his description of his transit through Gradgrind and Coketown(!). But really, he says, "'Neurology and the Soul': That's what the epilogue is about, what all my work is about."

December 13 (at Silberman's office)

Trying to put the goddamn Leg book to bed.

I sit in as Silberman's young associate editor, Ileene Smith, presents her condensation of the epilogue.

Oliver is absolutely hopeless dealing with editors ("Next time," he'd muttered before Ileene joined us, "I'm going to deal directly with the print-

*Jim Silberman, his editor at Summit Books.

ers and sidestep publishers and editors altogether"), so I stay on to mediate things.

I am momentarily put in mind of a passage from Walter Benjamin's *Illuminations*:

> The Latin word *textum* means "web." No one's text is more tightly woven than Marcel Proust's; to him nothing was tight or durable enough. From his publisher Gallimard we know that Proust's proofreading habits were the despair of the typesetters. The galleys always went back covered with marginal notes, but not a single misprint had been corrected; all available space had been used for fresh text.*

Ileene for her part has distilled the more than three hundred brilliant but somewhat chaotic pages of Oliver's epilogue and addenda into a coherent thirty pages, of which the first twenty-five are quite good. There's a flaw at page 25 that needs about five pages of fleshing out, and the rest is okay. I start by complimenting her, something Oliver would never think to do, and then focus quickly on the particular need—to expand the Kant section (it's the climax of the book and it needs to sing, it needs to swell and blossom)—so as to defuse Oliver's tendency to diffuse panic.

I tell Oliver what's needed here is five pages, not fifty, fifty will be *worse than useless*—five pages, Oliver!

And then I leave to let them get to work.

Ileene walks me to the door. "Dr. Sacks isn't going to take it all apart again, is he? I don't know if I can handle it if he takes it all apart again."

And it occurs to me that Oliver intimidates those who hold him in awe—that the way to deal with him in this sort of situation is as you would an eight-year-old prodigy, which is to say you need to blend amazement and respect with strict paternalistic forbearance.

Oh, Oliver . . . behave yourself!

※

---

*Walter Benjamin, *Illuminations*, ed. Hannah Arendt, trans. Harry Zohn (New York: Schocken Books, 2007), 202.

A headmaster once sent home a report card to young Oliver's parents with the following comment: "Oliver Sacks will go far if he doesn't go too far."

                                        ✳

I call Oliver the next day. "How'd it go?"

They were there until 12:30 a.m.

Oh dear, you must be tired.

"Well, that was just the beginning. Ileene had been calling the garage to make sure they'd stay open. They said they would. But I got lost getting there, and by the time I got there, they were closed. So I only got back to my house this morning at seven thirty!"

What did you do in the meantime? Did you go to a hotel?

"Oh, I walked around in an ambulatory daze, pausing to eat dinner every hour on the hour.

"I ate a great deal."

As he tells me the story at six that evening, he is eating roe. Carp roe. "I'm gobbling up a potential world of carp—a billion! A trillion! The roe produces a perseveration of both the mouth and the mind."

But he seems satisfied with the final product.

"It's *not* schmaltz," he says, answering Colin's misgivings. "There's thought there." Another audible slurp of roe. "It may be lubricated by schmaltz."

He continues downing universes.

"But my repetitions" (he is still worrying about the damn epilogue) "are not strictly repetitions. Rather, I approach and then reapproach from a different side, something after the fashion of Wittgenstein: to get my bearings.

December 19

I meet up with Oliver at Summit Books again, then off to a rambling lunch at the Beanstalk across the street.

"Come pick me up at twelve thirty," he'd told me over the phone. "By then I will have completed or, if not, abandoned it."

Our conversation turns to a perennial topic, a constant concern.

"I don't have reverence for the text, I take liberties," he acknowledges.

"But I *do* have reverence for the book of nature, and there I wouldn't so much as alter a comma.

"The littlest lie of a scientist will tear his science in half.

"I can't imagine that Freud, as a physician, would ever have sacrificed his patients to his theories—I feel the same way about Luria, and I feel the same way about myself . . . but, um, but and but and but" (Oliver in mid-monologue).

At which point he free-associates to the question of dearness.

"There was an editor at *Harper's*—an ex–think tanker, I have no doubt—who was inhumanly clever but also inhuman period. He objected to my calling my patients 'dear,' as in 'I saw a dear old woman this afternoon.' 'What is *dear?*' he asked me, proddingly, and suddenly all sense of dearness fled the world and I felt I was dying in interstellar space. The next morning, though, I was saved by a letter from Luria which began, 'My dear Dr. Sacks.'

"You might well ask, this *Harper's* fellow did, how can lithium carbonate be dear to one? But it can be, *and is* to me.

"With me, though, nowadays 'the dear' is often botanical.

"When my leg came back, I said, 'My dear old thing, you're home again.'

"It wouldn't be home—which is to say, dear sweet home—unless potassium carbonate were exactly like potassium carbonate. *That's* why truthfulness is so important."

Which brings us full circle.

"It has something to do with fidelity, too.

"Braefield" (his hellhole wartime boarding school) "was a world of fickle relations where no one was faithful to anyone. And the emotional *stability* of the inorganic world was crucial in saving me."

A pause. "In Ernest Jones's biography of Freud, there's a paragraph about Freud's respect for the *regular* fact, his *faithfulness* to it, even if it should take years to surface."

16

The Leg Book Shambles Toward Publication as Oliver Hazards a Neurology of the Soul (the First Half of 1984)

January 5

Oliver is back from London, and it looks like the Leg book is at long last locked into place.

And sure enough, while in London, Oliver, rid of that albatross, was on a tear, completing three new pieces: the review of a book on nineteenth-century neurology and psychiatry; that piece about his musical ladies; and another essay on that young woman who lost her proprioception.

He also visited Harold Pinter and Antonia Frasier, who greeted him with, "Oh, Dr. Sacks, do tell us some more neurological ghost stories." And he did—for three hours!

※

As I watched a special on TV the other evening about Jane Goodall and her wild chimpanzee subjects (Oliver and I often talked about Goodall), Oliver's perennial dilemma about the warring clinical versus naturalist tendencies within himself became somewhat clearer for me—this combination of scientific distance, reserve, observation as against the tendency toward empathy, emotion, touching. Indeed, touching itself became a seminally important moment: how remarkable that day when Goodall's chimps would let her touch them.

But beyond that, consider Goodall's ambivalent situation when the chimpanzees started killing each other: Should she intervene to stop the carnage? Or should she just observe this remarkable dark epiphany? She just observes. But on the other hand, when they contract polio: She laces their food with vaccine.

The key moment, though, in the Goodall enterprise came when she started giving the chimps names. It wasn't simply that an It became a Thou. In the process, description became *truer*. All sorts of things that were blurred in a merely statistical (more scientifically conventional) survey became vividly apparent once the chimps were seen as individuals.

Goodall's, like Sacks's, is thus a glorious example of romantic science: It can be accused of the same flaws (projection, anthropomorphizing the otherwise mute)—but finally, it evinces the same triumph (getting to places "objective" science could never reach, thereby limning the attenuated limits of such science).

January 15

Over lunch at my apartment, Oliver continues discoursing on his musical ladies and some other recent case histories he has been working on—indeed, he has no sooner arrived at my door than he has papers and drafts spread all about the dining table.

"Coming to look at the subject of nostalgia—the neurology of nostalgia—the only good reference I could find was myself.

"The theme here is mother love and home . . .

"I've added a footnote to 'The Lost Submariner,'" he says, stabbing for the *New York Review* galleys so as to show me. "Talking to Isabelle Rapin about Korsakoff syndrome, she told me about rare cases where such a retrograde amnesia appears in young children—with devastating results. They lose everything and in particular the memory of the early experiences of mother love and in such cases revert to deep autism."

A somber pause at the horror of that prospect, his eyebrows raising. Then, brightening: "I myself had a fit of musical nostalgia in London a few weeks ago. Eric suddenly said to me, Sherlock-like, 'So, you've been thinking of going to Vienna?' I was astonished, for yes, indeed, I had been.

"'How did you know?' I stammered, to which he replied, 'You've been humming *The Third Man* theme all morning.'

"I associate *The Third Man* with my first adolescent freedom—my first time abroad, a youthful foray."

From out of the pile of papers, Oliver now spears an essay by Esther

Salaman ("both an aunt of Jonathan Miller's and a niece of Proust's"*) entitled "A Collection of Moments."

"She's a novelist and this is a study of involuntary memory, and of autobiographies of childhood written in later life, and here, listen, she writes, 'Marcel says that the echo of his tears, in his traumatic memory of demanding his mother's kiss, never ceased, but was not audible until life grew quiet, like those convent bells which are drowned in the noise of daytime, and sound out again in the silence of the evening.'"†

In much the same way, Oliver himself, in writing about the second of his musical ladies, noted how she spoke of "a sense of impending presence" drifting back into the landscape of early childhood. A throwback to songs her mother had sung.

Neurologists, he points out, have spoken of epileptics in terms of "dreaming states" (Hughlings Jackson) and "psychical seizures" (Penfield).

"But I would like to speak of *spiritual seizures* as being significant and not merely trivial. In *Awakenings*, how when Rose sang 'Love's Old Sweet Song,' of course it was self-referential, but it was also a song precisely about the nostalgia of singing.

"My mother after age eighty used to be surprised by an upsurge of Edwardian song—to me, this evoked a feeling of imminent death."

Oliver now reaches into his satchel and pulls out a huge volume of the journal *Brain*. ("*Brain* as you can see was edited by Lord Brain! Which is to say that two of the greatest figures in twentieth-century neurology were Lord Brain and Sir Head!")

Flipping through *Brain*, Oliver now alights on an essay by Théophile Alajouanine on Dostoyevsky's epilepsy. "All you healthy people," Dostoyevsky once wrote, "cannot imagine the happiness we epileptics feel in the moment before our fit."

To which Oliver adds, "And everything which occurs in epilepsy can occur in migraine. Migraine aura, indeed, is a sort of slow-motion epilepsy."

---

*I had some trouble tracking down confirmation of this double characterization, so I recently wrote to Rachel Miller, who replied, "Total fabrication. Anyone called Salaman is my relation, not Jonathan's. There were two Esther Salamans. One was my mother's sister, a singer. The other, married to my mother's brother, was originally Esther Polianoski, who once worked with Einstein. On Jonathan's side, no Proust. But his mother's family were Bergsons. They lived in Sweden, but there was some fairly close relation to Henri Bergson." So go figure.

†Fascinating, of course, that the specific Proust memory that occasions this insight on later-life recollection of childhood (and in turn captures Oliver's attention) happens to be one of a traumatically ignored child's demand for his mother's attention. See page 31 above.

From migraine and epilepsy, our conversation drifts to drug-induced extremities. Did he ever consider himself addicted?

"Of course. Late in my California period, and then early on in New York, I was a full-out amphetamine addict."

How had he functioned as a doctor during all that time?

"The very worst period was in the autumn of '66 when I didn't even go to the hospital for two or three weeks." A pause. "Actually, December '65 was the worst of all. I was suffering from a bizarre broken heart I'd contracted the previous summer before I arrived in New York."

Presumably the German theater guy in Paris, I thought to myself. I'd been taking furious notes but now asked him: Did he want any of this talked about?

"I am very certain that I want no mention of my sexuality," he replied fiercely, *"it's not relevant."*

He was quiet for a moment. "Auden once told me of Paul Tillich's closet, how after his death, as they were emptying the rooms, they came upon a closet teeming with pornography of the lewdest sort—Auden told them to throw it out: *It wasn't relevant.*

"Well, I myself have always felt that Tillich, like Sartre, was something of an intellectual pervert. But I like to think of myself as having struggled hard and successfully at not being an intellectual pervert.

"I am well aware of the problem of the irritating continued existence on this planet of the person about whom one writes. I am vexed to my roots that I can't write about John the Touretter: furious that a perhaps major work is prevented from completion by the maniacal injunction of a paranoid psychotic.

"The drugs, yes, I can see where that might be relevant, though I'm not eager to see them written much of.

"The sex though . . .

"Well, finally, you will just have to write what you will and we'll see then."

Speaking of which . . .

"I've been reading *The Magic Mountain*," declares Oliver. "I am increasingly bothered by Mann—he is on the side of disease. He writes about pathology and calls it life. Hardly ever is normality portrayed except as a form of dullness. I react to the philosophy of morbidity more violently than to anything else.

"Hume, mechanical philosophy I find morally neutral.

"Kant and Leibniz allow for philosophy from the viewpoint of life.

"But romantic philosophy, and romanticism generally, is obsessed with death, whereas I am not." (This as opposed to his and Luria's notion of "romantic science," which is something else altogether.) "This exalting of disease and death. Mann, for instance, finds the world behind the music to be that of death, but how absurd to speak this way of Schubert!

"Nietzsche once said of Schopenhauer, 'He is an assassin of life.' And I think Mann's a killer. I think Sartre's a killer. And I think I'm fanatic enough to know whereof I speak!

"Hume was too sane to imagine a sick fantasy. With Freud and Schopenhauer, you come to a conception of religion springing out of morbidity and melancholy. But it's possible to imagine a religion arising from health, and oddly enough Nietzsche did that best.

"What I love in Tolstoy, for that matter, is precisely the existence of health and happiness alongside the morbid and tormented. Dostoyevsky understood the latter in a deeper way and he did not become the sort of nut Tolstoy was, but still . . .

"The point is, there's good magic and black magic. *I know all about black magic.* And I will have none of it anymore."

Two beats. "My own doctor has suggested I write a book on medicine from the point of view of health."

January 20

The *New York Review of Books* "Lost Mariner" piece is at the press. At the last minute, Oliver had added an addendum to a footnote based on the stuff Isabelle told him about Korsakoff syndrome in infants. Only now it turns out she was relating something Norman Geschwind at Harvard had told *her*, and even so Oliver seems to have embellished on the report.

And Oliver is freaking out!

As he tells me over the phone, he has "an enormous superego which is sometimes raised to psychotic dimensions," going on to say, "I have a terrible combination: an expansive generous imagination hooped to a wicked, recriminatory superego. Everything gets generalized into the accusation of forgery and lying. But it's not that I invent the truth," he tries to defend himself. "Rather, I intuit or imagine it.

"When I speak of that patient at Brooklyn Little Sisters who is afraid of light and sight, I *know* this is so even though he is aphasic. Or rather, I powerfully feel it to be so, and so do others.

"I sometimes articulate what the inarticulate would say if they could and will someday if they can."

At which point, a complete shift in tone: "By the way, I'll send you the last orthodox neurological study I ever wrote, in *Brain* in 1968: 'Oligodendroglioma with Remote Metastases.' In fact, it's the only neurological paper I've ever written, something of an homage to T.G.I. James, my chief at university in London, of whom I was fond, and who wrote up the only other such case."

Then again, perhaps not such a shift.

"It turns out that in that same volume of *Brain* I found a hilarious case study of a man who suffered from facial agnosia—couldn't even recognize himself in the mirror, had to stick out his tongue to confirm his intellectual surmise—and could only recognize his wife *when* she wore a hat!

"I do greatly appreciate this sort of corroboration, of validation.

"My pieces, if not precisely truthful descriptions, are veridical imaginations or extrapolations. Still, it's good to get corroboration in the media."

January 21 (typed letter)

Dear Ren,

Thank you for your sense and sensibility, your *sanity*, last night. I have written to Isabelle, and to Geschwind of Harvard, letters which (without being "confessional") are models of clarity, courtesy, candour, and with this (I think) the matter should be over, and I should feel free to turn back to *my own* concerns and work.

Over—but not over: I must take warning, and make resolve, because this *sort* of thing raises charged, and potentially quite dangerous issues and feelings—for me, at least, if not for

others; in phantasy, at least, if not reality. This sort of thing, this
realm—what is it? It embraces matters of quoting (or
misquoting), of alluding to, of my relation to . . . *the alive*, be
they patients, colleagues, or friends. And yet, being in the world
myself, perhaps I *have* to make such allusions to others . . .
or do I?
      [. . .]
      This business with Isabelle/Geschwind though brings
home to me that I must take *extreme care* in ever quoting, or
alluding to, a contemporary—a contemporary who is alive, and
perhaps touchy and vulnerable. And, by the same token, that
others must take extreme care *with me* . . . because *I* am alive,
and touchy, and vulnerable . . .[SB]

Noted.

January 23 (dinner at a Middle Eastern restaurant)

Oliver is thrilled with a new patient, a woman (at one of the Little Sisters
residences) who, virtually blind, is suffering or at any rate entertaining an
elaborate visual hallucinosis.

He pulls out a copy of *The New Yorker* scrawled over with notes.

"As you see, I'm now using *The New Yorker* to test for cognitive
recognition.

"Do *you*," he asks me, "ever have trouble keeping focused while taking notes of somebody talking?"

(Ha!)

"I could have killed today for a tape recorder. What a wonder!"

He gives me a copy of his typed notes: a summary.

"It's definitely in the visual apparatus or situation—*something* makes
her hallucinate, and it's not cerebral. Most interestingly, though, she is psy-
chically organizing her peripheral hallucinations. She is giving them personal shape and meaning. Fascinating.

"I once saw an older history professor from Harvard with a horror of a
case of diabetes: He'd had both eyes removed. After the second removal,
he suffered brilliant bright visual storms. I asked my father if he'd ever
heard of this, and he immediately said, 'Yes, nine times,' and gave me a

sixty-year history. It may have been the optic nerve got damaged in the eyeball's removal. It could also be that there's a *visual starvation* and the mind starts generating its own.

"The tragedy for this sad man, though, was that he furthermore had neuropathy of the arms, so that neither could he feel what he could no longer see.

"My father's favorite bedside reading is the *Dictionary of Musical Themes*. He loves music *indiscriminately* and he goes to sleep with a concert ringing in his ears.

"My early Tourette's piece, well before John, 'Witty Ticcy Ray' was the only piece I ever wrote in one go—I wrote it, sent it off to Mary-Kay at the *London Review*, and it was published as drafted—no second thoughts. Usually there are second, third, fifth, and tenth thoughts."

Dessert has arrived: a cheese plate. Presently only the square of hard cheddar remains, which, over the next several minutes, Oliver proceeds to efface by way of a sequence of infinitesimal symmetricalizing subtractions: He takes a narrow slice of hard cheddar, then three more to reestablish the square, then another, then three more, till at considerable length, somehow there is none left.

Meanwhile: "The first thing of any length I wrote my first year at Oxford was an essay on Theodore Hook, the early-nineteenth-century composer, writer of six hundred comic operas. He was a charming man, a genius, but somehow he had no center. In a way this essay was a precursor of my later case studies. I didn't do it for any class—simply the result of a month's reading in the Radcliffe Library. It is the study of a comic, not unhappy, genius that left no residue, that strangely aborted. Hook didn't exactly peter out; he just never coalesced.

"Both Jonathan and I are haunted by the notion that we throw off an infinite number of brilliant ephemera but nothing else, nothing of permanent value.

"Ah well," sighs Oliver, "perhaps I've become duller and deeper . . .

"Hook, though, was a prodigy. And the prodigy is under terrible pressure. The pressures of vanity, narcissism. He has to struggle through his facility to reach poetic depths. And usually doesn't. Early on I read a book on musical prodigies—twenty case histories of which only three made it.

"I must have felt such pressure, even then."

January 29

Oliver goes and breaks his other leg!

Or so I now hear from Joanna by phone (I am again in LA for the week)—she gives me his phone number at Montefiore, where I reach him, in traction.

And indeed, he has badly broken his right leg, shattered his kneecap, and dislocated his shoulder, when simply falling on a sheet of ice, walking to the post office on City Island. (He notes that he is so big these days that whichever bones were fractured upon contact with the ground were completely pulverized by the sheer reverberation of the subsequent crush of flesh.) He is all plastered up, his right arm strapped to his body for the next month at least to allow the shoulder to heal. After that, he won't be able to use a crutch since he mustn't jam pressure against the armpit.

"Silly damn thing to happen," he understates, "but at least now I'll be symmetrical! You remember how I symmetrized our cheese the other night?"

Come to think of it, back in 1963, Oliver had dislocated his left shoulder in a surfing accident!

What is your *immediate* horizon? I ask him.

"Oh, about two inches off the ground."

He relates how he called Colin Haycraft in England to tell him, and without missing a beat, Colin simply retorted, dryly, "Oliver, you'd do *anything* for a footnote."

And indeed, the whole psychopathology of the incident is striking: In 1972 his mother dies, he finishes *Awakenings*, which gets published the following year, he goes to Norway where he is attacked by a bull (cow?), his leg is demolished, for months it lies there, a doughy ghost (castration), it takes him ten years to finally come to grips with the experience (the paralysis may not have been psychosomatic, but the blockage certainly was), he finally finishes the damn book about the incident, the blockage lifts, case studies start pouring forth, and now he goes and breaks the other leg! And the right arm gets disabled to boot. Oh, Oliver!

And yet everything about this time seems different—in the city versus the wilderness, immediate versus delayed care, quick recovery—and, as Oliver (mercifully) says, "In a way I'm not terribly *interested* in this experience."

Meanwhile, he has finished "The Disembodied Lady," his piece on proprioception dysfunction, he tells me, by way of a tiny cramped scrawl with his right hand and a single finger-poke at the typewriter with his left.

February 7

I'm back in New York, and over the phone, Oliver complains: "Waves of basilisk-like boredom are flowing over me. The last time I was like this, I was too anxious to be bored. This time recovery seems to be going well (my present surgeon says he's never seen anyone recover muscle strength so quickly), but the boredom is debilitating."

February 8

I visit Oliver at Montefiore Hospital—his old haunt. He is decked out like Bacchus, or like the god Tiberinus, his plastered leg outstretched, his furry barrel chest hunched on one elbow (the other arm strapped tight to his side), a swath of white sheet draped across his midriff.

A friendly doctor is just leaving. They have agreed to keep him on heparin, a blood anticoagulant, partly to compensate for the rigidity of the leg (to avoid thromboses and phlebitis), and partly to provide an excuse for his continued residence in the hospital. Thus, for the moment, Oliver is an artificial hemophiliac.

"I've got hypermobile blood," he crows. "A nosebleed would kill me!" He laughs.

"It's funny," he says, "if you gaze down from the window over there, you can see the Headache Unit, where both my creativity and my descent into American medicine began."

A few days later, another bedside visit.

"This leg is boring to me," Oliver announces. "It's of no interest whatsoever.

"In fact, I begin to see how someone last time might have said, 'What's the problem?' and when I replied, 'My leg is depoeticized, dis-exalted, etc.,' they'd have replied, *But that's normal!*"

"Although my morbid and creative preoccupations last time did verge occasionally toward somewhat excessive heights, at least then my imagination had a leg to stand on. Here there is nothing to exercise my imagination, and imagination is different from fantasy.

"Back then, the thing with the surgeon"—the surgeon who'd attended Oliver when he arrived in London, and whom he assigns the name "Mr. Swan" in the book, had seemed to Oliver singularly officious, imperious, and oblivious to any and all of his concerns, deeming the whole operation and its sequelae, to hear Oliver tell it, utterly ordinary and beneath concern—"no doubt had the effect of inflaming though not distorting the experience. Had he behaved differently, I might have been able to let the experience cool. Instead, his attitude invested everything with a sense of fundamental doubt and misgiving (while Luria invested everything with a sense of unexplored territory).

"But still sometimes I wonder: Was it *just* a scotoma? Did I in fact inject neuropsychology with metaphysics?

"Still and all, it's one thing to have a scotoma, another to experience it as a focal godforsakeness . . . or is it?"

✳

Our conversation turns to the Grumman buses that are all being recalled by the MTA—fully a fifth of NYC's bus fleet!

"I know," Oliver exults, "I love it! I have a Grumman car. I'm staying in a Grumman hospital. I have been having a *Dunciad*-like vision of all the world reduced to Grummandry!"

✳

A few days after that, back at Oliver's bedside, trying to entertain him, or rather maybe to get him to entertain both of us, I ask, "What about your debacle with that larcenous colleague of yours during the mid- and later seventies? You've never told me that story."

Oliver veritably harrumphs. "Well," he says, "Dr. F was a decent, ordinary doctor colleague who, with the advent of Medicare and Medicaid, went quite mad with cupidity."

Oliver had all along been quite hopeless with regard to the Medicare bureaucracy so that at first after he'd been fired from Beth Abraham, a partnership in which Dr. F would handle all the paperwork seemed an ideal solution. Oliver averted his gaze: Dr. F handled all business details and Oliver signed whatever he was given.

This state of affairs, Oliver explains, presently led to a Medicare audit.

"Under strenuous questioning as to EEGs which I had signed off on, I averred to the auditors that I couldn't possibly remember every one— but outside I confronted Dr. F: 'That's not true. I *can* remember every one, and I did not remember four-fifths of those. You ought to know that you've been naughty.' He had me signing blank bills. I should have known, I should have realized, but I was oblivious.

"After 1976, far from drawing back, Dr. F lurched forward. He had me going to scandalous, so-called 'adult manors'—deplorable places, many of them run by Hasidic Jews (which provided a further turn of the screw)— mass-production assembly lines of sub-adequate care—many of which would subsequently be shut down . . .

"In the summer of '77, Isabelle Rapin, my conscience and my reality, told me, 'This man Dr. F is grossly criminal and you simply must dissociate yourself from him.'

"The final blowout came by way of my EEG technician, Chris. The EEG machine at one of these places was in terrible shape (broken pen spikes and so forth) and Chris told him, 'Dr. F, these readouts are simply unacceptable, they must be done again,' and he refused. Which led to the blowup.

"By Christmas 1977, we accomplished a legal separation, at immense cost. And then, several months later, there came another Medicare audit, this time of me alone. I didn't even connect the two. I went there proudly with my ninety-nine out of a hundred requested files. (Oddly, the only one I couldn't track down was for a patient called Sacks.)

"The first meeting, they complimented me on my thoroughness. The second meeting, though, quickly began to seem a kangaroo court. The questions were palpably dripping with insinuation: 'Dr. Sacks, you depart from medical protocol.'

"'That's only for children.'

"'Dr. Sacks, I can't read your records.'

"'Well, then you differ from everyone else who comes in contact with them. People not only read them, they positively relish them!'

"Then, during a break, a little bearded man came up to me and confidentially confided, 'As one beard to another, we're not interested in any of this but rather in what came before, in Dr. F . . .'

"At that moment I realized that all this was profoundly improper and that I needed a criminal lawyer. I got one—a good lawyer, who charged accordingly. Luckily letters from Dr. F existed, detailing our arrangement, and it quickly became obvious that though I may be ingenuous to a fault, I was no prime mover.

"I thought it was all over until a year ago when I got a $5,000 bill in triplicate, denying an earlier 1975 tax credit. My lawyer called Dr. F, who refused to pay."

A long sigh, a vacant gaze out the window.

"The thing, all told, has cost me $50,000 and years of moral misery. But this whole business with Dr. F was only possible because one charges per service. I mean, myself I do one EEG for every six patients. I find it harder and more tedious to earn money that way—to be done properly they should take an hour each. Dr. F would have them done in five minutes and read in thirty seconds, which was easy because they were in fact utterly unreadable.

"As a doctor working principally on the Medicare circuit, one is paid relatively too little for clinical exams and too much for tests: $7 for a clinical visit, but $35 for an EEG.

"Medicare and Medicaid insurance have had a baneful influence because they're organized on the basis of payment for service or commodity. A boy with a cold walks into a Medicaid clinic and $200 later—having been x-rayed and this and that—he walks out still sniveling. In Britain, by contrast, they have a capitation fee, which works out well—there isn't the temptation or the potential for unnecessary testing.

"Here CAT scans at $300 a pop are being ordered up like blood tests. When I'm off driving and my car radar device goes off, it's generally either because I'm passing a microwave oven or a CAT scan center. Unscrupulous doctors and unscrupulous patients collude in this mad, excessive testing."

What about rising medical costs, more generally? I ask.

"I recently received a bill for $200 following a three-minute appointment with a specialist," he replies. "I sent him a copy of the Hippocratic oath, underlining its prohibition against charging fellow doctors, and went on to ask, somewhat sarcastically, whether he really felt his time was worth $70 a minute. He apologized by return mail, saying the bill had been sent out by mistake and that the fee was artificially inflated, pushed up for insurance."

Meanwhile, Oliver goes on, truly vital medical research is falling by the wayside. "I just got word that over at Beth Abraham, R.B., our dear old postencephalitic piano player, has died and, incredibly, there has been no postmortem. Indeed, there has been no postmortem since 1972 on any of the postencephalitics. Ninety percent of our postencephalitics have died without any pathological study performed on these unique nervous systems.

"Postmortems—the classical way of learning pathology—are disappearing from the American scene. It's hard enough having to request permission to perform a postmortem from a relative without having to *charge* them for it . . .

"The only postmortems I've had for that matter have been with the Little Sisters. For example, Mother Genevieve at Queen of Peace once allowed us to do a postmortem on a twin with Huntington's disease—very important. There are patients at Beth Abraham of whom we will never know the cause of their illness!"

He shakes his head plaintively, muttering, "Unbelievable."

※

A few days later, and now Oliver is *really* bored. I have an idea. I call my friend Robert Krulwich, the (at that time) comically flecked business correspondent at National Public Radio (remember the mouse opera with which he contrived to explain interest rates?). As it happens, I'd gotten to know him over the past several months, since I am regularly dropping in to NPR's New York offices to opine on things Polish (I'd become one of their Rolodex pundits as well). Anyway, so now I call him and tell him to grab his tape recorder and come meet me at Montefiore: trust me. I then get Oliver to start telling Krulwich some stories for a change. And Scheherazade-like, across a series of sessions, Oliver starts lavishing him with oral versions of some of his recent case studies, which in turn now start showing up on *All Things Considered* (effectively seeding the ground for what will be Oliver's first bestseller, once we finally get past the release of the Leg book).

A few days later, he wants me to bring books.

I ask him if he'd like some of Martin Gardner's books of mathematical curiosa.

"Absolutely not!" he interrupts brusquely. "I know you and Eric love that sort of thing, but I can't abide it. I have consuming curiosity about nature but none about mathematics as such. For me, the delight and relish of problem-solving has to occur in a natural context and cannot be numbered one through twenty inclusive."

He also tells me how during the night he suffered a terrible fright, a night hypochondria, perhaps—spasms in his calf transmogrifying into imagined thrombosis, just waiting to dislodge and engulf his heart. In his ensuing night panic, he composed a new last will and testament, naming as his heirs his "literary children" and decreeing that his entire fortune should be given over to their care, Eric Korn and I (!) to be the executors of the estate. He hopes I won't mind.

Thankfully, nothing thrombotic or otherwise occurs, and the will in the meantime has been superseded many times over.

February 14

I call to ask Oliver if I can visit him at Montefiore later in the day. Will he be around?

"Will I be *around*?" he blusters, exultantly. "*Will I be around?* You might as well ask the question of the Grand Canyon! My dear boy, I am *geologically immobile.*"

In the event, two of the nurses from Beth Abraham, the Costello sisters, are at Oliver's bedside when I arrive, having delivered turkey sandwiches.

"Does Doctor like turnips?" one of them inquires.

He grimaces. "Oof, I'm afraid not. They remind me too vividly of my days at Braefield: It was mangel-wurzel and swedes. The turnip is a delicate sedate cousin of the mangel-wurzel. A swede is a ten-pound, monstrous, misshapen turnip, and the mangel-wurzel a forty-pound, overblown swede. Well, at Braefield it was swedes for breakfast, mangel-wurzel for lunch, and swedes *and* mangel-wurzel combined for dinner. For four years! So: No, thank you. But thank you for the thought."

Oliver recalls how Jonathan Miller, in his production of *Eugene Onegin*, included a minor character who "never seemed to be eating but by banquet's end had devoured the whole place—grape by grape. 'That's me, isn't it?' I said to Jonathan afterwards, and he just smiled.

"Sometimes," Oliver muses by way of association, "I do grow cannibalistic of my patients, I suppose. I become *voraciously* interested. I hold my breath with excitement."

Oliver feels his days of bodybuilding and weight lifting back in LA may have contributed to both of his leg accidents—this time, for instance, the ligaments around the knee simply snapped.

Another weight-lifter friend from that period, whom Oliver recently reencountered, currently has two plastic hips.

He asks me the next time to bring him that picture of himself squat-lifting at the California State Heavyweight Championship.

"I am thinking of writing a short sad piece for a weight lifters' magazine; I will call it, 'The End of a Squatter.'"

Meanwhile, by his bedside, Oliver has Nietzsche's *The Will to Power* (edited by Walter Kaufmann). He has clearly been through it dozens of times. There are layer upon layer of margin scribblings.

There is a passage (on page 428) where Nietzsche describes the exalted sensitivity of the artist, comparing it with a sick person's, in language that directly applies to John the Touretter. Oliver reads it to me, adding, "When he wrote this passage, he was already himself in a state of physiological exaltation.

"At my best, reading Nietzsche is like hearing myself think—only more exalted. I know *so exactly* what Nietzsche is thinking there."

February 18 (phone conversation)

Oliver is reading *Alan Turing: The Enigma*, the biography of the British computer and cipher scientist, pilloried in the fifties for his homosexuality. "A young genius driven to anxious suicide by his sexuality," says Oliver. "He reminds me of someone I know.

"When I was eighteen or nineteen, I read Harrod's biography of Keynes—it was the official biography, so there was no overt discussion of his homosexuality but one could, or at any rate *I* could, tell reading between the lines, and it was greatly heartening—as it was later with Thom Gunn and Auden—to find someone in whom integrity and distinction were melded to the homosexual. It helped dissipate the taint of the morally squalid . . .

"For all that, I don't have the feeling, though, that either Keynes's or Turing's *mind* was different for being homosexual."

March 13

Typewritten letter from Colin Haycraft at Duckworth, responding in his own delicious way to my letter to him about the galleys of the Leg book:

> Re: A LEG TO STAND ON by Oliver Sacks
> Dear Ren,
>   Very many thanks for your letter of February 27th. We had found most of the "literals" ourselves, but I was glad to have your reaction to the overuse of the word "joy" and its derivations. I remember removing hundreds of them in the typescript. I have now removed virtually all of them!
>   All the best.
>   Yours,
>   [signed] Colin

*

Pauline Kael on John Candy in *Splash* in the March 19 issue of *The New Yorker*:

> There's a certain amount of aggression built into a frame as big as Candy's: he simply occupies more space than other people do. But Candy doesn't have anything like John Belushi's insane volatility or the gleam in his eyes that told you he was about to go haywire and smash things up; Candy is the soul of amiability—it's just an awfully large soul.

April 18

Oliver is now home again, although he continues to return to the Burke rehabilitation center for daily outpatient therapy sessions.

He is terribly agitated because Mary-Kay has sent back galleys for the *London Review* version of his musical women piece, and it has undergone, to hear him tell it, "a terrible metamorphosis." It has been stripped of its neurological meditation, and the bare case studies, thus unadorned, have indeed been reduced to the "Two Gothic Tales" of the new title.

"Yes," Oliver huffs, "but do they have any interest beyond the Gothic?

They *do*, or rather they did, when it was clear that they illustrated the nature of experience and the organization of individuality and of personal originality in the brain—the interaction of a crude electrical explosion and an individual memory . . . Now, it reads like a couple of pieces of inadequate fiction. People will think I've entered my *anecdotage*, retailing bizarre tales of no significance."

He wonders if he is being punished for the disloyalty of having also begun to publish pieces in *The New York Review of Books*.

❋

The fact is that what with his increasing visibility, in both the *London Review of Books* and *The New York Review of Books*—and the general upsurge of case studies he has been publishing as he emerges from the penumbra of the Leg blockage—and now, too, the conversations with Krulwich over NPR, Oliver is becoming steadily more well known among the cognoscenti. And three months ago Bob Silvers arranged for him to give the prestigious Gallatin Lecture at the New York Public Library, now coming up next week.

"I have to avoid anticipation," Oliver tells me. "I'm fine on five minutes' notice or no notice whatsoever, but three months of anticipation wears me out in the extreme.

"I need to write another piece on Luria's and Goldberg's favorite subject: frontal lobe syndrome. I realized this and thought, who shall I choose? And immediately realized it was Harry, this engineer who blew an aneurism at age thirty-one and has since been a patient of Beth Abraham, a man who will score extremely well on an IQ test, is good at problems and puzzles, but who is not there as a person and because of that shows extraordinary lapses in judgment—defecating in the middle of conversation, violent outbursts, etc.

"It's different each time: with the two musical ladies, the case study generated the meditation; with frontal lobe, the meditation demanded an example; with 'Witty Ticcy Ray,' the two impulses were simultaneous."

April 20

We attend the Manhattan Theatre Club's production of Pinter's *Other Places* (with "A Kind of Alaska" as its last act, and Dianne Wiest in the Judi Dench role). Afterwards we all go out for a drink at the Churchill Tavern.

Oliver recounts how in 1973 Colin received a letter from Pinter telling him how moved he had been by *Awakenings* and how though he was now going to let it "submerge" beneath conscious attention, he expected that someday it would "resurface" in some creative form. Years passed without his giving it much thought and then one morning, suddenly, on waking, the line "Something . . . is . . . happening" was in his mind, and the rest of the composition occurred fairly quickly.

Oliver as inveterate naturalist: He recounts how he was recently undergoing his physical therapy for his leg, commenting to his therapist how his thigh muscle had long seemed especially adapted to powerful, consistent, but slow exertions; the therapist seemed interested, commented on the different kinds of muscle tissue, and jokingly suggested that they ought to perform a biopsy on the thigh to learn more.

"Yes, *let's!*" Oliver immediately insisted. "Pluck out a wedge, do take a pound of my flesh! Let's examine it together!" He was at most only half joking.

"I myself have always felt that terror is reduced by active investigation," he goes on to explain.

He also feels that no matter how grim the situation, laughter can be a palliative. "This is because the self who laughs is greater than the self who suffers—is momentarily *outside* the suffering self, liberated from it, laughing at it.

"Indeed," he goes on, "I've often had students who were rather astonished at my 'unprofessionalism' when suddenly I'd be laughing merrily at the bizarre exertions of an obviously suffering patient—but they were even more astonished when my laughter was quickly joined by that of the attending nurses and presently by the patient himself—and it was clear that if only for a moment, the pall of affliction, in Simone Weil's sense, had been lifted."

A walk through the city, and then back to my apartment. He comes in for coffee before heading home.

"I knew delirium as a child with my fevers and migraines and perhaps this is why as an adult, delirium does not so much threaten me. At any rate, I feel myself frayed at the edges but still whole at the center, although the fraying is definitely edging in, or perhaps subjacent to, the integrated part—I just hope the center can hold out till I have finished all my work."

April 25

Oliver calls, nervous about the lecture he is to give tomorrow night. "I suppose it's procrastination," he surmises, "but instead of preparing for the talk, I've launched out on a new story . . ."

I tell him I don't have time to hear the whole thing right now, I'm just rushing to an appointment, but could he summarize it? "Ah yes," he exudes. "Sudden unexpected outbreak of genius and salaciousness in an eighty-nine-year-old woman brought on by neurosyphilis."

All right then. Can't wait.

Later he explains: "This one concerns an eighty-nine-year-old Albanian lady who came into clinic with her ninety-two-year-old husband. She'd been enjoying a slow, dignified winding-down sort of existence, but now she was complaining that she was all abuzz, and indeed she was—she displayed a remarkable efflorescence, flirtatiousness, salaciousness, wit, intelligence, an absurd, dizzying vitality. 'Do you think,' she presently confided, 'that it could be Cupid's disease?' She explained that sixty-five years before, she had worked in a brothel in Salonika from whence she'd been rescued by her husband. Up to now, she'd had no complaint, but . . . We tested her, and her hunch proved correct: Spirochetes were *rioting* in her brain. It was a complex situation because in some ways she was enjoying her rejuvenescence, although in other ways she felt it undignified and she worried about the illness's progress into the future, that she might go right past the border into dementia. And what she wanted to know was, could we keep her *just as she was?*

"Well, as things developed, the question proved moot because a few weeks later she contracted pneumonia and quickly died . . .

"But it all reminded me of Mann's last story, *The Black Swan*—have you read it? About a menopausal woman in a sort of grief over the lapsing of her menstrual flow who seeks solace at a spa where she falls passionately in love, insanely in love, with a young man, whereupon her menstrual flow resumes. A few weeks later, she is dead, and in the autopsy they discover a huge tumor in her ovaries. And the question is, did her passion create the tumor, or the hormonal imbalance brought on by the tumor create her passion?"

Two beats: "A truly wicked old man, the late Mann."

The next morning over the phone, Oliver tells me that, still concerned about the coming talk, he'd decided to photocopy a few things in preparation (Descartes, Pascal, Nietzsche)—only now he has two hundred pages!

April 26

At the New York Public Library, Susan Sontag introduces Oliver as "one of the best living writers in the English language," following up in particular with an evocation and celebration of his "writerly style." She describes *Awakenings* as a "cascade of ideas" and "the most interesting speculation on allegory since Walter Benjamin" with "prose of an incandescent intensity," and Oliver's life meditation as focusing on "morbid processes and metaphysical sobriety."

Jasper Johns is seated behind me: it's that sort of crowd.

Oliver begins: "It's lovely and terrifying to be here.

"The title I've chosen for this talk, 'Neurology and the Soul,' is provocative and possibly mad. It self-consciously echoes James's 'Reflex Action and Theism,' and to the extent it contrasts materialism and vitalism, scientism and religion, body and soul, it is the oldest subject in the world, although it is particularly new today, what with the rise in such notions as artificial intelligence, robots, computers, etc."

Continuing on: "The Modern Age is traceable to Descartes, with his early insistence on viewing man as a machine, quoting the *Meditations*: 'I regard the human body as a machine, so built, put together of bone, nerve, muscle, vein, blood, and skin that still although it had no mind it would not fail to move in all the same ways as at present since it does not move by direction of its will or mind but only by arrangement of its organs.'

"And indeed, he was the first to consider that a human being just might be an automaton," though there would be many to follow, from Sherrington through Pavlov, all of them completely alienated from notions of soul, imagination, and the like."

On the other hand, Oliver suggests, if one has a mechanical view of human nature, a sort of dissociation may occur and one may oneself become more machinelike. He goes on to quote "a passage of great pathos from Darwin's autobiography" where the great man speaks of his loss of interest in music, how he has become "a machine for grinding particulars into theorems."

Throughout the lecture, Oliver props his glasses on his forehead, then drops them back down.

"Enough of an introduction," he finally says. "Now on to some neurological stories!

"For as a doctor, one is constantly confronted with neurological preparations, on the one hand, and existential stories and dramas, on the other.

"William James," he interrupts himself, "referred incessantly to 'the soul' in his conversation but banished the word from his physiology. 'Some day, though,' he nevertheless mused, 'perhaps souls will have their innings.'

"And I want to give souls their inning."

He then moves through a series of stories—many of the ones he'd been regaling his friends and colleagues and increasingly his readers with over the past several months, before eventually beginning to wrap things up.

"Perhaps two final examples," he suggests.

"People with Parkinsonism indeed begin to walk like robots. I recall a music teacher unmusicked by her Parkinsonism. But precisely to the extent that, as Eliot reminds us, 'You are the music while the music lasts,' just so the antidote to Parkinsonism is *music*. If the Parkinsonian suffers from inertia, the remedy at times can consist, precisely, in artfulness, art-fusedness.

"And then as well there is my own story." He goes on to rehearse some of the stations along his Leg journey (the book being due out now within a few weeks), concluding by noting how during recovery, he began to experience an almost hallucinatory in-playing of Mendelssohn, whereupon he recovered his own kinetic melody. "Nietzsche says one listens to music with one's muscles—that one is, precisely, moved.

"Walking is a melody and not just a mechanical consecution. It *is* mechanical but not *just* mechanical."

William Harvey as a young man, Oliver recalls, went to Galileo's lectures and the first part of his book on animal motion was a Galilean analysis. But, in his second half, he concluded that such an analysis was necessarily incomplete. Because animal motion is *essentially* graceful, musical, transcendental.

Pulling things together, Oliver now soars to his conclusion: The Cartesian notion of man as a machine is tremendously powerful, and indeed was absolutely necessary for the rise of an empirical, objective science.

But it is not enough. It cannot tell us about the personal, the "I," inside the physiological. A purely physiological explanation offends common sense and one's own egotism. Mechanistic neurology needs to be complemented by an existential neurology—of face, internal landscape, the individual.

"Until we achieve such a conjunction, we can never hope to fathom the mysteries of perception and action but will remain lost in the empty labyrinths of empiricism.

"We need, if it's not a contradiction in terms, a science of the individual, or at the very least one that does not do violence to the individual."

Much applause followed by a truly vivid and vivifying question-and-answer session.

One person asks what Oliver makes of the question of the transcendence of the soul.

"I can provide no sense to the notion of a dismembered soul. I am speaking precisely of the *embodiment* of the soul."

And what of Freud?

"Early Freud seemed focused on a drive theory, even though a drive theory is contradictory to human nature since a person would then merely be the algebraic sum of the drives. And yet, clearly, Freud was obsessed, enraptured by art. And Freud and Spinoza both conceived of analysis as a means of reducing bondage and liberating the *soul*, discussed as such."

And behaviorism?

"Ach, the infernal science: puppetry. Behaviorism deals with an impassive 'It' and makes no attempt to bring out the active 'I.' An active science would give support for the idea of freedom, provide the frame for the picture. Indeed, we've spent a century building the scaffolding. Now it's time to paint a few pictures."

Any influence from Susanne Langer?

"It's many years since I read Susanne Langer, or for that matter since I read anyone." ("Ha!" write I, in the margin of my notes.)

Do you believe in God?

"I believe in the divine: Mendelssohn is divine.

"I believe in grace: All natural movements are graceful.

"I believe in the mystical mathematics of heaven, which is to say grace beyond the algorithm of causality."

What about out-of-body experiences in those just returned from death's brink?

"Hell, one has a vision of heaven all the time!"

❋

Later that night, a group of us walk over for supper at a Brazilian restaurant on Forty-Seventh. (On the way, Oliver complains to me of having been a bit disconcerted by Sontag's celebration of his "writerly style," insisting "I'm not conscious of having a style; hell, I'm not conscious of being a writer, since I only try to express my thoughts.") Once there, as if at the Last Supper, Oliver starts passing out his two hundred photocopied pages of passages to us, his disciples.

"Oh damn," he says, "I was going to say something about Simone Weil and roots and being neurologically uprooted." "I'm getting exceedingly fond of Coleridge, all about the wonder of synthesis." "Oh bugger, I was going to read the first three pages of the *Pensées*." "Oh," finally, "oh, oh well."

May 5 (phone conversation)

"The thing that upsets people about a frontal lobe patient is his *indifference* until they realize that he is *truly indifferent*; that he means no harm, although he *means no good*; that he is precisely *meaningless*.

"In this way, such patients remind me of *bureaucracies*."

Bureaucratic inertia as a frontal lobe syndrome?

"Well, perhaps I wouldn't react as violently to bureaucracies if I could just see them as frontal lobe syndromes . . . I mean, I send out two thousand bills a year and encounter Arendtian error constantly—the banal absence of thought, feeling, sense—moral indifference.

"State law, appallingly, allows for the disposal of records after *five* years. There is, therefore, usually no medical record deeper than five years.

"On the other hand, one of the reasons for the growing uninhabitability of this house is that I myself have notes on every patient I have ever seen!"

❋

From Hermine Wittgenstein's recollection of her brother, included in *Recollections of Wittgenstein:**

> I said to him during a long conversation we had at that time that when I thought of him with his philosophically trained mind as an elementary school teacher it seemed to be like somebody wanting to use a precision instrument to open crates. Ludwig replied with an analogy that reduced me to silence. He said, "You remind me of somebody who is looking out through a closed window and cannot explain to himself the strange movements of a passerby. He cannot tell what sort of storm is raging out there or that this person might only be managing with difficulty even to stay on his feet."

John the Touretter?
Oliver?

※

Oliver also has me rereading William James's Gifford Lectures,† especially the one on "Religion and Neurology":

> But any object that is infinitely important to us and awakens our devotion feels to us also as if it must be *sui generis* and unique. Probably a crab would be filled with a sense of personal outrage if it could hear us class it without ado or apology as a crustacean, and thus dispose of it. "I am no such thing," it would say; "I am MYSELF, MYSELF alone."

> Medical materialism seems indeed a good appellation for the too simple-minded system of thought which we are considering. Medical materialism finishes up Saint Paul by calling his vision on the road to Damascus a discharging lesion of the occipital cortex,

---

*Edited by Rush Rhees (London: Oxford University Press, 1984), 4.
†William James, *Varieties of Religious Experience: A Study in Human Nature* (New York: The Modern Library, 1929), 10, 14–15, 23.

he being an epileptic. It snuffs out Saint Teresa as an hysteric, Saint Francis of Assisi as an hereditary degenerate . . .

And medical materialism then thinks that the spiritual authority of all such personages is successfully undermined.

Insane conditions have this advantage, that they isolate special factors of the mental life, and enable us to inspect them unmasked by their more usual surroundings. They play the part in mental anatomy which the scalpel and the microscope play in the anatomy of the body.

June 12 (a quiet dinner at 94 Hunan)

"I was speaking with my youngest postencephalitic today, a man who must have contracted the illness at birth, recovered, and then years later lapsed. He was talking about the hallucinations which infest his experience whenever he is administered certain drugs. He is phenomenally sensitive—the very slightest dosages provoking the very wildest, most vivid hallucinations. 'But they're okay with me,' he said, 'as long as they don't become so vivid that I feel *compelled* to participate. That way madness lies.'"

Which in turn gets Oliver talking about "Lilliputian hallucinations, in fever or drug states, accompanied by affect of *dreadless curiosity*. I had a patient," he continues, "who told me he saw the floor before him covered over with tiny musical instruments—infinitesimal violins, minuscule tubas. Such hallucinations often take the form of elves."

Question: Did hallucinations of elves precede their appearance in fairy tales, or do our feverish hallucinations rather order themselves into entities previously suggested by such fairy tales?

Meanwhile: "At Beth Abraham today I had an amazing conversation with a 'Yiddishe mama,' as she calls herself, who has been progressively disintegrating toward schizophrenia. Last month she'd told me that she believed the head nurse was head of the world and that she kept Negroes in a state of sexual suspense to prey on Yiddishe mamas.

"Today she told me that she herself was turning into a Negro.

"I asked her how long she'd been having these thoughts, and she vehemently protested, 'Don't ask me how long I've been having these

thoughts—ask me how long has this been happening, how long have I
been turning into a Negro.'

"'All right,' I asked, 'how long has this been happening?'

"'Eighteen days,' she replied.

"She'd been metaphysically offended by my reducing her calamity to
L-DOPA or whatever.

"'In the whole history of the universe, never has such a thing happened,' she proclaimed. 'Have you ever *heard* of Yiddishe mamas turning
into Negroes, just like that?'

"And of course her illusions were grounded in a sociological reality
there at Beth Abraham, where the lower staff is indeed almost entirely
black, simultaneously degraded and in a position of power."

May and June miscellany

Oliver drops by, lavish with ghost stories. Mainly he tells me of a patient
he once saw during medical school while doing rounds at Middlesex Hospital. This was a patient of Richard Asher's, the doctor teacher he respected
who later committed suicide. The year was 1957.

Asher had been paying a house call on another patient one afternoon
when he saw a seated figure in the corner, unearthly still.

"What's that?" he asked.

"That's Uncle Toby," came the reply. "He hasn't moved in seven years."

And sure enough, it seemed the family spoon-fed him slop from time
to time, he moved his bowels every couple of months, they moved his limbs
about every once in a while, but other than that he was immobile.

He was also very cold to the touch.

In fact, a few hours later when they got him to the hospital, his temperature on admission proved to be sixty-eight degrees! All his vital metabolic signs were way down, and his thyroid registered zero—absolutely
nothing (a possible cause of the low metabolism).

Slowly, over a period of weeks, the staff at the hospital "warmed him
up"—both with regard to body temperature and the synthetic thyroid sub-
stitute with which they now "topped him off." And gradually, he came
around. The first few days the sounds coming out of his mouth were like
a 78 rpm record being played at 16. But day by day, he pepped up to regular speed and seemed to be getting better.

When Oliver saw him, he recalls, the med students were being pushed to make a special effort not to mention the date or accidentally leave newspapers or the like—it was thought the shock would be too overwhelming. As far as Toby was concerned, he'd been out for maybe a day and it was still 1950.

"Fascinating," mused Oliver, recollecting the case. "Fascinating. Only sadly cut short."

Within a week or so of coming to, Uncle Toby began coughing blood. An X-ray revealed an intensely proliferating bronchial carcinoma—a virulently expanding lung cancer. And he was dead within two months.

Looking back through Toby's file, doctors came upon a 1950 chest X-ray. In hindsight, yes, they could notice the slightest trace, a dark smudge, of an incipient tumor. Lung cancer, Oliver explained, is one of the fastest-growing cancers. Apparently the carcinoma had been metabolically suspended, like Toby, for seven years. Perhaps the shutdown itself had constituted the body's own response to the only just blossoming carcinoma? And awakening him had awoken it . . .

Talking about Asher puts Oliver in mind of James Purdon Martin (1893–1984), who did his best work after retirement in 1960, during thirty years at Highlands Hospital in North Finchley (including work with a population of postencephalitics there). "He had been a humble, unnoticed neurologist," Oliver recalls, "no luminary and dismissed because of this—and yet he may have done the finest work of the lot of them. His book was finally published in 1967: *The Basal Ganglia and Posture.* A typically self-effacing title. I'd have given it a more dramatic title."

Like what?

"Oh, *The Salvation of Mankind*!"

※

On the dangers of overinterpretation: Oliver relates how back in his California days he once had a dream of a crowd chasing him, throwing a mirror at him, which upon breaking, shattered into a spangle of shards, each reflecting fragments of his face.

He'd told his shrink at the time about the dream and they'd hazarded the various obvious interpretations.

The next day, however, as he was watching himself pump iron at his gym, he suddenly noticed, in the reflection, that the ceiling mirror had come dislodged, was hurtling toward him, and indeed was shattering onto his leg—eventually requiring eighteen stitches.

He lets out a huge leonine yawn, then wonders, "Have you ever noticed how just prior to the yawn, our consciousness becomes a vast wide yawn-scape?"

Oliver talks about a conversation he had with Isabelle concerning learning and teaching, how a primary language cannot be taught through a system of rules and applications but rather must be learned through direct experience and inference.

"In this sense," he suggests, "I believe I am almost unteachable although I am a very good learner. This may be one of the reasons I'm ungrateful to my education . . .

"One of the things that struck me in coming to America was the richness of idiom combined with the paucity of vocabulary."

Another time he tells of a man in a Duncan Dallas film who, much as with the man who mistook his wife, could for example draw the spool of cotton thread placed before him in exacting detail and yet not identify what it was. "Which raises the question: Can you have a percept without a concept?

"Hughlings Jackson felt that aphasics could not form propositions or use propositional logic internally. One of the reasons Hughlings Jackson is generally unreadable, however, is precisely that he writes only in propositions.

"There is something about school which tends to hypertrophize the clever (which is required for test-taking) in a way that must be superseded if one is going to get on with living. I myself had a burst of the imaginative between the ages of ten and fourteen, which was then bludgeoned into cleverness for years thereafter and was not recovered—I did not really feel again, that is—until years later when, escaping school, I was rescued by the world of my patients.

"I was originally going to write the Leg book in kabbalistic terms, that is, beginning with tsimtsum—contracture (breakage), the plunge into nothingness—followed by the iridescent chaos of conceptual hypotheses, followed at long last by the phase of tikkun, with its redemptive action. And though in the end I decided not to be quite so explicit about that arc, you can still see it there inside, beneath the lineaments."

At dinner with some friends:

"I eat with a strange combination of appetite, inertia, and compulsion.

"Removed from my patients, I am like Antaeus removed from the earth.

"When I first reported to Shengold and he asked me in a word what my problem was, I replied, 'Changelessness.'

"For all my love of the case history, history itself came late within my own purview. My earliest passions were all for the eternal verities, the changeless, the starscape. In *Migraine* I spoke of the firmament of neurology, the constellations. What initially attracted me to the Parkinsonians was their stillness—the way they were like inert planets. It was only later that I became entranced by change—the Touretters, after all, are *pure* changefulness. A case history—any narrative for that matter—is about how freedom interacts with fate."

17

The Publication, at Long Last, of the Leg Book; Its Reception; Sancho Launches into His Profile and Is Stopped (the Second Half of 1984)

June 1984 (Blue Mountain meditations)

This time *I* am the one at Blue Mountain Center, trying to get Oliver down on paper. With the tide of his well-earned fame beginning to come in, the time has come for me at long last to move on from the endlessly diverting process of reporting and interviewing and note-taking.

I might also note that Joanna will be taking advantage of my time here to invite her parents out of Warsaw for the first time since the imposition of martial law, the first time Poles are being allowed such trips since then (and thus the first time she will be seeing them), and that they will be renting a cabin on the other side of the lake, to which I will be able to canoe (not swim back and forth and back and forth the way Oliver did all last summer). Unbeknownst to Joanna, I will be taking advantage of the occasion, in her presence and with her translating, to ask her parents for permission to marry her for real. We'll see how that works out . . .

During the day I am indexing my notes, more than fifteen volumes' worth, transcribing and reviewing my interviews, and generating various chronologies. Evenings, sitting around the dinner table before a rapt audience of fellow colonists and friends, the colony's administrators, Harriet and Allison and Ginny, and I spark Oliver stories off one another, as if— *exactly* as if—Oliver were some sort of wonder rabbi.

Talking to Oliver on the phone, I mention the chronology scroll I've been compiling, which is already several yards long.[SB]

"That's funny," he says, "I've been engaged in a chronological project of my own. The other day I noticed my bicycle's odometer turning to

1933—I continued to cycle through my childhood, my teens, my academic years. A few days ago, I reached 1984 and was seized by a superstitious fright that I would now certainly be hit by a truck with my broken odometer reading 1984. So I didn't stop till I'd raced it past 1990."

Did you just pull over, I asked him, and spin your wheels?

"No, no," he insisted, "that would have been cheating, that would have been confabulation, and the gods would then certainly have punished me—a truck would have leveled me on the spot!"

⁂

At dinner:

Herbert Shore, a theater-person colonist: "Does Oliver ever talk to himself?"

Kaye, who was in residence here last year: "Oh yes, especially when he's talking to you!"

⁂

Some possibly pertinent passages from W. Jackson Bate's *Samuel Johnson*, which I've taken to reading:*

> In the whirling of the psychological maelstrom in which he now found himself [at twenty], he learned far more than he had ever suspected, that the mind has "cliffs of fall / Frightful, sheer, no-man-fathomed," as Gerard Manley Hopkins later said out of his own self-experience, and the terror of this realization was afterward always present to Johnson. It may at first seem ironic that Johnson, who was to figure in literary history as its supreme exponent and symbol of practical common sense, of unremitting grip on concrete reality, should have begun his adult life in fear for his sanity. But just this explains the authority of his common sense over other minds and the cleansing power of his utterance. It was no bland virtue, but hard-won, through a fearful and prolonged baptism, and afterward maintained in lifelong struggle with himself.

*(New York and London: Harcourt Brace Jovanovich, 1975), 116, 118, 125, 125–26, 388–89, 599.

At the same time he had also been trying to throw himself into exertions that would pull his mind away from itself into some kind of unified activity. He would force himself to walk to Birmingham and back, a distance of thirty-two miles, in the hope that it could shake him into manageability. "Imagination," as he was later to say, "never takes such firm possession of the mind, as when it is found empty and unoccupied." Any activity—recreation or labor—can be "styled its own reward" if we recognize "how much happiness is gained, and how much misery escaped, by frequent and violent agitation of the body."

Another by-product of his attempt to control aggressions by turning them against himself was more conspicuous if less painful. For he now (age twenty) began to develop the embarrassing tics and other compulsive mannerisms that were to haunt him all his life—the sort of thing that led the artist William Hogarth to say that when he first saw Johnson (at the home of Samuel Richardson, standing by a window "shaking his head and rolling himself about in a strange, ridiculous manner"), he concluded Johnson was an idiot, whom his relations had put under the care of Mr. Richardson. Then, to Hogarth's surprise, this figure stalked over to where Richardson and he were sitting, and "all at once took up the argument and displayed such power of eloquence that" he (Hogarth) "looked at him with astonishment and actually imagined that this idiot had been at the moment inspired."

These obsessional traits took such a variety of forms as to have included almost every major category of tics or compulsive gestures. But they usually tend to have one common denominator: an instinctive effort to control—to control aggressions by turning them against himself (as Joshua Reynolds shrewdly said, "Those actions have appeared to me as if they were meant to reprobate some part of his past conduct") or they were employed to control anxiety or to reduce things to apparent manageability by compartmentalization, by breaking things down into units through measurement (counting steps, touching posts, and the like), just as he turned to arithmetic . . . when he felt his mind disordered.

[Thomas Tyers on Johnson, just after Johnson's death] "He was afraid of disorder seizing his head and took all possible care that his understanding should not be deranged. His imagination often appeared to be too mighty for the control of his reason."

[William Gerard Hamilton at the time of Johnson's death] "He has made a chasm which not only nothing can fill up, but which *nothing has a tendency to fill up*—Johnson is dead—let us go to the next best: But there is nobody—no man can be said to put you in mind of Johnson."

Oh, I find myself thinking, setting the book aside and turning out my bedside lamp, *one man can, one man can.*

June 25

Though letters from Oliver have been growing increasingly fretful with the approach of the imminent release of the Leg book, on this day it appears he has received a letter from his great friend and anchor Thom Gunn in response to an early mailing of the book, a copy of which he now passes along to me:

San Francisco, Calif.
June 4, 1984
Dear Ollie,
       I'm writing to you in London because you sent me your
book when you were just about to fly there, and that was only
the end of May. At last, the Leg Book, which contained many
a good surprise (considering I had already read a shortened
version) and was well worth waiting for. Different from your
other books, not only in subject matter, but different in
kind because of the subject matter. Personal and at times
subjective—but that is much of the point of the book isn't it?
One of the most marvelous passages is the description of the
migrainous scotoma on p. 69, into which Nurse Sulu enters, or
in a sense disappears. This is not only exquisitely written but it
forms an essential link in the chain of your small realisations
that add up to a larger understanding. (And I seem to

remember that it was not there in your short version, the
London Review of Books article that I can't lay my hands on at
present, living as I do in a state of perpetual disorganization
that looks like organization—as opposed to yours, which looks
honestly like disorganization, I think, remembering your
room on Christopher Street.) Another exceptional passage is
on pp. 46–47, the explanation of proprioception. And of course
the last which pulls everything together beautifully. At times,
in the more ecstatic parts of the book, you read like Melville, and
I admire Melville enormously, having read and reread him all
through two years ago: it involves going forward for stretches on
your nerve alone and is responsible for M at his best and worst
(*Moby Dick* best and worst *Pierre*). It is a great risk-taking, a kind
of effusion.

I think there are two small weaknesses in the book, both
due to a momentary loss of control; first with the first
description of the bull on p. 5, where you use the word huge(r) four
times, and also stupendous, enormous, vast, and great. By the time
I get to the last sentence ("IT became, first a monster and now
the Devil") I have a sense of leaving the clear-cut reality of the
mountain and of being led into a thicket of rhetoric. And yet a
central sentence is absolutely right: "It sat unmoved by my
appearance, exceedingly calm, except that it turned its vast
white face up towards me." That is startlingly right, but then we
get into language for its own sake, it seems to me. On the other
hand, when the bull returns in your dream, it is very real,
distorted monster as it was. The other passage I don't like is on
pp. 130–131, the part about the "sweet haven," too effusive.

Maybe I am wrong about these two passages, anyway, and
forgive me for mentioning them: because they certainly don't
harm the book as a whole (any more than occasional effusiveness
in Melville or Dickens harms their best books as wholes), which
is sturdy and astonishingly varied in texture and tone—a very
rich work indeed! Perhaps it is because of this richness and
variety, in fact, that the book can accommodate what I take to
be a couple of weaknesses. I feel properly honored that such a
fine book takes my name as its first two words—thank you!

And I enjoyed it, and learned from it, as I always do with your writing. I hope to see you here in July.

Love, Thom

P.S. Reading through this note, I am not sure I make it clear on what level I am criticizing your book. I consider you literally of Dickens and Melville level—up there, indeed, with them! It is not interesting to me just because it is written by a perceptive friend; it is "classic" in its importance.

Alas, any sense of respite offered Oliver by his friend's letter proved short-lived. In its June 21, 1984, issue, the *London Review of Books* (which, on June 17, 1982, had published a condensed version of what would finally become the Leg book; preceding that with "Witty Ticcy Ray" on March 19, 1982; and following up on May 19, 1983, with "The Man Who Mistook His Wife for a Hat" and May 3, 1984, with "Musical Ears") published a truly devastating review of *A Leg to Stand On*, by Michael Neve, a historian of medicine at the University of London and the Wellcome Institute and a member of the *LRB*'s editorial board. Recall that Mary-Kay Wilmers, the *LRB*'s deputy editor, had been closely involved in publishing Oliver all the way back to her days at *The Listener*, which had printed the earliest version of *Awakenings* and received both praise and reproval for doing so. Neve's review, by contrast, seemed almost precision engineered (I am speaking here of effect and not intent) to detonate virtually all of Oliver's anxieties about the entire enterprise.

Beginning with an overview of what Neve saw as Oliver's general project—a revival of the tradition of such literary-minded tellers of medical tales as S. Weir Mitchell in the nineteenth century, further leavened in the twentieth by the contributions of Henry Head on the one hand and A. R. Luria and the various Soviet neuropsychologists on the other—Neve went on to summarize how

Sacks is suggesting that neurology itself has had its own gaps. In ways that historians of neurology might well find interesting but highly selective, he is proposing an absence, an existential space that ought to have been filled, but wasn't, and which has held the science back. The full involvement of patients themselves, in the practical task of recovering the self that has been damaged or lost, is the largest of these missing parts. To complete the progress that the Russians started, Sacks calls for "a neurology of the self, of identity," a task of neurological completion which he (unconvincingly) proposes was resolved in the history of philosophy when Kant dealt with Hume's philosophy of identity and restored "the self" to an existence that was not fleeting or transitory.

Going on to note how:

> These are large, even rabbinical claims and hopes [. . .] Almost any reader, as indeed any television viewer of Sacks's L-DOPA patients, will start out longing for this completion to work out. This is a matter of resurrection, not only of the individual medical case, but of neurology itself [. . .] A lot is riding on 168 pages of a Duckworth book.

"Bearing in mind all the ground rules that medicine will have given him—the commitment to careful, even mundane observation, the skeptical business of listening and feeling," Neve avers how "Doctor Sacks is now to write about himself: and that, as everybody knows, is a damned hard business," following up that proviso with a critique that is equal parts bald ridicule:

> What "happened" to Oliver Sacks to make him become one of the patients at the neurological interface that he believes now exists? Basically, he behaved like a silly twit. He went on a holiday in Norway, in the peak of health, and went walking in the mountains. He was (like all prophets) alone, and had not bothered to tell anyone his whereabouts. He came to a field, which had a huge sign saying "BEWARE OF THE BULL!" He ignored it, came face to face with a large white bull (which appears to have resembled the Devil), panicked and ran. In flight, he fell, twisted his left leg, and had considerable difficulty getting himself back down the mountain. Fortunately, a night in the open was avoided when two passing Norwegians picked him up.

The main part of Sacks's tale follows from this incident, an
incident that, as it were, turns one into the Doctor's mother, making one want to give this burly man a hug and tell him not to go
to Norway and have no one know where he is. This sense of pro-
tectiveness towards a man bent on resolving all the mysteries of
human knowledge is reinforced when we learn that he has "fifty
books" in his rucksack and no change of clothes.

Sly innuendo:

> The story of his "becoming a patient" is partly the story of losing
> a sense that his left leg existed, but is partly also a story of be-
> ing "unmanned by medicine." It would be wrong to make too
> much of the Freudian possibilities at this point, but Sacks's hostil-
> ity to the male surgeon, a "Mr Swan," and a conception of medi-
> cine (from the patient's viewpoint) as unfeeling and masculine, are
> noticeable.

And downright incredulity:

> Now at this point, in the maternal way that the distressing if
> overblown story makes one come to feel, the advice might be:
> "Ollie, sit tight." But this would be useless, since, Verne-like,
> the journey must get stranger. Limbo awaits, introduced by a
> suitable quotation from the Book of Job. There is no longer a
> way round the fact that if Sacks's account of himself has now
> degenerated, into, most noticeably, literary ostentation and gen-
> eralized exaggeration, then this matters. By not adhering, with
> some care, to the delicacy of the necessary linguistic account
> [. . .], Sacks is jeopardizing the very connection between outer
> and inner, surgical and perceptual, neurological and metaphysi-
> cal, upon which the claims for his "existential neurology" must
> rest. [. . .]
>   The middle parts of the book, which might in a modest,
> Chekhovian manner have described distressing things (a foul
> migraine, with eerie results, a perfectly understandable despair)
> instead appear in an unbelievable 3D. He is sinking; he is in the

abyss; and yet "I kept reading *Dr Faustus* at this time, especially its passages on Hell—and Music." (When?) [. . .]

The determination to exaggerate leads to two dreadful things: the reader, irony of all ironies, starts to disbelieve the writer. And worse, the truthful tension that must hold, between the organic experience and the psychological experience, between the science and the subject, starts to fail, and a dreadful thought enters, as the second thing: that a man who is having a bad time, who one wants to get well, is making this stuff up.

Culminating, witheringly:

The possibility that Oliver Sacks's "existential neurology" is simply a way of talking about important things in unbelievable ways lingers in the mind. [. . .] The vexed relationship between subject and object that existentialism concerns itself with remains distressingly unclarified after *A Leg to Stand On*. Florid, fictive, without sufficient respect for the worldliness of pain and illness—let alone the need to be careful about what you say—the book takes its place among the more harmless products of medical egomania. I am very glad that Oliver Sacks got better, and I also wish that his autobiographical tale did not seem so full of the loneliness that comes with intellectual messianism.[SB]

The Neve review indeed sent Oliver reeling, as became clear in his correspondence with me and others across the weeks ahead. Thus, for example, in these typewritten letters:

July 1, 1984
Dear Ren,

I just got a couple copies of the US edition [of *A Leg to Stand On*, hereafter referred to by its initials ALTSO]—I think it looks handsome with its larger print, less crowded, easier on the eye—and herein one, with all my love.

I hope you are finding life at Blue Mountain enjoyable and perhaps productive (it is important that you enjoy it, even if it is not *overtly* productive) . . .

For myself, I get hints of something enjoyable and productive, but then the mood gets spoilt and dissipated. I was upset at a visious [sic] and vulgar notice in the London Review—quite an elaborate, sustained and malevolent "attack," not merely on ALTSO but on everything I have written, and on what (the author fancies) I am . . . It was quite stupid, fundamentally, but calculated to hurt nonetheless: what I found particularly unpleasant was the obvious ill-will, and the sense that the London Review, Mary-Kay in particular, invited or incited such a review—for it is by a member of their editorial board, and as such, so to speak, an "official" review. I can only think that Mary-Kay has now come to hate me—apparently because (in her words) I was "unfaithful" to the LRB and to her in submitting a piece to the New York Review of Books [Oliver had published his first piece there, "The Lost Mariner," earlier that year in the February 16 issue, following that up with the first chapter of ALTSO, "The Bull on the Mountain" on June 28]—and this being so, I have to be "punished." The mutilation of the Music piece was one slap in the face, and this vicious review by their "house hatchet-man" is the other.

Very unpleasant, very bizarre. Not (objectively) so much damaging, as sad. I think neurosis is the worst thing in the world—at least if it is indulged and allowed in the real world. God knows I am myself neurotic as hell, but (hopefully) I rise above it sometimes and don't let it contaminate work and thought. Whereas in this LRB business, it is precisely my work and thought, which cost me so dearly, which has been mutilated, or smeared, by others' neuroses—(Mary-Kay's gonads, I feel, and those of her boyfriend, the reviewer . . . horrible, incestuous, Freudian sexuality).*

---

*I had occasion recently to ask Wilmers for her take on this letter, and she had the grace and good humor to let Oliver's hyperventilating remarks pass without comment. She did note, however, that "Neve was in no sense the LRB's 'house hatchet-man.' I didn't 'hate' Sacks, or think he needed to be 'punished' for anything, even if I was disappointed that he took those pieces to The New York Review without offering them to us first (and I still think he shouldn't have done it). The prosaic truth is that, as always, we sent the book to the person we thought would write the best piece about it; Sacks's personal feelings (and mine) were neither here nor there."

I find that the feeling of this clouds my own mind, and makes it difficult for me to retrieve the tranquility, the elevation, I need for work. I can only recapture it vicariously, so to speak, by reading and rereading Helmholtz whom I love—I carry him around (as I did Hannah Arendt), I feel *safe* with him.

The letter breaks off at this point, continuing the next day:

July 2
   I had been going (I think) to send you a letter—had half typed it, but it was becoming morbid; I felt extremely morbid this morning, a morbidity I first took to be spiritual (*accidie*) until I got a tingling around the lips and a perceptual illusion [. . .]; and a slightly confused and dizzy feeling, I got a bit scared, and thought of a stroke. The attack (? migraine) and its accidie, after some hours, went away, and now I am "myself" once again—not too happy, but not melancholy-migrainous mad.
   Anyhow, it was very nice to get your letter, with its friendliness and its businesslike questions. I am relieved to hear there is some (internal and external) consistency in what I have said (and what has been said about me) in the past three years— the more so in that that lead review in the *London Review,* in addition to everything else, accuses me of confabulation—the words "disbelief" and "unbelievable" occur seven or eight times. Similar imputations of veracity/sanity appeared wholesale in that dreadful issue of *JAMA,* around December 15 [1970], and its poisonous effect lasted through January and into February, obnubilating any pleasure I might have got from the publication of *Migraine.* [. . .]
   Unfortunately, I too readily introject the accusations of the *JAMA* doctors, or (*LRB*'s) Mr. (Dr.?) Neve, and can hardly believe the good words of a [Gunn], a Gregory, a Luria . . . Eric tells me I must be more philosophical—and less "vain"—but I think vulnerability, rather than vanity, is the problem . . . though perhaps they go together, or at least share too great a dependence on the reactions of others . . . At the deepest level,

of course, there is no such dependence, and I judge myself and my thoughts evenly and justly.

[As for your comments in your most recent letter,] I think you are right to see my preoccupation with Order and Disorder as quite central. Curiously, I have at this very moment been reading a book on (one of my Victorian heroes) Hugh Miller, subtitled "Outrage and Order" . . . I enclose Neal Ascherson's introduction. You will note that Hugh Miller committed suicide. This (writes George Rosie, the biographer), ~~in a life "highly successful and flawed with tragedy,"~~ "lends a bleak symmetry to his life." I was thinking of this, I could think of nothing else, in my morbid mood this morning, and thought (as I do at times) that this would be the ending of my own life, if I don't end it "accidentally" beforehand . . . But not because I am torn between Order and Disorder, (though I am).

August 14, 1984
Dear Ren,

[. . .] I have a grief (and perhaps a grievance) about my "orphan" book, which cost me *so much*—and yet may be almost "valueless" for all that because the cost was in "private" feeling, in conflict, rather than in actual thought and achievement.

As you wisely say—as Eric says, as others say, as my own wiser self says—I must become immune alike to criticism and to praise. I *am*, to a considerable extent—at the deepest level certainly, the level I get to, not immediately, but after a while . . . But ALTSO, from the wicked Ward 23 incidents which set the whole train of events into motion, has been *so* charged with anxiety and guilt that this instantaneously gets reactivated by almost anything anyone says, at least anything adverse (and by the same token, if it is not adverse, I remain unreassured and feel that the critic is merely being "kind"— or deluded).

And then, on August 15, a long-delayed reply to Thom Gunn, a copy of which Oliver subsequently shared with me. He began by thanking Gunn for his wonderfully affirming letter, noting how, as Gunn had said, the book had been "a kind of effusion" (a characterization with which Oliver agreed though one over which to some degree he still agonized) but was nonetheless, despite all that, "rich and varied and sturdy" (this last having proved the word that most mattered to Oliver, since he now went on to note how he was being wracked by anxieties that both the book and he himself might simply be, as he put it, "flimsy"). Oliver went on to acknowledge that the eruptive (the blockage of many years followed by a sudden and projectile breakthrough) was a tendency he shared with many of his patients, especially the postencephalytics, but that the tendency toward effusion was not simply that, that it also, at its best, aspired to "the oceanic." Furthermore, while acknowledging the imputations of hyperbole and the merely rhetorical with which some critics were charging him, he went on to insist, in italics, that *this was the nature of the experience*," and how was he to represent the hyperbolic without to some extent succumbing to it? He had lived through "the very stuff of nightmare," and the book had in one sense been an attempt to exorcise such demons—but not, he hoped, only that.

Still, he now doubled back, "I don't think I will . . . ever want to write, anything so personal and subjective . . . again. There is a safety, a sanity, built into my case-histories"—he could *enter into* his patients' situations through the extension of a sort of "imaginative sympathy" without being *swept away.* And he seemed to have had enough of such privately charged transports.

In a postscript, he went on to castigate himself for the "cagey" if not downright "puny" quality of his comments the previous day, especially when compared to the tone of Gunn's "grand" missive. He confessed to an enveloping misery, to the ongoing sense of having "lost or forgotten" himself, going all the way back to the time of the accident. "I have 'forgotten' too the landscape of *ideas*, of concepts, which can also be so grand . . . [and] *I have lost my imagination*—both 'scientific' and 'bardic' . . . But *occasionally*, I dare think, and you help me think, occasionally, when I feel good, something extraordinary is given to me at times," concluding, "Your own letter was grand, and showed your grandness; and I can only hope that sometime I get a touch of my own back . . ."

He would, and he did . . . get a touch of his own back, that is. And in a big way. Though at first the caviling continued to bother him ("Every doubt that anyone can have I've had, only more strongly," he assured me at one point, regarding both the Awakenings and the Leg books), as the weeks passed, such concerns tended to fall away, especially with the arrival of further countervailing praise (at another point he related his gratification at a recent letter from a neurologist in California, at first doubting then confirming his formulations on peripheral neural damage: "Page one raised my hackles," Oliver reported, "but page two made them purr"). And he grew more and more preoccupied with the new patients, fresh clinical situations, and the ever-growing set of case studies (both in print and over the radio), and gratified by the admiration and adulation they were bringing him from wider and wider quarters (sometimes even the professional medical community, where a generational change in attitude appeared to be afoot). With its publication in 1985, *The Man Who Mistook His Wife for a Hat* would prove an international bestseller, eventually to be translated into more than twenty languages, and the years of his reclusive seclusion would be coming to an end.

Meanwhile, I had descended from my own Blue Mountaintop—my notes in order, my chronologies complete, my thoughts arrayed—and was getting set to launch into the writing proper of my extended profile.

❋

The elephant in the room, of course, was the question of Oliver's homosexuality—or not the homosexuality itself (who cared about that, except obviously Oliver himself, exquisitely, lashingly, continuously) so much as Oliver's attitude toward its possible revelation (which at the best of times had been torturously attenuated). Indeed, a good part of our relationship in those early years, as he slowly, tentatively, achingly revealed the dimensions of the calamitous blight, had consisted in my assuring him that (as I saw things, anyway), really, Oliver, *hardly anyone cares, certainly no one who matters*. Alas, to no avail.

Ironically, it had been around this theme that our conversations about Sartre had first begun. I was not unaware in such moments that I was to a certain extent casting myself in a role Sartre had glancingly condemned in a passage early on in *Being and Nothingness* in which he was endeavoring to specify exactly what he meant by "bad faith." At one point, he launches into an example of two male friends, one of whom (a straight fellow) is trying to get the other simply to admit that he is a homosexual, assuring him that he would have nothing against the fact but that what was

driving him crazy was his friend's refusal to be open and candid and simply sincere about such an obvious state of affairs. In Sartre's telling, the
straight fellow's friend refuses, saying that no, there were always extenuat-
ing circumstances, the first time he was in the army, the next he was in
prison for a short stint, and as for that thing the other day, you have to
admit that particular boy was exceptionally beautiful, and so forth. At
which point, Sartre, asking which of these two gentlemen can be said to
be in bad faith, surprisingly singles out the former, the one making the
demand for sincerity.

Because, no, Sartre insists, the other fellow is in fact not a homosexual "the way a rock is a rock," as discomfiting and anxiety-producing as
that fact may be for his straight sincerity-demanding friend. He, like all
of us (like any and every human being, that being the very definition of
what being human *is* for Sartre), is free at any and every moment to constitute himself in any way that he chooses. The sincerity-demanding friend's
insistence that he constitute himself otherwise is precisely what constitutes
his own bad faith (in this context Sartre counterposes "sincerity" to "authenticity," the latter, though far preferable and indeed a sort of ideal, at
best ever being provisional and momentary and itself perpetually subject
to calcification over time).*

Granted that this, like several of the other examples in this section of
Being and Nothingness (don't even get me started on the girl on a date), reads
oddly nowadays, at best dated if not downright politically incorrect. Still,
as I would acknowledge to Oliver, Sartre had been on to something. On
the other hand, I wasn't trying to get Oliver to "admit" that he was a
homosexual, only to stop giving himself such a hard time over the eventual-
ity, and if he could, to allow me in my telling of his life story to place
certain events in his formation in the context of others.

Which is where the black felt-tip pen (Oliver's obnubilating FBI-like
redaction of the better part of Sartre's book) had come in.

Nevertheless, I persisted.

One evening several months before I'd left for Blue Mountain, for example, after a long, wending conversation about him and his relationship
with his great California love, Mel, the disastrous ending of their idyll,
and his more than fifteen years of resolute celibacy since, I sighed (chan-

---

*Jean-Paul Sartre, *Being and Nothingness* (New York: Philosophical Library, 1956), 63ff.

neling my inner Sartre) and said, "Well, yes, Oliver, but who knows what the future will hold?," going on to recall the great line from Grace Paley's fortuitously titled story collection *Enormous Changes at the Last Minute* about how "Everyone, real or invented, deserves the open destiny of life," and following that up with my own lame insistence that "Life is always an open book." To which Oliver responded, emphatically, "I agree, absolutely. Everything is an open book, everything, that is, except sexuality. Or at any rate *my* sexuality. Which is as resolutely closed a book as any book can be."

Another time, after he mentioned how "I've recently been being visited by a certain nostalgia for the sexual, now that I am no longer monstrofied by obesity," I asked him if he'd even noticed the advent of gay liberation. It had suddenly occurred to me that the great epochal events surrounding Stonewall in the summer of 1969 had been transpiring only a dozen miles away during the very same months that he had been logging those twenty-two-hour days at Beth Abraham in the Bronx, at the very peak of the Awakenings drama: There was a good chance he hadn't noticed. "No," he acknowledged, "not at the time, though of course I have in the years since, and granted, with a certain gladness, though it has never felt like any of it had or has anything to do with me. You sound like my analyst, who assures me he's never met anyone less affected by gay liberation. But it's true: I remain resolutely locked in my cell despite the dancing at the prison gates."

The question, as I'd headed up to Blue Mountain that summer, was no longer so much whether I or anyone else was ever going to succeed in drawing Oliver out of his cell (helping to relax the tyrannical hold of that grim celibate resolve), nor even whether I was going to be able to convince him to let me write about the issue of his sexuality anyway—I certainly had no intention of outing him if he didn't want to be outed. Rather, the question had become whether it was going to be possible to tell his story without reference to that elephantine (hippopotamoid?) backdrop.

And there, as I steeped myself in my notes, sorting and indexing and contemplating, allowing the arc of my proposed piece gradually to gel, it seemed less and less likely that I was going to be able to do so. Because to the extent that *the* question—or at any rate one of the principal questions—about Oliver's life had continued to sharpen around that mystery of what had made him, and him virtually alone, certainly among his fellow doctors as he arrived at Beth Abraham in 1966, capable of recognizing that there was something essentially different about those various specific "living statues" scattered among the wider hospital community, and of imagining, most harrowingly and audaciously of all, that the patients in question might indeed be vitally alive somewhere deep inside—surely that capacity had everything to do (as Sister Lorraine surmised) with the precipitous depths of his own prior life experience, his sense of his own oddness, to be sure, of having been and still being damaged (the way "he belongs to and with the Community of the Refused," as his friend Bob Rodman had put it), and then of course the ferocious intensity with which he'd dealt with those feelings during the immediately preceding decade, bursting out of England, hell-bent for California: the extravagant bodybuilding (and its requisite tolerance for physical pain), the motorcycling (the Newtonian passion for speed), and then the drugs (the subsequent addiction to speed) and the insights into near-terminally distant extremities to which such passions had privileged him. He knew there might well be life in those statues because at times he himself had been as thoroughly, deeply entrammeled in his own solipsistic recesses.

But the thing is, there really was no way to tell *that* story without alluding to his mother's devastating maledictions and his consequent desperate need to burst free from such a strangulating atmosphere. Otherwise his California adventures would just come off as the hedonistic escapades of a wildly inchoate oddball, a senselessly masochistic thrill-seeker or the like.

Across the ensuing months, I told Oliver as much, and as the two of us pondered the dilemma, he balanced for a long while on the verge of agreeing, even going so far as to encourage me to go ahead "and we'll see," in the meantime coaching me on possible avenues of approach to the entire project.

Thus, for example, during the autumn, I invited Oliver to join me in an informal working seminar on narrative which grew out of the New York Institute for the Humanities at New York University, where I was a fellow: It was a remarkable biweekly gathering, including the likes of Susan Sontag, Janet Malcolm, and Jerome Bruner. And on November 6, he wrote me all excited about a session on Samuel Beckett, which I'd been forced to miss, and its implications for both of our work.

[Handwritten scrawl above typed pages]
11/8 I came to doubt this letter as soon as I wrote it, but will send it all the same
Dear Ren:

I have just come back from an exciting afternoon on Beckett—indeed it precipitated me into a bookshop to buy him, all of him. I would not mention this, nor write this letter, if I did not think something fundamental had been touched, which concerns you no less than, or *as*, it concerns me.

I don't know that I ever mentioned to you that I had a peculiar passion, practically a compulsion, for Beckett in the early 1950s—roughly speaking my Oxford days and a little beyond. [. . .] And now all this has got reignited, and makes sense, this afternoon.

What came up in the Narrative seminar was the *explosion* of the Narrative, the Narrator, in Beckett. I made an impertinent comment comparing Beckett to—*delirium* (in the sense of an endless saying, an endless changing, the absence of any fixed perspective or viewpoint; the absence of "tale" or "plot"; and the sense, perpetually, of waiting, or pending—for something always hinted, which never occurs). Bruner made an interesting comparison of Beckett with Wittgenstein—the taking back, the undermining, the subversion, of earlier thoughts, the explosion towards a half-nihilistic half-creative endless doubt. [. . .]

What this comes to is a sense that I must complete my present book of Tales [*The Man Who Mistook His Wife for a Hat*]—in order to get on, if I can, to a book of "*Anti-Tales*," which (as I now see them) would be four "Beckett-like" presentations—of Delirium, Dementia, Korsakoff's, and Tourette's. This movement to "anti-tales" may be making it difficult (as it makes it necessary) for me to complete my "Tales" . . . and I cannot help wondering if some of *your* difficulty—indeed you have half-expressed this—is that it may be difficult to tell *my* "Story," my "Tale," because it is also rich in elements of explosion, of "anti-tale" (in somewhat the same way as it might be difficult to present a straight "story" of Wittgenstein—reflected, perhaps, in that maddening, if

fascinating, book [Thomas Bernhard's] *Correction* that you gave
me . . .

There *is* (I like to think, I sometimes dare think) a
"development," a deepening, but I am not sure that it is in any
sense linear. Indeed, it may involve (dialectically, if not literally)
turning on myself, contradicting myself, subverting myself, all the
time, a half-destructive, half-creative contest between views. [. . .]

[For] there may be some sort of fragmentation which is
deeper and more truthful than any "unity." There is a sort of
explosion which is anarchic—and yet the deepest expression of
life and law.

I no longer know what I want to say. Nor do I believe it.
Nor have I said it. Nor did I think it. I don't think.

[Handwritten] *I have not written this.*

Love, Oliver[SB]

A few weeks later, Oliver began getting a bizarre series of phone
calls, one from a man identifying himself as Shapiro who claimed to
have been referred to him by a noted retired neurologist and friend of
Sheldon Novick, insisting (with badgering repetitive self-assurance) that
Oliver take him on as a patient. Which was already freaking him out.
Then, on top of this, a new caller, an elderly woman, began demanding
to see Oliver to get him to call off the murderous rampages of her patient,
one John P, holding Oliver responsible for John's indecent behavior, and
so forth.

Oliver, in a complete quandary (not having seen John the Touretter
since the debacle of their work together in 1978), hadn't a clue what to do,
and began suspecting that *both* callers might in fact be John, hounding
him and preparing his murder, as per earlier threats.

"That," he joked, cutting the tension, "would certainly solve all your
problems with regard to resolving my biography—what a perfect ending!"

In the event, the calls subsided and eventually just went away.

And near the end of the year, Oliver sent me another note:

Dear Ren,

Lovely seeing you last night [. . .] I do enjoy your company
now, fully, as a friend—it is a very good feeling, and it evolved

(or rather emerged) very slowly. At fifty, perhaps, one no longer forms real friends as one did earlier.

Hannah Arendt writes: "I met Auden late in life at an age when the easy knowledgeable intimacy of friendships concluded in one's youth can no longer be attained, because not enough life is left, or expected to be left, to share with each other. Thus, we were very good friends but not intimate friends."

I regard you, now, as a very good friend—I am not quite sure if I have any intimate friends—or whether, indeed, I am capable of "intimacy." Perhaps, defensively, I can only feel it at a distance, some safe "remove," where I do not feel too engaged.

I am not sure how you regard me, or feel to me, but I am sure that friendship is part of the feeling. It is possible that this itself may make writing about me difficult—which is why I have offered to keep a due distance. But equally, it is possible that this does not impede you, and may indeed make your task easier, and give it depth and warmth it would otherwise lack . . . Certainly, in my own "profiles" of patients, I find friendly feelings to them make it easier to write; and hostile feelings (as to John) almost impossible to write . . . though of course the friendliness is at a distance, or within reserve (there is a danger, otherwise, that it will degenerate into sentimentality—which I am afraid I am sometimes prone to . . . Eric has chided me for this, and I do feel it as a danger).[SB]

Notwithstanding the open-endedness of that last paragraph, as Oliver continued to dwell on our common challenges as writers of profiles, he also continued to worry about any coming revelations of his sexuality, and those worries did not subside. Indeed, in the end, they came to a head one evening a few weeks later during a brisk sunset walk in Riverside Park, when after a good deal of stammering and stuttering, of hemming and hawing, he at length seemed to come to his final resolve. "As I wrote you a few weeks back," he said, "I have come to value you as a dear friend, of whom as I say I don't have that many. I think what I was trying to say in that letter but never got around to saying is that I value you more in that role than as any sort of biographer. And although I deny nothing," he concluded, "I have lived a life wrapped in concealment and wracked by inhibition, and I can't see that changing now. So please I must ask you not to continue. I don't care what you do with all your material after I die. Just not now."

And that was that.*

---

*Over the ensuing years, I've had occasion to further mull over my attitude regarding the relative stakes in Oliver's position, or rather my own blithe assurance to him that hardly anyone would have cared one way or the other if he had simply acknowledged his sexuality. Bracketing the specifically biographical context in his case (the lingering trauma of his mother's maledictions, the virulence of homophobia specifically in the Britain of his formation as late as the fifties and the sixties—the chemical castration of Alan Turing in 1952, with "gross indecency" still being a criminal offense, the social milieu surrounding the Jeremy Thorpe scandal well into the seventies—and so forth), the wider social environment may not have been nearly as benign as I kept insisting. Certainly, homophobia was still widespread and could destroy careers and lives. At the same time, tens of thousands of men, and hundreds of physicians, and dozens of celebrities, had come out in the years since Stonewall—at least in New York City, it was no longer that much of a sensation in each individual case. (I sometimes wonder whether Oliver's hesitancy regarding direct political engagement, notwithstanding his love of Arendt, didn't have a lot to do with his internal conflicts over joining the wider struggles over gay liberation specifically, and conversely, whether his subsequent engagements with the deaf community, in the years ahead, may not have served, in addition to everything else, at least in some sense as a release valve for some of those internal pressures.)

Meanwhile, of course, the next great turn in the social history of homosexuality was starting to well up all around us during the very years of the conversations detailed in this book (1981–84), the catastrophic upsurge, that is, at first a trickle but by 1985 a horrendous floodtide, of the disease which would become known as AIDS, and all the crosscurrents of engagement, solidarity, and denial that it was going to bring forth. (Over the years, Oliver and I had occasion to note the fact that his own self-enforced celibacy after the mid-sixties, for all its torments, had obviously had the ancillary effect of sparing him exposure to the rampaging disease.) Who knows how vividly Oliver, as an increasingly beloved public intellectual, might have been able to engage with the debates around that issue, had he allowed himself to come out earlier.

The main point here, though, was that at no time was I ever going to be the one to out him against his will, I'd only have done so with his active concurrence, which, for whatever reasons, he felt he could not provide, so that in the end, back then in the mid-eighties, that was indeed that.

PART III

Afterwards

Oliver on our patio

18

Dear Friends (1985–2005)

But friends we stayed. Dear friends, and for the next thirty years.

Backtracking for a moment here, Joanna was indeed blindsided by that ricochet marriage proposal in the cabin by the lake up there at Blue Mountain (her father joyously catching the drift even before she did, jumping up to hug me much to her baffled consternation), and she and I were officially married, or at any rate celebrated a festive post-wedding party, later that year in Manhattan, with Oliver in happy attendance.

And Oliver would continue dropping by our West Ninety-Fifth Street apartment for dinners or weekend brunches on a regular basis.

Both of our writerly profiles and reputations now began to consolidate. I was appearing ever more regularly in *The New Yorker*, shuttling, as the people there took to saying, between political tragedies and cultural comedies. I was one of the three principal authors of the at the time still anonymous Notes and Comment pieces, alongside Jonathan Schell and presently Bill McKibben, this during the years of Reagan's blustering senescence and Bush Senior's belligerent sequel. In July 1984, I'd published the first of many pieces on David Hockney, in that instance on his Polaroid photo collages, pieces that came to be consciously counterpoised to an equivalent ongoing series on his polar opposite, Robert Irwin. In addition, in the months and years to follow, I'd cover the improbable discovery of a long-occluded first-generation abstract expressionist by a wildly fervent young promoter (self and otherwise) from Bangalore, India; an artist who drew money and spent his drawings, and the confounding legal quandaries such practices regularly led to; the nonagenarian failed

Oliver at our wedding, progressively shedding formalities

wunderkind, the onetime avant-garde conductor and subsequent musical lexicographer Nicolas Slonimsky; a rocket scientist turned investment banker who'd only ever really wanted to be a clown—to name just a few. (Funny thing about Slonimsky, who lived to be one hundred and one and a half, completely lucid till his hundred-and-first birthday, at which point a series of ministrokes over the ensuing couple of weeks robbed him of any sense of self, the only thing that survived unscathed being his vanity. He had no idea who he was, but he knew he was hot stuff and was quite happy to have you come visit and celebrate him as such. When I described the situation to Oliver, he said that just went to prove that the site of vanity in the brain had no necessary relationship to the site that warehouses what one might be vain about.) Parallel to those pieces, though, I was also covering the aftermath of torture in Brazil and Uruguay; calamities of exile among outcasts from Iraq, South Africa, and Czechoslovakia; and by decade's end, the resurgence of Solidarity in Poland and the ensuing onslaught of neoliberal capitalism, there and elsewhere. Passion pieces all, as I took to thinking about them—evocations of the moment (as the theorists of Solidarity used to parse things) when people or places stopped acting like the objects of other people's sentences and insisted on becoming the subjects of their own. When I eventually left the magazine, in 2001, to take up a position as the director of the New York Institute for the Humanities at NYU, the *New Yorker*'s librarian took me aside to tell me that during the twenty years of my residence there, I had managed to publish more column inches than any other writer during that same period. I don't know if that's true, but I did publish a lot, and in retrospect, it's funny, I can't see where there would even have been time or room for a big Sacks profile.

My own efflorescence, though, was of course as nothing compared to Oliver's, especially following the publication of his first breakout bestseller, *The Man Who Mistook His Wife for a Hat*, by Duckworth in England and Summit in the United States, in March 1986. (A question had arisen the previous year about the former, with Oliver's agent urging him to find a more efficient English outlet, and Oliver momentarily hesitating. "It's true that Colin doesn't exactly publish," he admitted one evening over dinner. "In fact, he *privishes*. His attitude is, 'Why should I give advances? I'm not the Bank of England. Why should I advertise? That's vulgar. My job is to see that the book is well edited, well printed, well noticed, well reviewed,

Sacks and Weschler
backstage and
onstage at a Lannan
Foundation event
in Santa Fe, New
Mexico

and then made available for paperback.'" In the end, though, out of
loyalty, Oliver had given the book to Colin, and deservedly so.) The legendary Peter Brook and his company would soon be fashioning a powerful
theatrical evening based on the book, hauntingly titled *The Man Who*, while
Christopher Rawlence and Michael Nyman turned the title story into a
successful chamber opera. Oliver was regularly appearing on NPR and
BBC and PBS, in both documentaries and newscasts, gradually (as he slowly
surmounted his default tendencies toward tongue-tied self-consciousness)
becoming everyone's favorite public neurologist (both impressively erudite
and impossibly cuddly).

For that matter, we began appearing together fairly regularly in ven-
ues around the country as interlocutors of each other.

And he was at last starting to feel at home at home. Indeed, in September 1985, as the much-hyped Hurricane Gloria took direct aim at New
York City and City Island in particular, he and some neighbors, though

repeatedly advised to evacuate, had instead spent a jolly afternoon in his mariner neighbor Skip's house, indulging in a hurricane party. At a certain point, the slashing winds suddenly stilled, the sea subsided, the sky came out dazzling blue—they were in the eye of the hurricane. "Everything went eerily calm," as he subsequently told me (and I for my own part continued to record, though now somewhat more haphazardly, in my notebooks, not quite sure why), "the waves went suddenly flat, there was a glory of birds swirling about overhead, a bevy of tropical butterflies that had been hoovered up the coast by the storm fluttering all about, the whole was transfused with a certain sinister benignity"—and Oliver (of course, naturally, for how could he not?) went for a swim! Indeed, he misjudged his return to shore, and when he was still a good twenty yards off, the back wall of the storm came smashing through, and the last segment of his swim turned pretty hairy. "The rocks and small boulders under the water as I came swimming in were splashing all about *like popcorn*," he recalled the next day, marveling and proudly showing off his bruises. In the end, though, Oliver had been underwhelmed by the storm's much-vaunted ferocity. "It makes me wonder," he concluded, "how America would react if it was ever faced with an actual reality."

Later that fall, as the waters in the sound cooled precipitously, Oliver took to joining me at the local New Rochelle Y to take laps in its indoor pool. From my notebooks:

> Massive solid physique swathed in grey fur. Black Speedo trunks, transparent black-rimmed face goggles, massive black flippers, fingerless webbed black leather gloves with implanted lead weights, and atop it all, covering the only hairless part of his body, a black swimming cap, like some daft rebbe's yarmulke. He lumbers forward, awkwardly, anxiously, gingerly.
>
> And yet, once in the water, his swimming is powerful, even, grace-flecked, godlike.
>
> And relentless: He ordinarily does 72 laps but can, and does on occasion, enter a fugue state in which he ends up swimming for hours on end.

I titled this entry "The Rebbe from the Black Lagoon."

While he was waiting for the royalties from his new book to start coming in, he was still limping along financially, so I got him a gig leading

weekly seminars at nearby Sarah Lawrence (on everything from Leibniz
to scotomas), and then, come the winter of 1986, a monthlong stint as a
Regents' Professor back in my old haunts at UC Santa Cruz.

From my notebook, re the latter:

> Two Februarys ago, OWS celebrated the completion of his Leg book
> by breaking his other leg, sliding on the ice outside the City
> Island post office. Last winter, OWS spent the whole while mor-
> tified that he'd slip again and resolved to never spend another
> entire winter in NYC. I thereafter set about securing him a
> monthlong Regents' Professorship at Cowell College at UCSC,
> all of which went swimmingly—only, as the appointed week
> approached, he seemed more and more anxious, so I decided to
> head out there myself for his first week, to try to make sure the
> graft didn't reject the host, or vice versa.
>
> Generally, things seemed to go well, but it took some doing.
> Before each of his presentations (T-Th seminars 3:15–5:15, Weds
> public lectures 8 pm), we'd set out on a ramble around the cam-
> pus: he'd be virtually incoherent, his thoughts careening out of
> control all over the lot, me trailing behind trying to impose struc-
> ture on the jumble. On Thursday [marine biologist] Todd New-
> berry and [Wittgenstein scholar] Bob Goff joined the walk so
> they'd know how to do it in the weeks thereafter. Again, my only
> contribution was the imposition of some sort of order in summa-
> tion. Still, though each time I had grave doubts that Ollie would
> be able to focus and pull it off, each time he surprised us all by
> (grace of graces!) pulling it off flawlessly.

Later that year, when Joanna and I found ourselves happily pregnant
(or however one characterizes that state when referring to an entire burgeoning family), we realized we'd likely have to move out of town (typically, all we were looking for at the time was one more room, a fact that
priced us clean out of Manhattan). In no small part, we chose the suburb
we did, Pelham, just beyond the Bronx city limits on the Long Island Sound
side of Westchester County, so as to be close to Oliver's City Island haunts,
only a couple of miles away, and sure enough, his dinner and weekend
brunch visits became all the more frequent.

Sara and Oliver

Joanna was continuing her rise through what had become Human Rights Watch, eventually becoming Human Rights Watch's first representative at the United Nations.

Our daughter, Sara Alice, was born on February 22, 1987,* and the next day Oliver agreed to be her godfather. She was not his only godchild (years later, late one woozy melancholy drunken evening, he would note in passing, almost unthinkingly, how he'd regularly fallen in love with brilliant straight young men, the godfather of whose children he later became), but he was *her* only godfather, and indeed more than that—really her only nearby grandfatherly figure. She'd grow to be very close to her Polish grandparents but only saw them sporadically, and both of my parents had passed on, such that as a result Oliver took on a larger-than-life role in her early years. Not to speak of the fact that he was *literally* larger than life. There are some marvelous photographs of him, in one of his more generously capacious phases, seated beside her comparatively infinitesimal self on a couch in our Pelham living room, genially reviewing a picture book.

---

*For my *New Yorker* Talk piece on the occasion of her birth, and some of the Oliveresque speculations to which that birth led me, see the SourceBook.

In later years he would regularly amaze and enchant her, bringing over a new Tourettic friend, a young Canadian sculptor named Shane Fistell, for example, for walks in the nearby forest (Shane bolting forth and back from the path to finger-tap tree after tree, provoking little Sara's sage whispered observation, "He's just like a *dog!*") or, some years later, spending hours around the living-room table at Oliver's house, with another of his friends, the eponymous "Anthropologist on Mars," Temple Grandin, the three of them deep in almost Talmudic disputations about the relative capacities of their favorite television character, Data on *Star Trek: The Next Generation.* Later still, when Oliver first met Patrick Stewart, the Shakespearean actor who played the commander Jean-Luc Picard, I don't know which of the two, Sara or Oliver, was initially the more gaga excited.

As Sara began acquiring language during her first eighteen months, Oliver became more and more fascinated by the process, and perhaps as a tangent to that fascination, he grew intrigued by the languages of the deaf (or maybe it was the other way around, who knows). At any rate, in the spring of 1988, when the students at Gallaudet University, the country's premier college for the deaf in Washington, DC, went on strike to protest the appointment of a non-signing president (and the implicit downplaying of the centrality of American Sign Language, increasingly at the core of a bourgeoning deaf pride movement), Bob Silvers, the editor of *The New York Review of Books*, convinced Oliver (though I doubt it took much convincing) to go down there to cover developments. Which is how it came to pass, a few days later, that in a scene worthy of Chaplin's Tramp in *Modern Times,* the famous visiting reporter Oliver Sacks presently found himself being pushed to the front of a demonstration march, holding a proud banner in his upraised fist. (It was in a profound sense Oliver's own political awakening as well, his first actual gesture as any sort of activist, all his prior love of Hannah Arendt notwithstanding.) And the book version of the ensuing reportages that would follow within a year, *Seeing Voices,* would prove one of his most vivid and consequential (not just for its celebration of the sinuous particularities of sign but also for its deep meditations on what it means for anyone "to talk to oneself," the role of language in such internal conversations, and the terrible deprivation of children born without access to language and denied a proper correlative).

His love of *Star Trek* notwithstanding, Oliver was still pretty much clueless when it came to the rest of popular culture. One afternoon, for example, he took to regaling me about a recent patient, a onetime hippie who'd become stuck in time, forever harking back to his love for a particular band. Oliver couldn't remember the band's name, it was something, he thought, like the Happy Corpses. The Grateful Dead? I suggested. Yes, exactly, the Grateful Dead! (In the years after the publication of the piece in question, "The Last Hippie," Oliver would get to know the group's lead drummer, Mickey Hart, and the two often traded notes on matters percusso-neurological.) Another afternoon, I received a panicky phone call from Oliver in his City Island home. In a great hurry, he explained that there was suddenly renewed interest from Hollywood in making a film out of *Awakenings*, and in fact things had advanced to the point where they were sending over actors to meet with him, and one was headed over right this minute, in fact, oh no, he could see the limo rounding the bend onto his little side street, only he had forgotten the name of the actor, he was going to be there any minute and it was all going to be a terribly embarrassing fiasco. Calm down, I tried to dulcify him, did he remember anything of what he'd been told about the actor in question? Well, he was being considered for the role of Leonard, the main patient character, and they'd told Oliver that he was famous for a film called *Taxicab* or something like that. Robert De Niro? I hazarded. "That's it!" Oliver exulted, flush with relief, just as the doorbell rang in the background. "Thank you, *thank you!*"

That conversation apparently went well, as did another with Robin Williams, who was being courted to play Oliver, and as did a third with the putative director (although after the fact in that instance Oliver called me, in a whole new lather of fraught confusion, because he'd taken the woman in question on a walk in the Botanical Garden and he'd thought her name was Penny Something but all the kids in the park kept running up to her, gigglingly, and addressing her as "Laverne," and what was *that* all about?).

The film actually came together and by 1989 was shooting in New York—in fact, at one point on City Island. The screenwriter had placed Oliver's 1969 home lodgings in a bungalow not unlike the one he'd interviewed him at on City Island a few years earlier (even though back in 1969, Oliver had in fact been living in that spare little apartment right beside

the hospital), so the film company had rented a similar house on the island for a series of on-site scenes. One evening Joanna and Sara and I went
over to watch the proceedings, and while the cinematographer and his crew
were adjusting lighting, we came upon Oliver, in a crisp white medical
smock, standing next to Robin-as-Oliver in identical garb. Sara, in my
arms, looked her godfather in his face, then Robin in his, then back and
forth once more, before settling on Robin and pronouncing, solemnly,
"You're not Ollie." Which cracked them both up.

Another time, Joanna and I went to join Oliver at an abandoned wing
of the old Kingsboro Psychiatric Center in Brooklyn, which the crew was
deploying as a stand-in for Beth Abraham. The place was often thronged
with extras, in many cases actual long-term patients, but on that particular afternoon, they were shooting an intimate scene with Williams and
De Niro alone. The blithe early days of L-DOPA are giving way to something
far more unsettling, and Leonard, having been one of the first to assay the
drug, is now one of the first to sense the raging onslaught of ever-wilder
side effects. At first they'd hoped it was just a matter of proper titration,
but this is the scene where Leonard realizes (in the screenplay, even before
the Sacks character) that they are never going to find their way back to
any proper balance, that this is just how things are going to be. Williams,
in his medical smock, was seated by the table where the scene was going
to play out, entertaining the crew with easy scattershot free-associative patter (he'd taken to describing the eccentric doctor he was playing to visiting press types as "a veritable cross between Arnold Schwarzenegger and
Albert Schweitzer"), while the camera and soundmen were adjusting their
levels, Penny Marshall was hovering over a video feed, and De Niro, off in
a corner in deep focused concentration, seemed to be psyching himself up,
rolling his shoulders and stomping his feet like a boxer preparing to enter
the ring. At length Marshall announced, "Okay, let's go," and Williams
instantaneously sobered up, with De Niro now lumbering over to take his
seat on the opposite side of the table, already in full drool, and picking up
a book.

"Action," muttered Marshall, quietly, and the scene played out,
De Niro, his jerks becoming more and more wild, his diction more tortured,
his head flailing all over the place, unable to focus on the opened book
before him and presently throwing it aside in exasperation, grunting, "I
can't read anymore, I can't keep my eyes on one place," and going on to

wail, "I've let everybody down." (Williams: "No.") "I've let you down." ("No, you have not!") "I'm grotesque." ("No, you are not, it's not true, and I will not listen to you talk like that.") "I am, I am, look at me, *look at me*," whereupon De Niro breaks down sobbing, and a tongue-tied Williams reaches over the table to grab his hand. Two beats, three, and Marshall sighed. "Cut." A completely stunning collaborative performance: Williams immediately relaxing back into his prior self, with a broad smile of accomplishment, but De Niro continuing to jerk and pound angrily, "Damn, fuck it all, damn it, DAMN IT"—everyone else trying to assure him that no, honestly, it had been a terrific take, couldn't have been better, but him continuing to curse and stab until suddenly calm washed over his body as he seemed visibly at long last to rise out of his character, smiling, because, yeah, of course, he knew that.

Marshall looked over at Miroslav Ondricek, her veteran cinematographer (the master behind such earlier films as *Loves of a Blonde* and *If . . .* and *Ragtime* and *Amadeus*), and he nodded that yes, they'd gotten it. So she called a break while the crew prepared for the next scene.

An interesting thing about Ondricek's presence: The crew's outerwear swag that fall had been a black army jacket with the word AWAKENINGS stitched in elegant engraver's green type across the back, and Ondricek at one point had taken a brief trip back to his hometown, Prague, just as the glorious dominoes of transformation started falling all across the eastern bloc, one country after the next, which is how it must have come to pass that just a few weeks later, when Ondricek's old sixties dissident buddy, the playwright Václav Havel, stood atop that balcony at the Castle, addressing the celebrating throng in the square below at the climax of the Velvet Revolution, the country's new leader was wrapped in a black lumber jacket with the splendid green logo AWAKENINGS improbably, uncannily scrawled across its back.

And speaking of costumes, at one point the filmmakers decided to slip Oliver into the film (Hitchcock-style), all gussied up as a department store Santa off to the side for a scene where the as yet untroubled, fully awakened Leonard made his merry way down Fifth Avenue among the shopping hordes. In the end the scene was scrapped from the film, but that explains how one evening a few weeks after Havel's star turn in Prague, back in Pelham, just before Christmas Eve dinner, there was a knock at the door and Sara went rushing to open it, only to find Santa Claus himself

Santa Sacks

standing there in full red-and-white regalia, though once he reached down
to pull her up onto his chest, Ho Ho Ho, she gazed into his face (the bushy
natural beard, the round spectacles) and broke out laughing, saying, "Wait,
you *are* Ollie!"

Months passed in postproduction, almost a full year, but Oliver kept
up his friendship with Williams (the two seemed to have an infinite
capacity to crack each other up, Oliver even coming to wonder whether
Williams's lightning powers of manic antic free-association didn't bear
some happy neurological kinship with Tourette's).

Finally came the release date, just before Christmas 1990, and Joanna
and I joined the legions of guests at the premiere at the Paris Theater in
Manhattan, followed by a gala dinner at the nearby Pierre Hotel. The film
proved surprisingly fine for a studio production, the performances uni-
formly excellent across the board, the pacing and arc true to life, and the
screenplay by Steven Zaillian quite faithful to the spirit of the book. The
two main ways in which the film veered from the actual story were that,
here, it was Oliver who, harboring messianic fantasies, first had to drag
his hospital administrators along with his schemes (rather than the other
way around), and that, Hollywood being Hollywood, the Oliver character

had to have a love interest, or at any rate an almost-love interest, an ador-
ing nurse (delicately turned by Julie Kavner) with whom the shy neurologist entertains a tentative, halting, and in the end entirely chaste and
fugitive romance.

The audience at the screening was thoroughly engrossed and enchanted
(offering a standing ovation at the end), and then we all ambled over to
the Pierre. Oliver was walking alongside me, glowing, and confirming, by
way of a side whisper, "Okay, I think I have this right, I kiss all the women
and shake hands with all the men, even though I'd much rather be doing
the opposite." But he indeed had it right, and was behaving entirely ap-
propriately, right through the lead-up to the dinner. Joanna and I were
seated at Oliver's table, on the other side of which was Penelope Ann Miller
(in a ravishing sleeveless gown), who'd played De Niro's brief love interest.
Each place setting featured a corporate gift from the sponsor (Ralph
Lauren or Calvin Klein or some such), perfume for the women and eau de
cologne for the men. Oliver, predictably starting to overheat, unscrewed
his bottle and splashed some on his face. And then did so again a few
minutes later, and again a few minutes after that. Presently he was actually pouring the stuff over his head, soon having emptied a good half of
the bottle. Robin came ambling over to give Oliver a hug and was stopped
cold, a good yard away, by the wall of perfumed stench. (Shades of cuttlefish and lavender!) "Whoa!" He seemed to bounce off it. But then, perfectly gauging the situation, he grabbed the bottle and proceeded to pour
the other half all over himself in madcap solidarity.

At one point, Miller got up to mill about, and I asked Oliver how he
had liked her performance in the film. Two beats, confusion: "She was in
the film?"

And life went on. These were the years, during the late eighties, following the publication of *The Man Who Mistook His Wife for a Hat* and the
consequent increase in his royalties, that Oliver began to assemble the support system that would sustain him through the rest of his life (from
helping him to recognize who had been in the growing number of films
rendered from his books, through putting together new ones, to just
running his life in general). To begin with there was Helen, his marvelous
and beloved once-a-week housekeeper and cook (who stocked his freezer
with a week's worth of meals every Thursday, especially including a gefilte fish somehow as sublime as his mother's). After she passed away in

1992, Joanna and I helped replace her with our own housekeeper, an efficient diminutive Guatemalan woman named Yolanda, who likewise grew into an almost equally beloved fixture in his household. Then there was Kevin Halligan, a lineman with the telephone company who one day paid a call on Oliver to suss out some trouble with his connection and stayed on to become his endlessly resourceful, endlessly bemused, all-around part-time handyman and bookshelf builder (and more, and more, bookshelves builder), presently taking on much the same roles in the nearby Weschler manor as well.

But most important without question was the arrival of Kate Edgar, a onetime managing editor in Jim Silberman's office at Summit Books, who'd moved to San Francisco but continued to help Jim by typing up some of Oliver's Leg drafts (becoming expert in deciphering the good doctor's atrocious handwriting, sometimes extemporizing when such deciphering proved impossible). Upon her return to New York, Oliver and she arrived at an arrangement whereby she would rent a car once a week to drive out to City Island and tidy up his office, helping to marshal the pieces that would presently become *The Man Who Mistook His Wife for a Hat*, a gig that gradually evolved into a full-time role as Oliver's office and life manager, in which role she would literally render possible the creative burgeoning of his final decades. "His work wife" being how she once described herself in jest—his "editor" as she would characterize her role at other times, his "assistant," his "mom." Kate in turn would bring in others, including Bill Morgan, who took on the project of archiving Oliver's prodigious medical notes, widely scattered manuscripts, graphomaniacal diaries and correspondence, and miscellaneous audio- and videocassettes; and the polymath Hailey Wojcik, who when she wasn't transcribing new material or attending to Oliver's ever-expanding correspondence had a side career going as a cutting-edge country rock performer. (Hailey's lives would sometimes blend into each other fetchingly, as in her classic anthem "Amnesia," the chorus of which runs, "Let's get hit over the head / Just not so hard that we're dead / But so hard we forget all the things that we said / and the things that we haven't said yet.")

On January 20, 1990, Oliver's father died in London at age ninety-five. One of the encomiums noted, "Known as Pop to relatives, friends and even to the Family Practitioner Committee, Dr. Sacks still had all the notes from his two million consultations with patients across the 73 years of his practice, and was regularly making house calls and otherwise seeing the 2,000 patients on his list up until his recent retirement." As I drove Oliver to the airport for his flight to London, where he would help arrange shiva and, more important, plan a new life situation for his brother Michael, Oliver described feeling "a vivid sense of the historical."

A year later, on January 25, 1991, Oliver briefly made all the tabloids when he ("Doctor Played by Robin Williams in Film") found himself being fired ("Awakenings Doctor Gets Pink Slip"), alongside close to twelve hundred others throughout New York, from the Bronx Psychiatric Center where he had been in active service since 1966. As he noted in an op-ed in *The New York Times*, "The medical care in state hospitals has been deteriorating steadily over the years, and now, one fears, it will be almost nonexistent. Such a situation is both tragic and unnecessary. The savings in money to the state will be relatively slight; the cost in human terms will be incalculable."

Notwithstanding which, Oliver continued to visit the facility on an occasional pro bono basis for years thereafter, regularly checking in on his own longtime wards.

Meanwhile, a few months later, Oliver was extremely moved at being honored with a presidential citation from the American Academy of Neurology before four thousand fellow practitioners at their annual convocation in Boston. Returning, he described "a sense of closure, of inclusion, of homecoming—and in particular of delight at all the *young* neurologists who came up to me, asking for their copies of my books to be autographed, declaring me their *hero*." Indeed, he had become a sort of father figure, much as Luria had been to him. Furthermore, he was vivified by "the blaze of fresh excitement in the field, not unlike particle physics in the 1920s."

During these same years, I published two pieces of my own, both political allegories drawing on my years with Oliver. The first, a Notes and Comment piece in *The New Yorker* on January 29, 1990, which is to say within a month of the climax of all the velvet revolutions sweeping Eastern Europe, deployed Oliver's story of the remarkable revival of Uncle Toby—and his tragic fate thereafter when the ferocious malignancy that had been held in abeyance across the many years of his body's metabolic shutdown came surging back to life with his revival, claiming his life within weeks—as a cautionary warning of things to come.[SB] (A few years later, Warren Zimmerman, the American ambassador to the disintegrating

Yugoslavian state, summoned the image of Uncle Toby in his accounts of
the unfolding horrors.) Likewise, a few months later, in a piece entitled
"Allegories of Eastern Europe" (*The Threepenny Review*, Fall 1990), I suggested that the definitive text on what to expect in the economies across
the collapsing Soviet Empire as neoliberal capitalism was being introduced
at turbo speed might not be some abstract financial treatise so much as
Oliver's *Awakenings* (talk about tribulations!) and casting Havel's wearing
of that black *Awakenings* jacket as he addressed the joyous throngs from
the castle's parapet in a decidedly more disconcerting light.[SB]

Meanwhile, on March 16, 1992, in a move that somehow signaled the
very end of whatever fantasies I may still have been harboring of being
able to profile Oliver in the magazine, he appeared in *The New Yorker* (now
Robert Gottlieb's *New Yorker*) for the first time under his own byline with
a marvelous short piece about his visit to a Tourettic surgeon in British
Columbia. There would be dozens of others to follow.

Notwithstanding which, I continued to file the occasional anecdote in
my ever so gradually expiring notebooks. Thus, for example, the film producer Neal Baer, who'd optioned the rights to "The Lost Mariner" for a
project that never quite gelled, recalling how one day, when he and Oliver
had been walking in the lee of the California Academy of Sciences in
San Francisco's Golden Gate Park, he'd been mortified when Oliver suddenly collapsed to the ground, belly-first, veritably trembling. Neal thought
he was having a stroke or a fit of some sort—but, no, he was just cooing.
"He'd encountered a rare fern he'd never seen before," Neal explained,
"and he was fervid with ecstasy and fellow feeling."

Another time Oliver reported how "in the olden days, whenever I got
depressed, I sometimes used to become convinced that I was contracting
Alzheimer's. One time, to test whether I indeed was, I forced myself to
write a précis, from memory, of Kant's *Prolegomena to Any Future Metaphysics*, and it turned out not all that bad—a bit dull, but then maybe so is
the original. At any rate, it became clear that the depression in question
was a matter not of facility but rather of vitality, which in itself provided
a sort of relief."

As may be gathered, Oliver's growing public and worldly success was
hardly a prophylactic to his ongoing elaborately neurotic swings. Peter Sel-
gin, one of his swimming buddies, reported Oliver's reaction, when they
were out driving to Lake Jeff and had stopped for a coffee in a village along

Sara conversing with Oliver at our Pelham home

the way, and returning to the car, he noticed he'd gotten dog shit on his shoe. "And it was the apocalypse," Peter laughed, recalling the scene, "a compounding calamity. He was going to have to burn his shoe, the gas pedal, the car, the street, the town—the entire world! The reaction was positively symphonic in its wild density. But then, later, he could and would laugh at himself."

Some similar reports were not always so risible. He could at times still become as awkwardly tongue-tied as ever. In another such sighting, in December 1992, my old LA friend Susie Einstein reported, "I just saw Oliver Sacks at LACMA speaking about mental patients' artwork in conjunction with the 'Outsider Art' show there. At the end of his talk he asked for questions from the audience. An older woman stood up, with a lengthy tale of how she'd had a stroke a year ago and suffered some changes as a result. She went on and on. O.S. interrupted her at one point, trying to speed things up—still she went on. Finally, she made reference to a character in the 'hat' book and then said ever since her stroke the most outstanding change in herself is that she's developed an intense crush on a man she's never met, though she's read all his books! The audience then swung its heads back to O.S., who was looking at his feet.

After a very pregnant pause he mumbled, 'I think the idea of questions was not a good one—that's all. Thank you and good night!' He's quite a character."

He was, of course, though sometimes not so haplessly benign. December 1994 found Oliver in another lather, this one far less excusable, as I noted in another of my now very occasional entries from one of my notebooks:

> An incident last night was not untypical of another side of Oliver which perhaps I ought to document more forthrightly—initially not that important although perhaps significant in what it adumbrates and in any case the sort of thing that would be essential to ever making up a full portrait:
>
> The phone rings and it is Oliver, sputtering with fury and righteous ire. It seems (at length) that he had gotten a new television in his office and had brought the office one back home and then indicated to a meltingly sweet neighbor of his that once he got this one hooked in, she and her children could have the one it was replacing. Apparently, she misunderstood (or knowing Ollie, she understood perfectly well and obeyed to the letter his own—subsequently revised—instructions).
>
> At any rate, he came home this evening and his old TV (with its precarious antenna) was gone and in its place was the office one. Trouble is, the neighbor or her husband appear not to have known how to attach it properly, or to attach the VCR, and the resultant reception is poor, etc. (I can just see them halfway into the operation and not knowing how to finesse the completion, or not even realizing that they'd failed to.)
>
> Anyway, Ollie is beside himself, *over the top* with histrionic, exaggerated rage. He can't believe this *violation*, after everything he's done for *that woman*, he feels as if he's been *raped*, the whole house is sunken with *moral turpitude*, his heretofore exemplary relationship with the neighbor is probably *permanently blackened* by this *egregious* moral lapse, this monstrous theft and on and on and on.
>
> Truly ugly and unpleasant stuff and really almost unforgivable in its vileness (I am talking about his response though I realize I am resorting to the very vocabulary of his reaction . . .) and

perhaps that's the wider point: Can one imagine what it must be like to have the capacity for such moralizing rage and to occasionally, often—almost always—have it become trained back on oneself? This is of course the voice—Oliver's interior voice—of his mother's deuteronomical cursing following his revelation of his homosexuality.

But Jesus, one occasionally does just want to grab Oliver by his lapels and to shout:

Grow up already! Get a life!

⁂

Later the following year, 1995, in a further effort to organize Oliver's life, Kate and Oliver acquired a small office space in an apartment building on Horatio Street in Greenwich Village, just a few blocks from Stonewall, as it happens, but Oliver continued to reside on City Island and to drop by our place for regular visits. I note one in particular from May 1997, which I felt worthy of recording in my notebook:

Oliver and I take a walk in our nearby forest following his European tour for *The Island of the Colorblind.*

He relates how in Zurich he had to restrain himself before the thronged audience at his reading (he always tries to include some locally appropriate autobiographical detail at each of his stops) from noting that he's always had a bit of a soft spot for Zurich since it was here that he experienced his *first orgasm*—at age twelve in the public pool . . . It was a few years after the war, he explained, and his parents were taking the kids on their first peacetime outing. He was agog at the splendors of war-spared Zurich, and one afternoon while floating on a cork raft in the middle of the public pool, he found himself feeling really good, and then better and better yet, incredibly good, and positively splendid, ecstatic with well-being. A bit later, in the changing room, he noticed his trunks were all sticky.

(Typically, he associates this with his love of swimming—I point out that all the surrounding half-naked boy-flesh might have had something to do with it, and though he doesn't reject this out of hand, he claims he'd never thought of that.)

He's publishing a swimming piece in one of the upcoming *NYer*s and relates how he's added a paragraph provoked by a recent St. Paul's School alumni publication where it emerged that St. Paul's had a vast and wonderful pool the entire time he was there, into which he never so much as dipped.

And why? Because, as the long-suppressed memories recently flooded in at his shrink Shengold's, during his adolescence he'd been affected by a disfiguringly shameful skin pestilence, a free-floating, rotting and pus-ey rash that cleared instantly with his arrival at Oxford but that was so humiliatingly unspeakable that he never appeared in trunks or shorts or bare-chested his entire adolescence.

And what was it? They could never find a cause. Was it perhaps an expression of his shame at his homosexuality—or was his attitude toward his budding homosexuality in turn shaped by this sense of the shameful? Did it perhaps shield him from having to act on his homosexual impulse? Who knows.

From there, conversation drifts into his stop in Rome where he had a bit of an Audrey Hepburn moment—his interpreter, a young man, tells him he'd arrived on a motorcycle and offers to let Oliver ride it around. Oliver takes a few ecstatic laps of the parking garage and then trundles about into the city with the young man in tow (unclear which is Peck and which Hepburn)—the two have dinner in his room, he falling "a little bit in love," as he seems to be doing a good deal of lately—but he typically doesn't make a move, nor apparently does he invite one (I can imagine he'd be an awe-inspiring figure), and nothing happens. As usual.

Alas.

For the record, I also note a melting in his contempt for one of his former nemeses around this time: the inclusion in my files of a photocopy of a piece by Douglas Hofstadter from the July 24, 1998, issue of the journal *Science* on "Popular Culture and the Threat to Rational Inquiry," with a note from Oliver hand-scrawled in red ink across the top: "I thought this essay marvelous!"

During these years, Oliver was becoming increasingly interested in his neurological artists, as he took to calling them: a series of cases displaying odd and often quite remarkable capacities for visual representation in a variety of patients. An accomplished artist who suddenly went completely color-blind and kept on painting, though now in grayscale. A young autistic savant, entirely infolded upon himself except for his vivid knack for depiction. An Italian immigrant in San Francisco beset by dazzlingly clear and sweet memories of his little village back home, which he was able to transcribe in oils. And so forth.

Oliver himself was beyond hopeless as an artist. Once, for example, he sketched out driving directions for me to his fabled Lake Jefferson Hotel on a little Post-it Note, which I subsequently retained in my files, treasuringly.

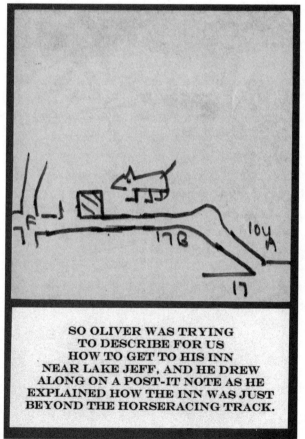

The Rat Track

To get there, it appears one had to pass the Monticello horse racing track (or, as one might be excused for imagining, based on Oliver's drawing, its rat racing track).

At any rate, on visits with such patients, he would often bring me along as a sort of aesthetic consultant—he didn't trust his own chops in that regard. Some of our most fascinating conversations concerned another astonishing (though somewhat more famous) young England-based Caribbean autistic artistic prodigy, Stephen Wiltshire, who Oliver spent a good deal of time with, even traveling to Russia with him, during those years. Actually, in this instance I don't recall meeting the shy phenom myself, but Oliver and I often discussed him, and Oliver would show me his drawings. Curiously, I note from my files that some of our most interesting exchanges involved not so much the boy's drawing as a sudden recent flowering of the musical, in particular Wiltshire's sudden passion for mimicking the Louis Armstrong version of the George David Weiss and Bob Thiele classic jazz standard "What a Wonderful World." At one point I sent Oliver a memo, starting with the piece's lyrics* and then expanding from there to note:

1. The first verse is all about visualization—it is the song of an artist, a seer, someone who experiences the world first and foremost *through his eyes.*
2. The third verse starts out being about race, people of all different sorts of races getting along. Is that significant given Stephen's race?
   The last half of that verse is the most poignant of all in Stephen's context ("I see friends shaking hands, saying how-do-you-do, They're really saying, I . . . love . . . you"). This is all about the sort of intersubjectivity of which, otherwise, Stephen seems precisely incapable. When you suggest that in singing his "autism disappears," are you saying that while he is singing he seems to have access to possibilities of intersubjective experience (such as those

---

*Although I cannot reproduce the piece's lyrics here, they are very easy to google up, and one might want to do so in tracking what follows.

suggested by the lyrics of the song) of which he is otherwise
incapable? And does he? Or what?

3. The fourth stanza ("I hear babies cry . . .") again is terrifically
poignant in Stephen's context, suggesting an openness to the
kind of experiential growth of which, again, he seems so
challenged in all other circumstances.

4. When Stephen sings "Oh what a beautiful world," is he
being or having reason to be consciously ironical? Would he
be capable of that? You may recall that the same rendition of
the song was used to quite lacerating effect in the film Robin
did just before *Awakenings*: *Good Morning, Vietnam*.

5. More generally, do the words have any meaning whatsoever
for him? Phrased differently, is singing this song with its
words any different for him than humming it would be? If
not, why doesn't he just hum or play the piano? Why, in
other words, does he enjoy *singing*? (For the external praise or
the internal experience?) What is his experience of the lyric?
Again, I ask all this because you say that while he is singing
it, his autism disappears, and I am trying to figure out what
you mean.

Oliver's responses were in some sense incorporated in "Prodigies," the
long piece he eventually wrote about Wiltshire for *The New Yorker* and then
included (as with "The Last Hippie") in *An Anthropologist on Mars*.

Some of our closest collaborations during this period, though, centered
around another of Oliver's discoveries. In this instance, he called one morning, saying, "You know how I always drag you along for visits with my
various neurological artists. Well, I realize that most of them are not necessarily great artists in the conventional meaning of that term: They are
oddities, prodigies, and the like. But I think I've come upon one fellow
who might really be a serious artist in every sense, and I need your
opinion."

And indeed, Ed Weinberger was something else altogether. A high-
level investment banker and alpha outdoorsman, Weinberger one fine
morning had found himself completely unable to get out of bed—he physically couldn't do it—and was soon diagnosed as presenting with a sudden
early-onset Parkinsonism that within months had him compressed into a

rictus clench. Whereupon he'd launched a second career, with great focus and concentration, designing incredibly intricate modernist furniture, tremblingly applying pencil to paper, only deploying tolerances more aerospace than carpentry (thousandths of an inch rather than the traditional sixty-fourths), conceptions so formidably rigorous that hardly anyone could be found to realize them, until a master cabinetmaker in coastal New Hampshire named Scott Schmidt began trying his hand, to truly extraordinary effect. Oliver and I visited Ed pretty regularly for a long while, Oliver always getting set to write up his case and then for some reason demurring, till eventually (with a survey show of the duo's work approaching), I asked him if he'd like me to write it up instead and he agreed, my account eventually appearing in *The New Yorker* under the title "The Furniture Philosopher" (and subsequently in my *Vermeer in Bosnia* collection).

On July 9, 1998, to celebrate Oliver's sixty-fifth birthday, Kate rented and staffed a cruise boat for a trip around Manhattan, and it was remarkable how crowded (and how varied) the party of celebrating guests proved to be (Oliver was no shy, retiring recluse any longer). His goddaughter Sara, now age eleven, had painted him a memento of the occasion portraying the Periodic Cruise as it sliced through the Cuttle Sea (flanked by merrily bobbing cuttlefish), slipping by Mendelejev Island, with its skyscrapers consisting of stacked elemental cubes, the orange sun setting in the distance. Later in the proceedings, when friends and colleagues started going to the microphone to offer their fervent toasts, Sara, seated next to me, grew increasingly annoyed that no women were taking the cue. Finally, she just shoved her way up to the mic and delivered her own, with Oliver beaming off to the side.

When later that year Oliver later finally decamped from City Island, that framed watercolor followed, soon to grace the guest bathroom in his elegant new book-lined apartment in the building next door to his new office, at the corner of Horatio and Eighth Avenue (with a magnificent view of the latter, coursing uptown toward Columbus Circle).

But Oliver kept driving out to visit us in Pelham, soon almost every weekend because he'd embarked on a new project, an autobiographical account of his chemical boyhood, the years immediately following his dreadful stint in the wartime boarding school, when he was saved by the periodic table and his beloved Uncle Tungsten. Oliver seemed intent on converting his goddaughter to the One True Faith, and with the comple-

Sara's drawing for Oliver's
sixty-fifth birthday

tion of each new chapter, he came over to read it to her—to all of us, but mainly to her: she beside him, listening solemnly rapt as he shuffled through the pages. And though in the end his ministrations never quite took (she was going to be a linguist), they were not without their effect. Later that semester, I got a call from Sara's teacher asking me to come in. It appears that the kids in class had been given a pop quiz in the form of an essay assignment: Why are human beings on earth? Fifteen minutes. The teacher wanted to show me what Sara had turned in:

> Why is the human on earth?
>
> I believe that there is, despite the fact that we humans have done so much damage to the world, a reason for our existance on this planet. I think we are here because the universe, with all it's wonder and balance and logic, needs to be marveled at, and we are the only species (to our knowledge) that has the ability to do so. We are the one species that does not simply except what is around us, but also asks why it is around us, and how it works. We are here because without us here to study it, the amazing complexity of the world would be wasted. And finally, we are here because the universe needs an entity to ask why it is here.

Not bad, I remember thinking at the time. It took Kant three volumes to get to the same place. But looking back on it today, I realize that who she was really channeling was her Kantian godfather.

Over the years, Sara had taken to traveling somewhere new almost every summer, accompanying both of her Polish grandparents to places they likely could never have gone before the fall of communism. In the summer of 2001, for a change she (now age fourteen) and her beloved grandfather Zenek traveled to the Canary Islands for a week by the beach, and on their last day they ventured out for one last swim, whereupon they got caught up in a riptide. As they were being dragged out to sea, both of them flailing fiercely, Zenek appears to have begun suffering a heart attack. Sara was at first at a loss as to what to do, he kept pushing her away, urging her to head back to shore. Eventually she did, mainly to seek help—she barely made it. Zenek alas did not. And she had to stand there alone as others rushed into the sea, presently to emerge with Zenek's body. All of which her mother and I back in New York only heard about some minutes later in a phone call from the hotel. As things developed, the fastest way we could join Sara was for her to board the very plane she and Zenek were scheduled to take back to Warsaw, and for us to meet her there, where a few days later we got this letter (typewritten, by fax) from Oliver:

July 20, 2001
Dear, stricken Weschler family,

I don't know whom I should write to, or what I can say.

What an awful thing to happen. I never knew your grandfather well, Sara, (it was difficult because of the language gap), but he seemed so strong and affectionate and playful and tender, all at once—and I knew, too, because we sometimes swam together, that he was a careful and powerful swimmer. I am sure there was no way to know (or avoid) that fatal tide— and you must see it as a freak accident which nobody—least of all yourself—could have done anything about.

I feel more than I can say, Joanna, for you too—because I know what a deep bond there was between the two of you. And I wonder, too, how your poor mother is managing.

And I feel intensely for you, too, Ren, not least because there have been other sudden deaths, deaths-by-accident, in your family . . .

If there is any way I can help, other than being a godfather and a friend and a neighbor, you must let me know.

My deepest sympathy, again, to you all,
Oliver

Later that summer of 2001, after twenty years at *The New Yorker*, I quit in order to take the helm at the New York Institute for the Humanities at New York University, where Oliver was now a fellow too, and he frequently agreed to participate in our public offerings, including one early on that I recall with particular warmth, an evening entitled "To Be Young and On Fire: Pre-Adolescent Intellectual Passion," pairing Oliver with fellow fellows Susan Sontag and Freeman Dyson.

Meanwhile, Oliver's primary focus seemed to be turning from the neurology of the visual to that of the aural, and in this regard, I was of no value to him whatsoever. Indeed, I was so musically hapless that it became a running joke between us, especially since by all genetic counts I ought to have been some sort of musical marvel. My mother's father had been that eminent Viennese transplant, Weimar Berlin modernist composer Ernst Toch, who following the rise of Hitler had fled, eventually alighting in Hollywood, where his modernist idiom was deemed perfect for chase scenes and horror effects, though he did go on to win the Pulitzer Prize for a late-career upwelling of symphonies. My father's mother, Angela Weschler, had been the head of the Vienna Conservatory of Music's piano department, and my father for his own part had been quite a proficient and inspired amateur jazz pianist. None of it mattered: The genes all seemed to cancel each other out in my case. My immediately younger brother and I both took piano lessons for years, and at a certain point my grandfather even composed a canon for the two of us, which, following months of practice, we were paraded before him to perform on his Blüthner piano. Following which, unbeknownst to me at the time, he apparently turned to my grandmother and said, "The younger one, maybe, there might be a chance; the older one is completely hopeless." All I knew was that suddenly the pressure to practice and go on with my lessons seemed to fade away.

But it was strange, because as Oliver kept probing, it was clear that I had quite a good sense of rhythm, I could keep a beat, conduct symphonic records, and was not a bad dancer; I had a thoroughly adequate musical memory (I could recall tunes and hum them; indeed, ask me anytime and I will regale you with a hummed version of the two-part canon my grandfather wrote for my brother and me). The thing is—and I admit it's weird—in any given melody I simply can't make out whether the successive notes are going up or down. The first four notes of Beethoven's Fifth Symphony, for example: I can tell the first three notes are the same, but does the fourth one go up or down? Beats me, and I can't even get myself to remember. Put me in front of a piano, and I will happily play you the first two notes of my grandfather's canon (which are the same: middle C), but then I am at an utter loss and have to stab about haplessly, stumbling toward the next. This failing goes along with certain other odd idiosyncrasies, as Oliver was at pains to worry out. For example, no matter how often I try, I can't recall whether the fork goes on the right or the left, I have to rely on mnemonic crutches, such as the fact that both "fork" and "left" have four letters, whereas "spoon," "knife," and "right" all have five—

and I have to do so *every single time.* Similarly, although I have quite a good sense of direction, when *giving* directions I often flip right and left, this even though I have them correct in my mind's eye; so when it comes to directions, don't ever listen to me! I am a very slow reader (very much the opposite of Oliver).*

Though it's even stranger than all of that, because when I talk about my own writing, or teach writing to others, all of my metaphors are musical: "This next paragraph needs to be syncopated slightly differently," "You need a rest there, maybe even a pause," "Maybe now you should shift from the major to a minor key for the next several pages," and so forth. My grandfather used to speak of a piece of music's "architectonic"—by which he meant architecture across time rather than space: "the sequential exposition of material across time in a formful manner" being another way he used to put it—and this is exactly how I think about narrative, as passages of compression and then spaciousness, vaults and alcoves and buttresses and the like. Indeed, when I am struggling through any sort of writerly blockage, I often spend hours deploying a big boxful of wooden blocks, many of them self-designed, across our dining-room table, not thinking about the subject matter of my blockage at all, just noodling around with form as such. (In the old days, when Sara and her kindergarten friends would come traipsing in after school, she'd have to yell, pre-emptively, "Don't touch those blocks! Those are Daddy's blocks!")

And it's even weirder than that, because often when I am writing and things are going really well, I will unconsciously find myself humming up a storm, even pacing my sentences to the cadences of the piece I am humming, and often, after I'm finished and the hummed orchestra continues to reverberate in my head, I will realize it's *one of my grandfather's pieces*!

And yet, because of that up-and-down-deaf business, I don't especially like going to concerts, because I can't make out the very things that must

---

*All of this might have something to do with the family legend regarding the origin of our last name, Weschler, which is actually quite unusual; take a look in any phone book and you'll see how there are all sorts of Wechslers, a name that straightforwardly derives from the Yiddish for "money changer," as with all those "Wechsel" signs you see at European airports. But what's with our spelling? Well, goes the family account, Weschler is Yiddish for "dyslexic money changer," which in turn, by simple Darwinian selection, accounts for why there are so few of us.

enthrall the people who do, the way notes and themes weave in and out of each other and the like. (Oliver, by contrast, loved going to concerts, in part because he could make these things out to a highly developed degree, though in truth, in larger part it was because they kept the lights on, however dimly, and he could scribble away in his notebook all the while.)

Anyway, all of this fascinated Oliver, he used to quiz me on it, and we were always intending to hook me up to an EEG machine so he could poke and prod and try to pinpoint the peculiarity—only we never got around to it. I (or rather my manifest oddness) did however eventually rate a full-page mention in "Things Fall Apart: Amusia and Dysharmonia," a chapter of *Musicophilia*, the book he was developing all the while, which came out, to considerable acclaim, in 2008.

Meanwhile, Oliver began turning his attention to a similarly odd, though far more consequential, scotoma of his own, the fact that, as he began to acknowledge, he had suffered from a curious sort of face blindness his entire life, a facial agnosia, a neurological condition more technically known as prosopagnosia. He had a terrible time recognizing people by their faces, and specifically their faces (as opposed, say, to their voices or postures or gaits), even people he knew, even people he knew quite well (even Kate, even Joanna, even me), *even himself* (he was given to begging pardon when bumping up against the bearded figure coming toward him in a long mirror—and sometimes just the opposite: I was once returning from the bathroom at a diner and saw him primping his beard while gazing intently upon the actual bearded fellow the next banquette over, who was staring back at him in some bewilderment).

Sometimes the effects could be quite amusing. "I often tend to recognize similarities in style over substance," he once confided when our conversation turned to his problem. "The other day, for instance, I walked up to a couple of men and asked if they were brothers. 'Brothers?' one of them shot back. *'Brothers? Are you out of your mind? Can't you see that we're father and son? My hair is white and his is jet-black!'*" But other times they could be almost paralyzingly debilitating. He dreaded parties and other sorts of social occasions, even to an extent his own birthday parties. He knew he would fail to recognize cherished friends and, almost as bad, in an attempt to compensate, strike up intimate conversations with complete strangers. He'd be causing offense on all sides. And I gradually came to realize that what so often passed with Oliver for strangulated shyness, stammering awkwardness, or even insufferable arrogance simply rose from the fact that he had no idea whatsoever whom he was talking to. It was a syndrome that had cast a long shadow across his life.

Nor was he by any means alone in this, as became dazzlingly clear a few years later when he published a piece on the subject in *The New Yorker*. Much as had happened earlier when his pieces on Tourette's or the autism spectrum had opened readers' eyes to the presence of such folk all around them (and brought a corresponding measure of surcease to those struggling in self-imagined isolation with the conditions, and to their families), hundreds of people began writing in with their own stories and their appreciation at being recognized, their surpassing relief at having their secret torment named and explained and acknowledged. Most famously, perhaps, it turned out that the great artist Chuck Close had long suffered from the same perplex (that's in part what his giant gridded facial portraits had been all about, an attempt to overmaster the difficulty), and Oliver and Chuck began appearing together onstage and on the radio (specifically on Robert Krulwich's public radio show, *Radiolab*) to discuss their mutual travails, in conversations that were both deeply heartening and uproariously funny.

Of course, Oliver's prosopagnosic tendencies also tracked uncannily with some of the deficits he kept locating, probing, and memorializing in the lives of several of his patient-subjects—not least, in this instance, the man who mistook his wife for a hat, another instance where Oliver's preternatural capacity for empathy seemed rooted in a sense of fellow feeling, of recognition all the more remarkable in that it was all about a fellow inability, precisely, to recognize anyone at all!

19

A Digression on the Question of Reliability and the Nature of Romantic Science

But—and here I want to shift keys, maybe even modulate from the major down to a minor register for a while before returning to the main chrono-logical procession (which now, alas, is beginning to rush toward its conclusion)—the thing is that Oliver's blithe confession of his own prosop-agnosia shaded into a wider concern on the part of many regarding the ex-tent to which this albeit thoroughly engaging chronicler (who couldn't even keep faces straight, for God's sake) could be relied upon more generally: The ongoing suspicion, that is, that he was sometimes making things up, exag-gerating, fantasticating, seeing more than was there, or even things that weren't there.* All the variations on Michael Neve's critique.†

---

*See as well, for example, this passage from Alan Bennett's diaries, *Keeping On Keeping On* (New York: Farrar, Straus and Giroux, 2016), 235–36:

> Chatwin—like Sebald, Kapuscinski and Oliver Sacks—operates on the borders of truth and imagination, dodging over the border into fantasy as and when it suits and making them difficult to pin down. Defenders of Chatwin like Fran-cis Wyndham dismiss criticism of this as 'English, literalist or puritanical'—in my case all three. One tells the truth or one makes it up, not both at the same time.
>
> One tells the truth. It isn't just a whim. Or so I tell myself. Such characters trouble me.

Or so I tell *myself.*

†Curiously, such a catalog of aspersions might have been thought to include an instance to which Oliver himself continually used to allude, one he never seemed able to shake: the slashing wholesale rejection of his 1970 letter to *The Journal of the American Medical Associa-tion*, the one in which he'd tried to alert his colleagues to the wild side effects he and his colleagues were beginning to encounter with the L-DOPA they'd been administering to

As for the original misgiving here, the question of whether Oliver's admitted prosopagnosia might be seen to undercut his reliability on other scores, it seems to me that the very opposite was the case. For one thing, he lavished a far more focused level of attention on his patients than on others in his social world. (He once recalled for me how the remarkable photographic memory that had helped him sail through college and medical school completely disappeared soon thereafter. At first he fretted that he might be entering an early-onset Alzheimer's. But in fact, he came to understand that his wide-ranging memory was just becoming more selective, and focusing in particular on his patients.) Beyond that, it may well have been in compensation for the prosopagnosia that he started taking such thorough case notes on every single patient interview he undertook, taking the notes in the first place and then retaining them long after he was legally required to. (I myself can relate to the latter: I have a terrible innate memory for specific incidents and conversations, even just a few hours after the fact—spoons and forks all over again—which is one of the reasons I am such a ferocious note-taker; as a reporter, I'm not unlike the severe asthmatic who overcompensates himself into becoming a professional soccer player. And something similar may have been going on with Oliver as well.)

As for the wider misgiving, however—the nagging suspicion that Oliver at least occasionally exaggerated or confabulated or the like, or that the things he was seeing were at best anecdotal and of no wider medical use—misgivings that Oliver confessed to sometimes having himself (as he said of his Leg book, every charge that was being waged against him, he had at one point or another hurled against himself, only more severely), the question, that is, of his general trustworthiness, relevance,

---

their patients. The fact is (and this sort of confirms the wider point), if you go back and actually look at the letters that *JAMA* published in response to Sacks et al.'s, they weren't nearly as dismissive and cutting and thoroughly rejectionist as Sacks himself kept remembering; rather, they were relatively measured, pointing out that the patients Sacks and his colleagues were dealing with were much more extremely impacted by their Parkinsonism than the average sorts of patients most doctors would be encountering, such that the Sacks side effects might not be expected to show up everywhere else. (The fact that later on such side effects *did* begin showing up everywhere else, albeit to a lesser degree, is beside the point here; what's germane is how wildly Oliver himself continually exaggerated the purdah-shaming tone of the letters in question in his own recollection of them, as if he had been utterly cast out of the profession.)

and reliability, there it seems to me that a wider-ranging consideration may be in order.

After all, as sympathetic a friend and colleague as Jonathan Miller had at one point in our conversation conceded how "you begin to wonder. When you visit the cases he talks about, none of them really exhibit any of the features that he claims they have. A lot of medical people I think are very, very suspicious of what he says about the cases he talks about in *Awakenings.* And I know friends of mine who've actually seen them say they are not quite what he says." And indeed, these sorts of reservations were often expressed to me, especially in the early days when I was just getting started on my profile, by doctors and medical writers with whom I would broach the subject.

However, such misgivings were directly countered by the countless testimonials I collected during the years of my research, from colleagues and patients and reporters and friends and documentarians alike, to the effect that as unlikely and almost unbelievable as many of Oliver's reports might have seemed, they'd all seen it, too, and could corroborate his descriptions and vouch for his clinical trustworthiness.

ISABELLE RAPIN

Well, there's no doubt that many people don't see his work as serious science. But for example, remember how he described that very rapid change in some of his patients, how they would go from being totally Parkinsonian to completely not, just like that, in an instant. When he described that in *Awakenings,* people thought he was making it up, but today this phenomenon is called the "on-off effect" and is well known and well recognized. So you see, I think he's an excellent observer.

DUNCAN DALLAS

As I say, when you first saw the patients who'd survived the time of Tribulation, you didn't really believe all the things Oliver was ascribing to them, but the more time you spent with them, the more you began to realize how their inner lives were in fact still quite *dense* with experience, and then, when coupled with the films Oliver himself had been taking earlier on, both before and after L-DOPA, you could see that it was all true.

MARGIE KOHL

Whatever other license Oliver may take at times, what he says about the patients is true.

He trained me. I am a fantastic observer today, and it is all thanks to him. "Go in there," he would say, "and tell me what you see." Most neurologists are so stuck in their checklists and their Medicare-mill fifteen-minute drills that they miss everything; Oliver missed nothing.

And when I asked her directly about the charge that Oliver made things up, Kohl responded emphatically:

I know the charge is *not* true, and I was there. Sure, he would occasionally attribute a higher vocabulary to some of the patients— Maria, for instance, was uneducated and he made her language flow, but this was as much as anything out of respect for her, an honoring and cherishing of her—and in a wider sense he embellished nothing. And many of the patients did talk fluently and with great subtlety.

But you had to be willing to sit at the bedside and listen. They didn't just up and tell you these things. You had to establish rapport and a context.

With Leonard, for instance, most people had never gotten to him because (and I am speaking here of the years before L-DOPA) they wouldn't spend the time with him: He was very slow, each letter might take a minute for him to spell out on his board, and everyone else would limit themselves to yes or no questions. But Oliver sat it out.

And even, elsewhere in our conversation, Jonathan Miller himself:

Well, he is unreliable only in the sense that it would be very difficult to accommodate some of his work within the body of neurology as it stands today. On the other hand, he also appeals to and represents some aspects of classical neurology which the modern reductionist neurology hasn't accommodated *itself* to. This curious sort of infinity that does exist within each individual self, which simply doesn't get treated in ordinary neurology.

Beyond such testimonials, in further adjudicating the question of Oliver's overall reliability, one needs to consider the sorts of distinctions Oliver himself has made: How, for example, he may at times not see things directly but "imagines" his way to the truth, which is to say that he gives articulation to the otherwise inarticulate through an act of active imaginative projection, one that he subsequently confirms through further observations (and corroborates in the prior literature). Such a method may indeed run counter to the strictures of conventional positivist science, with its insistence on valuing only that which can be measured and quantified (ideally by way of double-blind and peer-reviewed experiments), but Oliver's entire point is that certain things cannot be quantified (such as, precisely, the *depth* of experience—"Sometimes," he once told me, "I feel like I am not so much interested in phenomena as in the *resonance* of phenomena, what it is like to *live* with the phenomena"), and that such quantifying studies by definition have to carve out a scrupulously circumscribed portion of clinical reality, when what he is often trying to gauge, access, evoke, and address is the wider reality, in its entirety, of the patient's experience.

Here, as well, we are broaching into the terrain of his entire critique regarding the necessary limitations of computers and artificial intelligence ("Although people regularly talk about 'personal' computers, inter*face* is the one thing you can't do with them"), which is almost always a stand-in for his critique of positivism in general. Not that positivist research is without its uses (far from it!), but that positivism can only take one so far, and it doesn't get to dictate the lack of validity of anything beyond its ken. Just because something can't be quantified doesn't mean it is not there (here we verge back on the terrain of Jane Goodall and the qualitative change in her capacity for observation that occurred when she started giving her chimpanzees names rather than assigning them numbers). "The other day," Oliver told me at one point, regarding his colleague and former Luria student, "I called Nick Goldberg 'my bête noire and favorite adversary' and he was honored. Anyway, Nick says neurology is hardware and neuropsychology is software. But isn't there anything else? Granted, sickness is stripping people down to their robotics—and damaged robotics at that—and I *know* robotics. Indeed, I know it better than most. But I also know that there's more than robotics to human experience. Admittedly, as there is a robot in me, there is also a roboticist. But there's also an eideticist. And you have to get from the Robot to the Creature, which is what Kant is all about."

This, too, is where Leibniz comes in for Oliver. What he particularly treasured in Leibniz was his monadology, the notion that reality was made up of a vast latticework of wholes, every one of which reflected back the entire infinity of the universe (the whole business of the macro in the micro, the infinite one could find reflected in even the most infinitesimal, an essentially kabbalistic notion, and indeed, Leibniz was consulting with kabbalists when he was developing it), and that therefore, as a result, the true doctor (and Oliver considered Leibniz "the ultimate physician") has to deal with the whole person (one infinite monad to another, an "I" to a "Thou"), not just the fragmented facets delivered forth by all the ever more narrowly siloed specialists and their ever more narrowly slicing and dicing quantitative diagnostic tools.

Granted, Oliver sometimes pushed this critique too far. But here I'm reminded of a seminal clarification the great religious historian Donald Nicholl offered us back in my days at Santa Cruz: He spoke of the value of heresies, and more specifically of the way that in the decades of the early church fathers, heresies were defined as long-suppressed aspects of the truth that then got idolatrized as the whole truth. Their problem was hence not so much one of verity as one of proportion. And in those terms, it seems to me that when it came to his critiques of positivism, more often than not Oliver stayed on the proper side of right relation. (Even though he once quipped to me how "At my symbolic best, I aspire to Donne, at my conceptual best, to Wittgenstein, but sometimes, I grant, I get overDonne.")

But there was a still-wider issue here, that of the very nature and facticity of narrative itself (whether any story, any tale, can ever be strictly true*), a question to which Oliver alluded in another typewritten letter he sent me some months after the first round of attacks on his Leg book.

---

*The sort of thing that E. L. Doctorow was getting at in his novel *The Waterworks* when he has his narrator explaining, regarding one of the book's principal characters, how "I withhold here the circumstances of our first sight of Satorius. I want to keep to the chronology of things but at the same time to make their pattern sensible, which means disrupting the chronology. After all there is a difference between living in some kind of day-to-day crawl

January 11, 1985

Dear Ren

The reviews which bothered me most of ALTSO (in the
LRB, and a very similar one in the *TLS*, I don't think you saw
it) [were those that contained] the imputation that I had lied . . .
here, and therefore everywhere as well. And of course, this
readily ties in with self-doubt and accusation, and conceivably,
too, an impulse to lie (or at least to "enhance": the *TLS* reviewer
spoke of "dramatic enhancement," and you yourself said yesterday,
"Ollie, come on!").

I could not, I think, lie "phenomenologically" (I mean,
about phenomena)—because I love them too much, and they
do not *admit* of any lies.

Or, as he'd put it that other time: "It wouldn't be home [. . .] unless
potassium carbonate were exactly like potassium carbonate. *That's* why
truthfulness is so important."

Continuing on:

I may indeed (this is difficult for me to judge, because I am
so intuitive, and there is a borderland somewhere between
"glimpsing" and "guessing") say more than I am absolutely
sure of—this was the case with "Dr. P," [the original man who
mistook his wife] and therefore of the extreme pleasure when
I came across Macrae's description of an almost identical case.

What is very important to think clearly on, though, and to
discuss—and I think I will follow your advice and do this at
the next Narrative seminar—is the business of "telling a tale,"
finding or imposing dramatic organization, *over and above, but
never violating* a phenomenological description. And the business
as to whether there "is" any such organization in reality, e.g., in
the case of being ill, or sustaining some damage . . . Michael
Neve, in the *LRB*, felt "the story" took over, had to proceed

---

through chaos, where there is no hierarchy to your thoughts, but a raucous equality of them,
and knowing in advance the whole conclusive order . . . which makes narration . . . suspect"
(New York: Random House, 1994), 123.

with its own inexorable momentum. There may be something
in this, but not in the pejorative way he means. The 1974
experience *was* organized "dramatically," the 1984 one [when
Oliver broke his other leg on the eve of the Leg book's
publication] was not (was hardly an "experience," just a boring,
meaningless consecution of events . . .)

   The extent, generalizing, to which "Life" is just a boring,
meaningless consecution of events . . . and the extent to which it
constitutes, is constituted on, organized as, experienced as . . . a
story . . . (this would have been your challenge too, perhaps not
unlike Shengold's, in trying to make a "narrative" of my "life.")
   [. . .]
Anyhow, love, Oliver[SB]

Luria reserved the term "romantic science" for the sorts of extended
storytelling he chose to engage in across the latter half of his life in *The
Man with a Shattered World*, *The Mind of a Mnemonist*, and the like (in con-
tradistinction to the other kind of more conventional scientific investigation at which he also excelled) and for the sorts of truths he felt could only
be arrived at by such storytelling. And Oliver followed his hero in that
characterization.

   The passage from my conversation with Jonathan Miller, quoted earlier in this chapter (about how one couldn't help but begin to wonder about
Oliver's veracity), was itself sandwiched between two countervailing senses
of the situation. I'd begun by asking about the various imputations of exaggeration and the like, and he'd shot back: "But they're all true! And at
the same time, yes, completely mad."*

   And onward through the point about his friends who've seen some of
the instances in person and claim that things are not precisely as Oliver
says they are: "But the fiction is so luminous and so beautiful that in a
way, it's beside the point, because the fictions become more important. And
the facts seem almost like impudent irrelevancies. There's a tremendous
overlap between him and Borges in some ways."

---

*One is momentarily reminded of Adorno's remark to the effect that nothing is true in psy-
choanalysis except the exaggerations (especially if one is one's editor, Alex Star!). In addition
to their all being true, all the truths are fictions, so that it gets so you can't separate them
out. It isn't that they're invented. But you begin to wonder . . .

Ryszard Kapuściński and Oliver at our home in Pelham, Joanna in the background

During the twenty years that I used to teach my annual Fiction
of Nonfiction classes (surveying all the fictive elements of narrative nonfiction, from form and structure through voice and tone and irony and freedom and so forth), toward the end of the course, when we arrived at Oliver's
prose, I deployed a slightly different coinage: Rhapsodic Nonfiction. Here,
I hooped Oliver and Ryszard Kapuściński (both of whom had often found
their strict veracity called into question) as each being instances of the sort
of practitioner who first approaches his subject across one sort of daily and
immediate writing (daily dispatches as the premier foreign correspondent
for the Polish Press Agency, in Kapuściński's case; those 500-word clinical notes for every patient he saw across his entire career, in Oliver's), and
then years later might return to the same material in a conspicuously different register. Thus, for example, Kapuściński begins his legendary account of the final days of Ethiopia's Haile Selassie, *The Emperor,* "In the
evenings I listened to those who had known the Emperor's court."

"In the evenings," which is to say when he had finished with his day
job (filing those news reports). And "listened," past tense, which is to
say back then and over there. You can almost hear him swirling the
whiskey in his snifter as he launches into his reverie-like tale before an
intimate and rapt audience now that he is back home after his years of

wandering. And as I argued in that "Allegories of Eastern Europe" piece, Kapuściński's text, when it was published in 1978 in Warsaw, seemed to operate at four levels simultaneously: as more or less straightforward reportage; as a prophetic allegory of the situation in Poland at that very moment, deep into the corrupt regime of the Communist Party chieftain Edward Gierek and just two years from the coming upsurge of Solidarity (let those with ears to hear, hear); as a more general allegory of the precarious dynamics of any and every sort of imperial court; and finally, as literature of the highest order, where it took its rightful place on the shelf alongside Calvino, García Márquez, Kafka, and, yes, Borges. (Jonathan Miller, incidentally, once mounted a remarkably evocative adaptation of Kapuściński's *Emperor* on the London stage.)

Oliver's rhapsodic writings arise in a similar context, for not only can he do the other—he has, repeatedly, every day through his entire career, and to remarkable documentary effect—but these tales are pitched slightly differently, and they shimmer to similar effect (hence all the references to Arabian Nights entertainments and so forth, both on his own part and on that of others). He is writing for a different audience (though one that he dearly hoped would come to include his medical colleagues, responding in a slightly different way from their usual reaction) and not asking to be judged by the same actuarial quantitative peer-reviewed standards as more conventional medical researchers (though even he himself occasionally grew confused on this last point).

And yet, in another sense, he was asking to be so judged. Or rather, he was trying to advocate for and model a different sort of medicine on behalf of chronic, often institutionally warehoused and largely abandoned patients, especially those with massively enveloping syndromes that set them off at a nearly infinite remove, the sort of patients often referred to as "hopeless" or "mere vegetables." And here—and this is something Oliver's blithe critics often failed to notice—narrative of this sort was *part of the therapy itself.* Helping to turn an It back into an I, in Sister Lorraine's evaluation. Or maybe a patient (an object) back into an agent (a subject). The therapy in question had to be intensely collaborative—patients who had been treated as mere thrown-away objects might well have long since lost any sense of their own capacity for agency and subjectivity. Trying to puzzle out their story, Oliver would often spend hours at a time with any single one of them (out of both compassion and fascination on his own part). Such people were privileged witnesses to and actors along the very remotest stretches of human possibility, and as such had marvelous stories to offer about such extreme vantages and experiences. The way a Parkinsonian can be jump-started, as it were, into fluid action by the mere extension of a friend's helping hand, so Oliver would offer his collaboration, sharing the self-organizing capacity for narrative. Doctor and patients would work out (literally, "make up") their stories together, and in so doing the doctor would help his patients to re-compose themselves. As such, narrative was not unlike Oliver's beloved music, in that it allowed patients to be moved by what moved them. And the animating surround to the entire exercise was nothing less than love, understood, granted, in an impersonal Eliotian sense. (But just try to quantify that!)*

And the marvel of the whole thing was that, as the years passed, Oliver, by way of his stories (and in particular the tenor of those stories, the quality of their attentiveness), along with the example set by a few other similar visionaries, actually began to turn the tide on how conventional neurology was being taught and practiced. Not at all bad for a series of "mere anecdotes."

---

*It occurs to me in this context that this model of the doctor, by way of painstaking attention and concourse, helping the patient to make up, compose, and narrate into being a therapeutic way of thinking about the extremity of his or her specific existential situation, might in turn account for the singularly knotty problems Sacks himself got into with his Leg book—all the convolutions and blockages involved in its writing, and, once finally written, the text's exceptional susceptibility to all the Nevian sorts of critique—precisely because, in the particular instance in question, doctor and patient were one and the same person. Sacks had been all by himself, chasing his own tail, the necessary (self-)love all bollixed up with equally strong doses of self-doubt and self-loathing. He never achieved any Eliotian distance whatsoever.

20

His Own Life (2005–2015)

Beginning in late 2005, Oliver faced a serious cancer scare, the discovery of a slowly expanding tumor in his right eyeball whose otherwise seemingly successful (high-tech focused-radiation) treatment, by December 2007, had nevertheless cost him the use of that eye, and hence his stereoscopic vision. We'd long talked about stereoscopic vision, and about his early passion, going back to his youth, for stereopsis, stereo-optical equipment, stereo-photography, and the neurology of binocular vision.*

That complete loss of vision in his right eye was particularly ironic since just recently he'd been returning with renewed concentration to this earlier passion and its tangent possibilities, in large part because of his exchanges over the previous year with a delightful new correspondent, a professor of neurobiology at Mount Holyoke College named Susan Barry, who late in life had managed, through rigorous visual exercises, to acquire a stereoscopic vision she'd never before had and was able to describe the transformative effect in luminously observant prose. "Stereo Sue," as Oliver referred to her, was featured in Oliver's June 19, 2006, *New Yorker* piece, one that would subsequently be included in his 2010 collection, *The Mind's Eye.*

On July 9, 2008, when Oliver celebrated his seventy-fifth birthday at the New York Botanical Garden, I was off somewhere reporting, but this time Sara was one of the official speakers and, now age twenty-one, she

---

*See, for example, the letter dated March 8, 1985.[SB]

charmed the crowd with tales of the way he had long enchanted and informed her.

Shortly thereafter Oliver (more than thirty-five years into his self-enforced celibacy) met a marvelous younger man, maybe in his mid to late forties, a fellow writer, recently transplanted to New York from San Francisco, by the name of Billy Hayes (they met, as it happens, after Oliver had been asked to blurb Hayes's *The Anatomist*, about Henry Gray of *Gray's Anatomy* fame), and over a period of some months, ever so tentatively at first, Oliver finally allowed himself to fall in love and to accept the fact that Billy had likewise fallen in love with him. (I say "allowed himself"; the fact is that he had been falling in love and being fallen in love with regularly, constantly, over the preceding thirty-five years, it's just that he'd always foresworn the budding connections.) There was something different now, though: perhaps the recent close shave with mortality, equally likely the extraordinary caliber and quality of Billy himself, something all of Oliver's friends could immediately discern, for Billy was elegant, and circumspect, and kind. Oliver was almost comically besotted, anxiously asking after our opinions and making sure that we were still of the same opinion, primping and flushing like some hyperventilating teenager, and Billy and Oliver started traveling pretty much everywhere together.*

In the meantime, under Kate's expert management, Oliver's life became more and more full. In 2009, he spent a few weeks at the MacDowell Colony in Peterborough, New Hampshire, where he was presumably wrapping up *The Mind's Eye* or beginning to focus on his next book, *Hallucinations*, in which he would be divulging further details of his own earlier drug experiments alongside the cases of other witnesses to such epiphanies.

Oliver was now regularly communing with the likes of Gerald Edelman, Francis Crick, and Carleton Gajdusek, and closer to home, such stellar colleagues as Torsten Wiesel, Roald Hoffmann, Eric Kandel, Bob Wasserman, Ralph Siegel, and Orrin Devinsky. He and Kate made regular appearances at my institute luncheons, and he continued to let himself be featured at many of our events. We saw him every once in a while out

---

*Beyond that, I defer to Billy's account of the ensuing years in his gorgeously lyrical elegiac 2017 memoir, *Insomniac City*.

in Pelham, but he was busy, we were busy. Sara was away at college and then, for several years, in Africa (her initial interest in African languages having spilled over into a wider passion for the place and its people as a whole)—and so we all tended to drift somewhat apart for a while. (Sara surmises, too, that Oliver was now happily getting directly from Billy many of the sorts of things he used to rely on the rest of us for, albeit in sublimated form.)

In 2013, with my NYU gig coming to an end, I began taking on a variety of other side postings, and in particular accepted an offer from the eminent dancer and choreographer Bill T. Jones to curate a weeklong festival every April called Live Ideas, held at his New York Live Arts facility on West Nineteenth Street: twenty events over five days devoted to a single figure or subject as a way of promulgating Jones's own convictions about "the *embodiment* of ideas," the interpenetration, that is, of body and (variously) mind or spirit or soul. Since 2013 was also going to see Oliver's eightieth birthday, I suggested we focus our first festival on him (and the next, in 2014, on James Baldwin, on the occasion of the ninetieth anniversary of *his* birth), with sessions (in Oliver's case) ranging from ferns and bodybuilding to chemistry and philosophy, with individual panels devoted to Oliver's impact on the worlds of Tourette's and Parkinson's and the deaf, and contributions from (as well as direct original commissions to) the worlds of film, theater, dance, and music. Jones agreed enthusiastically, Oliver less so (shy, abashed, and histrionically involuted, as per usual). He gave his grudging consent but promised at most to come to only one event (a public conversation between himself and Robert Krulwich).

Nevertheless, he agreed to all my other plans with one notable exception. As part of my full portrait of "The Worlds of Oliver Sacks," I had wanted to devote an entire session to the poetry of his two great friends, Thom Gunn and W. H. Auden (to be read by an already quite eager contingent of New York poets)—but that Oliver nixed outright. "You know what that's code for." He pointed an accusatory finger at me. (What? I asked. Great English poets, once resident in America, who've in the meantime died?) Even though he was now openly living and regularly being seen about town with Billy, at that late stage he still could not abide any wider public acknowledgment, even one so glancing, of his homosexuality.

In the end, the festival went off almost flawlessly—and Oliver attended every single event.* We'd found a box of old Super 8 film reels in Oliver's closet, his documentation of the Awakenings patients, and I was able to get them digitized and to commission Bill Morrison to fashion a short original documentary ("Re:Awakenings") out of them, with music provided by Philip Glass. Tobias Picker conducted the Orchestra of St. Luke's in Sacks-inspired works by Picker and Michael Nyman; we commissioned an original dance piece from Donna Uchizono. We had all sorts of panels on all sorts of aspects of the Sacks universe: Stereo Sue led us through some of her stereoscopic exercises; the marathon swimmer Lynne Cox and astronaut Marsha Ivins both waxed eloquent on extremes of embodiment; the philosophers Alva Noë and Colin McGinn took a deep dive into mind-body conundrums; Roger Hanlon from Woods Hole talked cephalopods, and Dennis Stevenson from the New York Botanical Garden even lugged over a truly huge cycad—all by way of tribute.

But perhaps the most profoundly moving evening consisted of a matched pair of productions of Harold Pinter's "A Kind of Alaska," the first in a standard (albeit powerfully rendered) spoken version, and then again (perhaps to even more powerful effect) an original production in American Sign Language by a troupe of deaf actors—followed by a talk-back session where the deaf actors and others were able to address Oliver directly, thanking him for the enormous impact his witness and involvement in deaf culture had made in their lives.

Oliver was quite overwhelmed by the general outpouring of love and appreciation. He had recently launched into the writing of his autobiography, and, perhaps thus reassured, he now finally resolved to come clean about his sexuality, in his own words and in his own good time.

Not quite two years later, in early February 2015, Sara (recently back in the States and now attending a crash master's program in African studies at Columbia) and I went over to visit Oliver at his apartment, and he proudly pulled out the thick tranche of his autobiographical manuscript and, as in the good old days, started reading from it to us. At one point, he noted that he'd wanted to title the thing "My Own Life," in keeping with the title Hume had given his late-life self-accounting. But Kate was dubious and instead had insisted on the alternative, *On the Move*, with a

---

*For videos of several of the events, go to the festival's YouTube page: https://www.youtube.com/playlist?list=PLUlBGrV6VKCgzE2hkANkrNlrjCkP4l8za.

terrific photo of a leather-jacketed, clean-shaven young Oliver astride a fierce BMW on the cover. Oliver read on for some minutes, marvelous passages about his youth and his days in California, but something was clearly bothering him. He would interrupt himself, anxiously hemming and hawing, until finally he just blurted it out: "You're not in it, Ren."

What? "You're not in the book." No problem, I assured him, I didn't care (and I didn't, though later maybe I did, some, though then again, not so much—I don't know). "There just wasn't room, we had to make choices." Greatly relieved by my apparent calm, he started to return to the text, only to interrupt himself once again. "And I'm not giving any interviews!"

Which was funny, because literally the next day I got a call from Cullen Murphy, an editor pal from my days feeding *The Atlantic* pieces that Tina Brown had declined, who himself had in the meantime moved on to *Vanity Fair*. "Did you see?" he asked. "Sacks is about to publish his autobiography and he himself is going to be talking about all the stuff he wouldn't let you mention all those years ago. Maybe you could interview him for us." To which I snapped, "He's not giving any interviews!" Though then again, it occurred to me, almost immediately, maybe he would let me rifle through those old notebooks of mine, without bothering him further, so as to publish some of my notes from those days. Cullen was game, and so (it turned out) was Oliver, and in the days ahead I pulled together a quick 13,000-word cull, passed it along, and *Vanity Fair* committed to publishing a bit more than half of the thing.

Hardly had I turned that original manuscript in, though, than we received a handwritten letter from Oliver:

February 16, 2015
Dear Ren (and Joasia and Sara),

Sad news to report—I have metastasis in the liver, from the melanoma I had in my eye (in '05)—I'm very glad I was granted nine good, happy, productive years before it decided to spread [. . .] These metastases are not too treatable and (while one cannot be precise) I have only a matter of months to live.

I hope these are "easy" months, relatively, so I can see friends and family and enjoy life and (being me) write—but I have to go to the hospital for a few days tomorrow for a special treatment and will not be feeling well for a couple of weeks after that—I have felt, and looked, well up to this point which makes the death sentence seem almost unreal.

Dear Ren, you have been such an important & loving & faithful friend these last 35 years (or more)—and you, Joasia, and godchild Sara, have added a special warmth to this old bachelor's life. So let's see a lot more of each other in the months to come.

Love, Oliver

A few days later, on Thursday, February 19, readers of *The New York Times* opened their morning papers to the first of a series of utterly remarkable, brave, forthright, heartfelt, and profoundly sane open letters from the dying doctor, this one headlined "My Own Life."*

"Awww," said Sara, her eyes glistening as she put the paper down that morning, "look how he finally got to use his title!"

The next few weeks would indeed prove really tough on Oliver. The quartet of his remarkable final pieces from *The New York Times* would, soon after his death, be published in a small book entitled *Gratitude* (introduced by Kate and Billy, flanked by several of Billy's poignant photos of Oliver). But in some ways one of the most astonishing pieces of writing from that last year of Oliver's life ran in *The New York Review of Books* in its issue of April 23, under the title "A General Feeling of Disorder" and described, in truly harrowing terms, the discomforts of those first weeks after his mid-February surgical procedure.†

The procedure itself ("threading a catheter up to the bifurcation of the hepatic artery, and then injecting a mass of tiny beads into the right hepatic artery, where they would be carried to the smallest arterioles, blocking these, cutting off the blood supply and oxygen needed by the metastases—in effect, starving and asphyxiating them to death") proved entirely straightforward, and the tiny beads performed their magic precisely as planned. The problem (also entirely expected though no less the agonizing for all that) came when the metastases, by this point taking up fifty percent of his liver tissue, proceeded to die and fall away, with all of

---

*It is available on the *New York Times* website.
†That piece was included in the next posthumous collection the Sacks collective put out, *The River of Consciousness* (New York: Knopf, 2017).

that toxic dead tissue having to be disposed of in the usual manner, for starters by the macrophages of the immune system—a process which rendered Oliver deathly ill and profoundly uncomfortable for almost two weeks. "On day ten," though, Oliver reported, "I turned a corner—I felt awful, as usual, in the morning, but a completely different person in the afternoon. This was delightful, and wholly unexpected: there was no intimation, beforehand, that such a transformation was about to happen." By the end of a further two days, "I suddenly found myself full of physical and creative energy and a euphoria almost akin to hypomania. I strode up and down the corridor in my apartment building while exuberant thoughts rushed through my mind." As if to prove his complete rejuvenescence, by the end of the article he was quoting his beloved Nietzsche, from *The Gay Science*, to the effect that

> Gratitude pours forth continually, as if the unexpected had just happened—the gratitude of a convalescent—for *convalescence* was unexpected . . . The rejoicing of strength that is returning, of a reawakened faith in a tomorrow and the day after tomorrow, of a sudden sense and anticipation of a future, of impending adventures, of seas that are open again.*

And indeed, the procedure had killed off eighty percent of the tumors in Oliver's liver, leaving it, in his surgeon's vivid description, "like a chunk of Swiss cheese." One good thing about the liver is that it is devoid itself of pain neurons, so that liver cancer, unlike many others, is in itself largely painless. Another good thing about the liver is that almost uniquely among human organs, it grows back. The bad thing in this instance was that as it grew back, so would the tumors, so Oliver's blessed reprieve, while much longer in the end than most of us (including him) were expecting, was never going to be permanent.

Once he had recovered, I sent over, with some trepidation, the 13,000-word version of my *Vanity Fair* piece, and to my great relief, the next morning he called, incredibly happy with the result: They would have to publish all of it, he insisted. I told him I was glad he liked it but, no, they'd

---

*A passage he'd also cited, incidentally, years earlier, as the epigraph to the Convalescence section of *A Leg to Stand On*.

only be publishing 7,500 words, which was still a lot for them. Nonsense, he insisted, he'd have his agent, Andrew Wylie, call them and demand they publish the whole thing! I told him I doubted that was how it worked: Even Andrew Wylie was not going to trump Graydon Carter. But Oliver harrumphed, we'd see (we did, Andrew didn't, and the piece eventually ran at 7,500 words)—and notwithstanding all of that, he now veritably ordered me to get back to the original project and to publish the whole of the book I'd been planning to thirty years earlier. There: Matter settled.

At one point in April, the three of us Weschlers went to visit him at his apartment and found him in excellent form. Improbably, he informed us, he had developed a mad taste for liver and was eating it in great gobs ("I've become a latter-day Prometheus!" he crowed). He was curious about the future, he told us, "but mainly the nineteenth-century future"—he'd been reading a lot of H. G. Wells. As far as the twenty-first century went, he continued, he harbored more wistful curiosity about coming developments in chemistry and physics than in biology. He quizzed Sara on several of the specimens of pure elements with which he'd surrounded himself at his desk, and being his goddaughter, she did quite well.

He showed us how he was continuing to write up a storm, essay after essay, and surprisingly, he was even trying his hand at a children's book, an introduction to the chemical elements. I'm not sure if he ever finished that one, but that day he was especially delighted to show us how, in his

Oliver quizzing Sara on the elements

Our last photos with Oliver

notebook, as he'd been approaching the element sodium, some sort of drug-induced delirium appeared to have kicked in. Look! See how his hand-writing had abruptly disintegrated into delightfully indecipherable loop-de-loops! He laughed proudly. He told us how he and Billy and Kate would be going to England in early May, by way of a farewell tour; they intended to hole up in various comfortable hotel rooms and entertain a veritable procession of friends. After which he and Billy had plans to visit a lemur sanctuary in North Carolina (one of Oliver's few sorrows was that he had never made it to Madagascar, with its dazzling wealth of unique insular wildlife variations, but this was going to come close).

But first, in late April, in the loft at De Niro's Tribeca restaurant, Oliver presided at the festive launch of his autobiography—Knopf had rushed the publication through, under the circumstances (and *Vanity Fair* had followed close behind, releasing my piece just a few days later). At one point, the chief of neurology at Columbia rose to toast Oliver, informing the assembled throng of well-wishers that these days, fully seventy percent of those young students who applied to intern in neurology mentioned Oliver Sacks in their letters of application. Other similarly laudatory toasts followed, and a thoroughly good time was had by all. Or, at any rate, almost all.

For here Oliver departed from Hume. While he enjoyed loving relationships and friendships and had no real enemies (give or take the stray ex-boss or super-Touretter), no one who knew him, as he'd acknowledged in that first *Times* piece, would say that he was a man of mild disposition. On the contrary, he was a self-described "man of vehement disposition, with violent enthusiasms, and extreme immoderation in all [his] passions." And he remained one to the very end.

What apparently happened was that someone at the party, a young woman, came up to him suppressing sobs, tears streaming down her cheeks, and Oliver pushed the young lady away, for he would have none of that. In his prosopagnosiac way, he seemingly convinced himself that this had been Sara, and later on, as the party was winding down and Sara came over to hug him good night, he brusquely pushed her away as well.

It hadn't been Sara. But Oliver would not be assuaged. According to Kate's recollections, he may have believed she had been "emotional" during an earlier visit, not at the party—in any case, in the weeks that followed, no amount of dissuading or clarifying would appease him, and he refused to entertain any further visits from her. At his eighty-second birthday party on July 9, this time at his apartment (and who among us had thought he was going to make it that far?), when Sara came over to hug him, he again pushed her away. That very morning, Oliver had learned that his illness was progressing rapidly, and he was understandably eager to husband his resources—he was, after all, striving to complete writing projects, recover from surgeries, and bid farewell to many people. But his behavior stung all the same.

Sara, being Sara, was devastated. Her almost weekly requests to visit were being regularly rebuffed. Kate said she was trying to bring Oliver around, but we all knew how stubborn he could get, and in any case, he was now progressively weakening (for that matter I didn't really see him anymore myself). For Sara and myself, it was such an odd and sad and disquieting dark note, an apparent throwback to earlier near-solipsistic petulances, in what was otherwise (witness those *Times* pieces) proving to be the virtual master class he seemed to be giving everyone else in how to go about this business of dying. All of which was also and at the same time completely genuine and overwhelmingly true (it's just that, in addition, even if only minimally so, he was also Oliver in every other way as well, and to the very end, and his goddaughter just had the bad luck to find herself on the receiving end of some of the less admirable parts).

In the end, Sara gave up waiting and prepared to return for a few weeks of late-summer thesis research in Uganda. But first, before leaving, she sent Oliver a letter, fashioned out of handmade stationery and wrapped in an elaborate periodic table–themed handmade envelope. (She made no photocopy, but she did take some blurry iPhotos of the letter before sending it, and she recently allowed me to see those, and sanctioned my quoting from them here.)

Aug 6, 2015
Dear Oliver,

I've been writing this letter in my head for almost six months now, and I still don't know quite what to say. I was going to have it ready on your birthday and made the stationery accordingly (note the "Pb" boxed off on the flap of the envelope) but didn't manage it then. Afterward, I thought I'd wait with it till some visit, but I guess that wasn't in the cards. Now I'm leaving for Uganda again, so I suppose I should really get out the words I have been meaning to put down all this while.

I do need to tell you something first though, neurotic as it may seem: whoever came up to you in tears at your book party, I swear to God it wasn't me. It may seem silly to specify that but I have been given to understand that my supposed lachrymosity is the reason I was not allowed to see you this summer. And that's a pity for me, because it's some sort of misunderstanding. The last time I cried in front of you I was 11 years old (I initially told Kate 3, but that was a mistake)—I

can describe the scene in perfect detail, down to what we were
each wearing that evening. As for who it was who cried in front
of you at your party, I cannot say. All I know is that as much as
I have cried *about you* in the last six months, I have never and
would never burden you by crying *in front* of you. All irrelevant
now, I suppose. But I didn't want to leave that misunderstanding
hanging between us. Chalk it up to a quirk of my scrupulous
and obsessive-compulsive neurology.

But to get to my point in this letter. . . . . .

A couple months back when my father was pulling together
the material for the *Vanity Fair* piece we came across an old
picture of you reading to me from a picture book when I
was perhaps four years old. The photo tickled me for reasons
I cannot quite explain, but I suppose in a way it seemed like a
nice visual metaphor for the way I've related to you throughout
my life. In the shot, I am tiny—so small that, even with my legs
outstretched my feet don't make it to the edge of the couch.
You, by contrast, seem too big for everything—the couch, the
book in your hands, the little girl beside you, the very dimensions
of the photograph! And that's very much how I remember you
when I look back on my childhood, a burly, hulking presence
(with a seemingly endless appetite, and a penchant for startling
and exuberant vocalizations). I was both fascinated and
frightened by you. And, in a sense, that has never truly worn off.

Over the years, the gap in our sizes has of course narrowed.
But you've continued to loom large in my life, and around you
I often still feel like that little girl on the sofa—dwarfed and
dazzled now not by your heft, but by your intellect and
creativity. The fact that I got to grow up listening to you and
my father conversing/discussing/rhapsodizing about the world
has been one of the great delights and privileges of my life thus
far. You may not even remember this, but there was a stretch
when I was twelve or thirteen when each weekend you came to
our house (you were still on City Island back then) and read to
us from your draft of *Uncle Tungsten*. Those afternoons were
deeply formative for me: a demonstration of the writing process,
the role that writing could play in a person's life, and just what

a true life of the mind could look like. Several years later, when you had the treatment for the eye tumor, I remember hearing from Kate how you had her bring you elements from your collection to see which ones responded to the radiation. I'm jumping around here; I know this is not the most organized note.—But I just remember being so struck by that, seeing it as such a valuable model for a life in which every experience, however trying, could be treated as an occasion for wonder and inquiry.

I have been so lucky to grow up around you, to have spent so much of my childhood getting to listen to you and observe you. I think that as a kid, because I spent so much time around you and my father, I kind of assumed that all people grow up to be vibrant, creative intellectuals. I thought it would come naturally with adulthood. Now, as an adult myself, I see that it is not as simple as that. I find myself constantly falling short of the ideal I have always seen in you, and I often fear that I will never live up to the sort of example of intellectual engagement and creative fervor you and my father offered me.

All of that is okay, though, I realize. It is nice to have something to strive for. I feel profoundly blessed to have had you as such a dear (and towering) figure in my life. And the example you set for me (however unconsciously) will continue to guide me throughout my adulthood. Thank you for showing me how rich and fascinating the world can be if looked at the right way. That has been a tremendous gift to this not-so-little-anymore goddaughter of yours.

Love,
Sara

Alas, Oliver was really weakening by the day now, and he never did get a chance to respond to Sara's note in writing. A week later, though, in Uganda, Sara did receive an email from Kate, with her transcription of his dictation. He began by thanking Sara for her letter and especially for its lovely periodic table stationery. He went on to urge her to stop comparing herself to anyone (and in particular himself or her parents). "You are very talented in your own ways, and you will find your own path—indeed, you

seem to be already well launched on it." Noting the long road spooling
forth before her into the future, he continued, "I know that you will make
the most of life, of your unique talents and desires. I hope that you will
feel free to pursue your own passions." In closing he bid her farewell, sent
his love, and signed off as her godfather, Oliver.

And though I don't want to speak for Sara, my sense is that that note
did end up making a world of difference to her.

※

The next day, Sunday, August 16, *The New York Times* published the last
of Oliver's dispatches, a lyric evocation of "Sabbath," summoning at the
outset memories of how his mother and her seventeen brothers and sisters
had all had an Orthodox Jewish upbringing, and how while his had not
been quite as strict or rigorous, Friday evenings still mattered enormously
(the way, come the early afternoon, she would rush home from the hospital and start preparing "the gefilte fish and other delicacies for Shabbos,"
and then, come sunset, "would light the ritual candles, cupping their flames
with her hands, and murmuring a prayer.")

Concluding, several paragraphs later:

> And now, weak, short of breath, my once-firm muscles melted
> away by cancer, I find my thoughts, increasingly, not on the super-
> natural or spiritual, but on what is meant by living a good and
> worthwhile life—achieving a sense of peace within oneself. I find
> my thoughts drifting to the Sabbath, the day of rest, the seventh
> day of the week, and perhaps the seventh day of one's life as well,
> when one can feel that one's work is done, and one may, in good
> conscience, rest.

Precisely two weeks later, as that week's Sabbath gave way to night-
fall and then to early morn, at 5:25 a.m., I was woken by the ping of an
incoming text from Kate: "Oliver died peacefully this morning at home.
Talk soon."

Strange, in that the overwhelming initial feeling for me was one of
gladness and gratitude. I almost wanted to say Amen. Only he'd have given
me that look. Or not. I wonder.

I indeed spoke with Kate a few hours later, and she related how she and the rest of them (Hailey had come back from Nashville for the previous several weeks, where she'd joined her replacement, a young woman improbably named Hallie, and Yolanda as well, and of course Billy) were all feeling strangely similar, more glad than sad, though we all expected that that initial sense might of course subside with time. She said that Oliver's passing was largely painless to the very end. And that he'd been writing, or at least dictating, till two days before taking his leave.

(What is it that Rabbi Jesus says in the end, up there on the cross? "It is done." Or as it gets translated alternatively, "It is accomplished." Or maybe better: "It is *achieved*.")

※

Then I called Sara on her cell on what was in any case her last day in Uganda and found her at a street café in Kampala. She knew immediately. "It's Oliver," she said, before I could utter a word. "He's gone."

A few minutes later she texted me:

"It seems to me that one ought to rejoice in the fact of death— ought to decide, indeed, to earn one's death by confronting with passion the conundrum of life"
—the line I just read, returning to my James Baldwin

In the wake of the Baldwin festival a few months earlier, she'd been reading *The Fire Next Time*.

Anyway, the point being that Oliver did confront the conundrums of life just so, exactly thus, they both did, so may we all learn to, so may we all.

※

Sara made it back home the next day (at the airport in Entebbe, she reported, on all the TV monitors CNN had been scrolling "Doctor played by Robin Williams in film, dies"), and we all went to Oliver's to sit . . . well, not shiva exactly but something commemorative and celebratory and almost joyous. And at the same time a bit teary. Billy was there, of course, with all five of his sisters, who'd come in to support him (maybe that explained things, I found myself thinking: his preternatural grace and gentleness). So was pretty much everyone else. And so was the rotund jolly

Jamaican nurse, Maureen Wolfe (!), who'd only known Oliver five short days but had clearly become completely enamored. His heart and lungs, she told me, were like nothing she'd ever encountered. "Had it not been for the cancer, he'd have lived to be a hundred!" She was, she said, used to predicting the trailing off of the people she dealt with late in their lives, but the doctor had proved completely unpredictable: repeatedly rallying; asking for food; waking up to ask both that the air conditioner be turned up and that he be provided a blanket, the blue one, for his extremities; rousing himself from deep slumber to greet her ("Oh, how good to see you again") each time she entered the room. This afternoon she'd brought along both of her daughters, who were training to be nurses, just so they could see the home of this good man she'd been talking about so incessantly.

In Oliver's bedroom, his walking cane (its handle wrapped in its usual web of rubber bands) lay spread diagonally across the blue bedspread in the darkening gloam of the evening. No one else was in there, except I suddenly noticed, on the far side, huddled together on the carpet with their backs to the bed, facing the window, Sara and Yolanda (the housekeeper, after all, of *Sara's* childhood), snuggling, commiserating.

Yolanda was telling Sara stories of how Oliver, growing more and more dear with every passing week toward the end, used to correct her manglings and mispronunciations of English, clarifying for her the difference, say, between "on TV" and "on the TV" and carefully writing the words on the whiteboard in the kitchen, so that she would remember. She related how, during the last few days, once he'd become confined to his bed, they'd filled his room with ferns and minerals and stuffed cephalopods, "all his friends," she said, and they both laughed.

And then she related how every once in a while, in those last few days, he'd wake up and ask for "*su sopita de pescado.*" Just that morning *The New Yorker* had posted their last little piece of Oliver's, a short essay about his mother's sublime gefilte fish, and the way that no one ever made it nearly as well again except for his beloved housekeeper Helen, back in Mount Vernon and his early days on City Island, who'd go with him to Arthur Avenue each Thursday morning to rustle up the ingredients for, as she always called it, his "filter fish."

Su sopita de pescado: Sara was now parsing the implications of the phrase for us, a few hours later, as we drove back home to Pelham. "His little fish soup. Meaning, of course, his gefilte fish. But actually the use of the diminutive *sopita* there is so sweet, because you'd usually use that form only if you were talking to a child. 'Come on, baby, don't you want to eat your *sopita de pescado?*' And Oliver himself in that 'Filter Fish' piece talked about gefilte fish being the ambrosia of his infancy and the meal that would see him out of this life as well."

Thirty-five years ago I was a staff writer for *The New Yorker*, and I was working on a biography of Oliver Sacks. I had about fifteen notebooks full of interviews. We were meeting for dinner two or three nights per week. But at some point he asked if I could leave out the fact that he was gay. And I couldn't do it. His sexuality tied him up in knots. And I thought those knots helped explain why he became such an amazing neurologist. So I agreed to stop writing, but we remained good friends. Shortly before he died last year, he called me and asked me to finish the book. So I'm trying to figure out where to begin. Thirty years ago I was going 100 mph in an aircraft carrier, and I was asked to stop on a dime. Now I've got to figure out how to start it back up.

—an entry on *Humans of New York*

Postscript

And so I set to work, as per Oliver's late-life instructions, to put this book together. Or rather didn't. For almost a year, I hesitated and dawdled, resisting and procrastinating. Instead, I wrote two other books. And still I couldn't seem to jump-start myself. (One always needs to be careful writing about somebody else's writing block: the stuff's contagious. Just ask Joseph Mitchell.)

One afternoon, not writing, I wandered over to the Guggenheim instead, to take in the sly and wry Fischli and Weiss show. I was relaxing for a moment on one of those benches along the ramp, when a young fellow came up to me and introduced himself as Brandon Stanton and explained that he ran a little weblog operation called *Humans of New York*. Oh yeah, I assured him, I know about you. And so, oh, that was good because maybe then I knew how he liked to take pictures of random people around town, and would I mind if he took one of me. Not at all, go ahead. Whereupon he took a few snapshots and then came back to say that he always asked a question to go along with the photo, and today's question was: What sort of work are you currently doing? Whereupon I replied regarding the work that I wasn't.

And a few days later I got a call from Sara's best college friend Niwa, a Tanzanian cultural-geography grad student at the University of Wisconsin, shouting over the line, "Parent, you've been Humanized!"

And indeed. There I was on Stanton's website, kvetching away.

I was about to enter my fifteen minutes of viral anonymous fame, because even though my own name wasn't indicated anywhere in the post, presently hundreds and then thousands of commenters were weighing in, urging me forward, suggesting that I just tell that story, that would be a great way to begin, come on, you can do it, they all promised to buy the book, how hard could it be, just get in there and write what you know, and you obviously knew him . . .

You guys do it, I wanted to say, *if it's so damn easy.*

But instead I did go back to my desk. And started compiling this book.

Love you, Oliver,
miss you every day.

Late photo of Oliver

Acknowledgments

We were all so young then. Strange, today, to realize how long ago much of the work, or at any rate the chronicling and the reporting on this book, transpired. Such that many of the people with whom I spoke and who were so generous with their time and remembrances, people I would love to have acknowledged here (and had have them here to receive that acknowledgement), have now passed. Thus, for example, Dick Lindenbaum (d. 1992), Colin Haycraft (d. 1994), Orlan Fox (d. circa 1999), Bob Rodman (d. 2004), Thom Gunn (d. 2004), Carmel Ross (d. 2006), Duncan Dallas (d. 2014), Eric Korn (d. 2014), Margie Kohl (d. 2016), and Isabelle Rapin (d. 2017). Not to mention Oliver himself, of course (d. 2015). The upper canopy just keeps thinning away, the giants toppling, exposing the rest of us down here in the middle story to the relentless glare of mortality. And yet some of my fond interlocutors are still around—Jonathan and Rachel Miller, Jonathan Cole, and Sister Lorraine (though she's in the meantime transferred to another Little Sisters home, this one in Totowa, New Jersey)—and it gladdens me that they *are* here to appreciate, I hope, how much I treasured my hours with them.

Them and all the others in Sacksworld: Kate Edgar, Hailey Wojcik, Yolanda Rueda, the late Kevin Halligan (d. 2012), and of course more recently Billy Hayes. The Awakenings patients, those still living back then in the early eighties (now all dead, alas), who honored me with their stories—and all those other patients of Oliver's who put up with my presence on his rounds. Doctors Mark Homonoff, Nick Goldberg, Orrin Devinsky, and "Stereo Sue" Barry. Fellow journalists (and Sacksologists) Mary-Kay

Wilmers of the *London Review of Books*, Steve Silberman of *Wired* magazine, and Robert Krulwich of NPR and *Radiolab*. The photographers Don Usner and John Midgley, and mutual friends Peter Seldon, Baynard Woods, Carl Ginsburg, John Hastings, Jonathan Mahler, Alva Noë, Shane Fistell, Lowell Handler, Bill Morrison, Andrzej and Rebecca Rapaczynski, Stanley and Jane Moss, and the late Ryszard Kapuscinski (d. 2007) and Jonathan Schell (d. 2014).

Ric Burns and Leigh Howell and their whole cohort at Steeplechase Films. Bill T. Jones and Bjorn Amelan and theirs at NY Live Arts (conveners of the 2013 inaugural NY Live Arts Live Ideas Festival, centered on "The Worlds of Oliver Sacks").

The staff and supporters, respectively, of the Blue Mountain Center (in the Adirondacks), where much of the work on the earlier version of this book took place in the mid-eighties, and the MacDowell Colony, in whose good graces I somehow managed to revive the project more recently.

My indefatigable agent, Chris Calhoun, and this book's eminently sage and sensible editor, Alex Star, his aide Dominique Lear, this book's deft designer, Jonathan Lippincott, and my own utterly unflappable sometime assistant Laura deBuys.

My own dearly beloved family (and often, it seemed, Oliver's as well), Joasia and Sara, who at any rate sometimes had to forebear us both, gilding and gladdening our lives all the while.

And finally, of course, again and always, Oliver himself. Boy, could that man drive a person crazy, but he always drew you back with his impishly joshing self-awareness, his bounding curiosity, his profound wisdom, and his essential *dearness*—and it is that dearness, in the end, that pervades the air surrounding his never-lapsing memory. Bless you, dear Oliver, and thank you.

Thinking is thanking.

Index

"OS" refers to Oliver Sacks. Page numbers in *italics* refer to illustrations.

ILLUSTRATION CREDITS

Frontispiece: Oliver in the water: James Estrin / *The New York Times* / Redux
Page 36: Bob Rodman: Kathy Rodman
Page 42: Thom Gunn: Mike Kitay
Page 92: Margie Kohl: Andrew Inglis
Page 114: W. H. Auden: Peter Mitchell / Camera Press / Redux
Page 114: A. R. Luria: The Alexander Luria website, Luria.ucsd.edu
Page 130: Oliver and Pop: Lowell Handler
Page 140: Oliver and Eric Korn: Kathy Rodman
Page 161: Jonathan and Rachel Miller: The Miller Family
Page 178: Colin Haycraft: Gerald Duckworth & Co.
Page 228: Joanna Stasinska: The Weschler Family
Page 304: Oliver on the patio: The Weschler Family
Page 306: Oliver shedding formalities: The Weschler Family
Page 308: Sacks and Weschler: Copyright © Don Usner
Page 311: Sara and Oliver: The Weschler Family
Page 316: Santa Sacks: The Weschler Family
Page 321: Sara conversing with Oliver: The Weschler Family
Page 325: The Rat Track: The Weschler Family
Page 329: Sara's drawing for Oliver: The Weschler Family
Page 344: Ryszard Kapuściński and Oliver: The Weschler Family
Page 354: Oliver quizzing Sara: The Weschler Family
Page 355: Last photos with Oliver: The Weschler Family
Page 364: *Humans of New York* post: Courtesy of Brandon Stanton
Page 367: Late photo of Oliver from *Wired* magazine: John Midgley

A NOTE ABOUT THE AUTHOR

Lawrence Weschler, a longtime veteran of *The New Yorker* and a regular contributor to *The New York Times Magazine*, *Vanity Fair*, *McSweeney's*, and NPR, is the director emeritus of the New York Institute for the Humanities at New York University and the author of nearly twenty books, including *Seeing Is Forgetting the Name of the Thing One Sees*, a life of the artist Robert Irwin; *Mr. Wilson's Cabinet of Wonder*, about the Museum of Jurassic Technology; *Everything That Rises: A Book of Convergences*; *A Miracle, a Universe: Settling Accounts with Torturers*; and *Vermeer in Bosnia*.